LINUX
KERNEL
INTERNALS

LINUX
KERNEL
INTERNALS

Second Edition

Michael Beck
Harald Böhme
Mirko Dziadzka
Ulrich Kunitz
Robert Magnus
Dirk Verworner

 **Addison-Wesley**

Harlow, England • Reading, Massachusetts • Menlo Park, California • New York
Don Mills, Ontario • Amsterdam • Bonn • Sydney • Singapore • Tokyo • Madrid
San Juan • Milan • Mexico City • Seoul • Taipei

Translated from the German edition *Linux-Kernel-Programmierung* published by Addison-Wesley (Deutschland) GmbH.

Addison Wesley Longman Limited
Edinburgh Gate
Harlow
Essex
CM20 2JE
England
and Associated Companies throughout the World

Translated and typeset by 46
Cover designed by Senate
Printed and bound in the United States of America.

First printed 1997. Reprinted 1998 and 1999

ISBN 0–201–33143–8

British Library Cataloguing-in-Publication Data
A catalogue record for this book is available from the British Library.

In memoriam,

Dirk Verworner

Foreword

Creating an operating system has been (and still is) an exciting project, and has been made even more rewarding through the extensive (and almost uniformly positive) feedback from users and developers alike.

One of the problems for people wanting to get to know the kernel internals better has been the lack of documentation, and fledgling kernel hackers have had to resort to reading the actual source code of the system for most of the details. While I think that is still a good idea, I'm happy that there exists more documentation like this explaining about LINUX use and internals.

I hope you have a good time with LINUX and this book.

Linus Torvalds

Preface

This is the second edition of our book about the LINUX kernel. The book has been updated to cover the 2.0 version of the kernel, which is a milestone in the development of LINUX. LINUX 2.0 is now the standard UNIX desktop operating system, giving you all the power of free UNIX software which has been developed over more than 25 years, together with a growing number of commercial applications. It is both stable and open. There are no hidden secrets. If you want to solve a problem, you can get the source code. Such a philosophy is exactly what this book is about. We tell you about the LINUX kernel so, you, the experienced computer user, are always in control.

It seems that a lot of early LINUX hackers, like ourselves, are now professional software developers. As such, it is always helpful to know something about operating systems. At least you will have seen some pieces of really good code. When we started to play with LINUX, we did it for fun. Now there is a real return. Seen in this light, this book is a good investment.

Recently some hackers told us that LINUX is boring. They want to have the excitement of something really cool and new, and the joy of seeing something grow from scratch. To us, though, developments such as a project to develop a LINUX graphical user interface supporting a unique look-and-feel still seem very exciting. Such developments will make LINUX usable for the famous 'rest of us'. For a lot of people LINUX is a better UNIX than UNIX. We would really love to use a better Windows than Windows. Or to put it another way: simply make LINUX more like the Macintosh.

As in every preface, we want to thank all the people who made this edition possible. We have to mention here Fiona Kinnear from Addison Wesley Longman. This edition would not have been published without her commitment.

As LINUX users we thank the LINUX community as a whole, for building software the way we want it. May this book be a contribution to that effort.

Michael Beck, Harald Böhme, Robert Magnus
Berlin
Mirko Dziadzka
Furtwangen
Ulrich Kunitz
Frankfurt am Main

Contents

1 LINUX – the operating system

Linux is obsolete!

Andrew S. Tanenbaum

1.1 Main characteristics	1.2 LINUX distributions

LINUX is a freely available UNIX-type operating system. Originally developed only for the PC, it now runs on Digital Alpha and Sparc workstations as well. Further ports, for example to the Amiga and the PowerPC, are under development and are already relatively stable.

LINUX is compatible with the POSIX 1003.1 standard and includes large areas of the functions of UNIX System V and BSD 4.3. Substantial parts of the LINUX kernel with which we will be concerned in this book were written by Linus Torvalds, a Finnish student of computer science. He placed the program source codes under the *GNU Public License*, which means that everyone has the right to use, copy and modify the programs free of charge.

The first version of the LINUX kernel was available on the Internet in November 1991. A group of LINUX activists quickly formed, and continues to spur on the development of this operating system. Numerous users test new versions and help to clear the bugs out of the software.

The LINUX software is developed under open and distributed conditions. 'Open' means that anyone can become involved if they are able. This requires LINUX activists to be able to communicate quickly, efficiently and above all globally. The medium for this is the Internet. It is therefore no surprise that many of the developments are the product of gifted students with access to the Internet at their universities and colleges. The development systems available to these students tend to be relatively modest; and it is no doubt for this reason that LINUX is the 32-bit operating system that uses the smallest resources, without sacrificing functionality.

As LINUX is distributed under the conditions of the GNU Public License, the full source code is available to users. This allows anyone to find out how the system works and trace and remove any bugs. However, the real attraction for the authors of this book lies in 'experimenting' with the system.

Needless to say, LINUX has its drawbacks. It is just as much of a 'programmer's system' as UNIX. Cryptic commands, configurations which are difficult to follow and documentation which is not always comprehensive make the system far from easy to use – and not only for beginners. However, it appears that many users accept this downside to escape the number of limitations (technical as well as financial) found in proprietary systems such as MS-DOS, Windows, or commercial UNIX derivatives for the PC. In the meantime many books on LINUX accessible to beginners have been written in addition to the *Linux Documentation Project* (LDP).

LINUX systems are used in software houses, by Internet providers, in schools and universities and in private homes. There is no computer magazine that does not regularly report on this operating system. The German LINUX market alone is worth several million Marks per year. Considering LINUX simply as a pure hackers' toy no longer does justice to reality.

Although there are ports to other hardware architectures, most users still run LINUX on Intel 386 or compatible systems. Owing to the wide availability of these systems, there are almost no problems under LINUX with peripheral device drivers. As soon as a new PC expansion board is on the market, some LINUX user will implement a driver for that board.[1] Since version 2.0, LINUX also supports multi-processor systems based on Intel and Sparc architectures.

To ensure reasonable performance under LINUX, the PC should have at least 8 Mbytes of RAM, but if the X Window system is being used as the graphical user interface, at least 16 Mbytes are needed. With double that amount, performance remains acceptable even when you are running several compilers in the background and trying to edit a text in the foreground. However, for special applications such as modem/fax servers or firewalls, 4 Mbytes are sufficient.

In principle, LINUX supports any readily available UNIX software. Thus, object-oriented programs can be written in GNU C++ or graphics created under the X Window system. Games such as Tetris will run, as will development systems for graphical user interfaces. With their built-in network support, LINUX computers can be linked into existing networks without problems.

---

[1] Manufacturers who do not release information on the functioning of their hardware do not benefit from this.

1.1 Main characteristics

LINUX will meet all the demands made nowadays of a modern, '.
operating system.

- *Multi-tasking*
  LINUX supports true preemptive multi-tasking. All processes run entirely
  independently of each other. No process needs to be concerned with
  making processor time available to other processes.

- *Multi-user access*
  LINUX allows a number of users to work with the system at the same time.

- *Multi-processing*
  Since version 2.0, LINUX also runs on multi-processor architectures. This
  means that the operating system can distribute several applications (in
  true parallel fashion) across several processors.

- *Architecture independence*
  LINUX runs on several hardware platforms, from the Amiga to the PC to
  DEC Alpha workstations. Such hardware independence is achieved by
  no other serious operating system.

- *Demand load executables*
  Only those parts of a program actually required for execution are loaded
  into memory. When a new process is created using fork(), memory is not
  requested immediately, but instead the memory for the parent process is
  used jointly by both processes. If the new process subsequently accesses
  part of the memory in write mode, this section is copied before being
  modified. This concept is known as *copy-on-write*.

- *Paging*
  Despite the best efforts to use physical memory efficiently, it can happen
  that the available memory is fully taken up. LINUX then looks for
  4 Kbyte memory pages which can be freed. Pages whose contents are
  already stored on hard disk (for example, program files) are discarded.
  All other pages are copied out to hard disk. If one of these pages of
  memory is subsequently accessed, it has to be reloaded. This procedure
  is known as *paging*. It differs from the *swapping* used in older variants of
  UNIX, where the entire memory for a process is written to disk, which is
  certainly significantly less efficient.

- *Dynamic cache for hard disk*
  Users of MS-DOS will be familiar with the problems resulting from the
  need to reserve memory of a fixed size for hard disk cache programs such
  as SMARTDRIVE. LINUX dynamically adjusts the size of cache memory
  in use to suit the current memory usage situation. If no more memory is

available at a given time, the size of the cache is reduced to free memory. Once memory is again released, the area of the cache is increased.

- *Shared libraries*
  Libraries are collections of routines needed by a program for processing data. There are a number of standard libraries used by more than one process at the same time. It therefore makes sense to load the program code for these libraries into memory only once, rather than once for each process. This is made possible by *shared libraries*. As these libraries are loaded only when the process is run, they are also known as dynamically linked libraries or, in other operating system environments, as *dynamic link libraries*.

- *Support for POSIX 1003.1 standard and in part System V and BSD*
  POSIX 1003.1 defines a minimum interface to a UNIX-type operating system. This standard is now supported by all recent and relatively sophisticated operating systems. LINUX (since version 1.2) fully supports POSIX 1003.1. Meanwhile there are even LINUX distributions that have gone through the official certification process and therefore have the right to call themselves officially 'POSIX compatible'. Additional system interfaces for the UNIX System V and BSD development lines are also implemented. Software written for UNIX can generally be ported directly to LINUX.

- *Various formats for executable files*
  It is naturally desirable to be able to run under LINUX programs which run in different system environments. For this reason, emulators for MS-DOS and MS-Windows are currently under development. LINUX can also execute programs from other UNIX systems conforming to the iBCS2 standard. This includes, for example, many commercial programs used under SCO UNIX. Also, in ports to other hardware architectures (for example Sparc and Alpha), care is taken that the individual 'native binaries' can be executed. Thus, there is a wealth of commercial software available to the LINUX user without its having been specially ported to LINUX.

- *Memory protected mode*
  LINUX uses the processor's memory protection mechanisms to prevent the process from accessing memory allocated to the system kernel or other processes. This is a major contribution to the security of the system. An erroneous program can therefore (theoretically) no longer crash the system.

- *Support for national keyboards and fonts*
  Under LINUX, a wide range of national keyboards and character sets can be used: for example, the *Latin1* set defined by the International Organization for Standardization (ISO) which also includes European special characters.

● *Different file systems*

LINUX supports a variety of file systems. The most commonly used file system at present is the Second Extended (*Ext2*) File System. This supports filenames of up to 255 characters and has a number of features making it more secure than conventional UNIX file systems.

Other file systems implemented are the MS-DOS file system and the VFAT file system for accessing MS-DOS or Windows 95 partitions, the ISO file system for accessing CD-ROMs and the NFS for accessing the file systems of other UNIX computers present in the network. Less widely spread are the AFF file system for accessing the Amiga Fast File system, the UPS and the SysyV file systems for accessing UNIX file systems of other manufacturers, HPFS for accessing OS/2 partitions and the Samba file system for accessing file systems exported from Windows computers. Other file systems, such as the Windows NT file system used under Windows NT, are under development and available as beta versions. What commercial operating system can offer such a range?

● *TCP/IP, SLIP and PPP support*

LINUX can be integrated into local UNIX networks. In principle, all network services, such as the Network File System and Remote Login, can be used. SLIP and PPP support the use of the TCP/IP protocol over serial lines. This means that it is possible to link into the Internet via the public telephone network using a high-speed modem.

1.2   LINUX distributions

To install LINUX, the user requires a distribution. This consists of a boot diskette and other diskettes or a CD-ROM. Installation scripts enable even inexperienced users to install runnable systems. It helps that many software packages are already adapted to LINUX and appropriately configured: this saves a lot of time. Discussions are constantly taking place within the LINUX community on the quality of the various distributions; but these frequently overlook the fact that compiling a distribution of this sort is a very lengthy and complex task.

Internationally widely used are the RedHat, the Debian and the Slackware distributions. Which of these distributions is used is just a matter of taste. Distributions can be obtained from FTP servers, e-mail systems, public-domain distributors and some bookshops. Sources of supply can be found by consulting specialist magazines or the LINUX newsgroups in Usenet.

Compiling the kernel

A system is anything with no system to it,
hardware is anything that clatters when you drop it,
and software is anything for which there is a logical explanation
why it's not working.

Johannes Leckebusch

Before we go on to study the inner life of the LINUX kernel in the following chapters, we will first take a look at the source and compiled versions of the kernel.

2.1   Where is everything?

As the source codes have already grown to a quite considerable size, different parts of the kernel can be found in different directories.

In the LINUX system, the sources can normally be found under /usr/src/linux. In the following chapters, therefore, the pathnames given are always relative to this directory. The exact directory structure is shown in Figure 2.1.

Ongoing porting to other architectures has resulted in changes as compared with version 1.0 of the kernel. Architecture-dependent code is held in the subdirectories of **arch/**. This at present contains the directories **arch/alpha/** for the DEC Alpha, **arch/i386/** for the Intel 386 and compatible processors, **arch/mips/** for the MIPS architecture, **arch/ppc** for the PowerPC architecture and **arch/sparc/** for the port to Sparc workstations. As LINUX is mainly used on PCs, we will only be considering this architecture in what follows.

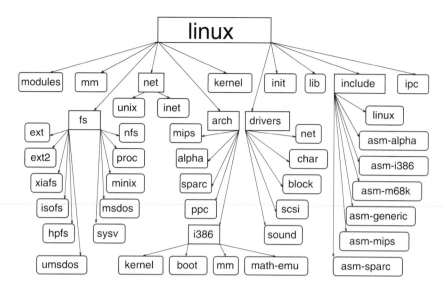

Figure 2.1   The directory structure of the LINUX sources.

For the most part, the LINUX kernel is nothing other than a 'standard' C program. There are only two real differences. The usual entry function, familiar in C programs as `main(int argc, char **argv)`, appears in LINUX as `start_kernel(void)` and is not given any arguments. In addition, the environment for the 'program' does not yet exist. This means that there is a little preparatory work to be done before the first C function is called. The assembler sources which take care of this are held in the directory **arch/i386/boot/**. They also configure the hardware, so this section is highly machine-specific.

The appropriate assembler routine loads the kernel. It then installs the interrupt service routines, the global descriptor tables and the interrupt descriptor tables, which are only used during the initialization phase. Address line A20 is enabled, and the processor switches to Protected Mode.

The **init/** directory contains all the functions needed to start the kernel. Among the functions held here is `start_kernel()`, which was mentioned above. Its task is to initialize the kernel correctly, taking account of the boot parameters passed to it. As well as this, the first process is created without using the system call `fork`, that is, 'manually'.

The directories **kernel/** and **arch/i386/kernel/** contain, as their names suggest, the central sections of the kernel. This is where the main system calls (such as `fork`, `exit`, and so on) are implemented. In addition, the mechanism used by all system calls to switch to system mode is defined. Other important sections are time management (system time, timers, and so on), the scheduler, the DMA and interrupt request management and signal handling.

Memory management sources for the kernel are stored in the directories **mm/** and **arch/i386/mm/**. This takes care of requesting and releasing kernel memory, saving currently unused pages of memory to hard disk (paging), inserting file and memory areas at specified addresses (*see* the *mmap* system call, page 373) and the virtual memory interface.

The virtual file system interface is in the **fs/** directory. The implementations of the various file systems supported by LINUX are held in the respective subdirectories. The two most important file systems are *Proc* and *Ext2*. The *Proc* file system is used for system management; *Ext2* is at present 'the' standard file system for LINUX.

Every operating system requires drivers for its hardware components. These are held in the **drivers/** directory and can be classified into groups according to their subdirectories. These comprise:

- **drivers/block/**
  the device drivers for block-oriented hardware (such as hard disks),

- **drivers/cdrom/**
  the device drivers for proprietary CD-ROM drives (no SCSI or IDE drives),

- **drivers/char/**
  the drivers for character-oriented devices,

- **drivers/isdn/**
  the ISDN drivers,

- **drivers/net/**
  the drivers for various network cards,

- **drivers/pci/**
  PCI bus access and control,

- **drivers/sbus/**
  access and control of Sparc machines' S buses,

- **drivers/scsi/**
  the SCSI interface, and

- **drivers/sound/**
  the sound card drivers.

The drivers listed here are partially architecture-dependent and would properly belong to the **arch/*/** directory, where – in **arch/i386/math-emu/** – the emulation of the maths co-processor's floating-point arithmetic is already located. This only comes into use if no maths co-processor is present.

The **ipc/** directory holds the sources for classical inter-process communication (IPC) as per System V. These include *semaphores, shared memory* and *message queues*.

The implementations of various network protocols (TCP/IP, ARP, and so on) and the code for sockets to the UNIX and Internet domains have been stored in the **net/** directory. As is usual in other systems, the user can access lower protocol layers (for example, IP and ARP). Because of its complexity, this section has not yet been completed.

Some standard C library functions have been implemented in **lib/**, so that programming in the kernel can use the conventions of programming in C.

The modules generated when the kernel is compiled are held in the **module/** directory and can be added to the LINUX kernel later, at run-time. This directory will therefore be empty until the first compilation is run.

Probably the most important directory for programming close to the kernel is **include/**. This holds the kernel-specific header files. The **include/asm-i386/** directory contains the architecture-dependent include files for Intel PCs. To simplify access, the symbolic link **include/asm/** points to the current architecture directory.

As the header files may change from version to version, it is simpler to set up links in **usr/include/** to the two subdirectories **include/linux/** and **include/asm**. Thus, when LINUX kernel sources are changed, the header files are updated automatically.

2.2 Compiling

In essence, a new kernel is generated in three steps. First, the kernel is configured by

```
# make config
```

This runs the Bash script `Configure`, which reads in the `arch/i386/config.in` file, which is located in the architecture directory and holds the definitions of the kernel configuration options and default assignments, and interrogates it to see which components are to be included in the kernel. `arch/i386/config.in` resorts to the `Config.in` files contained in the directories of the individual subsystems of the kernel. Easier-to-handle configuration scripts can be called with

```
# make config
```

for a menu-driven console installation or with

```
# make xconfig
```

for a menu-driven installation under the X Window system.

During this process, the two files `<linux/autoconf.h>` and `.config` are created. The `.config` file controls the sequencing of the compilation run, while `<linux/autoconf.h>` takes care of conditional compiling within the kernel sources. The `.config` file is used if `Configure` is called again, to determine the default responses to individual questions. A fresh configuration will thus return the last values as the defaults. The command

```
# make oldconfig
```

ensures that the default values are accepted without further interrogation. This enables a `.config` file to be included in a new version of LINUX so that the kernel is compiled with the same configuration.

Expansion packages for the kernel will extend the `config.in` file by entries in the form:

```
bool 'PC-Speaker and DAC driver support' CONFIG_PCSP n
```

so that they can be added to or removed from the configuration. Further facilities for configuring the LINUX kernel are described in the next section, but are not required as a rule.

In the second step, the dependencies of the source codes are recalculated. This is done by means of

```
# make depend
```

and is a purely technical procedure. It uses the capability of the GNU C compiler to create dependencies for the *Makefiles*. These dependencies are collected in the `.depend` files in the individual subdirectories and subsequently inserted into the Makefiles.

The actual compilation of the kernel now begins, with the simple call:

```
# make
```

After this, the `vmlinux` file should be found in the uppermost source directory. To create a bootable LINUX kernel,

```
# make boot
```

must be called. As only a compressed kernel can be booted on PCs, the result of this command is the compressed, bootable LINUX kernel `arch/i386/boot/zImage`.

However, other actions can be initiated using `make`. For example, the target `zdisk` not only generates a kernel but also writes it to diskette. The target `zlilo` copies the generated kernel to `/vmlinuz`, and the old kernel is renamed `/vmlinuz.old`. The LINUX kernel is then installed by means of a call to the Linux loader (LILO), which must however be configured beforehand (*see* Appendix D.2.4).

For work on sections of the LINUX kernel (for example, writing a new driver) it is not necessary to recompile the complete kernel or check the dependencies. Instead, a call to

```
# make drivers
```

will cause only the sources in the `drivers/` subdirectory, that is, the drivers, to be compiled. This does not create a new kernel. If a new linkage to the kernel is also required,

```
# make SUBDIRS=drivers
```

should be called. This approach can also be used for the other subdirectories.

A large number of device drivers and file systems not linked into the kernel can be created as modules. This can be done using

```
# make modules
```

The modules created by this can be installed by means of

```
# make modules_install
```

The modules will be installed in the subdirectories `net`, `scsi`, `fs` and `misc` in the `/lib/modules/kernel_version` directory.

2.3   Additional configuration facilities

In special circumstances it may be necessary to change settings within the sources. Normally, however, one should try not to change the configuration in the kernel sources at run-time.

The following pages describe the files in the LINUX kernel to which changes can be made.

●   **Makefile**
This is the only file to which changes cannot be avoided if the user does not have a 'standard PC'. This file is used to set the hardware architecture on which the kernel should run by means of

```
ARCH = i386
```

Other values currently possible for `ARCH` are `alpha` and `sparc`. Additional architectures are already partly supported, but not yet completely integrated into the standard kernel. Furthermore, it is possible to generate a kernel with SMP (Symmetric Multi-Processing) support by entering the line

```
SMP = 1
```

It is also possible to define the root device, the screen mode used and the size of a RAM disk. However, as these can also be specified at a later stage by means of the `rdev` program (*see* Appendix B.3) or by means of parameter passing by the LINUX loader (*see* Appendix D.2.5), they should not be changed in the Makefile.

- **drivers/char/serial.c**
  There is normally no problem with the serial interfaces, as most PCs only possess two of these and they use by default IRQs 4 (COM1) and 3 (COM2). If more interfaces are available because of special hardware (such as an internal modem or a fax card, and so on), automatic IRQ recognition and support for various special cards (the AST Fourport card and others) can be brought in. All this needs is for the preprocessor macros (for example `CONFIG_AUTO_IRQ`) to be defined at the start of the file, which also gives an explanation of this and other macros. As well as this, the default settings for the serial interfaces in the `rs_table[]` field can also be changed. This contains entries conforming to the `async_struct` structure:

```
/* UART CLK    PORT IRQ      FLAGS      */
{ BASE_BAUD, 0x3F8, 4, STD_COM_FLAGS },                /* ttyS0 */
     ...
{ BASE_BAUD, 0x000, 0, 0 },    /* ttyS14 (user configurable) */
{ BASE_BAUD, 0x000, 0, 0 },    /* ttyS15 (user configurable) */
     ...
```

Here, the entries for `ttyS14` and `ttyS15` are intended for the user's own configuration. Once the kernel has been recompiled, the devices `/dev/ttyS14` (and `cua14`) and `/dev/ttyS15` (and `cua15`) can be used. If these do not yet exist, they must be set up.

It only remains to mention that the parameters can also be changed at system run-time by means of the `setserial` program (*see* Appendix B.10).

- **drivers/char/lp.c**
  The parallel interfaces are generally run in *polling mode* (*see* Section 7.2), which means that they are constantly interrogated by the device driver.[1]

---

[1] The parallel interface is, of course, only polled when a process accesses it.

If there is frequent use of the parallel interface, this can at times become something of a nuisance, as it uses computer time unnecessarily. For this reason, there is a facility to set up IRQs for the individual interfaces in this file. In addition, a fourth parallel interface can be added or I/O addresses altered by changing the `lp_table[]` field at the end of the file. This field has the following structure:

```
struct lp_struct lp_table[] = {
    /* PORT IRQ FLAGS CHARS          TIME        WAIT      QUEUE BUF */
    { 0x3bc, 0, 0,LP_INIT_CHAR,LP_INIT_TIME,LP_INIT_WAIT,NULL,NULL},
    { 0x378, 0, 0,LP_INIT_CHAR,LP_INIT_TIME,LP_INIT_WAIT,NULL,NULL},
    { 0x278, 0, 0,LP_INIT_CHAR,LP_INIT_TIME,LP_INIT_WAIT,NULL,NULL},
};
#define LP_NO 3
```

As with serial interfaces, the behaviour of a parallel interface can be changed at run-time through appropriate I/O control calls or the `tunelp` program (*see* Appendix B.11).

● **drivers/net/CONFIG**
If the automatic recognition of network cards is not working, it can sometimes be necessary to fix permanent settings of I/O addresses, IRQs or DMA channels. The precise configuration of such a card can be laid down in this file. The file will be added to the Makefile later.

Alternatively, the corresponding network driver can be compiled as a module and configured when the module is loaded.

● **drivers/net/Space.c**
For some network cards the facilities in the CONFIG file are no longer sufficient.

This file contains the initial configurations of the network devices. This allows the device structures eth1_dev, and so on, defined as constants, to be altered.

```
static struct device eth1_dev = {
/* NAME RECVMEM MEM I/O-BASE IRQ FLAGS NEXT_DEV    INIT      */
   "eth1", 0,0,  0,0, 0xffe0, 0, 0,0,0, &eth2_dev, ethif_probe};
```

Here, the I/O address 0xffe0 means that this device is not checked to see if it is present. This can be avoided by entering a zero for the automatic test or the relevant I/O address. By use of the boot parameter

ether=*irq, port, mem_start, mem_end, name*

the settings can be changed on later start-up of the system.

- **include/linux/fs.h**

  For LINUX computers in larger networks it may be necessary to manage more than 64 file systems. The number of file systems is, however, limited to 64 by the preprocessor macro NR_SUPER. Here, this specification can be altered.

- **include/linux/tasks.h**

  The maximum possible number of processes (NR_TASKS) is limited to 512 in this file and can be altered if necessary for big servers (*see also* Section 3.1.2).

This is a far from exhaustive survey of the configuration facilities in the LINUX kernel. Other facilities will be described in the course of the following chapters.

In conclusion, it should be stressed once again that the changes to the kernel sources described in this section are usually not required and should only be carried out when necessary.

Introduction to the kernel

Dijkstra probably hates me.

Linus Torvalds

3.1   Important data structures   3.3   Implementing system calls
3.2   Main algorithms

This chapter will focus on the basic structure of the LINUX kernel and the interplay of its main components, to provide a foundation for understanding the following chapters. However, before we start, a few more general remarks on the LINUX kernel are in order.

LINUX was not designed on the drawing board but developed in an evolutionary manner, and is continuing to develop. Every function of the kernel has been repeatedly altered and expanded to get rid of bugs and incorporate new features. Anyone who has been personally involved in a major project of this sort will know how quickly program code can become impossible to follow and liable to error. In the face of this, Linus Torvalds, as coordinator of the LINUX Project, has managed to keep the kernel organized in an easy-to-follow form and constantly cleared it of hangovers from earlier versions.

Despite this, the LINUX kernel is certainly not in every respect a good model of structured programming. There are 'magic numbers' in the program text instead of constant declarations in header files, inline expanded functions instead of function calls, `goto` instructions instead of a simple `break`, assembler instructions instead of C code, and many other less than elegant features. Many of these distinctive features of unstructured programming, however, were deliberately included. Large parts of the kernel are time-critical; so the program code is optimized for good run-time behaviour rather than easy readability. This distinguishes LINUX from, for example, MINIX (*see* Tanenbaum,

1990) which was written as a 'teaching operating system' and never designed for everyday use. LINUX, in contrast, is a 'real' operating system and, as such, its kernel is structured remarkably well.

The aim of this book is to explain the main functioning of the LINUX kernel. Therefore, the algorithms introduced in this and the next chapter represent a compromise between the original source codes and understandable program code, but attention has been paid to making the changes easy to follow.

General architecture

Since UNIX came on the scene, the internal structure of operating systems has changed radically. At that time it was revolutionary for most of the kernel to be written in a higher programming language, C; now it is taken for granted. The present trend is towards a microkernel architecture, such as that of the Mach kernel (*see* Tanenbaum, 1986) or the kernel of Windows NT. The experimental UNIX MINIX (*see* Tanenbaum, 1990) and the Hurd system currently under development are further examples of microkernel-based systems. Here, the actual kernel provides only a necessary minimum of functionality (inter-process communication and memory management) and can accordingly be implemented in a small and compact form. Building on this microkernel, the remaining functions of the operating system are relocated to autonomous processes, communicating with the microkernel via a well-defined interface. The main advantage of these architectures (apart from a certain elegance) is a system structure which is clearly less trouble to maintain. Individual components work independently of each other, cannot affect each other unintentionally and are easier to replace. The development of new components is simplified.

This in itself results in a drawback to these architectures. Microkernel architectures force defined interfaces to be maintained between the individual components and prevent sophisticated optimizations. In addition, in today's hardware architectures, the inter-process communication required inside the microkernel is more extensive than simple function calls. This makes the system slower than traditional monolithic kernels. This slight speed disadvantage is readily accepted, because current UNIX hardware is generally fast enough and because the advantage of simpler system maintenance reduces development costs.

Microkernel architectures undoubtedly represent the future of operating system development. LINUX, on the other hand, came into being on the 'slow' 386 architecture, the lower limit for a reasonable UNIX system. Exploiting all possible ways of optimizing performance to give good run-time behaviour was a primary consideration. This is one reason why LINUX was implemented in the classical monolithic kernel architecture. Another reason was undoubtedly the fact that a microkernel architecture depends on careful design of the system. Since LINUX has grown by evolution, starting from the fun of developing a system, this was simply not possible.

In spite of its monolithic foundation, LINUX is not a chaotic collection of program code. Most components of the kernel are only accessed via accurately defined interfaces. A good example of this is the Virtual File System (VFS), which represents an abstract interface to all file-oriented operations. We will be taking a closer look at the VFS in Chapter 6. But the chaos is apparent in the detail. At time-critical points, sections of programs are often written in 'hand-optimized' C code, making them difficult to follow. Fortunately, these program sections are quite rare and, as a rule, fairly well annotated.

The complete LINUX kernel in version 2.0 for the Intel architecture consists of around 470 000 lines of C code and some 8000 lines of assembler. By way of comparison, version 1.0 had only 165 000 lines and version 1.2 about 270 000 lines of C code.

Table 3.1 gives details of approximately how much of the program code is taken up by each component. The assembler coding is principally used in emulating the maths co-processor, booting the system and controlling the hardware. This is only to be expected. However, it can also be seen that something as 'secondary'[1] as implementing the file systems, the device drivers or the network accounts for a large proportion of the kernel sources. On the other hand, the central routines for process and memory management (that is, the kernel proper, in a microkernel context) only take up around 5 per cent, a relatively small amount of the code.

It is possible to separate most device drivers from the kernel. They can be loaded as autonomous, independent modules at run-time as required (*see*

Table 3.1 Proportions of source text accounted for by the individual components.

	C code without header files	Assembler instructions
Device drivers	377 000	100
Network	25 000	
VFS layer	13 500	
13 file systems	50 000	
Initialization	4 000	2800
Co-processor		3550
'Remainder'	20 000	

[1] Lectures on operating systems as a rule concentrate on memory management, scheduling and inter-process communication, and only very seldom deal with other components such as file systems or device drivers.

Chapter 9). Thus LINUX successfully tries to make use of the advantages of a microkernel architecture without, however, giving up its original monolithic design.

Processes and tasks

As seen by a process running under LINUX, the kernel is a provider of services. Individual processes exist independently alongside each other and cannot affect each other directly. Each process's own area of memory is protected against modification by other processes.

The internal viewpoint of a running LINUX system is a different matter. Only one program – the operating system – is running on the computer, and can access all the resources. The various tasks are carried out by co-routines – that is, every task decides for itself whether and when to pass control to another task.[2] One consequence of this is that an error in the kernel programming can block the entire system. Any task can access all the resources for other tasks and modify them.

Certain parts of a task run in the processor's less privileged User Mode. These parts of the task appear from the outside (to someone looking into the kernel) to be processes. From the viewpoint of these processes, true multi-tasking is taking place. Figure 3.1 should make this clear.

In the following pages, however, we will not be making any precise distinction between the concepts of tasks and processes, but using the two words to mean the same thing. When a task is running in the privileged System Mode, it can take one of a number of states. Figure 3.2 shows the most important of these. The arrows in this diagram show the possible changes of state. The following states are possible:

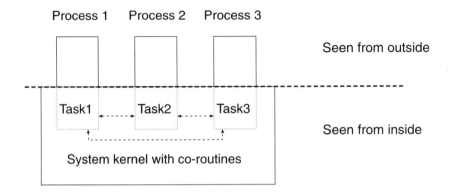

Figure 3.1 The process as seen from outside and from inside.

---

[2] This is also known as cooperative multi-tasking.

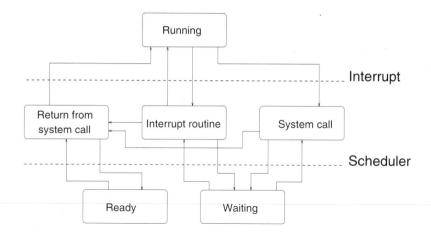

Figure 3.2   Chart of states within a process.

- *Running*
  The task is active and running in the non-privileged User Mode. In this case the process will go through the program in a perfectly normal way. This state can only be exited via an interrupt or a system call. In Section 3.3 we will see that system calls are in fact no more than special cases of interrupts. In either case, the processor is switched to the privileged System Mode and the appropriate interrupt routine is activated.

- *Interrupt routine*
  The interrupt routines become active when the hardware signals an exception condition, which may be new characters input at the keyboard or the clock generator issuing a signal every 10 milliseconds. Further information on interrupt routines is provided in Section 3.2.2.

- *System call*
  System calls are initiated by software interrupts. Details of these are given in Section 3.3. A system call is able to suspend the task to wait for an event.

- *Waiting*
  The process is waiting for an external event. Only after this has occurred will it continue its work.

- *Return from system call*
  This state is automatically adopted after every system call and after some interrupts. At this point checks are made as to whether the scheduler needs to be called and whether there are signals to process. The scheduler can switch the process to the 'Ready' state and activate another process.

- *Ready*

  The process is competing for the processor, which is however occupied with another process at the present time.

Processes and threads

In many modern operating systems a distinction is made between processes and threads. A thread is a sort of independent 'strand' in the course of a program which can be processed in parallel with other threads. As opposed to processes, threads work on the same main memory and can therefore influence each other.

Linux does not make this distinction. In the kernel, only the concept of a task exists which can share resources with other tasks (for example, the same memory). Thus, a task is a generalization of the usual thread concept. More details can be found in Section 3.3.3.

3.1   Important data structures

This chapter describes important data structures in the LINUX kernel. Understanding these structures and how they interact is a necessary foundation for understanding the following chapters.

3.1.1   The task structure

One of the most important concepts in a multi-tasking system such as LINUX is the *task* (or *process*). The data structures and algorithms for process management form the central core of LINUX.

The description of the characteristics of a process is given in the structure `task_struct`, which is explained below. The first components of the structure are also accessed from assembler routines. This access is not made, as it usually is in C, via the names of the components, but via their offsets relative to the start of the structure. This means that the start of the task structure must not be modified without first checking all the assembler routines and modifying them if necessary.

```
struct task_struct
{
    volatile long state;
```

The `state` variable contains a code for the current state of the process. If the process is waiting for the CPU to be assigned or if it is running, `state` takes the value `TASK_RUNNING`. If, on the other hand, the process is waiting for certain events (known as blocking system calls) and is therefore at present idle, `state` takes the value TASK_INTERRUPTIBLE or TASK_UNINTERRUPTIBLE. The difference between these two values is that in the TASK_INTERRUPTIBLE state a task can be reactivated by signals, whilst in the TASK_UNINTERRUPTIBLE state it is typically waiting directly or indirectly for a hardware condition and therefore will not accept any signals. TASK_STOPPED describes a process which has been halted, either after receiving an appropriate signal (SIGSTOP, SIGSTP, SIGTTIN or SIGTTOU) or when the process is being monitored by another process using the *ptrace* system call and has passed control to the monitoring process. TASK_ZOMBIE describes a process which has been terminated but which must still have its task structure in the process table (*see* the system calls *_exit* and *wait* in Section 3.3.3). There is also the TASK_SWAPPING constant, although it is not yet used in version 2.0. The keyword volatile indicates that this component can also be altered asynchronously from interrupt routines.

```
long counter;
long priority;
```

The counter variable holds the time in 'ticks' (*see* Section 3.2.4) for which the process can still run before a mandatory scheduling action is carried out. The scheduler uses the counter value to select the next process. counter thus represents something like the dynamic priority of a process, while priority holds the static priority of a process. The scheduling algorithm (*see* Section 3.2.5) uses priority to derive a new value for counter when necessary.

```
unsigned long signal;
unsigned long blocked;
```

The signal variable contains a bit mask for signals received for the process; blocked contains a bit mask for all the signals the process intends to handle later – that is, those for which processing is at present blocked. As these two components are 32-bit quantities,[3] LINUX supports no more than 32 signals. Removing this limitation would require modifications at various points in the kernel. This signal flag is evaluated in the routine ret_from_sys_call(), which is called after every system call (*see* Section 3.3) and after slow interrupts (*see* Section 3.2.4).

```
unsigned long flags;
int errno;
int debugreg[8];
```

flags contains the combination of the system status flags PF_ALIGNWARN, PF_PTRACED, PF_TRACESYS, PF_STARTING and PF_EXITING.

---

[3] This only applies, of course, when LINUX is running on 32-bit Intel architecture. A higher value will apply for the port to Alpha machines.

`PF_PTRACED` and `PF_TRACESYS` indicate that the process is being monitored by another process with the aid of the system call *ptrace*. Interested readers will find further information on this system call in Section 5.4 and Appendix A.

`PF_STARTING` and `PF_EXITING` indicate that the process is just being initiated or terminated. There are more flags (defined in `include/linux/sched.h`), but these are only used for process accounting (system call *acct*) and are not explained here. The `errno` variable holds the error code for the last faulty system call. On return from the system call, this is copied into the global variable `errno` (*see* Section 3.3). The `debugreg` variable contains the 80x86's debugging registers. These are at present used only by the system call *ptrace*.

```
struct exec_domain *exec_domain;
```

LINUX can run programs from other systems with an i386 base conforming to the iBCS2 standard. As the various iBCS2 systems differ slightly, a description of which UNIX is to be emulated for each process is kept in the `exec_domain` component for the process.

This completes the hard-coded part of the task structure. The following components of the task structure are considered in groups for the sake of simplicity.

Process relationships

All processes are entered in a doubly linked list with the help of the two following components:

```
struct task_struct *next_task;
struct task_struct *prev_task;
```

The start and end of this list are held in the global variable `init_task`.

In a UNIX system, processes do not exist independently of each other. Every process (except for the process `init_task`) has a parent process, which has created it using the system call *fork()* (*see* Section 3.3.3 and Appendix A). There are therefore 'family relationships' between the processes, which are represented by the following components:

```
struct task_struct *p_opptr; /* original parent */
struct task_struct *p_pptr;  /* parent */
struct task_struct *p_cptr;  /* youngest child */
struct task_struct *p_ysptr; /* younger sibling */
struct task_struct *p_osptr; /* older sibling */
```

The `p_pptr` variable is a pointer to the parent process's task structure. To enable a process to access all its child processes, the task structure holds the

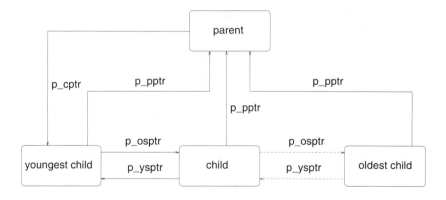

Figure 3.3 'Family relationships' between processes.

entry for the last child process created – the 'youngest child'. The child processes for the same parent process are similarly linked together as a doubly linked list by p_ysptr (next younger sibling) and p_osptr (next older sibling). Figure 3.3 should clarify the 'family relationships' between processes.

The scheduler uses a list of all processes that apply for the processor. It is implemented as a doubly linked list with the help of the two following components:

```
struct task_struct *next_task;
struct task_struct *prev_task;
```

Here too, the external variable init_task describes the start and end of this list.

Memory management

The data for each process needed for memory management are collected, for reasons of simplicity, in their own substructure

```
struct mm_struct mm[1];
```

The components of this are:

```
unsigned long start_code, end_code, start_data, end_data;
unsigned long start_brk, brk,
unsigned long start_stack,start_mmap;
unsigned long arg_start, arg_end, env_start, env_end;
    ...
```

which describe the start and size of the code and data segments of the program currently running. Further information is given in Chapter 4.

The structure `task_struct` has two more components relating to memory management. When a process is operating in System Mode, it needs its own stack (differing from that for the User Mode). The address of the stack is stored in

```
unsigned long kernel_stack_page;
```

For the MS-DOS emulator (or, more precisely, for the system call *vm86*) there is also the

```
unsigned long saved_kernel_stack;
```

in which the old stack pointer is stored.

Process ID

Every process has its own process ID number, `pid`, and is assigned to a process group, `pgrp,` and a session, `session`. Every session has a leader process, `leader`.

```
int pid, pgrp, session, leader;
```

To handle access control, every process has a user ID, `uid,` and a group ID, `gid`. These are inherited by the child process from the parent process when a new process is created by the `fork` system call (*see* Section 3.3.3 and Appendix A). However, for the actual access control the effective user ID, `euid`, and the effective group ID, `egid`, are used. A new feature in LINUX is the component `fsuid`. This is used whenever identification is required by the file system. As a general rule, `(uid==euid)&&(gid==egid)` and `(fsuid==euid)&&(fsgid==egid)`.

Exceptions arise for so-called set-UID programs, where the values of `euid` and `fsuid`, or those of `egid` and `fsgid`, are set to the user ID and the group ID for the owner of the executable file. This makes a controlled distribution of privileges possible.

As a rule, `fsuid` always takes the value of `euid`; and in other UNIX systems or older versions of LINUX the effective user ID `euid` was always used in place of `fsuid`. However, LINUX's *setfsuid* system call allows `fsuid` to be altered without changing `euid`. This means that daemons can limit their rights when accessing file systems with `setfsuid` (to the rights of the user for whom they are providing services), but they will retain their privileges. The reason this was introduced was a security gap in the NFS daemon. To limit its rights for file system access, this had set `euid` to the user ID of the requesting user. The file access then worked as expected, but it also allowed the user to send signals to the NFS daemon. This was not the desired result, and changes have now been made. Similar considerations apply for the component fsgid and the system call *setfsgid*.

```
unsigned short uid, euid, suid, fsuid;
unsigned short gid, egid, sgid, fsgid;
```

Like most modern UNIX derivatives, LINUX allows a process to be assigned to a number of user groups at the same time. These groups are considered when checking the access permissions to files. Each process may belong to a maximum of NGROUPS groups, which are held in the groups component of the task structure. It may seem odd at first sight that a different data type is used here for the group ID gid than for the groups field, but can be explained by the fact that groups can also hold the value NOGROUP==-1 for unused entries.

```
int groups[NGROUPS];
```

Files

The file-system-specific data are stored in the substructure:

```
struct fs_struct fs[1];
```

This contains the four components:

```
int count;
unsigned short umask;
struct inode * root;
struct inode * pwd;
```

A process can affect the access mode of newly created files via the system call *umask*. The values set using *umask* are also stored in the component umask. Under UNIX, every process has a current directory, pwd,[4] which is required when resolving relative pathnames and can be changed by means of the system call *chdir*. Every process has in addition its own root directory – root – which is used in resolving absolute pathnames. This root directory can only be changed by the superuser (system call *chroot*). As this is only rarely used (for example, in anonymous FTP), this fact is not well known. The count variable is reserved for future expansions.

A process opening a file with open() or creat() is given a file descriptor by the kernel to use in referencing the file in future. File descriptors are small

---

[4] The abbreviation pwd most probably derives from the UNIX command pwd – Print Working Directory – which outputs the name of the current directory.

integers. The file descriptors are assigned to the files under LINUX via the `fd[]` field in the substructure:

```
struct files_struct files[1];
```

This has four components:

```
int count;
fd_set close_on_exec;
fd_set open_fds;
struct file * fd[NR_OPEN];
```

File descriptors are used as an index in the `fd[]` field. This locates the file pointer assigned to the file descriptor, and with its help the file itself can then be accessed. `open_fds` is a bit mask of all file descriptors used.

The component `close_on_exec` in the `files` substructure contains a bit mask of all file descriptors used that are to be closed when the system call *exec* is issued. The data type `fd_set` is large enough to hold `NR_OPEN` (256) bits. Again, `count` is used as a reference counter.

Timing

Various times are measured for each process. Under LINUX, times are always measured in 'ticks'. These ticks are generated by a timer chip every 10 milliseconds and counted by the timer interrupt. In Sections 3.1.6 and 3.2.4 we will be considering timing under LINUX in more detail.

The `utime` and `stime` variables hold the time the process has spent in User Mode and System Mode, respectively, while `cutime` and `cstime` contain the totals of the corresponding times for all child processes. These values can be polled by means of the *times* system call.

```
long utime, stime, cutime, cstime, start_time
```

`start_time` contains the time at which the current process was generated.

UNIX supports a number of process-specific timers. One of these is the system call *alarm*, which ensures that the SIGALARM signal is sent to the process after a specified time. Newer UNIX systems also support interval timers (*see* system calls *setitimer* and *getitimer* on page 324).

```
unsigned long timeout;
unsigned long it_real_value, it_prof_value, it_virt_value;
unsigned long it_real_incr, it_prof_incr, it_virt_incr;
struct timer_list real_timer;
```

The components it_real_value, it_prof_value and it_virt_value contain the time in ticks until the timer will be triggered. The components it_real_incr, it_prof_incr and it_virt_incr hold the values required to reinitialize the timers after they run out. real_timer is used for the implementation of the real-time interval timer. More information on this is given in the description of the timer interrupt in Section 3.2.4.

Inter-process communication

The LINUX kernel implements a system of inter-process communication which is compatible with System V. Among other things, this provides semaphores. A process can occupy a semaphore, thereby blocking it. If other processes also wish to occupy this semaphore, they are halted until the semaphore is released. This uses the component

```
struct sem_queue *semsleeping;
```

When the process is terminated, the operating system must release all semaphores occupied by the process. The component

```
struct sem_undo *semundo;
```

contains the information required for this.

Miscellaneous

The following components do not fit any of the above groups.

```
struct wait_queue *wait_chldexit;
```

A process executing the system call *wait4* must be halted until a child process terminates. It joins the wait_chldexit wait queue in its own task structure, sets the status flag to the value TASK_INTERRUPTIBLE and passes control to the scheduler. When a process terminates, it signals this to its parent process via this queue. There is more on this in the section on wait queues (*see* Section 3.1.5), the section on the system calls *_exit* and *wait* (Section 3.3.3) and the source texts for the kernel function sys_wait4() (kernel/exit.c).

```
struct sigaction sigaction[32];
```

Every process can decide how it wishes to react to signals. This is specified in the sigaction structure (*see* page 327).

```
struct rlimit rlim[RLIM_NLIMITS];
```

Every process can check its limits for the use of resources by means of the system calls *setrlimit* and *getrlimit* (*see* page 325). These are stored in the rlim structure.

```
int exit_code exit_signal;
```

The return code for the program and the signal by which the program has been aborted. These data can be polled by a parent process after completion of the child process.

```
char comm[16];
```

The name of the program executed by the process is stored in the component comm. This name is used in debugging.

```
unsigned long personality;
```

As mentioned earlier, LINUX supports, via the iBCS interface, the execution of programs from other UNIX systems. Together with the exec_domain component described above, personality is used to give a precise description of the characteristics of this version of UNIX. For standard LINUX programs, personality takes the value PER_LINUX (defined as 0 in <linux/personality.h>).

```
int dumpable:1;
int did_exec:1;
```

The dumpable flag indicates whether a memory dump is to be executed by the current process if certain signals occur.

A rather obscure semantic in the POSIX standard requires, when calling *setpgid*, to distinguish whether a process is still running the original program or whether it has loaded a new program with the system call *execve*. This information is monitored using the flag did_exec.

```
struct desc_struct *ldt;
```

This entry has been included especially for the WINE Windows emulator, which needs more information and different memory management routines as compared with a standard LINUX program.

Another important component in the task structure is binfmt. This describes the functions responsible for loading the program.

```
struct linux_binfmt *binfmt;
struct thread_struct tss;
```

The `thread_struct` structure holds all the data on the current processor status at the time of the last transition from User Mode to System Mode. All the processor registers are saved here to enable them to be restored on return to User Mode. In addition (unlike LINUX version 1.0), this now includes the components

```
struct vm86_struct * vm86_info;
unsigned long screen_bitmap;
unsigned long v86flags, v86mask, v86mode;
```

to describe the 8086 emulation implemented by the system call *vm86*.

LINUX supports several scheduling algorithms. Besides the classic scheduling (SCHED_OTHER) there are now two real-time scheduling algorithms (SCHED_RR and SCHED_FIFO) described in POSIX.4. Each process can be assigned to one of these scheduling classes which, together with the real-time priority, is stored in the `task` structure

```
unsigned long policy; /* SCHED_FIFO, SCHED_RR, SCHED_OTHER */
unsigned long rt_priority;
```

There is more information on this in Section 3.2.5.

Since LINUX 2.0 the kernel supports Symmetric Multi-Processing. Thus, for each task the kernel needs to know on which processor the task is running.

```
#ifdef __SMP__
   int processor, last_processor;
   int lock_depth;
#endif
} /* struct task_struct */
```

3.1.2   The process table

Every process occupies exactly one entry in the process table. In LINUX, this is statically organized and restricted in size to NR_TASKS.

```
struct task_struct *task [NR_TASKS];
```

In older versions of the LINUX kernel, all the processes present could be traced by searching the task[] process table for entries. In the newer versions this information is stored in the linked lists `next_task` and `prev_task`, which can be found in the `task_struct` structure. The external variable `init_task` points to the start of the doubly linked circular list.

```
struct task_struct init_task;
```

This is initialized with the first task `INIT_TASK` when the system is booted (described in Section 3.2.3). Once the system has been booted, this is only responsible for the use of unclaimed system time (the idle process). For this reason, it is rather in a class of its own and should not be regarded as a normal task.

Many of the algorithms in the kernel have to take note of every individual task. To make this easier, the macro `for_each_task()` has been defined as follows:

```
#define for_each_task(p)        \
    for( p = &init_task ; ( p = p->next_task) != &init_task ; )
```

As can be seen, `init_task` is skipped. In version 1, the entry for the currently running task could be obtained via the global variable

```
struct task_struct current;
```

As version 2.0 supports multi-processing (SMP), this had to be extended – now there is a current task for each processor.

```
#define current current_set[smp_processor_id()]
task_struct *current_set[NR_CPUS];
```

The entry `task[0]` has a special significance in LINUX. `task[0]` is the `INIT_TASK` mentioned above, which is the first to be generated when the system is booted and has something of a special role to play. This process is frequently accessed in the kernel via `task[0]`; so this assignment should not be altered.

The static size of the process table is an anachronism in modern UNIX operating systems. In LINUX, there are historical reasons for it. It is simpler to reserve a field than to use dynamic memory management. However, development within LINUX tends towards the removal of static limitations, such as the maximum number of processes. The components `next_task` and `prev_task` have therefore been added to the `task_struct` described above; together with `init_task`, these enable all active processes to be referenced. It is now no longer necessary to hold all the process entries in a table.

3.1.3   Files and inodes

UNIX systems traditionally make a distinction between the file structure and the inode structure. The inode structure describes a file, which gives the term 'inode' a number of meanings. Both the data structure in the kernel and the data structure on the hard disk describe files (each from their own viewpoint), and are therefore called inodes. In the following, we will always be referring to the data structure in memory. Inodes contain information such as the file's owner and access rights. There is *exactly one* inode entry in the kernel for each file used in the system.

File structures (that is, data structures of the `struct file` type), on the other hand, contain the view of a process on these files (represented by inodes). This view on the file includes attributes, such as the mode in which the file can be used (read, write, read+write), or the current position of the next I/O operation.

File structure

The structure `file` is defined in `include/linux/fs.h`

```
struct file
{
   mode_t f_mode;
   loff_t f_pos;
   unsigned short f_flags;
   unsigned short f_count;
   struct file *f_next, *f_prev;
   struct inode * f_inode;
   struct file_operations * f_op;
   ...
};
```

The `f_mode` component describes the access mode in which the file was opened (read-only, read+write or write only); `f_pos` holds the position of the read/write pointer at which the next I/O operation will be carried out. This value is updated by every I/O operation and by the system calls *lseek* and *llseek*. Note that the offset is stored in the kernel as a 64-bit word of the type `loff_t`. This enables LINUX correctly to handle files larger than 2 gigabytes (2^{31} bytes).

Additional flags controlling access to this file are contained in `f_flags`. These can be set when a file is opened with the system call *open* and later read and modified using the system call *fcntl*. The variable `f_count` is a simple reference counter. A number of file descriptors may refer to the same file structure. As these are inherited through the system call *fork*, the same file structure may also be referenced from different processes. When a file is opened, f_count is initialized to 1. Every time the file descriptor is copied (by the system calls *dup*, *dup2* or *fork*) the reference counter is incremented by 1, and every time a file is closed (using the system calls *close*, *_exit* or *exec*) it is decreased by 1. The file structure is only released once there is no longer any process referring to it.

All file structures present in the system form part of a doubly linked list through their components f_next and f_prev. The global variable

```
struct file * first_file;
```

constitutes the start of this list.

The inode (the actual description of the file) is referenced by f_inode, whereas f_op refers to a structure of function pointers referencing all file operations. By comparison with other UNIX systems, LINUX supports a very large number of file system types. Each of these file systems implements accesses in a different way. For this reason, a 'virtual file system' (VFS) has been implemented in LINUX. The idea is that the functions operating on the file system are not called directly, but via a function specific to the file (system). The file-system-specific operations are part of the file or inode structure, which corresponds to the principle of virtual functions in object-oriented programming languages. Comprehensive information on the VFS is given in Section 6.2.

Inodes

The inode structure

```
struct inode
{
```

is also defined in include/linux/fs.h. Many of the components of this structure can be polled via the system call *stat*.

```
dev_t i_dev;
unsigned long i_ino;
```

The component i_dev is a description of the device (the disk partition) on which the file is located, while i_ino[5] identifies the file within the device. The (dev, ino) pair thus provides an identification of the file which is unique throughout the system.

---

[5] Here, too, ino stands for the inode, referring in this case to the block number of the data structure on the hard disk, describing the file on the external memory device.

```
umode_t i_mode;
uid_t i_uid;
gid_t i_gid;
off_t i_size;
time_t i_mtime;
time_t i_atime;
time_t i_ctime;
```

These components describe the access permissions to the file, its owner (user and group), the size i_size in bytes, and the times of the last modification (i_mtime), the last access (i_atime) and the last modification to the inode (i_ctime).

```
struct inode_operations * i_op;
...
```

Like the file structure, the inode also has a reference to a structure containing pointers to functions which can be used on inodes (*see* Section 6.2.4). Further information on inodes is given in Section 6.2.

3.1.4   Dynamic memory management

Under LINUX, memory is managed on a page basis. One page contains 2^{12} bytes. The basic operations to request a free page are the functions

```
unsigned long __get_free_pages(int priority,
        unsigned long order, int dma);
#define __get_free_page(priority) \
        __get_free_pages((priority),0,0)
#define __get_dma_pages(priority, order) \
        __get_free_pages((priority),(order),1)
```

which are defined in the file mm/swap.c. The value of priority controls the behaviour of __get_free_page() if not enough pages are free in main memory. The following values are legal for priority: GFP_BUFFER, GFP_ATOMIC, GFP_KERNEL, GFP_NOBUFFER and GFP_NFS. order describes the number of pages to be reserved, which is 2^{order}. If dma is not equal to 0, memory is requested that can be addressed by the DMA component.

Although __get_free_page() represents the basic operation to request a page, it should not be used in this form. A more suitable function is

```
unsigned long get_free_page(int priority);
```

which additionally initializes the requested memory to zero. This is important for two reasons. Firstly, some parts of the kernel expect freshly requested memory to be initialized to zero (for example, the system call *exec*). Secondly, this is a security measure: if the page has already been used it may contain another user's data (for example, passwords), which should not be made available to the current process.

C programmers will as a rule be accustomed to using `malloc()` and `free()` to manage memory. There is similar provision in the LINUX kernel: the function

```
void *kmalloc(size_t size, int priority);
```

works in an analogous way to `malloc()`. The argument `priority` indicates how `kmalloc()` is to request new pages of memory using `get_free_page()`. `kmalloc()` can request blocks of memory up to an extent of 128 kbytes. In LINUX version 1.0 there was still a limit of 4072 bytes. The counterpart to `kmalloc()` is the function

```
void kfree( void * ptr);
```

which releases an area of memory previously requested using `kmalloc()`. There is more information on how memory management operates under LINUX in Chapter 4.

3.1.5 Queues and semaphores

Often a process will be dependent on the occurrence of certain conditions. For example, the system call *read* has to wait until the data have been loaded into the process's area of memory from the hard disk, or a parent process is using *wait* to wait for the end of a child process. In each of these cases it is not known how long the process will have to wait.

This 'wait until condition met' is implemented in LINUX by means of wait queues. A wait queue is nothing other than a cyclical list containing as its elements pointers to the process table.

```
struct wait_queue {
  struct task_struct * task;
  struct wait_queue * next;
};
```

Wait queues are very sensitive creatures and are often modified from interrupt routines. They should therefore only be modified using one of the two functions below. By blocking the interrupts, these make sure that the wait queue is not modified from an interrupt routine at the same time. Consistency is thus guaranteed.

```
void add_wait_queue(struct wait_queue **queue,
    struct wait_queue *entry);

void remove_wait_queue(struct wait_queue **queue,
    struct wait_queue *entry);
```

The `queue` variable contains the wait queue to be modified, and `entry` the entry to be added or removed.

A process wishing to wait for a specific event now enters itself in a wait queue of this type and relinquishes control. There is a wait queue for every possible event. When the relevant event occurs, all the processes in its wait queue are reactivated and can resume operation. This semantic is implemented by the functions:

```
void sleep_on(struct wait_queue **p);
void interruptible_sleep_on(struct wait_queue **p);
```

These set the process status (`current->state`) to `TASK_UNINTERRUPTIBLE` or `TASK_INTERRUPTIBLE` respectively, enter the current process (`current`) in the wait queue and call the scheduler. The process then voluntarily relinquishes control.

It is only reactivated when the status of the process is set to `TASK_RUNNING`. This is generally done by another process calling the functions

```
void wake_up(struct wait_queue **p);
void wake_up_interruptible(struct wait_queue **p);
```

to 'wake up' all the processes entered in the wait queue.

```
void sleep_on( struct wait_queue **queue )
{
   struct wait_queue entry = { current , NULL };
   current->state = TASK_UNINTERRUPTIBLE;
   add_wait_queue( queue , &entry );
   schedule();
   remove_wait_queue( queue , &entry );
}

void wake_up( struct wait_queue **queue )
{
   struct wait_queue *p = *queue;
   do
   {
     p->task->state = TASK_RUNNING ;
     p = p->next;
   } while ( p != *queue );
}
```

With the aid of wait queues, Linux also provides semaphores. These are used to synchronize accesses by various kernel routines to shared data structures. These semaphores should not be confused with semaphores provided for user programs in UNIX System V.

```
struct semaphore {
    int count ;
    struct wait_queue *wait;
};
```

A semaphore is taken to be occupied if `count` has a value less than or equal to 0. All the processes wishing to occupy the semaphore enter themselves in the wait queue. They are then notified when it is released by another process. There are two auxiliary functions to occupy or release semaphores:

```
void down( struct semaphore * sem )
{
    while( sem -> count <= 0 )
        sleep_on( sem->wait );
    sem -> count -- ;
}

void up( struct semaphore * semd )
{
    sem -> count ++;
    wake_up( & sem -> wait );
}
```

3.1.6 System time and timers

In the LINUX system, there is just one internal time base. It is measured in ticks elapsed since the system was booted, with one tick equal to 10 milliseconds. These are generated by a timer chip in the hardware and counted by the timer interrupt (*see* Section 3.2.4) in the global variable `jiffies`. All the system timings mentioned below always refer to this time base.

Why do we need timers? Many device drivers like to be sent a message when the device is not ready. And in addition, there is sometimes a time gap before the next set of data can be sent when a slow device is being used.

To support this, LINUX provides a facility to initiate functions at a defined future time. In the course of LINUX's development, two forms of timer have come about. On the one hand, there are 32 reserved timers of the form:

```
struct timer_struct {
    unsigned long expires;
```

```
    void (*fn)(void);
} timer_table[32];
```

Each entry is given a pointer to a function `fn` and a time `expires` at which the function is to be called. A bit field

```
unsigned long timer_active;
```

indicates which entries in the `timer_table[]` are valid. This kind of timer is obsolete and only used for certain device drivers.

For normal applications, there is a more recent interface of the form:

```
struct timer_list {
    struct timer_list *next;
    struct timer_list *prev;
    unsigned long expires;
    unsigned long data;
    void (*function)(unsigned long);
};
```

The entries `next` and `last` in this structure are used for the internal management of all the timers in a doubly linked sorted list. At the start of this list is the variable `timer_head`. The component `expires` gives the time at which the function `function` is to be called with the argument `data`. The two functions

```
extern void add_timer(struct timer_list * timer);
extern int  del_timer(struct timer_list * timer);
```

are used in the administration of the timer list. Note that `add_timer()` changes the meaning of the component `expire`. As an argument for `add_timer()`, `expire` describes the time interval after which the timer is to run out. Once `add_timer()` has entered the structure on the list, `expire` signifies the time at which the function is to be called. In version 1.0 of LINUX, the semantics of the `expire` component were exactly the other way round.

3.2 Main algorithms

This section describes the main algorithms for process management.

3.2.1 Signals

One of the oldest facilities for inter-process communication under UNIX consists of signals. The kernel uses signals to inform processes about certain events. The user typically uses signals to abort processes or to switch interactive programs to a defined state.

All signals are sent by the function `send_sig()`. For this function, alongside the arguments giving the signal number and a description of the process which is to receive the signal (or, more precisely, a pointer to the entry for the process in the task structure), there is a third argument – the priority of the sender. At present, only two priorities are supported. The signal can be sent from a process, or it can be generated by the kernel. The kernel can send a signal to any process, while a normal user process is only allowed to do so under specific conditions. It must either possess superuser rights or have the same UID and GID as the receiving process. An exception to this is the `SIGCONT` signal, which may be sent from any process in the same session.

If there is authority to send the signal and the process is not inclined to ignore this signal, it is sent to the process. This is done by setting the bit for the signal number in the `signal` component of the task structure for the receiving process. The signal has then been sent. There is no immediate treatment of the signal by the receiving process: this happens only after the scheduler has returned the process to the `TASK_RUNNING` state (*see* Section 3.2.5). In addition, the kernel has the possibility of sending signals by means of the `force_sig()` function. This ensures that the signal is delivered even when the process has blocked the signal or – worse – wants to ignore it.

When the process is reactivated by the scheduler, but before it is switched to User Mode, the routine `ret_from_sys_call` (Section 3.3.1) is run. If signals are waiting for the current process, this calls the `do_signal()` function, which takes over the actual signal handling.

We have not yet dealt with the matter of how this function causes the signal handling routine defined by the process to be called. This problem was solved by a clever stratagem allowing the `do_signal()` function to manipulate the stack and the registers of the process. The process's instruction pointer is set to the first instruction in the signal handling routine, and the parameters for the signal handling routine are added to the stack. Now, when the process resumes operation, it appears to it as if the signal handling routine has been called like a normal function.

This is how it is done in principle; but in the actual implementation there are two additional features.

Firstly, LINUX claims to be **POSIX**-compatible. The process can specify which signals are to be blocked while a signal handling routine is running. This is implemented by the kernel adding further signals to the signal mask `current->blocked` before calling the user-defined signal handling routine. There is a problem, however: the signal mask must be restored to its original state after the signal handling routine has terminated. To deal with this, an instruction which activates the system call *sigreturn* is entered on the stack as the return address of the signal handling routine. This then takes care of the clearing-up operations at the end of the user-defined signal handling routine.

The second addition is an optimization. If a number of signal handling routines need to be called, a number of stack frames are set up. As a result, the signal handling routines are executed one after the other.

3.2.2 Interrupts

Interrupts are used to allow the hardware to communicate with the operating system. Programming interrupt routines will be examined in more detail in Section 7.2.2. Here, we are more interested in the principles governing the execution of an interrupt. The relevant code is held in the files arch/i386/kernel/irq.c and include/asm/irq.h.

There are two types of interrupt in LINUX: fast and slow. We could even say there are three, with the third type represented by system calls, which are also triggered via interrupts. However, this chapter will only deal with hardware interrupts.

Slow interrupts

Slow interrupts are the usual kind. Other interrupts are legal while they are being dealt with. After a slow interrupt has been processed, additional activities requiring regular attention are carried out by the system – for example, the scheduler is called as and when required. A typical example of a slow interrupt is the timer interrupt (Section 3.2.4). The processing of an interrupt involves the following activities.

```
PSEUDO_CODE IRQ(intr_num, intr_controller, intr_mask)
{
```

First, all the registers are saved with SAVE_ALL and receipt of the interrupt is confirmed to the interrupt controller with ACK. At the same time, further receipt of interrupts of the same type is blocked.

```
SAVE_ALL; /* macro in include/asm/irq.h */
ENTER_KERNEL; /* macro in include/asm/irq.h SMP lock */
ACK(intr_controller, intr_mask);
```

In the case of a multi-processor system, the call to the ENTER_KERNEL routine is used to synchronize the processors' access to the kernel.

The nesting depth of the interrupts is noted in the variable intr_count, after which further interrupts are enabled and the interrupt routine itself is called. This is also provided with a copy of the set of registers for the interrupted process. The registers are used by some of the interrupt handlers (for example, the timer interrupt) to determine whether the interrupt has interrupted the user process or the kernel.

```
        ++intr_count;
        sti();
        do_IRQ(intr_num, Register)
```

Once the interrupt routine has been successfully executed, the interrupt controller is informed that interrupts of this type can again be accepted. In addition, the interrupt counter is decremented.

```
        cli();
        UNBLK(intr_controller, intr_mask)
        --intr_count;
```

A jump into the assembler routine `ret_from_sys_call()` is then made. This takes care of more general administration tasks after any slow interrupt or system call (hence its name). This function never returns. It restores the registers saved with `SAV_ALL` and carries out the `iret` required at the end of an interrupt routine.

```
        ret_from_sys_call();
    } /* PSEUDO_CODE IRQ */
```

Fast interrupts

Fast interrupts are used for short, less complex tasks. While they are being handled, all other interrupts are blocked, unless the handling routine involved explicitly enables them. A typical example is the keyboard interrupt (`drivers/char/keyboard.c`).

```
        PSEUDO_CODE fast_IRQ(intr_num, intr_controller, intr_mask)
        {
```

First, as before, registers are saved – but only those which are modified by a normal C function. This means that, if assembler code is to be used in the handling routine, the remaining registers must be saved beforehand and restored afterwards.

```
        SAVE_MOST; /* macro in include/asm/irq.h */
```

The interrupt controller is also informed and the variable `intr_count` incremented in the same way as for slow interrupts. This time, however, no further interrupts are accepted before the interrupt handler itself is called (`sti()` is not called).

```
        ENTER_KERNEL; /* macro in include/asm/irq.h */
        ACK(intr_controller, intr_mask);
```

```
++intr_count;
do_fast_IRQ(intr_num)
UNBLK(intr_controller, intr_mask)
--intr_count;
LEAVE_KERNEL
```

This completes the interrupt handling. RESTORER_MOST returns the saved registers to their previous values and then calls iret to continue the interrupted process.

```
RESTORE_MOST; /* macro in include/asm/irq.h */
} /* PSEUDO_CODE fast_IRQ */
```

3.2.3   Booting the system

There is something magical about booting a UNIX system (or, for that matter, any operating system). The aim of this section is to make the process a little more transparent.

Appendix D explains how LILO (the LINUX LOader) finds the LINUX kernel and loads it into memory. It then begins at the entry point start: which is held in the arch/i386/boot/setup.S file. As the name suggests, this is assembler code responsible for initializing the hardware. Once the essential hardware parameters have been established, the process is switched into Protected Mode by setting the protected mode bit in the *machine status word*.

The assembler instruction

```
jmp 0x1000 , KERNEL_CS
```

then initiates a jump to the start address of the 32-bit code for the actual operating system kernel and continues from startup_32: in the file arch/i386/kernel/head.S. Here more sections of the hardware are initialized (in particular the MMU (page table), the co-processor and the interrupt descriptor table) and the environment (stack, environment, and so on) required for the execution of the kernel's C functions. Once initialization is complete, the first C function, start_kernel() from init/main.c, is called.

This first saves all the data the assembler code has found about the hardware up to that point. All areas of the kernel are then initialized.

```
asmlinkage void start_kernel(void)
{
    memory_start = paging_init(memory_start,memory_end);

    trap_init();
    init_IRQ();
    sched_init();
```

```
        time_init();
        parse_options(command_line);
        init_modules();

        memory_start = console_init(memory_start,memory_end);
        memory_start = pci_init(memory_start,memory_end);
        memory_start = kmalloc_init(memory_start,memory_end);

        sti();

        memory_start = inode_init(memory_start,memory_end);
        memory_start = file_table_init(memory_start,memory_end);
        memory_start = name_cache_init(memory_start,memory_end);
        mem_init(memory_start,memory_end);

        buffer_init();
        sock_init();
        ipc_init();

    ...
```

The process now running is process 0. It now generates a kernel thread which executes the init() function.

```
        kernel_thread(init,NULL,0);
```

Subsequently, process 0 is only concerned with using up unused CPU time.

```
        cpu_idle(NULL);
```

The init() function carries out the remaining initialization. It starts the bdflush and kswap daemons which are responsible for synchronization of the buffer cache contents with the file system and for swapping.

```
    static int init()
    {
        kernel_thread(bdflush, NULL, 0);
        kernel_thread(kswapd, NULL, 0);
```

Then the system call *setup* is used to initialize the file systems and to mount the root file system.

```
        setup();
```

Now an attempt can be made to establish a connection with the console and to open the file descriptors 0, 1 and 2.

```
if ((open("/dev/tty1",O_RDWR,0) < 0) &&
    (open("/dev/ttyS0",O_RDWR,0) < 0))
        printk("Unable to open an initial console.");

(void) dup(0);
(void) dup(0);
```

Then an attempt is made to execute one of the programs /etc/init, /bin/init or /sbin/init. These usually start the background processes running under LINUX and make sure that the getty program runs on each connected terminal – thus a user can log in to the system.

```
execve("/etc/init",argv_init,envp_init);
execve("/bin/init",argv_init,envp_init);
execve("/sbin/init",argv_init,envp_init);
```

If none of the above-mentioned programs exists, an attempt is made to process /etc/rc and subsequently start a shell so that the superuser can repair the system.

```
pid = kernel_thread(do_rc, "/etc/rc", SIGCHLD);
if (pid>0)
    while (pid != wait(&i))
            ;

while (1)
{
    pid = kernel_thread(do_shell,
        execute_command ? execute_command : "/bin/sh",
        SIGCHLD);
    if (pid < 0)
    {
        printf("Fork failed in init");
        continue;
    }
    while (1)
        if (pid == wait(&i))
            break;
    printf("child %d died with code %04x",pid,i);
    sync();
}
return -1;
}
```

The procedure described above is meant only to give an overview of what happens when a system is started. Owing to hardware initialization (MMU, SMP) and handling of exceptions (UMSDOS, INITRD), the reality is far more complicated.

3.2.4 Timer interrupt

All operating systems need a way of measuring time and keeping a system time. The system time is usually implemented by arranging the hardware to trigger an interrupt at specified intervals. These interrupt routines take over the time 'counting'. Under LINUX, system time is measured in 'ticks' since the system was started up. One tick represents 10 milliseconds, so the timer interrupt is triggered 100 times per second. The time is stored in the variable

```
unsigned long volatile jiffies;
```

which should only be modified by the timer interrupt. However, this method only provides an internal time base.

Applications, on the other hand, are more interested in the 'actual time'. This is held in the variable

```
volatile struct timeval xtime;
```

which is also updated by the timer interrupt.

The timer interrupt is called relatively often and is therefore somewhat time-critical. Therefore, its implementation in the 2.0 kernel is no longer as clear as it was in version 1.0.

The interrupt routine proper simply updates the variable `jiffies` and marks the bottom half routine (*see* Section 7.2.4) of the timer interrupt as active. This is called by the system at a later point (after handling other interrupts) and carries out the rest of the work. Since several timer interrupts can occur before the handling routines become active, the timer interrupt also increments the variables

```
unsigned long lost_ticks;
unsigned long lost_ticks_system;
```

so that these can later be evaluated in the bottom half routines.

`lost_ticks` counts the timer interrupts that have passed since the last call of the bottom half routine, whereas `lost_ticks_system` counts the timer interrupts during whose occurrence the interrupted process was in System Mode.

```
void do_timer(struct pt_regs *regs)
{
    ++jiffies;
    ++lost_ticks;
    if(!user_mode(regs))
            ++lost_ticks_system;
    mark_bh(TIMER_BH);
    if (tq_timer)
            mark_bh(TQUEUE_BH);
}
```

The real work is then carried out by the bottom half routines of the timer
interrupt.

```
void timer_bh(void)
{
    update_times();
    run_old_timers();
    run_timer_list();
}
```

Here, run_old_timers() and run_timer_list() process the functions for updating the system-wide timers described in Section 3.1.6, which also comprise the
real-time timers of the current task. update_times() is responsible for updating
the times.

```
static inline void update_times(void)
{
    unsigned long ticks;

    ticks = xchg(&lost_ticks, 0);

    if (ticks)
    {
        unsigned long system;

        system = xchg(&lost_ticks_system, 0);
        calc_load(ticks);
        update_wall_time(ticks);
        update_process_times(ticks, system);
    }
}
```

Here, `xchg()` is a function which reads the memory address specified in the first argument and sets the value specified in the second argument in an *atomic* way. Atomic means that this *read-and-set* cycle cannot be interrupted, either by an interrupt or by a second processor possibly present in the system. This guarantees that no ticks are lost even if a new timer interrupt occurs during the processing of this routine. `update_wall_time()` now updates the *real time* `xtime`, while `update_process_time()` is used to update the times of the current process.

```
static void update_process_times(unsigned long ticks,
    unsigned long system)
{
    unsigned long user = ticks - system;
```

First, the `counter` component of the task structure is updated. When `counter` becomes zero, the time slice of the current process has expired and the scheduler is activated at the next opportunity.

```
current->counter -= ticks;
if (current->counter < 0)
{
    current->counter = 0;
    need_resched = 1;
}
```

Then, the `utime` and `stime` components of the task structure are updated for statistical purposes.

```
current->utime += user;
current->stime += system;
```

Under LINUX it is possible to limit a process's 'CPU consumption' resource. This is done by means of the system call *setrlimit*, which can also be used to limit other resources of a process. Exceeding the time limit is checked in the timer interrupt, and the process is either informed via the `SIGXCPU` signal or aborted by means of the `SIGKILL` signal.

```
psecs = (current->stime + current->utime) / HZ;
if (psecs > current->rlim[RLIMIT_CPU].rlim_cur)
{
    /* Send SIGXCPU every second.. */
    if (psecs * HZ == current->stime + current->utime)
        send_sig(SIGXCPU, current, 1);
```

```
        /* and SIGKILL when we go over max.. */
        if (psecs > current->rlim[RLIMIT_CPU].rlim_max)
            send_sig(SIGKILL, current, 1);
    }
```

Subsequently, the interval timers of the current task must be updated. When these have expired, the task is informed by a corresponding signal.

```
    unsigned long it_virt = current->it_virt_value;
    unsigned long it_prof = current->it_prof_value;

    if (it_virt)
    {
        if (it_virt <= user)
        {
            it_virt = user + current->it_virt_incr;
            send_sig(SIGVTALRM, current, 1);
        }
        current->it_virt_value = it_virt - user;
    }

    if (it_prof)
    {
        if (it_prof <= ticks)
        {
            it_prof = ticks + current->it_prof_incr;
            send_sig(SIGPROF, current, 1);
        }
        current->it_prof_value = it_prof - ticks;
    }
}
```

3.2.5   The scheduler

The scheduler is responsible for allocating the 'processor' resource (that is, computing time) to the individual processes. The criteria by which this is done vary from operating system to operating system. UNIX systems prefer traditional interactive processes to enable short response times to be achieved and so make the system appear subjectively faster to the user.

In compliance with the POSIX standard 1003.4, LINUX supports various scheduling classes which can be selected via the sched_setscheduler() system call.

On the one hand, there are real-time processes in the scheduling classes SCHED_FIFO and SCHED_RR. Real time does not mean 'hard real time' with guaranteed process switching and reaction times, but 'soft real time'. When a process with higher real-time priority (described in the `rt_priority` component of the task structure) wishes to run, all other processes with lower real-time priorities are thrust aside.

The difference between `SCHED_FIFO` and `SCHED_RR` is that a process of the `SCHED_FIFO` class can run until it relinquishes control or until a process with higher real-time priority wishes to run. A process of the `SCHED_RR` class, in contrast, is also interrupted when its time slice has expired or there are processes of the same real-time priority. Thus, a classic *round robin* procedure is realized among processes of the same priority.

On the other hand, there exists the scheduling class `SCHED_OTHER` which implements a classic UNIX scheduling algorithm. According to POSIX 1003.4, every real-time process has a higher priority than any process of the scheduling class `SCHED_OTHER`.

The LINUX scheduling algorithm is implemented in the `schedule()` function (`kernel/sched.c`). It is called at two different points. Firstly, there are system calls which call the `schedule()` function (usually indirectly by calling `sleep_on()`; *see* Section 3.1.5). Secondly, after every system call and after every slow interrupt, the flag `need_resched` is checked by the `ret_from_sys_call` routine. If it is set, the scheduler is also called from here. As at least the timer interrupt is called regularly and sets the `need_resched` flag if necessary, the scheduler is activated regularly.

The `schedule()` function consists of three parts. Firstly, those routines that must be called regularly are started. Theoretically, this would belong in the timer interrupt (Section 3.2.4), but for reasons of efficiency has been placed in the scheduler. Secondly, the process with the highest priority is determined. Here, *real-time* processes always take precedence over 'normal' ones. Thirdly, the new process becomes the current process, and the scheduler has accomplished its task.

Unfortunately, the real source code of the scheduler has become relatively unclear in kernel version 2.0. The reason for this lies partly in the restructuring carried out for efficiency reasons, but for a substantial part also in the new multi-processor support.

Therefore, we will present a highly simplified version of the `schedule()` function. Among other things, the details needed for SMP support have been omitted.

```
asmlinkage void schedule(void)
{
    int c;
    struct task_struct * p;
    struct task_struct * prev, * next;
    unsigned long timeout = 0;
```

```
    prev = current;
    next = &init_task;
```

First the bottom halves (*see* Section 7.2.4) of the interrupt routines are called, then all routines that are registered for the scheduler in the task queue (*see* Section 7.2.5). Both kinds of routines are time-uncritical routines and have been taken out of the interrupt handlers for efficiency reasons. However, as these routines may well manipulate information capable of influencing the scheduling (for example, changing a task back into the TASK_RUNNING state), they must be processed here at the latest.

```
    if (bh_active & bh_mask)
    {
        intr_count = 1;
        do_bottom_half();
        intr_count = 0;
    }


    run_task_queue(&tq_scheduler);
```

If schedule() was called because the current process must wait for an event, it is removed from the run queue. If the current task belongs to the SCHED_RR scheduling class and the task's time slice has expired, it is placed at the end of the run queue and thus after all other ready-to-run tasks belonging to the SCHED_RR scheduling class.

The run queue is a list of all processes applying for the processor, and is doubly linked by the components prev_run and next_run of the task structure.

```
    if( prev->state != TASK_RUNNING )
    {
        del_from_runqueue(prev);
    }
    else if (prev->policy == SCHED_RR && prev->counter == 0)
    {
        prev->counter = prev->priority;
        move_last_runqueue(prev);
    }
```

Next, the scheduling algorithm itself is carried out, that is, the process in the run queue that has the highest priority is sought. Here, real-time processes have a higher priority than 'normal' processes.

```
restart_reschedule:
  next = &init_task;        /* next process */
  next_p = -1000;           /* and its priority */

  for( p = init_task->next_run; \
      p != &init_task ; p = p->next_run)
  {
      if( p->policy != SCHED_OTHER )
          weight = 1000 + p->rt_priority;
      else
          weight = p->counter;
      if( weight > next_p)
      {
          next_p = weight; next   = p;
      }
  }
```

If next_p is greater than 0, we have found a suitable candidate. If next_p is less than 0, there is no ready-to-run process and we must activate the idle task. In both cases, next points to the task to be activated next. If next_p is equal to 0, there are ready-to-run processes, but we must recalculate their dynamic priorities (the value of counter). The counter values of all other processes are recalculated as well. Then we restart the scheduler, but this time with more success.

```
if( next_p == 0 )
{
    for_each_task(p)
    {
        p->counter = (p->counter / 2) + p->priority;
    }
    goto restart_reschedule;
}
```

At this point, either next contains a ready-to-run process (next_p > 0), or there is no ready-to-run process (next_p < 0) and next points to init_task. In any case, the task pointed to by next will be activated:

```
    if( prev != next )
        switch_to(prev,next);
} /* schedule() */
```

This concludes the description of the scheduler. We stress again that the above source text is a highly simplified version of the scheduler which, in our opinion, is however complete enough to understand the scheduler's way of functioning.

3.3 Implementing system calls

The range of functions in the operating system is made available to the processes by means of system calls. In this section we will look at implementing system calls under LINUX.

3.3.1 How do system calls actually work?

A system call works on the basis of a defined transition from User Mode to System Mode. In LINUX, this is only possible using interrupts. The interrupt 0x80 is therefore reserved for system calls.[6]

Normally, the user will always call a library function (such as fork()) to carry out a certain task. This library function (as a rule generated from the _syscall macros in <asm-i386/unistd.h>) writes its arguments and the number of the system call to defined transfer registers and then triggers the 0x80 interrupt. When the relevant interrupt service routine returns, the return value is read from the appropriate transfer register and the library function terminates.

The actual work of the system calls is taken care of by the interrupt routine. This starts at the entry address _system_call(), held in the arch/i386/kernel/entry.S file. Unfortunately, this routine is written entirely in assembler. For better readability, it will be illustrated here by a C equivalent. Wherever symbolic labels occur in the assembler text, we have shown them as labels in the C text.

The parameters sys_call_num and sys_call_args represent the number of the system call (*see* <linux/unistd.h>) and its arguments.

```
PSEUDO_CODE system_call( int sys_call_num , sys_call_args )
{
_system_call:
```

First, all the registers for the process are saved.

```
SAVE_ALL; /* macro in entry.S */
```

If sys_call_num represents a legal value, the handling routine assigned to the system call number is called. This is entered in the sys_call_table[] field (defined in the arch/i386/kernel/entry.S file). If the process's PF_TRACESYS flag is set, it is monitored by its parent process. The work entailed in this is taken care of by the syscall_trace function (arch/i386/kernel/ptrace.c), which amends the state of the current process to TASK_STOPPED, sends a SIGTRAP signal to the parent process and calls the scheduler. The current

---

[6] This applies to LINUX system calls on the PC. The iBCS emulation supported on the PC by LINUX uses a different procedure – the so-called lcall7 gate.

process is interrupted until the parent process reactivates it. As this is done before and after every system call, the parent process has total control over the behaviour of the child process.

```
if (sys_call_num >= NR_syscalls)
   errno = -ENOSYS;
else {
   if (current->flags & PF_TRACESYS) {
     syscall_trace();
     errno=(*sys_call_table[sys_call_num])(sys_call_args);
     syscall_trace();
   }
   else
     errno=(*sys_call_table[sys_call_num])(sys_call_args);
}
```

The actual work of the system call is now complete. Before the process can continue, however, there may still be some administrative tasks to deal with. In fact, the following code is run not only after every system call, but also after every 'slow' interrupt, and therefore includes some instructions which are only of significance to interrupt routines. As it is perfectly possible for interrupt routines to be nested one within another, the variable intr_count manages the nesting depth of the interrupt routines. If it is not zero, another interrupt routine has been interrupted and ret_from_sys_call() immediately returns.

```
ret_from_sys_call:
   if (intr_count)
     goto exit_now:
```

As interrupts can have a bottom half (*see* Section 7.2.4), the function do_bottom_half() calls all the bottom halves marked as being active.

```
if (bh_mask & bh_active) {
handle_bottom_half:
   ++intr_count;
   sti();
   do_bottom_half()
   --intr_coun;
}
sti();
```

From this point, interrupts in general are re-enabled. Although interrupt routines run with blocked interrupts (for example, fast interrupts or interrupts which call cli()), the following actions may be affected by interrupts.

If scheduling has been requested (`need_resched!=0`), the scheduler is called. This causes another process to become active. The `schedule()` function will only return once the process has been reactivated by the scheduler.

```
    if (need_resched)
    {
reschedule:
        schedule();
        goto ret_from_sys_call;
    }
```

If signals have been sent for the current process and the process has not blocked receipt of them, they are now processed. The function `do_signal()` has been described in detail in Section 3.2.1.

```
    if (current->signal & ~current->blocked))
    {
signal_return:
        do_signal();
    }
```

This completes the necessary work, and the system call (or interrupt) returns. All the registers are now restored and the interrupt routine is then terminated by the assembler instruction `iret`.

```
exit_now:
    RESTORE_ALL;
} /* PSEUDO_CODE system_csll */
```

3.3.2   Examples of simple system calls

In this section we take a closer look at the implementation of some system calls. This will also demonstrate the use of the algorithms and data structures introduced above.

getpid

The *getpid* call is a very simple system call – it merely reads a value from the task structure and returns it:

```
asmlinkage int sys_getpid(void)
{
    return current->pid;
}
```

nice

The system call *nice* is a little more complicated: *nice* expects as its argument a number by which the static priority of the current process is to be modified.

All system calls which process arguments must test the arguments for plausibility.

```
asmlinkage int sys_nice(long increment)
{
    int newpriority;
```

Only the superuser is allowed to raise his/her own priority. Note that a larger argument for `sys_nice()` indicates a lower priority. This makes the name `increment` for the argument of *nice* a little confusing.

```
if (increment < 0 && !suser())
    return -EPERM;
```

`suser()` checks whether the current process has superuser privileges.[7]

The new priority for the process can now be calculated. Among other things, a check is made at this point to ensure that the new priority for the process is within a reasonable range.

```
newpriority = ...

if (newpriority < 1)
    newpriority = 1;
if (newpriority > DEF_PRIORITY*2)
    newpriority = DEF_PRIORITY*2;
current->priority = newpriority;
return 0;
} /* sys_nice */
```

pause

A call to *pause* interrupts the execution of the program until the process is reactivated by a signal. This merely amounts to setting the status of the current process to `TASK_INTERRUPTIBLE` and then calling the scheduler. This results in another task becoming active.

---

[7] The function not only checks this, but also records in the task structure when it was called successfully. This can be used to detemine whether a process has used superuser privileges or not. Thefore, the `suser()` condition should only be carried out *after* all other interrogations which might lead to a failure of the system call. Unfortunately, this rule is not always observed in the current LINUX kernel.

The process can only be reactivated if the status of the process is returned to TASK_RUNNING, which occurs when a signal is received (*see* Section 3.2.5). The system call *pause* then returns with the fault ERESTARTNOHAND and carries out the necessary actions for the handling of the signal (as described in Section 3.2.1).

```
asmlinkage int sys_pause(void)
{
    current->state = TASK_INTERRUPTIBLE;
    schedule();
    return -ERESTARTNOHAND;
}
```

3.3.3 Examples of more complex system calls

We will now turn to rather more complex system calls. This section examines the system calls for process management (*fork*, *execve*, *_exit* and *wait*).

fork

The system call *fork* is the only way of starting a new process. This is done by creating a (nearly) identical copy of the process that has called *fork*.

As a matter of fact, *fork* is a very demanding system call. All the data of the process have to be copied, and these can easily run to a few megabytes. In the course of developing UNIX, a number of methods were adopted to keep the demands of *fork* as small as possible. In the frequently occurring case where *fork* is followed directly by a call to *exec*, it is not necessary to copy the data, as they are not needed. In the UNIX systems from the BSD family, therefore, the system call *vfork* has been set up. Like *fork*, it creates a new process, but it shares the data segment between the two processes. This is a rather dubious approach, as one process can affect the data of the other process. To keep this interference as limited as possible, further execution of the parent process is halted until the child process has either been terminated by *_exit* or has started a new program with *exec*.

Newer UNIX systems, such as LINUX, for example, take a different approach, using the *copy-on-write* technique. The thinking behind this is that a number of processes may very well access the same memory at the same time – provided they do not modify the data.

Thus, under LINUX, the relevant pages of memory are not copied on a call to *fork*, but used at the same time by the old and new processes. However, the pages used by both processes are marked as write-protected – which means that they cannot be modified by either process. If one of the processes needs to carry out a write operation on these pages of memory, a *page fault* is triggered by the memory management hardware (MMU), the process is interrupted and the kernel is informed. At this point, the kernel copies the pages of memory concerned and assigns the writing process a copy of its own. This procedure is completely transparent – that is, the processes themselves are unaware of it. The great advantage of this copy-on-write method is that uneconomical copying of memory pages is only carried out when it is actually needed.

A concept which exists alongside that of a process in current operating systems is that of a 'thread' – an independent sequence of events within a process. A number of different threads may be processed in parallel and independently of each other during the execution of a process. The main way this differs from the concept of a process is that the different threads within a process operate on the same area of memory and can therefore affect each other. There are a variety of approaches to implementing threads. Simple variants, such as the widely used Pthread library, manage without any support from the kernel of the operating system. The disadvantage of these methods is that the scheduling of the individual threads has to be carried out by the user program: the kernel sees it as an ordinary process. As a result, a blocking system call (for example, a *read* originating at the terminal) blocks the entire process and thus all the threads. The ideal situation would be one in which only the thread which has used the system call were to block. However, this requires support for the thread concept by the kernel. Later versions of UNIX (for example, Solaris 2.x) provide this support.

LINUX supports threads by making available the (LINUX-specific) system call *clone*, which provides the necessary kernel support to implement threads. It works in a similar way to *fork* – that is, it creates a new task. The main difference is that with *clone* both tasks can work with common data (for example, a common area of memory, a common pid, and so on) after the system call. Up to now, however, there does not appear to be any implementation of the POSIX thread interface based on *clone*.

As *fork* and *clone* essentially do the same thing, they are implemented by a common function, which is simply called in a different way depending on the system call used.

```
asmlinkage int sys_fork( struct pt_regs regs)
{
    return do_fork(SIGCHLD, regs.esp, &regs);
}

asmlinkage int sys_clone(struct pt_regs regs)
{
    unsigned long clone_flags;
    unsigned long newssp;

    clone_flags = regs.ebx;
    newsp = regs.ecx;
```

```
    if(!newsp)
      newsp = regs.ecx;
    return do_fork(clone_flags, newsp, &regs);
  }
```

The actual work is done by the function do_fork():

```
int do_fork(unsigned long clone_flags,
                   unsigned long usp, struct pt_regs *regs)
{
  int nr;
  int error = -ENOMEM;
  unsigned long new_stack;
  struct task_struct *p;
```

First, the memory space required for the new task structure is allocated and a spare entry in the task[] array is found.

```
  p = (struct task_struct *) kmalloc(sizeof(*p), GFP_KERNEL);
  if (!p)
      goto bad_fork;

  new_stack = alloc_kernel_stack();
  if (!new_stack)
      goto bad_fork_free_p;
  error = -EAGAIN;
  nr = find_empty_process();
  if (nr < 0)
      goto bad_fork_free_stack;
  task[nr] = p;
```

The child process p inherits all the parent process's entries.

```
  *p = *current;
```

However, some of the entries need to be initialized for a new process.

```
  p->did_exec = 0;
  p->swappable = 0;
  p->pid = get_pid(clone_flags);
  p->next_run = NULL;
  p->prev_run = NULL;
  ...
  p->start_time = jiffies;
  p->swappable = 1;
```

```
p->exit_signal = clone_flags & CSIGNAL;
p->counter = current->counter >> 1;

init_waitqueue(&p->wait_chldexit);
init_timer(&p->real_timer);
```

Now the substructures in the task structure are copied. Depending on the value of the `clone_flags`, data structures will be either copied or shared. This is where the differences between the system calls *fork* and *clone* are put into effect.

```
if (copy_files(clone_flags, p))
        goto bad_fork_cleanup;
if (copy_fs(clone_flags, p))
        goto bad_fork_cleanup_files;
if (copy_sighand(clone_flags, p))
        goto bad_fork_cleanup_fs;
if (copy_mm(clone_flags, p))
        goto bad_fork_cleanup_sighand;
copy_thread(nr, clone_flags, usp, p, regs);
```

Finally, the state of the new task is set to `TASK_RUNNING` so that it can be activated by the scheduler. The old task (the parent process) returns from the system call with the process identification number (PID) of the new process.

```
wake_up_process(p);
return p->pid;
```

If something has gone wrong, data structures requested up to that moment must be released.

```
bad_fork:
    ...
    return error;
}
```

The `copy_thread()` function which is called in the above coding is also responsible for initializing the registers for the new process. Among other things, the instruction pointer p->tss.eip is set to the start of the `ret_from_sys_call()` routine, so that the new process begins processing as if it were the one which had issued the *fork* call. At the same time, the return value is set to zero to enable the program to tell the parent process and child process apart by reference to the different return values.

execve

The system call *execve* enables a process to change its
LINUX permits a number of formats for executable files.
recognized by the so-called 'magic numbers' – the initia
tradition, every UNIX system uses its own format for exe(
last few years two standards have developed: the COF
The trend clearly favours the ELF format, as it drastically ...
dling of dynamic libraries. Interested readers can find more information on ...
ELF format in the References at the back of this book under 'ELF'.

Both formats are now supported by LINUX. In addition, LINUX supports
the script files used in the BSD world. If a file begins with the pair of characters '#!', it is not loaded directly, but passed for processing to an interpreter
program specified in the first line of the file. The familiar version of this is a
line in the form

```
#!/bin/sh
```

at the start of shell scripts. Executing this file (that is, issuing an *execve*) is
equivalent to executing the file /bin/sh with the original file as its argument.
The following gives (heavily abridged) the annotated source text of do_execve().

```
static int do_execve(char *filename, char **argv, char **envp,
                     struct pt_regs * regs)
{
```

First, an attempt is made to find the file relevant to the executing program (its
inode) by reference to the name of the program. The structure bprm is used to
store all the data about the file.

```
struct linux_binprm bprm;

retval = open_namei(filename, 0, 0, &bprm.inode, NULL);
bprm.filename = filename;
bprm.argc = count(argv);
bprm.envc = count(envp);

restart_interp:
```

After this, the access permissions for the file can be checked:

---

[8] COFF stands for *Common Object File Format* and ELF stands for *Executable and Linkable
Format*.

```
if (!S_ISREG(bprm.inode->i_mode)) {
    retval = -EACCES;
    goto exec_error2;
}
...
```

By examining the first block of the file, the way in which the file should be loaded can be determined. To do this, the first 128 bytes of the file are read in:

```
retval = read_exec(bprm.inode,0,bprm.buf,128);
if (retval < 0)
    goto exec_error2;
```

Now, on the basis of the first bytes of the file, an attempt can be made to load the executable file. LINUX uses a separate loading function for each file format it is familiar with. They are each called in turn and 'asked' whether they can load the file. If the file can be loaded, execve() terminates successfully; if not, it returns ENOEXEC.

```
for( fmt = formats; fmt ; fmt = fmt->next )
{
    if (!fmt->load_binary)
        break;
    retval = (fmt->load_binary)(&bprm, regs);
    if (retval >= 0) {
        iput(bprm.inode);
        current->did_exec = 1;
        return retval;
    }
    if( retval != -ENOEXEC )
        break;
}

return(retval);
} /* do_execve() */
```

As this shows, the actual work is done by the function fmt->load_binary(). Let us take a closer look at a function of this type:

```
int load_aout_binary(struct linux_binprm *bprm,
                    struct pt_regs *regs)
{
```

The buffer `bprm->buf` contains the first 128 bytes of the file to be loaded. First, this section of the file is inspected to confirm that it is in the correct file format. If not, the function returns the fault `ENOEXEC`, after which `do_execve()` can test for other formats. These tests also extract from the header various items of information which will be needed later.

```
struct exec ex;

ex = *((struct exec *) bprm->buf);
if ((N_MAGIC(ex) != ZMAGIC && N_MAGIC(ex) != OMAGIC &&
   N_MAGIC(ex) != QMAGIC) ||
   ex.a_trsize || ex.a_drsize ||
   bprm->inode->i_size < ex.a_text+ex.a_data+ ..... )

{
   return -ENOEXEC;
}
...
fd_offset = N_TXTOFF(ex);
...
```

If these tests have been concluded successfully, the new program is loaded. The first action at this stage is to release the process's memory, which still contains the old program. After this release has taken place, `execve()` can no longer go back to the old program. If a fault occurs while the file is being loaded, the current process will have to be aborted.

```
flush_old_exec(bprm);
```

Now the task structure can be updated. At this point, a note that the program is in a LINUX-specific format is entered into the `personality` component.

```
current -> personality  = PER_LINUX;

current->mm->start_code = N_TXTADDR(ex);
current->mm->end_code   = current->mm->start_code + ex.a_text;
current->mm->end_data   = current->mm->end_code + ex.a_data;
current->mm->start_brk  = current->mm->end_data;
current->mm->brk        = ex.a_bss + current->mm->start_brk;
current->mm->rss        = 0;
current->mm->mmap       = NULL;
current->suid           = bprm->e_uid;
current->euid           = bprm->e_uid;
current->fsuid          = bprm->e_uid;
   ...
```

The file containing the new program is opened. The text and data segments are then inserted into memory using do_mmap(). Note that do_mmap() is not loading the file at this point, but only updating the page tables and thus telling the paging algorithm where to find the pages of memory to be loaded when it needs them. Paging is described in Section 4.4.

```
fd = open_inode(bprm->inode, O_RDONLY);

file = current->files->fd[fd];

error = do_mmap(file, N_TXTADDR(ex), ex.a_text,
    PROT_READ | PROT_EXEC,
    MAP_FIXED | MAP_PRIVATE | MAP_DENYWRITE | MAP_EXECUTABLE,
    fd_offset);
error = do_mmap(file, N_TXTADDR(ex) + ex.a_text, ex.a_data,
    PROT_READ | PROT_WRITE | PROT_EXEC,
    MAP_FIXED | MAP_PRIVATE | MAP_DENYWRITE | MAP_EXECUTABLE,
    fd_offset + ex.a_text);
sys_close(fd);
```

Now the BSS segment is loaded. Under UNIX, it contains the non-initialized data for a process. This is done by the function set_brk(). Initialization of the registers and, in particular, the instruction pointer for the new program is then carried out; this is the job of the function start_thread(). When the system call *execve* completes its work, program execution for the process continues from the new address.

```
set_brk(current->mm->start_brk, current->mm->brk);
current->mm->start_stack = ...;
start_thread(regs, ex.a_entry, p);
return 0;
} /* load_aout_binary */
```

In reality, the functions do_execve() and load_aout_binary() are considerably more complicated than this, partly because of the necessary fault and exception handling.[9] As well as this, we have left a number of 'unimportant' details out of this illustration – 'unimportant' in the sense that they are unnecessary to an understanding of the basic principles of do_execve(). Those who wish to explore these functions seriously and perhaps implement a new file format will find they cannot avoid a study of the original sources.

---

[9] It can happen, for example, that older LINUX binaries cannot be loaded using do_mmap(). This means that load_aout_binary() has to load the program code and data in full and cannot fall back on 'demand loading'.

exit

A process is always terminated by calling the kernel function `do_exit`. This is done either directly by the system call *_exit* or indirectly on the occurrence of a signal which cannot be intercepted.

As a matter of fact, `do_exit()` does not have much to do. It merely has to release the resources claimed by the process and, if necessary, inform other processes. However, this gives rise to a good deal of detail; so, once again, the following illustration of the `do_exit()` function is heavily abridged. For example, we shall not take account of actions necessary for clean management of the process groups.

```
NORET_TYPE void do_exit(long code)
{
```

First, the process releases all structures that it occupies.

```
del_timer(&current->real_timer);
sem_exit();
kerneld_exit();
exit_thread();
__exit_mm(current);
__exit_files(current);
__exit_fs(current);
__exit_sighand(current);
```

The parent process is informed of the termination of a child process. In some cases, it will already be waiting for this event via the system call *wait*. When a process completes its work, all the child processes must be given a new parent process. By default, all child processes are inherited by process 1. If it no longer exists, they are bequeathed to process 0. All this is done by the exit_notify() function.

```
exit_notify();
```

All the clearing-up operations have now been completed. No memory space is needed for the process any longer (except for the task structure), and it becomes a zombie process. It will remain a zombie process until the parent process issues the system call *wait*.

```
current->state = TASK_ZOMBIE;
current->exit_code = code;m
```

Finally, do_exit() calls the scheduler and allows other processes to continue. As the status of the current process is TASK_ZOMBIE, the schedule() function does not return to this point.

```
    schedule();
    /* NOTREACHED */
} /* do_exit */
```

wait

The system call *wait4* enables a process to wait for the end of a child process and interrogate the exit code supplied. Depending on the argument given, *wait4* will wait for a specified child process, a child process in a specified process group or any child process. Similarly, it can be specified whether *wait4* will actually wait for a child process to end or only react to child processes which have already been completed. As all these distinctions are rather boring, the following illustration shows a modified version of *wait4* with semantics more or less corresponding to those of *wait*. (Normally, *wait* is a library function which calls *wait4* with appropriate arguments.)

```
    int sys_wait( ... )
    {
    repeat:
```

The function sys_wait() consists of two parts. First, it tests whether there is already a child process in the TASK_ZOMBIE state. If there is, we have found the process we are looking for and sys_wait() can return successfully. Before it does so, however, it picks up statistical data (system time used, exit code, and so on) from the child process's process table and then releases its task structure. This is the only time a process entry can be removed from the process table.

```
    nr_of_childs = 0;
    for (p = current->p_cptr ; p ; p = p->p_osptr) {
      ++nr_of_childs;

      if(p->state == TASK_ZOMBIE) {
        current->cutime += p->utime + p->cutime;
        current->cstime += p->stime + p->cstime;
        if (ru != NULL)
          getrusage(p, RUSAGE_BOTH, ru);
        flag = p->pid;
        if (stat_addr)
          put_fs_long(p->exit_code, stat_addr);
```

```
        release(p);

        return flag;

      }
    }
```

If there is no child process, `sys_wait()` returns immediately.

```
    if (nr_of_childs == 0)
      return 0;
```

However, if there are child processes, it waits for one of the child processes to end. To do this, the parent process enters itself in the relevant wait queue in its own task structure. As we have already seen, on the _exit system call every process wakes up all the processes waiting in this wait queue via the `wake_up()` function. This guarantees that the parent process is informed of the end of a child process.

```
    interruptible_sleep_on(&current->wait.chldexit);
```

The signal `SIGCHLD` sent by `do_exit()` on terminating the child process is ignored. If a signal is received in the meantime (`interruptible_sleep_on()` can, after all, be interrupted by another signal) the system call is terminated with an error message. In all other cases, we know that there is now a child process in the `TASK_ZOMBIE` state, and we can start looking for it again from the top.

```
    current->signal &= ~(1<<(SIGCHLD-1));

    if (current->signal & ~current->blocked)
      return -EINTR;

    goto repeat;

  } /* sys_wait */
```

3.3.4   Implementing a new system call

Now that we have examined a few system calls, we will see in this section how a new system call can be implemented in LINUX. This should always be done with care, as programs using an operating system which has been modified in this way are no longer portable.

The example we shall use to document the implementation of a new system call is fairly academic in character. This is because in principle LINUX already contains all the important system calls. It concerns the implementation of a semaphore for process synchronization.

```
#include <linux/wait.h>
#include <linux/errno.h>
#include <asm/system.h>
#include <linux/sched.h>
```

If a process wishes to occupy a semaphore which is already occupied, the process must wait for the semaphore to be released. We therefore need to set up a wait queue.

```
static struct wait_queue * semop_wait = NULL;
```

We shall use the variable `sem_pid` to store the state of the semaphore. If the semaphore is not occupied `sem_pid` will hold a value of 0; otherwise it will contain the process number of the occupying process.

```
static long sem_pid; /* 0 ==> not used */

int sys_semop(int semop_type)
{
   int ret = 0;
   int ok = 0;
```

If `semop_type` has a value of 1, we wish to occupy the semaphore. If `sem_pid` matches our own process ID, the process has already successfully occupied the semaphore and we can return successfully.

Otherwise, we wait via `interruptible_sleep_on()` until the variable `sem_pid` has a value of 0. Note here that the `interruptible_sleep_on()` function may return, even though the semaphore is occupied. This may be for one of two reasons. On the one hand, a number of processes may have been waiting in the wait queue. These will then all be woken into the `TASK_RUNNING` state by `wake_up()`. The process which is first to be reactivated by the scheduler may then occupy the semaphore. `interruptible_sleep_on()` may also return if it is interrupted by a signal. In this case, we will simply return with an appropriate error code.

```
switch(semop_type) {
case 1: /* occupy semaphore */
   if(sem_pid == current->pid) return 0;
   while(sem_pid != 0)
```

```
{
    interruptible_sleep_on(&semop_wait);
  if(current->signal & ~current->blocked)
    return -EINTR;
}
/* Here always holds sem_pid == 0 ! */
sem_pid = current->pid;
return 0;
```

Note that no critical areas ('race conditions') are involved here, as the process cannot be interrupted by another process while it is in System Mode (that is, during a system call), but must always voluntarily relinquish control. This means that it is not possible for another process to occupy the semaphore between `sem_pid` being tested for zero and its being set.

If `semop_type` has a value of zero, the semaphore is to be released. We only allow the semaphore to be released by the process which has previously occupied it. Once the semaphore has been released (`sem_pid==0`), all the processes waiting in the `semop_wait` wait queue are reawakened via the `wake_up_interruptible()` function.

```
case 0: /* release semaphore */
  if (!sem_pid) return 0;
  if (sem_pid == current->pid) {
    sem_pid = 0;
    if(semop_wait)
        wake_up_interruptible(&semop_wait);
    return 0;
  }
  return -EPERM;
default:
  return -EINVAL;
}
} /* sys_semop */
```

What happens if a process occupies the semaphore but is then aborted for some reason? The semaphore remains occupied and can no longer be used or released. It is a good idea, therefore, to include the release of the semaphore in the _exit_ system call. All this requires is an additional line

```
sys_semop(0);
```

in the function `sys_exit()`.

This completes the implementation of our new system call. There are a number of ways of linking it into the kernel. The traditional method involves inserting the new system call permanently into the kernel. The following will describe how this is done. However, the newly supported kernel modules enable new system calls to be added to the kernel at run-time. This will be covered in Chapter 9.

Here we describe the traditional method. First, the system call must be given a name and a unique number. For every system call known to the system, the file <linux/unistd.h> contains an entry of the form

```
#define __NR_system call name    system call number
```

We add our system call at the next available number:

```
#define __NR_semop     141
```

The arch/i386/kernel/entry.S file holds the initialized table:

```
_sys_call_table:
        .long _sys_setup            /* 0 */
        .long _sys_exit
        .long _sys_fork
...
        .long _sys_llseek           /* 140 */
        .space (NR_syscalls-140)*4
```

Here we add, at position 141(__NR_semop), a pointer to the function handled by our system call. In our case, therefore, the result will be:

```
_sys_call_table:
        .long _sys_setup            /* 0 */
        .long _sys_exit
        .long _sys_fork
...
        .long _sys_llseek           /* 140 */
        .long _sys_semop
        .space (NR_syscalls-141)*4
```

Following the convention, we store the above source text for our new system call in the file kernel/semop.c. It is advisable to use our own files for our own system calls, as this makes porting to a later version of the LINUX kernel easier.

Once we have added the file semop.o to the entry for OBJS in the Makefile, we are almost finished. A new kernel can now be generated and installed, as described in Chapter 2, and this will support the new system call.

We should also set up a library function allowing the user actually to use the new system call. To do this, we use the following short C program:

```
#include <linux/unistd.h>

_syscall1(int, semop, int, semop_type)
```

The macro `_syscall1` in `<asm-i386/unistd.h>` then expands this into the following function definition:

```
int semop(int semop_type)
{
  long __res;
  __asm__ volatile ("int $0x80"
    : "=a" (__res)
    : "0" (__NR_semop),"b" ((long)(semop_type)));
  if (__res >= 0)
    return (int) __res;
  errno = -__res;
  return -1;
}
```

Alternatively, we could also use the library function `syscall()` to call the new system call.

4 Memory management

*Data memories consist of thousands of memory cells.
This means that the individual cells must be arranged
according to a purposeful and as far as possible
simple system.*

John S. Murphy

The quotation above is taken from a book originally published in 1958. The demands made of memory management systems have changed radically since then, and hardly any applications can get by on only a few thousand memory cells. But the need for simplicity and purposefulness is as relevant as ever.

A multi-tasking system like LINUX makes particular demands of memory management. The memory belonging to a process and that used by the kernel need to be protected against access by other processes. This protection is vital to the stability of a multi-tasking operating system. It prevents a process from writing at random into other processes' areas of memory, causing them to crash. This can be caused in a C program, for example, simply by exceeding the limits of a field variable.

Dubious programming methods, such as uncontrolled modification of system data, will certainly be used if they are not specifically excluded. Memory protection stops programmers affecting the stability of the system as a result of programming tricks.

Primary memory (RAM) has always been a scarce resource, and still is. As the amount of working memory regularly available has grown, the memory requirements of applications have grown with it – and software for LINUX, such as the GNU C compiler or the X Window system, is no exception. Given that a multi-tasking system like LINUX can run a number of processes at the same time, it is possible that the memory requirements of all the processes to be run may exceed the size of working memory. The memory management system should be capable of solving this problem by using secondary memory (for example, areas of the hard disk). It may also be necessary to run processes whose memory requirement itself exceeds the size of primary memory.

If two process instances of a program are run in quasi-parallel, at least the data for the two processes must be stored in different physical areas of memory. This means that the data for the corresponding variables in each process will be stored at different physical addresses. By far the most elegant method of dealing with this problem is to introduce a virtual address space for each process. The programmer can then design his/her program without regard to the actual locations of the code and data in the physical address space. Mapping the virtual addresses onto the physical addresses is the responsibility of the operating system's memory management system.

Memory protection prevents two processes exchanging data by changing areas of memory used by both. In this case, inter-process communication must be carried out using system calls. But the use of a system call is bound up with a large complex of operations such as multiple saving of registers to the stack, saving of areas of memory, and so on. If processes were able to share certain areas of memory, inter-process communication would be more efficient.

This concept of *shared memory* is not restricted to communication with processes. For example, areas of files could also be mapped into a process's memory: this could often save many repeated system calls to read and write the file.

The efficient implementation of a state-of-the-art system for memory management would be impossible without hardware support. As LINUX is also intended to run in the future on systems not based on Intel architecture, an *architecture-independent memory model* has to be defined. This memory model must be so universal that it can be used in conjunction with the memory architectures of a wide range of different processor types. This chapter starts by introducing this architecture-independent memory model. The implementation of the model for the i386 processor family is then presented. CPUs in this family will be referred to as x86 processors. To demonstrate the flexibility of the memory model, we then look at its implementation on the DEC Alpha architecture.

The second part of this chapter explains how the architecture-independent memory model is used to implement memory management. This brings in the memory management algorithms used by LINUX. It should be noted that other algorithms and approaches to memory management have been used and are still used by other systems. Readers interested in knowing more are referred to Bach (1986).

4.1 The architecture-independent memory model in LINUX

A typical computer today has at its disposal a number of levels of memory with different access times. The first level mostly consists of cache memory within the processor. A second level of cache is frequently implemented, using SRAM chips with a fast access time of around 20 ns. In almost all cases, the actual working memory consists of inexpensive DRAM chips with access times around 70 ns. As far as programming is concerned, the cache levels are transparent once they have been initialized by the BIOS code. For this reason, the cache levels are not mapped by the architecture-independent memory model and the term *physical memory* is used to refer to RAM in general.

4.1.1 Pages of memory

The physical memory is divided into *pages*. The size of a memory page is defined by the PAGE_SIZE macro in the asm/page.h file. For the x86 processor, the size is set to 4 Kbytes, while the Alpha processor uses 8 Kbytes.

4.1.2 Virtual address space

A process is run in a *virtual address space*. In the abstract memory model, the virtual address space is structured as a kernel segment plus a user segment. Code and data for the kernel can be accessed in the kernel segment, and code and data for the process in the user segment. A virtual address is given by reference to a segment selector and the offset within the segment. When code is being processed, the segment selector is already set and only offsets are used: thus, C pointers only hold offsets. In the kernel, however, access is needed not only to data in the kernel segment but also to data in the user segment, for the passing of parameters. For this purpose, the put_user() and get_user() macros are defined in the asm/segment.h file. A pointer to the datum to be copied is passed as an argument; the pointer type is used to determine the number of bytes to be copied. The additional functions memcpy_tofs() and memcpy_fromfs() are defined to allow the copying of any number of bytes to and from the user segment.

The segment selectors for the kernel data (KERNEL_DS) and the user data (USER_DS) are defined in asm/segment.h. Functions to read the current data segment selector (get_ds()) and to read and set the selector register used for the user segment in the kernel (get_fs() and set_fs()) are available. These allow system functions within the kernel to be called up. The code for this system function assumes that all the pointers passed to the function point to the user segment; if the segment selector register for the user segment – FS in x86 processors – is set so that it points to the kernel segment, the kernel segment is accessed via user segment access functions such as get_user_byte(). By carrying out a conversion on the segment selector register, a system function can be given pointers to the kernel segment. This method is used, for example, by the UMSDOS file system to simulate a UNIX file system in an MS-DOS file system, where the MS-DOS file system is accessed via system functions.

The *memory management unit* (MMU) of an x86 processor converts the virtual address into a *linear address*. The linear address space is limited to 4 Gbytes by the width of the linear address, which is 32 bits. As all the segments have to be mapped into the linear address space, the size of the user segment is restricted to 3 Gbytes via the macro `TASK_SIZE`. The remainder of the address space is available to the kernel segment.

The Alpha processor does not support segmentation of the virtual address space. Here, the offset of a virtual address is identical to the linear address, which means that the offset addresses for the user segment are not permitted to overlap with the offset addresses for the kernel segment. As the Alpha processor works with 64-bit addresses, however, this is not a serious handicap, as the linear address space runs to 2^{64} bytes. Functions to access the user segment are defined, but access the offset addresses directly. The functions to set and read the segment selector registers set a bit in the flags of the task status segment. This bit is used for the checking of system call arguments.

4.1.3   Converting the linear address

The linear addresses require conversion to a physical address by either the processor or a separate *memory management unit* (MMU). In the architecture-independent memory model, this *page conversion* is a three-level process, in which the address for the linear address space is split into four parts. The first part is used as an index in the page directory. The entry in the page directory refers to what in LINUX is called a *page middle directory*. The second part of the address serves as an index to a page middle directory. Referenced in this way, the entry refers to a page table. The third part is used as an index to this page table. The referenced entry should as far as possible point to a page in physical memory. The fourth part of the address gives the offset within the selected page of memory. Figure 4.1 shows these relationships in graphical form.

The x86 processor only supports a two-level conversion of the linear address. Here, the conversion for the architecture-independent memory model can be assisted by means of a useful trick. This defines the size of the page middle directory as one and interprets the entry in the page directory as a page middle directory. Of course, the operations to access page conversion tables will also have to take this into consideration.

The linear address conversion must be given a three-level definition in the architecture-independent memory model because the Alpha processor supports linear addresses with a width of 64 bits. An address conversion in only two levels would result in very large page directories and page tables if a

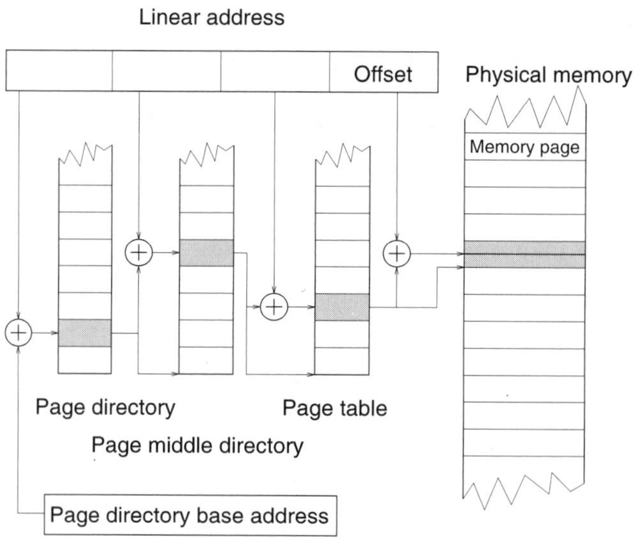

Linear address

Figure 4.1 Linear address conversion in the architecture-independent memory model.

reduction of the useful linear address to 32 bits were to be avoided. In porting the memory model to the Alpha architecture it was found that one page (8 Kbytes in the Alpha processor) was used for each page directory and page table. This limits the number of entries per level to 1024. As the base address for the page directory is also managed by the page directory, the size of the virtual address space is limited to $1023 \times 1024 \times 1024 \times 8192$ bytes, or 8184 Gbytes – just below 8 terabytes; 2 terabytes = 2^{41} bytes of this will be made available to a user segment.

4.1.4 The page directory

Data types, functions and macros for access and the modification of the page tables and directories are defined in the files `asm/page.h` and `asm/pgtable.h`.

An entry in the page directory is a `pgd_t` data type. To provide better support for the type check in C, it is defined as a structure. This value must be accessed via the macro `pgd_val()`.

- **`pgd_alloc()`**
  Allocates a page for the page directory and fills it with zeros.
- **`pgd_bad()`**
  Can be used to test whether the entry in the page directory is valid.
- **`pgd_clear()`**
  Deletes the entry in the page directory.

- **pgd_free()**
  Releases the page of memory allocated to the page directory.

- **pgd_none()**
  Tests whether the entry has been initialized.

- **pgd_offset()**
  Returns the pointer to the entry in the page directory for a linear address.

- **pgd_page()**
  The address of the page to which the entry in the page directory refers – usually the base address of a page middle directory.

- **pgd_present()**
  Shows whether the entry in the page directory refers to a page middle directory.

- **pgd_set()**
  The entry in the page directory is set to the base address of a page middle directory.

- **SET_PAGE_DIR()**
  This macro/function resets the page directory base address for a task.

4.1.5 The page middle directory

Entries in the page middle directory are of the pmd_t data type. Access is by the macro pmd_val(). The following functions are defined:

- **pmd_alloc()**
  Allocates a page middle directory to manage memory in the user area.

- **pmd_alloc_kernel()**
  Allocates a page middle directory for memory in the kernel segment. All entries are set to invalid.

- **pmd_bad()**
  Tests whether the entry in the page middle directory is valid.

- **pmd_clear()**
  Deletes the entry in the page middle directory.

- **pmd_free()**
  Releases a page middle directory for memory in the user segment.

- **pmd_free_kernel()**
  Releases a page middle directory for memory in the kernel segment.

- **pmd_none()**
  Tests whether the entry in the page middle directory has been set.

- **pmd_offset()**
  Returns the address of an entry in the page middle directory to which the address in the argument is allocated: the correct directory entry must be passed as a further parameter.

- **pmd_page()**
  Returns the base address of the page table to which the entry refers.

- **pmd_present()**
  Tests for the presence of the page table relating to the entry in the page middle directory.

- **pmd_set()**
  Sets the entry in the page middle directory to the base address of a page table; it is not defined for the x86 architecture.

4.1.6 The page table

An entry in the page table is defined by the data type pte_t. As before, there is a macro pte_val(), which provides access to the value of the data type. The most important task of the page table entry is to address a page in physical memory.

In addition, a page table entry contains a number of flags which describe the legal access modes to the memory page and their states. LINUX must map these architecture-dependent flags onto architecture-dependent attributes. The 'presence' attribute indicates whether or not the page is present in the virtual address space. There is one attribute each for reading from and writing to the memory page and for executing code. One attribute indicates whether the memory page has been accessed – in other words, this attribute describes the 'age' of the page. The 'dirty' attribute is set when the contents of the memory page has been modified.

The following attribute combinations are defined as macros of the pgprot_t type:

- **PAGE_NONE**
  No physical memory page is referenced by the page table entry.

- **PAGE_SHARED**
  All types of access are permitted.

- **PAGE_COPY**
  This macro is historical and identical to PAGE_READONLY.

- **PAGE_READONLY**
  Only read or execute access is allowed to this page of memory. With write access, an exception is generated which allows this error to be handled. The memory page can be copied, and the page table entry can be set to the physical address of the new page and its attributes to PAGE_SHARED. This is exactly what is meant by 'copy-on-write'.

- **PAGE_KERNEL**
  Access to this page of memory is only allowed in the kernel segment.

Table 4.1   Semantics for the combinations of protection attributes for x86 processors.

Attribute combination	x86 semantics
---	---
--x	r-x
-w-	rwx
-wx	rwx
r--	r-x
r-x	r-x
rw-	rwx
rwx	rwx

As well as these, `asm/pgtable.h` holds definitions of the macros `__P000` to `__P111` and `__S000` to `__S111` which, together with the `_PAGE_NORMAL()` macro, enable any combination of protection attributes to be defined. The bit positions in the macro names are interpreted as 'xwr'. For the macros beginning with `__P`, the position of the 'write' attribute is interpreted as the 'copy-on-write' attribute.

The x86 architecture does not support all combinations of the 'read', 'write' and 'execute' attributes. Table 4.1 shows the semantics of all the possible attribute combinations, using the classical UNIX 'rwx' notation.

A range of functions have been defined to manipulate the page table entries and their attributes. Note that the functions are described here by reference to the attributes explained above. For architectures which do not support all the attributes for pages defined in the architecture-independent memory model, the semantics may vary from those given here.

- **`mk_pte()`**
  Returns a page table entry generated from the memory address of a page and a variable of the `pgprot_t` type, which describes the memory protection for the page.

- **`pte_alloc()`**
  Allocates a new page table.

- **`pte_alloc_kernel()`**
  Allocates a new page table for memory in the kernel segment.

- **`pte_clear()`**
  Clears the page table entry.

- **`pte_dirty()`**
  Checks whether the 'dirty' attribute is set.

- **pte_exec()**
  Checks whether the execution of code in the referenced page of memory is permitted, that is, whether the 'execute' attribute is set.

- **pte_exprotect()**
  Clears the 'execute' attribute.

- **pte_free()**
  Releases the page table.

- **pte_free_kernel()**
  Releases the page table responsible for managing the pages in the kernel segment.

- **pte_mkclean()**
  Clears the 'dirty' attribute.

- **pte_mkdirty()**
  Sets the 'dirty' attribute.

- **pte_mkexec()**
  Sets the 'execute' attribute, permitting code in the page to be executed.

- **pte_mkold()**
  Sets the 'age' attribute, that is, the system now assumes that this memory page has already been accessed.

- **pte_mkread()**
  Sets the 'read' attribute to allow read access to the page.

- **pte_mkwrite()**
  Sets the 'write' attribute to allow write access to the page.

- **pte_mkyoung()**
  Clears the 'age' attribute.

- **pte_modify()**
  The protection attribute for the page of memory referenced by the page table entry is modified as defined in the parameter.

- **pte_none()**
  Checks whether the page table entry is set.

- **pte_offset()**
  Returns a pointer to the page table entry referencing the page of memory to which the address passed as a parameter refers. However, the parameter passed must be the entry in the page middle directory valid for this page.

- **pte_page()**
  Returns the address of the page referenced by the page directory entry.

- **pte_present()**
  Checks whether a page in physical memory is referenced by the page table entry.

- **pte_rdprotect()**
  Clears the 'read' attribute to protect the page referenced by the page table entry against read accesses.

- **pte_read()**
  Checks whether the 'read' attribute is set.

- **pte_write()**
  Checks write authorization for the referenced page by testing the 'write' attribute.

- **pte_wrprotect()**
  Sets the 'write' attribute to activate write protection for the referenced page.

- **pte_young()**
  Checks that the 'age' attribute is not set, that is, that the page has not yet been accessed.

- **set_pte()**
  Sets the page table entry.

4.2 The virtual address space for a process

As we have already mentioned in the last section, the virtual address space of a LINUX process is segmented: a distinction is made between the kernel segment and the user segment. For the x86 processor, two selectors along with their descriptors must be defined for each of these segments. The data segment selector only permits data to be read or modified, while the code segment selector allows code in the segment to be executed and data to be read.

In x86 architecture, the user process can modify its local descriptor table, which holds the segment descriptors, by making use of the system call *modify_ldt*. This enables a process to enlarge its local address space by additional segments. This facility is used, for example, by the Windows emulator WINE to imitate MS-Windows segment-based memory management.

4.2.1 The user segment

In User Mode, privilege level 3 on x86 processors, a process can access only the user segment. As the user segment contains the data and code for the process, this segment needs to be different from those belonging to other processes, and this means in turn that the page directories, or at least the individual page tables for the different processes, must also be different. In the system call *fork*, the parent process's page directories and page tables are copied for the child process. An exception to this is the kernel segment, whose page tables are shared by all the processes.

The system call *fork* has an alternative: *clone*. Both system calls generate a new thread, but in *clone* the old thread and the thread generated by *clone* can fully share the memory. Thus, LINUX regards threads as tasks which share their address space with other tasks. The handling of additional task-specific resources, such as the stack, can be controlled via parameters of the system call *clone*.

The structure of the user segment during execution in ELF format is shown in Figure 4.2. The user segment for any process, other than the idle process (process no. 0), is initialized by the loading or mapping of a binary file carried out by the system call *execve*. A process generated by *fork* inherits the structure of its parent process.

The shared libraries shown in the user segment need some explanation. Originally, the entire code of a program was statically linked into one binary. This led to the effect that, with the growth of the libraries, binaries became ever larger. In order to prevent this, the libraries were stored in separate library files and loaded at program start. However, owing to restrictions in the `a.out` format, the shared libraries were linked to static addresses. Thus, all shared libraries had to lie on different addresses. With ELF, a file structure and some methods were defined which made this superfluous and allowed shared libraries to be loaded during program execution. With a flexible design, shared libraries unknown at compile time could now be linked into a program. Perl's automatic modules are a good example, where the shared libraries are mapped at dynamically determined addresses. However, the libraries must have been generated as position-independent code (PIC), that is, there must be no absolute address references in the compiled code.

LINUX still supports the classic `a.out` format. Here, however, the user segment is structured in a different way. The program text starts at virtual address 0, and the dynamic libraries are mapped at static addresses between the heap and the stack. Because of the fixed address allocation and the much more laborious way of generating shared libraries in the `a.out` format, this binary format has been superseded.

In addition, Linux can handle scripts as true binaries. When a script is called, the interpreter specified in the first line after the character combination `#!` is started with the script as its argument. Java programs are supported in a similar way. The interpreter must be made known to the system beforehand by describing the pseudo-files `/proc/sys/kernel/java-interpreter` and `/proc/sys/kernel/java-appletviewer` with their corresponding paths.

The environmental variables and arguments for a process are stored at the top end of the user area as a sequence of character strings ending in zeros. Below this are the pointer tables for the arguments and the environmental variables to which a C program will refer using `argv` and `environ` respectively. Below this, the stack starts.

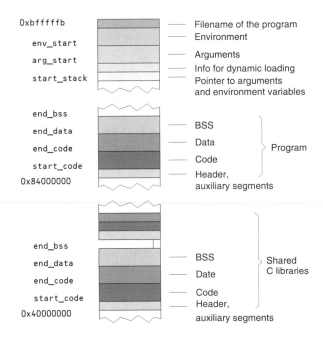

Figure 4.2 Structure of the user segment for a process with a binary file in ELF format.

4.2.2 Virtual memory areas

As a shared library can be very large, it would not be a good idea if all of its code were constantly being loaded into physical memory. We can be sure that the processes running at any one time will not be using all of the functions in a library simultaneously. Loading the code for unused functions squanders memory resources and is unnecessary. Even in larger programs there will certainly be sections of code which will never be touched by a process because (for example) certain program features are not used. Loading these parts of the program is just as wasteful as loading the unused sections of a library.

If two processes are being run by the same executable file, the program code does not need to be loaded into memory twice. Both processes can execute the same code in primary memory. It is also possible that large parts of the data segments of these processes will match. These can also be shared between the processes, provided neither process modifies these data. Only when a process modifies a page of memory does a copy-on-write need to be performed.

If a process reserves very large amounts of memory, the allocation of free pages of physical memory would be extravagant. The process will only use these pages fully at a later stage, and possibly not even then. The way to get round this problem is to use copy-on-write, by which an empty page of memory is referenced more than once in the page tables for the process. It is only after a modification has been made at a specific address in the user segment that this page needs to be copied and mapped to the appropriate point in the linear address space.

It is clear from this that the separate areas of the user segment must have different attributes for the page table entries for the memory page, different handling routines for access errors and different strategies for saving to secondary memory. It was for this reason that the abstract concept of virtual memory was introduced during the development of LINUX. A virtual memory area is defined by the data structure `vm_area_struct`.

```
struct vm_area_struct {
/* parameters for virtual memory area */
  struct mm_struct * vm_mm;
  unsigned long vm_start;
  unsigned long vm_end;
  pgprot_t vm_page_prot;
  unsigned short vm_flags;
/* AVLtree for virtual memory area of a process,
 * sorted by address. */
  short vm_avl_height;
  struct vm_area_struct * vm_avl_left;
  struct vm_area_struct * vm_avl_right;
/* singly linked list of areas of virtual memory of a process
 * sorted by address */
  struct vm_area_struct * vm_next;
/* for areas with an inode, the doubly linked circular list
 * inode->i_mmap */
/* for area of shared memory, the list of mappings */
/* otherwise unused */
  struct vm_area_struct * vm_next_share;
  struct vm_area_struct * vm_prev_share;
/* more */
  struct vm_operations_struct * vm_ops;
  unsigned long vm_offset;
  struct inode * vm_inode;
  unsigned long vm_pte;                         /* shared mem */
};
```

The components `vm_start` and `vm_end` determine the start and end addresses of the virtual memory area managed by the structure.

The structure `vm_mm` is a pointer to a part of an entry in a process table. The protection attributes for pages of memory in this area are fixed by `vm_page_prot`. Information on the memory area type is held in `vm_flags`. This includes the current access permissions to the memory area and rules as to what protection attributes can be set.

The virtual memory areas for a process are managed in two places: an AVL tree, sorted by address, and a singly linked list, also sorted by address. For special purposes, such as the mapping of a file or the use of System V shared memory, fields for a doubly linked circular list are also defined.

The inode pointer vm_inode refers to the file or the hardware device whose contents have been mapped to the virtual memory area starting at the offset vm_offset. If this pointer is set to NULL, the process is referred to as 'anonymous mapping'. If a virtual memory area is mapped anonymously, all the page table entries for this area point to one and the same page of memory, which is completely set to NULL. If the process then writes to a page in this area, a new physical page is initialized by copy-on-write handling routines and entered in the page table. In this way, LINUX only allocates pages of memory for anonymous areas of virtual memory if these are accessed by writing. This mechanism is used in the system call *brk*. The vm_pte field is used when System V's shared memory is implemented.

As the virtual areas of memory are merely reserved, any attempt to access memory in one of these areas will produce a page error, because either no entry in the page directory as yet exists for the page, or else the referenced page of memory does not allow write access. The processor generates a page error exception interrupt and activates the appropriate handling routine. This routine then calls up an operation to provide the required pages in memory. There are pointers to these operations in vm_ops. As well as these, vm_ops also contains pointers for additional operations which organize the initializing and release of a virtual memory area. The structure vm_operations_struct defines the possible function pointers enabling different operations to be assigned to different areas.

```
struct vm_operations_struct {
  void (*open)(struct vm_area_struct * area);
  void (*close)(struct vm_area_struct * area);
  void (*unmap)(struct vm_area_struct *area, unsigned long,
    size_t);
  void (*protect)(struct vm_area_struct *area, unsigned long,
    size_t, unsigned int newprot);
  void (*sync)(struct vm_area_struct *area, unsigned long,
    size_t, unsigned int flags);
  void (*advise)(struct vm_area_struct *area, unsigned long,
    size_t, unsigned int advise);
  unsigned long (*nopage)(struct vm_area_struct * area,
    unsigned long address, unsigned long page,
    int write_access);
```

```
        unsigned long (*wppage)(struct vm_area_struct * area,
          unsigned long address, unsigned long page);
        void (*swapout)(struct vm_area_struct *,
          unsigned long, pte_t *);
        pte_t (*swapin)(struct vm_area_struct *, unsigned long,
          unsigned long);
    };
```

The functions protect(), sync(), advise() and wpprotect() are not used by
version 2.0. Memory access errors in cases where write access to the memory
page is illegal are handled in the central routine do_no_page() instead of by the
wpprotect() call.

The open() function is called if a new virtual memory area is mapped to
the user segment. To remove the mapped area of memory again, the function
close() is called. If a file has been mapped to the virtual memory area, the
changed data must be written back to the file itself. The function unmap() is
used to indicate that part of the data mapped to the virtual memory area is
being cleared. The virtual memory area is then split at the unmapped area.

Errors caused by attempts to access a page which is not present in physical memory and which has not been copied to secondary storage are handled
by nopage(). The only job of this function is to load the page to the page in
physical memory referenced by the parameter page.

The function swapout() copies to secondary storage the page within the
memory area pointed to by the offset given as a parameter. When this function
is called, a check is made to ensure that the 'dirty' bit for this page has been
set. It is not possible for this function to return an error. The function
swapin() reloads the page of memory whose offset has already been calculated
relative to the component vm_offset in the virtual memory area's data structure. If the function fails it will return BAD_PAGE; otherwise it returns the
appropriate page table entry.

The function sync() writes changes in the memory area back to the
inode associated to that memory area.

In the LINUX kernel, virtual memory areas for a process can be set up
using the function do_mmap.

```
        int do_mmap(struct file * file, unsigned long addr,
                    unsigned long len, unsigned long prot,
                    unsigned long flags, unsigned long off)
```

At the do_mmap() call, file is either null or should point to a data structure of
the file type with a function pointer for mmap entered in its operation vector.
The argument len gives the length of the memory area to be mapped and off
the offset in the file indicated by file. If file is NULL, an empty page of
memory of the size given by len will be mapped to the user segment of the
process. This is also known as anonymous mapping.

Table 4.2 Values for `prot` as argument of the `do_mmap()` function.

Value	Meaning
PROT_READ	Area can be read
PROT_WRITE	Area can be written to
PROT_EXEC	Area can be executed
PROT_NONE	Area cannot be accessed (not supported at present)

In `prot` the calling process specifies the access protection to be given to the virtual memory area. The options for this are summarized in Table 4.2.

Attributes for the virtual memory area are given in `flags`. MAP_FIXED can be used to specify that the memory area should be mapped exactly at the given address. Care should be taken in this case to ensure that any virtual memory areas previously mapped to this address have been removed. The flags MAP_SHARED and MAP_PRIVATE control the handling of memory operations in the virtual memory area: MAP_SHARED specifies that all write operations will be carried out on the same pages of memory, while for MAP_PRIVATE any write access will cause the pages to be duplicated. In other words, setting MAP_PRIVATE switches on the 'copy-on-write' attribute for the pages concerned. The limitations of x86 architecture mean that it is not possible to achieve a complete implementation of `do_mmap()` for x86 processors.

4.2.3 The system call *brk*

At the start of a process the value of the `brk` field in the process table entry (*see also* Section 3.1.1) points to the end of the BSS segment for non-statically initialized data. By modifying this pointer, the process can allocate and release dynamic memory: this is usually done when the standard C function `malloc()` is called. The allocation of memory must of course be linked to the necessary changes to the page directory for the process. As this can only be done under the control of the kernel, an appropriate system call is needed.

The system call *brk* can be used to find the current value of the pointer or to set it to a new value. If the argument is smaller than the pointer to the end of the process code, the current value of `brk` will be returned. Otherwise an attempt will be made to set a new value.

The new value is checked for consistency. Thus, a new value will be rejected if the memory required exceeds the estimated size of the space currently available in primary and secondary memory. As well as this, a check is made on the current limits for the size of process memory. The process is also prevented from setting `brk` to a value which would overlap with the stack or a virtual memory area that has already been mapped.

After the consistency checks, the kernel function `sys_brk()` calls `do_mmap()` to map a private and anonymous memory area between the old and new values of `brk`, corrected to the nearest page boundary, and return the new `brk` value. The first write access to a page in the virtual memory area will cause a copy of the memory page mapped via copy-on-write to be created. The copy can then be modified as required. `sys_brk()` returns the new `brk` value.

4.2.4   Mapping functions

The C library provides three functions in the header file `sys/mman.h`.

```
#include <sys/mman.h>

extern caddr_t mmap (caddr_t addr, size_t len,
                     int prot, int flags, int fd, off_t off);
extern int munmap (caddr_t addr, size_t len);
extern int mprotect (caddr_t addr, size_t len, int prot);
extern int msync;
```

The `mmap()` function makes use of the system call *mmap*, which in turn calls `do_mmap()`. The file descriptor `fd` must be opened before the call. For anonymous mapping, the additional flag `MAP_ANON` needs to be used.

The `munmap()` function makes use of the system call *munmap* to remove memory areas mapped to the user segment.

The library function `mprotect()` implements the protection attributes for a memory area in the user segment, using the macros `PROT_NONE`, `PROT_READ`, `PROT_WRITE` and `PROT_EXEC` mentioned above. The implementation of this function is based on the system call *mprotect*. This system call will of course check whether an area of memory has been mapped at this point and whether the new protection attributes are legal for the area.

It should be mentioned that, in x86 architecture, the semantics of setting the attributes `PROT_WRITE` and `PROT_EXEC` will cause `PROT_READ` to be set for all of these operations. In addition, the attribute `PROT_EXEC` is implicitly set when `PROT_READ` is set.

Furthermore, additional functions for synchronizing the working memory with the disk contents and the fixing of mapped memory areas in RAM are supported, so that since LINUX 2.0 the whole range of `mmap` functionality is available.

4.2.5   The kernel segment

When a system function is initiated, the process switches to system mode. In x86 architecture, a LINUX system call is generally initiated by the software interrupt 128 (0x80) being triggered. The processor then reads the gate descriptor stored in the interrupt descriptor table. This is a trap gate descriptor pointing to the assembler routine `system_call` in `arch/i386/entry.S`. The processor jumps to this address with the segment descriptor in the CS register pointing to the kernel segment. The assembler routine then sets the segment selectors in the DS and ES registers in such a way that memory accesses will read or write to data in the kernel segment.

As the page tables for the kernel segment are identical for all processes, this ensures that any process in system mode will encounter the same kernel segment. In the kernel segment, physical addresses and virtual addresses are the same except for the virtual memory areas mapped by `vmalloc()`.

Alpha architecture does not support segments, which means that the kernel segment cannot start at address 0. A `PAGE_OFFSET` is therefore provided between the physical and virtual addresses, which is determined by the start address of the kernel segment in the virtual address space.

In an x86 processor, the next step involves loading to the segment register FS a data segment selector pointing to the user segment. Accesses to the user segment can then be made using the `put_user_` and `get_user_` functions mentioned earlier. This may cause a general protection error, if the referenced address is above the segment boundary 0xc0000000. It is also possible that the operation may be attempting to access an address inside a write-protected page of memory. As the 386 ignores the write-protection bits when it is in system mode, however, this could cause problems if the page concerned has only been mapped by copy-on-write. This means that a user process would be able to modify other processes' memory when using a system routine. Users of 486 and Pentium machines have the advantage that these also take account of the protection bits in system mode. On a 386, the handling routine for write protection must be called explicitly. Action must also be taken in the kernel to prevent attempts to access virtual addresses in the user segment for which no virtual memory area has been defined. Interrupting the code in the kernel segment with the `SIGSEGV` signal would result in inconsistencies in kernel data structures which have just been modified by the interrupted process.

```
#define VERIFY_READ  0 /* before read access */
#define VERIFY_WRITE 1 /* before write access */

int verify_area(int type, void * addrs, unsigned long size);
```

To avoid these problems, system routines have to call the `verify_area()` function before they access the user segment. This checks whether read or write access to the given area of the user segment is permitted, investigating all the virtual memory areas affected by the area involved. If there are write-protected pages in the area, a 386 will call the handling routine for write-protect errors. If access to the specified area of memory is permitted, the function returns zero.

4.2.6   Static memory allocation in the kernel segment

Before a kernel generates its first process when it is run, it calls initialization routines for a range of kernel components. These routines are able to reserve memory in the kernel segment. The initialization routine for character-oriented devices is called as follows by `start_kernel` in the `init/main.c` file:

```
memory_start = console_init(memory_start,memory_end);
```

The initialization function reserves memory by returning a value higher than the parameter `memory_start`. The memory between the return value and `memory_start` can then be used as desired by the initialized component.

4.2.7   Dynamic memory allocation in the kernel segment

In the system kernel, it is often necessary to allocate dynamic memory, for example for temporary buffers. In the LINUX kernel, the functions used for this are `kmalloc()` and `kfree()`. These are implemented in the file `mm/kmalloc.c`.

```
void * kmalloc (size_t size, int priority);
void kfree (void *obj);
#define kfree_s(a,b) kfree(a)
```

The `kmalloc()` function attempts to reserve the extent of memory specified by `size`.

The memory that has been reserved can be released again by the function `kfree()`. The `kfree_s()` macro is provided to ensure compatibility with older versions of the kernel, in which `kfree_s()`, with an indication of the size of the area allocated, was faster; but a more recent implementation of `kmalloc()` has wiped out this difference. Version 1.0 of LINUX only allowed memory to be reserved up to a size of 4072 bytes. After repeated reimplementation, it is now possible to reserve memory of up to 131 048 bytes – just a whisker short of 128 Kbytes.

To increase efficiency, the memory reserved is not initialized. When it is used, it is important to remember that the process could be interrupted by the `kmalloc()` call. The function `__get_free_pages()` may be called and, if no free pages are available and other pages therefore need to be copied to secondary storage, this may block.

In the LINUX kernel 1.2, the `__get_free_pages()` function can only be used to reserve contiguous areas of memory of 4, 8, 16, 32, 64 and 128 Kbytes in size. As `kmalloc()` can reserve far smaller areas of memory, however, the free memory in these areas needs to be managed. The central data structure for this is the table `sizes[]`, which contains descriptors for different sizes of memory area. These descriptors include two pointers to linear page descriptor lists. One of these lists manages memory suitable for DMA, while the other is responsible for ordinary memory. One page descriptor manages each contiguous area of memory. The name page descriptor derives from an earlier implementation of `kmalloc()` in which only one page of memory was reserved at a time and the largest area of memory that could be reserved using `kmalloc()` was no larger than 4 Kbytes. This page descriptor is stored at the beginning of every memory area reserved by `kmalloc()`. Within the page itself, all the free blocks of memory are managed in a linear list. All the blocks of memory in a memory area collected into one list are the same in size.

The block itself has a block header, which in turn holds a pointer to the next element if the block is free, or else the actual size of the memory area allocated in the block. This structure makes for very effective implementation of a free memory management system inspired by the Buddy system[1] but allowing for the particularities of the x86 processor. Figure 4.3 shows a possible content for this structure.

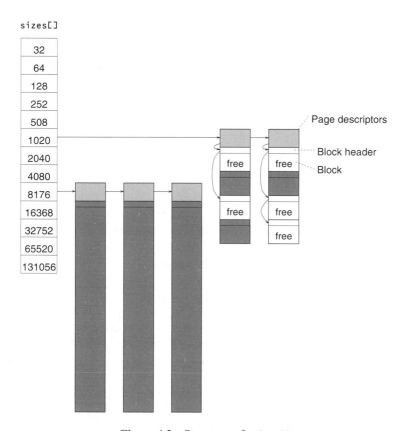

Figure 4.3 Structures for `kmalloc`.

---

[1] The Buddy system is explained in Tanenbaum (1986).

The kmalloc() algorithm searches for a free block in all the memory areas in charge of blocks suitable for the size required. If none can be found, a new memory area with free blocks must be set up. Once the block is found or made available, it is marked as occupied and removed from the list of free blocks in its memory area.

The implementation of kfree() thus also becomes clear. If blocks are still occupied in the memory area where the free block is located, the block that has been released will be entered in the list of free blocks. If the memory area consists completely of free blocks it will be released in its entirety.

In older versions of the kernel, kmalloc() provided the only facility for dynamic allocation of memory in the kernel. In addition, the amount of memory that could be reserved was restricted to the size of one page of memory. The situation was improved by the function vmalloc() and its counterpart vmfree(). Using these, memory in multiples of a page of memory can be reserved. Both functions are defined in mm/vmalloc.c.

```
void * vmalloc(unsigned long size);
void * vmfree(void * addr);
```

A value which is not divisible by 4096 can also be entered in size, and will then be rounded up. If areas smaller than 4072 bytes are being reserved, it makes more sense to use kmalloc(). The maximum value for size is limited by the amount of physical memory available. The memory reserved by vmalloc() will not be copied to external storage, so kernel programmers should take care not to overuse the function. As vmalloc() calls the function __get_free_page(), the process may risk being locked out in order to save pages of memory to external storage. The memory that has been reserved is not initialized.

After size has been rounded up, an address is found at which the area to be allocated can be mapped to the kernel segment in full. As we have mentioned, in the kernel segment the entire physical memory is mapped from its start, so that the virtual addresses are the same as the physical addresses apart from an offset dependent on the architecture.

With vmalloc(), the memory to be allocated must be mapped above the end of physical memory, as __get_free_page() (*see* Section 4.4.2) only allocates individual pages, and not necessarily consecutive ones. In x86 architecture, the search begins at the next address after physical memory, located on an 8 Mbyte boundary. The addresses here may already have been allocated by previous vmalloc calls. One page of memory is left free after each of the reserved areas, to cushion accesses exceeding the allocated memory area.

The free pages are mapped by vmalloc() to the address range in memory which has just been located. If it is necessary to generate new page tables, these are entered in the *memory map* as reserved pages.

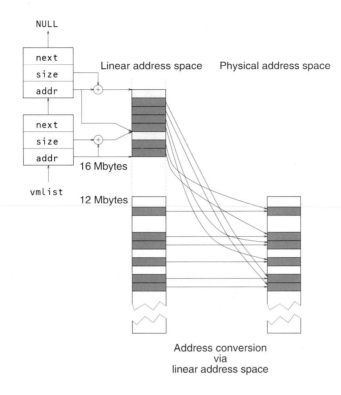

Figure 4.4   Operation of `vmalloc()`.

Kernel addresses set up in this way are managed by LINUX very simply, using a linear list. The related data structure `vm_struct` contains the virtual address of the area and its size, which also includes the page not entered in the page table. As mentioned above, this is intended to intercept cases where the address range is exceeded. This means that the memory area that has been reserved is smaller by one page than the value held in `vm_struct`. As well as this, there is a pointer to the last element in the list and a component `flags` which is not used.

The clear advantage of the `vmalloc()` function is that the size of the area of memory requested can be better adjusted to actual needs than when using `kmalloc()`, which requires 128 Kbytes of consecutive physical memory to reserve just 64 Kbytes. Besides this, `vmalloc()` is limited only by the size of free physical memory and not by its segmentation, as `kmalloc()` is. Since `vmalloc()` does not return any physical addresses and the reserved areas of memory can be spread over non-consecutive pages, this function is not suitable for reserving memory for DMA.

4.3 Block device caching

When judging the performance of a computer system, the speed of access to block devices plays a decisive role. LINUX makes use of a dynamic cache system which employs primary memory left unused by the kernel and the processes as buffer for block devices. If the requirement for primary memory increases, the space allowed for buffering is reduced. Since version 2.0, block device caching is complemented by the file-oriented memory page caching described further below. Thus, for block devices there is a not very orthodox division of tasks between the two cache systems: file-oriented memory page caching is used for read operations, whereas write operations resort to the block buffer cache. Memory page caching can, in a way, be interpreted as an addition to block buffer caching, using temporary block buffer heads (*see below*) for reading in order to avoid administering data in two cache systems simultaneously. In connection with write operations this can lead to additional copying of data into the memory page cache. This does not really matter because, compared to read operations, write operations occur far less frequently. One can, however, still think about optimization, which would finally lead to management of the same data in the two cache systems.

4.3.1 Block buffering

Files are held on block devices, which can process requests to read or write blocks of data. The block size for a given device may be 512, 1024, 2048 or 4096 bytes. These blocks must be held in memory via a buffering system. The device itself should only be accessed in two events: a block may be loaded if it is not yet held in the buffer; and a block may be written if the buffer contents for the block no longer match what is held on the external medium. To handle the latter case, the respective block in the buffer is marked as 'dirty' after a modification. There may be a delay in performing this write operation, however, as the valid contents of the block are held in cache. A special case applies for blocks taken from files opened with the flag `O_SYNC`. These are transferred to disk every time their contents are modified.

   The implementation of the buffer cache in LINUX was originally based, with slight modifications, on the concept described by Maurice J. Bach (1986) in *The Design of the* UNIX® *Operating System*. The changes that have been made in the meantime, however, justify our referring to a separate LINUX buffer cache system.

   As mentioned earlier, the buffer cache manages individual block buffers of varying size. For this, every block is given a `buffer_head` data structure. For simplicity, it will be referred to below as the 'buffer head'. The definition of the buffer head is in `linux/fs.h`:

```
struct buffer_head {
  /* first cache line */
  unsigned long b_blocknr; /* block number */
  kdev_t b_dev;            /* device (B_FREE: buffer free ) */
  kdev_t b_rdev;           /* real device */
  unsigned long b_rsector; /* real position of buffer on
                            * hard disk */
  struct buffer_head * b_next; /* hash list */
  struct buffer_head * b_this_page;
                           /* circular list of buffers inside
                            * one memory page */

  /* second cache line */
  unsigned long b_state;   /* buffer status bitmap */
  struct buffer_head * b_next_free;
  unsigned int b_count;    /* number of users of block */
  unsigned long b_size;    /* block size */

  /* speed-uncritical area */
  char * b_data;  /* pointer to data block (1024 bytes) */
  unsigned int b_list;     /* list for buffer */
  unsigned long b_flushtime; /* time from which (dirty) buffer
                              * should be written back */
  unsigned long b_lru_time;  /* time of last use of buffer */
  struct wait_queue * b_wait;
  struct buffer_head * b_prev; /* doubly linked hash list */
  struct buffer_head * b_prev_free; /* doubly linked list
                                     * of buffers */
  struct buffer_head * b_reqnext;   /* request queue */
};
```

The data structure is organized in such a way that frequently requested data lie very close together and can be possibly kept in the processor cache.

The pointer b_data points to the block data in a specially reserved area of physical memory. The size of this area exactly matches the block size b_size. This area and the buffer head together form the block buffer. The value of b_dev specifies the device on which the relevant block is stored, and b_blocknr the number of this block on the storage medium used by the device. As it is possible that the referenced device is a pseudo-device which combines several block devices (such as several partitions on a hard disk), there are the additional pointers b_rdev and b_rsector which reference a real sector on a real device.

The number of processes currently using the block buffer is held in b_count. The bitmap variable b_state combines a series of status flags. The block buffer matches the disk contents if the BH_Uptodate flag is set. The block buffer must be written back to the medium if BH_Dirty is set. If BH_Lock is set, access to the block buffer is locked: in this case, processes must wait in the wait queue b_wait. The flag BH_Req indicates whether the block belonging to the buffer has been requested from a device. For a block buffer marked as 'dirty', b_flushtime shows in jiffies the time from which the block buffer should be written back to the device. When the block is marked 'dirty', its b_flushtime is set to the current time plus a delay parameter. The buffer is then only written back to the disk if no write access has been carried out over a lengthy period. b_lru_time holds the time at which the buffer was last accessed by a buffer management procedure.

The additional flags BH_Touched and BH_Has_aged are used to determine the time when the block can be removed from memory if additional memory is needed.

The BH_FreeOnIO flag marks a buffer head which is used only temporarily for input and output on block devices. This flag is mainly used for reading data into the memory page cache.

4.3.2   The update and bdflush processes

The update process is a LINUX process which at periodic intervals calls the system call *bdflush* with an appropriate parameter. All modified buffer blocks that have not been used for a certain time are written back to disk, together with all superblock and inode information. The interval used by update as a default under LINUX is five seconds.

bdflush is implemented as a kernel thread and is started during kernel initialization in init/main.c. In an endless loop, it writes back the number of block buffers marked 'dirty' given in the bdflush parameter (default is 500). Once this is completed, a new loop starts immediately if the proportion of modified ('dirty') block buffers to the total number of buffers in the cache becomes too high. Otherwise, the process switches to the TASK_INTERRUPTIBLE state.

The kernel thread can be woken up using the wakeup_bdflush() function. If the wait parameter is set when this function is called, the function will wait until the bdflush process has completed a circuit of the loop.

The bdflush kernel thread is always activated when a block is released by means of brelse(). It is also activated whenever new block buffers are requested or the size of the buffer cache needs to be reduced, meaning that old block buffers – but not 'dirty' ones – have to be discarded.

The bdflush kernel thread can be configured during operation using the system function sys_bdflush() and a range of parameters. Table 4.3 lists the individual parameters with their default values and a short description.

The advantage of the combination of bdflush and update should be clear. They keep to a minimum the number of 'dirty' block buffers in the buffer

Table 4.3 Parameters for the `bdflush` process.

Parameter	Default value	Description
`nfract`	25	Fraction of 'dirty' buffer blocks above which the `bdflush` process is activated, expressed as a percentage
`ndirty`	500	Maximum number of buffer blocks which may be written each time `bdflush` is activated
`nrefill`	64	Number of clean block buffers generated by calling `refill_freelist()`
`nref_dirt`	256	Number of 'dirty' block buffers at which `bdflush` is activated in `refill_freelist()`
`clu_nfract`	15	Fraction of buffer cache searched for free clusters (*Ext2* file system), expressed as a percentage
`age_buffer`	3000	Ticks by which writing a 'dirty' data block buffer is delayed
`age_super`	500	Ticks by which writing a 'dirty' superblock or inode block buffer is delayed
`lav_const`	1884	Constant used in calculating the load average
`lav_ratio`	2	Value specifying the threshold for the pad average of a given block size below which the number of block buffers for this block size is reduced

cache. The different write delays give preference to the blocks which are important to the consistency of file systems (blocks for inodes and superblocks).

4.3.3 List structures for the buffer cache

LINUX manages its block buffers via a number of different lists. Free block buffers are managed in circular doubly linked lists. A list of this type is maintained by the table `free_list[]` for every possible block size. Blocks held in `free_list[]` are marked by `B_FREE` (`0xffff`) entered in the `b_dev` field in their buffer heads. This makes it easy to determine that a free block buffer has been entered in another list. The table `nr_free[]` contains the number of free block buffers for every possible block size. These values must of course match with `free_list[]`.

Block buffers in use are managed in a set of special LRU (least recently used) lists. In older LINUX versions, the block buffers were sorted into the LRU lists by the time of last usage. As continuous re-sorting of lists is very expensive, this is no longer done, and old block buffers are now marked by the status flags `BH_Touched` and `BH_Has_aged`. The individual LRU lists are collected in the table `lru_list[]`. The indices in this table specify the type for the block buffers entered in each of the LRU lists. Table 4.4 shows the indices

Table 4.4 The various LRU lists.

LRU list (index)	Description
BUF_CLEAN	Block buffers not managed in other lists – content matches relevant block on hard disk
BUF_UNSHARED	Block buffers formerly (but no longer) managed in BUF_SHARED
BUF_LOCKED	Locked block buffers (b_lock != 0)
BUF_LOCKED1	Locked block buffers for inodes and superblocks
BUF_DIRTY	Block buffers with contents not matching the relevant block on hard disk
BUF_SHARED	Block buffers situated in a page of memory mapped to the user segment of a process

available, followed by the type of the related LRU list. Like the lists of free blocks, the LRU lists are doubly linked circular lists, linked by means of the pointers prev_free_list and next_free_list. A block buffer is sorted into the correct LRU list by the function refile_buffer.

The buffer blocks used are referenced in the table hash_table[]. Memory for the table is reserved on start-up of the system via vmalloc(), and its size will depend on the primary memory available. It is used to trace block buffers by reference to their device and block numbers. The procedure used for this is open hashing; the hash lists are implemented as doubly linked linear lists using the pointers b_next and b_prev in the buffer head. The hash function used is defined as follows:

```
#define _hashfn(dev,block) (((unsigned)(dev^block))%nr_hash)
```

4.3.4 Using the buffer cache

To read a block, the system routine calls the function bread(). This is defined in the fs/buffer.c file.

```
struct buffer_head * bread(kdev_t dev, int block, int size)
```

First a check is made as to whether there is already a buffer to the device dev for the block block, by accessing the block buffer hash table. If the buffer is found and if the BH_Uptodate flag is set, bread() terminates by returning the block buffer. If the flag is not set, the buffer must be updated by reading the external medium, after which the routine can return.

The block is read using the function ll_rw_block(), which generates the appropriate request for the device driver. It is implemented in ll_rw_blk.c in the drivers/block/ directory. However, after issuing the device driver request, the current process has to wait for the request to be processed. The memory block returned by bread() should be released once it is no longer required, by using brelse().

A variant of the bread() function is breada(). Depending on the block device to be read from, this function reads not only the block requested into the buffer cache but also a number of following blocks. However, breada() only waits for the requested block to be read. The remaining blocks are read asynchronously.

A modified ('dirty') block buffer must be written to the block device once the time specified in b_flushtime has been reached. This is carried out using either the bdflush kernel thread or the update process.

For reading and writing memory pages from and into working memory, the brw_page() function is available.

```
int brw_page(int rw, struct page *page,
             kdev_t dev, int b[], int size, int bmap)
```

This function writes or reads the blocks whose numbers are contained in the table b[] to or from the page page of size size of the device dev. bmap is a flag which indicates that the block number 0 is interpreted as a block of zeros. For the data held in the memory page, temporary buffer heads are generated, which means that the read or written data is not permanently managed in the block buffer cache.

However, LINUX also provides the classical system calls *sync* and *fsync*. The *sync* call writes back all modified buffer blocks in the cache, including inodes and superblocks, without waiting for the end of the write requests, while *fsync* writes back all the modified buffer blocks for a single file, and waits for the write operation to be completed. In LINUX this operation is implemented by writing back all 'dirty' block buffers of the device on which the file is stored. Both functions call sync_buffers().

```
static int sync_buffers(kdev_t dev, int wait);
```

The dev parameter can be set to 0, so as to update all the block devices. The wait parameter determines whether the routines will wait for the write request to be performed by the device drivers. If not, the entire buffer cache is inspected for modified block buffers. If any are found by sync_buffers() it will generate the necessary write requests to the device drivers by calling the ll_wr_block() routine.

A more complicated situation arises if the routine is required to wait for successful execution of the write operation. This involves going through the entire buffer cache three times in all. In the first pass, the appropriate requests are generated for all the modified blocks which are not locked. The second pass waits for completion of all the locked operations. It could happen, however, that during the first pass a buffer locked by a read operation is modified by another process while the routine is waiting; so write requests are also generated for modified buffers during this second pass. The third pass only involves waiting for all the operations which have locked buffers to be completed. This demonstrates a particular advantage of asynchronous control of the device drivers. While block buffers are being written to the block devices during the first pass, LINUX can already be searching for the next modified block buffer.

When required, the buffer cache can use the computer's entire available RAM apart from a small reserve of memory pages. The number of pages for this reserve is determined by the variable `min_free_pages`. This has a minimum value of 16 and is otherwise dependent on the size of available main memory.

4.4   Paging under LINUX

The RAM memory in a computer has always been limited and, compared to fixed disks, relatively expensive. Particularly in multi-tasking operating systems, the limit of working memory is quickly reached. Thus it was not long before someone hit on the idea of offloading temporarily unused areas of primary storage (RAM) to secondary storage (for example, a hard disk).

The traditional procedure for this used to be the so-called 'swapping', which involves saving entire processes from memory to a secondary medium and reading them in again. This approach does not solve the problem of running processes with large memory requirements in the available primary memory. Besides this, saving and reading in whole processes is very inefficient.

When new hardware architectures (VAX) were introduced, the concept of *demand paging* was developed. Under the control of a *memory management unit* (MMU) the entire memory is divided up into pages, with only complete pages of memory being read in or saved as required. As all modern processor architectures, including the x86 architecture, support the management of paged memory, demand paging is employed by LINUX. Pages of memory which have been mapped directly to the virtual address area of a process using `do_mmap()` without write authorization are not saved, but simply discarded. Their contents can be read in again from the files which were mapped. Modified memory pages, in contrast, must be written into swap space.

Pages of memory in the kernel segment cannot be saved, for the simple reason that routines and data structures which read memory pages back from secondary storage must always be present in primary memory. The most straightforward way of making sure that this is the case is to lock all of the kernel segment pages against saving.

LINUX can save pages to external media in two ways. In the first, a complete block device is used as the external medium. This will typically be a partition on a hard disk. The second uses fixed-length files in a file system for its external storage. The rather loose approach to terminology characteristic of

LINUX has resulted in these areas being referred to, confusingly, as swap devices or swap files. It would be more correct to call them paging devices and paging files. However, as the two not quite correct terms have now become standard, they will be used here: the term 'swap space' below may refer to either a swap device or a swap file.

A common structure is defined for swap devices and swap files. The first 4096 bytes contain a bitmap. Bits that have been set indicate that the page of memory for which the number in the swap space matches the offset of the bit at the start of the space is available for paging. From byte 4086 the character string 'SWAP_SPACE' is also stored as an identifier. This means that only 4086 × 8 − 1 = 32 687 pages of memory (130 784 Kbytes) can be managed in a swap device or swap file. Given the size of hard disks usual today, this is not a lot. In addition, it is possible to manage a number of swap files or devices in parallel. LINUX specifies this number as 8 in MAX_SWAPFILES; but this value can be increased to 63. The space available for swap files should, however, be enough for actual applications in nearly all cases.

Using a swap device is more efficient than using a swap file. In a swap device, a page is always saved to consecutive blocks, whereas in a swap file, the individual blocks may be given various block numbers depending on how the particular file system fragmented the file when it was set up. These blocks then need to be found via the swap file's inode. On a swap device, the first block is given directly by the offset for the page of memory to be saved or read in. The rest then follow this first block. When a swap device is used, only one read or write request is needed for each page, while a swap file requires a number, depending on the proportion of page size to block size. In a typical case (when a block size of 1024 bytes is used) this amounts to four separate requests, to read areas on the external medium which may not necessarily follow one after the other. On a hard disk, this causes movements of the read/write head, which in turn affect the access speed. The system call *swapon* logs on a swap device or file to the kernel.

```
int sys_swapon(const char * swapfile, int swapflags);
```

The parameter swapfile is the name of the device or file. The priority of the swap space can be specified by the swapflags flags. The SWAP_FLAG_PREFER flag must be set, while the bits in the SWAP_FLAG_PRIO_MASK specify the positive priority of the swap space. If no priority is specified, the swap spaces are automatically assigned a negative priority, with the priority decreasing with each call to *swapon*. The system routine completes an entry for the swap space in the swap_info table. This entry is of the swap_info_struct type.

```
struct swap_info_struct {
  unsigned int flags;
  kdev_t swap_device;
```

```
      struct inode * swap_file;
      unsigned char * swap_map;
      unsigned char * swap_lockmap;
      int lowest_bit;
      int highest_bit;
      int cluster_next;
      int cluster_nr;
      int prio;                        /* swap priority */
      int pages;
      unsigned long max;
      int next;                        /* next entry on swap list */
};
```

If the SWP_USED bit in flags is set, the entry in the swp_info table is already being used by the kernel for another swap space. The kernel sets flags to SWP_WRITEOK once all the initialization stages for the swap space have been completed. If a structure refers to a swap file, the inode pointer swap_file will be set; otherwise the device number of the swap device will be entered in swap_device. The swap_map pointer points to a table allocated via vmalloc() in which each page in the swap space has been allocated one byte. This byte keeps a count of how many processes are referring to this page. If the page cannot be used, the value in swap_map is set to 0x80, or 128. The table swap_lockmap provides one bit for each page in the swap space. If set, the bit indicates a current access to the page. No new read or write requests may then be generated. The integer component pages holds the number of pages in this swap space that can be written to, while the values of lowest_bit and highest_bit define the maximum offset of a page in the swap space. The integer max contains the value of highest_bit plus one, as this value is frequently required. prio holds the priority assigned to the swap space.

New pages to be swapped are stored sequentially in clusters in the swap space. This serves to prevent excessive head movements of the hard disk during consecutive swapping of memory pages and is controlled by the variables cluster_nr and cluster_next of the swap_info_struct structure.

The system call *swapoff* may be used to attempt to log off a swap file or device from the kernel. However, this requires enough space to be available in the memory or in the other swap spaces to accommodate the pages in the swap space that is being logged off.

```
      int sys_swapoff(const char * swapfile);
```

4.4.1   Page cache and management

For each memory page, a data structure page or mem_map_t is managed in the kernel in a table pointed to by mem_map. Data is organized in such a way that data that belong together are stored in a cache line (16 bytes).

```
typedef struct page {
  /* these must be first (free area handling) */
  struct page *next;
  struct page *prev;
  struct inode *inode;
  unsigned long offset;
  struct page *next_hash;
  atomic_t count;
  unsigned flags;           /* atomic flags, some possibly
                             * updated asynchronously */
  unsigned dirty:16, age:8;
  struct wait_queue *wait;
  struct page *prev_hash;
  struct buffer_head * buffers;
  unsigned long swap_unlock_entry;
  unsigned long map_nr;  /* page->map_nr == page - mem_map */
} mem_map_t;
```

The pointers `prev` and `next` are used for the management of this data structure in doubly linked circular lists.

`inode` and `offset` specify the file or offset from which the memory page was read. For each inode there is a list in which all pages are entered that have been read from the file belonging to the inode. `next_hash` and `prev_hash` are used to reference the page in a hash list, which is part of the hash table `page_hash_table`. The hash function consists of the inode address and the offset in the page's file. When a read request is made for a page from a file, the hash table is checked for the existence of that page first. If it is found there, it does not have to be read with the aid of the file system. Thus, file-oriented caching which supports arbitrary file systems (in particular NFS) is implemented. Also, normal file system read operations, such as `read()`, access data via the page cache.

Back to the page structure: the number of users of a page is held in `count`. The `buffer_head` pointer references the block buffer if the page is part of a block buffer. `map_nr` indicates the page number, while `swap_unlock_entry` specifies the number of the page in swap space to be unlocked after the memory page has been read. The `wait` queue contains the entries of the tasks which are waitin for the page to be unlocked. Table 4.5 explains the meaning of the individual flags stored in `flags`. `age` holds a value regarding the age of the page; the variable `dirty` is currently not used.

4.4.2 Finding a free page

When physical pages of memory are being reserved, the kernel function `__get_free_pages()` is called. This is defined in the `mm/page_alloc.c` file.

Table 4.5 Memory page flags.

Flag	Description
PG_locked	The page is locked.
PG_error	This flag indicates an error condition.
PG_referenced	This page has been recently accessed.
PG_uptodate	The page matches the hard disk contents.
PG_free_after	The page should be released after an I/O operation.
PG_decr_after	The counter nr_async_pages is decremented after reading the page.
PG_swap_unlock_after	After reading from the swap space, the page should be unlocked by calling the swap_after_unlock_page() function.
PG_reserved	The page is reserved.

```
unsigned long __get_free_pages(int priority,
                     unsigned long order, int dma)
```

The parameter priority controls the way the function is processed. The permissible values are shown in Table 4.6.

GFP_ATOMIC is intended for calls to __get_free_pages() from interrupt routines, and GFP_BUFFER is used in buffer cache management to prevent pages from processes being discarded or, worse, buffers wiped. If other values are used for priority, it is possible that the process may be interrupted and scheduling may be called.

The second parameter, order, specifies the order of size for the memory block of consecutive pages that is being reserved. A block of order o is 2° pages in size. The LINUX kernel only allows orders of size smaller than the macro NR_MEM_LISTS (default value 6). This means that only blocks with a size of 4, 8, 16, 32, 64 or 128 Kbytes can be allocated. The third parameter, dma, specifies that the pages to be reserved should be suitable for DMA.

If __get_free_pages() is able to reserve the right block, it returns the address of the block. The current implementation ensures that the block will begin at an address which is divisible by its size in bytes.

The kernel manages the table free_area[] to allow for this. One table entry contains a doubly linked circular list of free memory blocks in the different orders of size. The header element references its own entry. The pointer map references a bitmap with one bit reserved for two consecutive memory blocks in the same order of size. The bit is set if one of the two blocks is free and the other may be only partly reserved. Figure 4.5 shows example contents of maps for the first three orders of size.

Table 4.6 Priorities for the function **__get_free_pages()**.

Priority	Description
GFP_BUFFER	Free page to be returned only if free pages are still available in physical memory.
GFP_ATOMIC	The function __get_free_page must not interrupt the current process, but a page should be returned if possible.
GFP_USER	The current process may be interrupted to swap pages.
GFP_KERNEL	This parameter is the same as GFP_USER.
GFP_NOBUFFER	The buffer cache will not be reduced by an attempt to find a free page in memory.
GFP_NFS	The difference between this and GFP_USER is that the number of pages reserved for GFP_ATOMIC is reduced from min_free_pages to five. This should clearly speed up NFS operations.

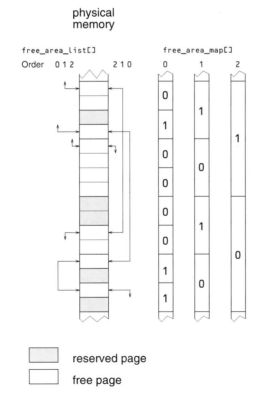

Figure 4.5 Example of contents of maps in **free_area_map[]**.

The LINUX implementation ensures that there are never two consecutive memory blocks free which could be combined into a larger block. This can sometimes mean that no blocks are free for the smaller orders of size. If a request for one of these is made, the higher-order block will have to be split. The EXPAND macro in mm/page_alloc.c updates the relevant free_area data structures accordingly.

The function __get_free_pages() attempts to reserve a block of memory from the list of free blocks relating to the right order of size. If this is not possible, calls with the parameter GFP_BUFFER or GFP_ATOMIC will return without result. In the remaining cases, the function try_to_free_page() is called. If a free page was found, a jump to the start of __get_free_pages() is carried out. If try_to_free_page() is not successful, __get_free_pages() returns zero, indicating that LINUX was unable to find any free memory.

```c
int try_to_free_page(int priority, int dma, int wait)
{
  static int state = 0;
  int i=6;
  int stop;

  /* we don't try as hard if we're not waiting.. */
  stop = 3;
  if (wait)
    stop = 0;
  switch (state) {
    do {
    case 0:
      if (shrink_mmap(i, dma))
        return 1;
      state = 1;
    case 1:
      if (shm_swap(i, dma))
        return 1;
      state = 2;
    default:
      if (swap_out(i, dma, wait))
        return 1;
      state = 0;
    i--;
    } while ((i - stop) >= 0);
  }
  return 0;
}
```

As this shows, a maximum of six passes are made in the attempt to find at least one free page. In the course of this, the various functions are called with a rising sequence of priorities. The static variable `state` ensures that each call to `try_to_free_page()` starts a different function, which ensures that calls to the different functions are equitably distributed.

The function `shrink_mmap()` attempts to discard memory pages that are part of the memory page cache or the buffer cache and currently have only one user. Only those memory pages or block buffers that have not been referenced since the last cycle are discarded. The number of inspected memory pages depends on the priority used to call `shrink_mmap()`.

The function `shm_swap()` attempts to save memory space reserved using the shared memory function in System V's inter-process communication routines (*see* Chapter 5). The function `swap_out()` is intended to swap out or discard pages of memory from the processes' user segments. It is a very interesting function, as it uses a procedure which makes a less intensive search for discardable or pageable pages in processes which have recently been swapped in and out frequently. This makes use of a calculated value `swap_cnt`, which indicates for each process how many pages of memory should be saved before `swap_out()` moves on to the next process. The search for discardable or pageable pages by `swap_out()` always begins after the page of the process at which the function was quit the previous time. In Tanenbaum (1986) this procedure is called a 'clock algorithm'. The priority parameter controls the maximum number of processes inspected by `swap_out()` during a call.

In older LINUX versions, `swap_out()` was calculated using a special algorithm. LINUX 2.0 simply uses a coefficient which indicates how many pages of memory per 1024 pages of a process are to be inspected (*see* `linux/swapctl.h`).

The `swap_out()` function now attempts to save pages for the process it has just been searching in, using the `swap_out_process()` function. This function searches the individual virtual memory areas in the user segment for pages which can be paged out. This involves searching through the page directories and then calling `try_to_swap_out()` for the individual page table entries. In `try_to_swap_out()` a page from the process's virtual address area is checked to see whether it is in fact in memory and not reserved. If the 'age' attribute in the `mem_map` data structure is 0, the file is saved. Pages get younger when they are accessed, and older when they are not. Thus, the pages most recently used are not paged out so quickly.

For a 'dirty' page, either the virtual memory area's `swapout()` operation is called, or the page of memory is swapped out if it is used by only one process. An invalid value is entered in the page table, in which the swap space and the address within the swap space are stored. A page of memory which is already present in the swap space, or can simply be loaded, is simply deleted from the page table. It may happen that the page cannot yet be released if it is used by several processes.

The `kswapd` kernel thread running in the background is activated every time the number of free pages falls below a critical level. In this case, the kernel thread repeatedly calls the `try_to_free_page()` function.

A block of memory is released using `free_pages()`. When the number of users of a page has reached 0, the page is again entered in the `free_area[]` data structures.

The function `get_free_page()` and the macro `__get_free_page()` reserve a free page in memory. The function `get_free_page()` also sets the content of the page to 0. Both use `__get_free_pages()` to carry out their task.

A number of consecutive pages can be released using the function `free_pages()`. The macro `free_page()` calls `free_pages()` for exactly one page.

4.4.3 Page errors and reloading a page

If the x86 processor is unable to access a page, it will generate a page fault interrupt. An error code is written to the stack and the linear address at which the interrupt was triggered is stored in register CR2.

Under LINUX, the routine `do_page_fault()` is now called.

```
void do_page_fault(struct pt_regs *regs)
                              unsigned long error_code);
```

It is passed the values of the registers when the interrupt occurred and the error number. The routine searches for the virtual memory area of the currently active process in which the address in the user segment which caused the fault is to be found.

If the address is not in a virtual memory area, the routine checks whether the flag `VM_GROWSDOWN` for the next virtual memory area is set. An area of this sort provides memory for the stack and may grow downwards. The `do_page_fault()` routine takes care of the necessary expansion. If the next virtual memory area cannot be expanded, `do_page_fault()` sends a `SIGSEGV` signal to the process which caused the error. This segmentation violation signal will be familiar to any serious UNIX programmer.

If an address pointing to the kernel segment was the cause of the access error, a check is made on whether this involved a test on the write protection bit, which is ignored by x86 processors in System Mode. When the write protection bit is ignored in the kernel segment, special treatment by the `verify_area()` function is required, otherwise kernel alarm messages will be printed out at the console by `printk()`, along with a variety of debugging information, and the process causing the error will be terminated.

If the address is in a virtual memory area, the legality of the read or write operation is checked by reference to the flags for the virtual memory area. If it was legal, the page error handling routine calls `do_no_page()` or `do_wp_page()`. Otherwise the `SIGSEGV` signal is sent again.

```
void do_no_page(struct task_struct * tsk,
      struct vm_area_struct * vma,
      unsigned long address, int write_access)

void do_wp_page(struct task_struct * tsk,
      struct vm_area_struct * vma,
      unsigned long address, int write_access)
```

The do_wp_page() function checks whether a write-protected page is located at the given address in the first place. If it is only referenced once, the write protection is simply cancelled. If it is referenced a number of times, a copy of the page is generated and entered without write protection to the page table for the process which caused the error.

If a non-empty entry is present in the page table without its presence attribute set, the function do_no_page() calls the do_swap_page() function. If no nopage() handling routine has been defined for the virtual memory area, an empty page is mapped to the memory area. Otherwise a check is now made to establish whether the page can be shared with another process. If not, the nopage() handling routine is called.

```
static inline void do_swap_page(struct task_struct * tsk,
      struct vm_area_struct * vma, unsigned long address,
      pte_t * page_table, pte_t entry, int write_access)
```

If no swapin() routine has been defined for the virtual memory area given as a parameter, the swap_in() function is called.

```
void swap_in(struct task_struct * tsk,
      struct vm_area_struct * vma,
      pte_t * page_table, unsigned long entry,
      int write_access)
```

This function reads in the page. The number of the relevant swap space and the page number in the swap space are given in entry.

The page in the swap space is released using swap_free(). This decrements the appropriate reference counter in the swap_map.

The swap_in() routine for a virtual memory area loads a page. In the next chapter, this function will be examined with respect to System V's shared memory.

Inter-process communication

*Is simplicity best
Or simply the easiest?*

Martin L. Gore

There are many applications in which processes need to cooperate with each other. This is always the case, for example, if processes have to share a resource (such as a printer). It is important to make sure that no more than one process is accessing the resource – that is, sending data to the printer – at any given time. This situation is known as a *race condition* and communication between processes must prevent it. However, eliminating race conditions is only one possible use of inter-process communication, which we take in this book to mean simply the exchange of information between processes on one or more computers.

There are many different types of inter-process communication. They differ in a number of ways, including their efficiency. The transfer of a small natural number between two processes could be effected, for example, by one of these generating a matching number of child processes and the other counting them.

This example, which is not meant entirely seriously, is of course very unwieldy and slow and would not be considered. *Shared memory* can provide a faster and more efficient answer to the problem.

A variety of forms of inter-process communication can be used under LINUX. These support resource sharing, synchronization, connectionless and connection-oriented data exchange or combinations of these. Synchronization mechanisms are used to eliminate the race conditions mentioned above.

Connectionless and connection-oriented data exchange differ from the first two variants by different semantic models. In these models, a process sends messages to a process or a specific group of processes.

In connection-oriented data exchange, the two parties to the communication must set up a connection before communication can start. In connectionless data exchange a process simply sends data packets, which may be given a destination address or a message type, and leaves it to the infrastructure to deliver them. The reader will already be familiar with these models from everyday life: when we make a telephone call we are using a connection-oriented data exchange model, and when we send a letter we rely on a connectionless model.

It is possible to implement one concept (for example, semaphores) based on another (for example, connectionless data exchange). LINUX implements all the forms of inter-process communication possible between processes in the same system by using shared resources, kernel data structures and the 'wait queue' synchronization mechanism. Although semaphores are available in the kernel for synchronization, these themselves rely on wait queues.

LINUX processes can share memory by means of the System V shared memory facility. The file system has been implemented from the start to allow files and devices to be used by several processes at the same time. To avoid race conditions when files are accessed, various file locking mechanisms can be used. System V semaphores can be used as a synchronization mechanism between processes in a computer.

Signals are the simplest variant of connectionless data exchange. They can be understood as very short messages sent to a specific process or process group (*see* Chapter 3). In this category, LINUX still provides message queues and the datagram sockets in the INET address family. The datagram sockets are based on the UDP section of the TCP/IP code and can be used so as to be transparent to the network (*see* Chapter 8).

The available methods for connection-oriented data exchange are *pipes*, *named pipes* (also known in the literature as FIFOs),[1] UNIX *domain sockets* and *stream sockets* in the INET address family. Stream sockets are the interface to the TCP part of the network and are used to implement services such as FTP and TELNET, among others. These are also examined in Chapter 8. The use of the socket program interface does not always amount to inter-process communication, as the opposite number on the network need not be a process. It could for example be a program in an operating system, with no process concept.

Maurice J. Bach's book *Design and Implementation of the* UNIX® *Operating System* (1986) introduces the system call *ptrace* as a variant of inter-process communication. This can be used by a process to control the operation of

---

[1] FIFO stands for 'First In, First Out', which describes the action of a pipe very well.

Table 5.1   Types of inter-process communication supported by LINUX.

	Kernel	Processes	Network
Resource sharing	Data structures, buffers	System V shared memory, files, anonymous `mmap`	
Synchronization method	Wait queues, semaphores	System V semaphores, file locking, lock files	
Connectionless data exchange	Signals	Signals, System V message queues, UNIX domain sockets in datagram mode	Datagram sockets (UDP)
Connection-oriented data exchange		Pipes, named pipes, UNIX domain sockets in stream mode	Stream sockets (TCP)

another process right down to single-step processing and modify both the memory and the registers for this process. It is especially used in debugging work. Its implementation will be discussed in this chapter.

Table 5.1 gives a summary chart of the types of inter-process communication supported by LINUX. As NFS is based on datagram sockets, the facility to send files over an NFS system is not included. In version 2.0, the system call *mmap* is fully implemented, which means that shared memory can be effected via anonymous mapping as in BSD systems. The System V Transport Library Interface is not supported.

5.1   Synchronization in the kernel

As the kernel manages the system resources, access by processes to these resources must be synchronized. A process will not be interrupted by the scheduler so long as it is executing a system call. This only happens if it locks or itself calls schedule() to allow the execution of other processes. In kernel programming it should be remembered that functions like __get_free_pages() and down() can lock. Processes in the kernel can, however, also be interrupted by interrupt handling routines: this can result in race conditions even if the process is not executing any functions which can lock.

Race conditions between the current process and the interrupt routines are excluded by the processor's interrupt flag being cleared when the critical section is entered and reset on exit. While the interrupt flag is cleared, the processor will not allow any hardware interrupts except for the non-maskable interrupt (NMI), used in PC architecture to indicate RAM faults. In normal operation, the NMI should not occur. This method has the advantage of being very simple but has the drawback that, if used too freely, it slows the system down.

In standard operation it can happen that processes in the kernel need to wait for specific events, such as a block being written to the hard disk. The current process should lock to allow other processes to execute.

As already mentioned in Section 3.1.5, this is where wait queues come in. A program can enter itself in a wait queue using the functions `sleep_on()` and `interruptible_sleep_on()`. The pair of functions `wake_up()` and `wake_up_interruptible()` switch the process back to the `TASK_RUNNING` state. These routines in turn use the functions `add_wait_queue()` and `remove_wait_queue()`, which add or delete entries in a wait queue. However, they are also used by interrupt routines to ensure that race conditions are prevented. This is implemented as follows:

```
struct wait_queue {
    struct task_struct * task;
    struct wait_queue * next;
};
```

The wait queue is a singly linked circular list of pointers in the process table.

```
extern inline void add_wait_queue(struct wait_queue ** p,
                                   struct wait_queue * wait)
{
    unsigned long flags;

    save_flags(flags);
    cli();
    __add_wait_queue(p, wait);
    restore_flags(flags);
}
```

This shows very clearly how mutual exclusion via the interrupt flag works. Before entry to the critical area, the processor's flag register is stored in the variable `flags`, and the interrupt flag is cancelled by `cli()`. On exit, `flags` is written back and the interrupt flag returned to its old value by `restore_flags()`. A simple `sti()` would only be correct if interrupts had been permissible beforehand, which might not be the case. The critical region is defined separately in an inline function `add_wait_queue()` which allows the code to be used in other critical regions without having to disable the interrupts again.

```
extern inline void __add_wait_queue(struct wait_queue ** p,
                 struct wait_queue * wait)
{
  struct wait_queue *head = *p;
  struct wait_queue *next = WAIT_QUEUE_HEAD(p);

  if (head)
    next = head;
  *p = wait;
  wait->next = next;
}
```

In __add_wait_queue(), the structure wait is inserted in the list referenced by
the pointer p. The function remove_wait_queue() has essentially the same structure as add_wait_queue().

```
extern inline void __remove_wait_queue(struct wait_queue ** p,
  struct wait_queue * wait)
{
  struct wait_queue * next = wait->next;
  struct wait_queue * head = next;

  for (;;) {
        struct wait_queue * nextlist = head->next;
        if (nextlist == wait)
                break;
        head = nextlist;
  }
  head->next = next;
}
```

```
extern inline void remove_wait_queue(struct wait_queue ** p,
                 struct wait_queue * wait)
{
  unsigned long flags;

  save_flags(flags);
  cli();
  __remove_wait_queue(p, wait);
  restore_flags(flags);
}
```

These two functions are used to implement kernel semaphores. Semaphores are
counter variables which can be incremented at any time, but can only be decremented if their value is greater than zero. If this is not the case, the decrementing

process is blocked. Under LINUX, it is entered in a wait queue for a semaphore. The implementation chosen under LINUX 2.0 is somewhat more complicated than the naive approach:

```
struct semaphore {
  int count;
  int waiting;
  struct wait_queue * wait;
};
```

The value of the semaphore is the sum of `count` and `wait`. Incrementing can be carried out with up(), decrementing with down().

The following pseudo-code explains the functioning of down():

```
__pseudo__ void down(struct semaphore * psem)
{
    while (-psem->count <= 0) {
            psem->waiting++;
            if (psem->count + psem->waiting <= 0)
                    do {
                            sleep_uninteruptible(psem->wait);
                    } while (psem->count < 0);
            /* normalization of semaphore */
            psem->count += psem->waiting;
            psem->waiting = 0;
    }
}
```

The actual implementation is more complex, in order to allow up() system calls from within interrupt handling routines and avoid having to lock the interrupts in down() and up(). What we see, however, is that in the case of success only the count variable is decremented. Thus, if we need to block anyway, more operations must be executed. The normalization allows the simple loop structure of the function.

In the best case, only one variable need be incremented in up().

```
__pseudo__ void up(struct semaphore) {
    if (++psem->count <= 0) {
            /* normalization of semaphore */
            psem->count += psem->waiting;
            psem->waiting = 0;
            wake_up(psem->wait);
    }
}
```

This clever mechanism allows `up()` and `down()` to be implemented as inline assembler routines which in principle consist only of incrementing and decrementing instructions, together with a conditional jump into the code for more complex cases.

5.2 Communication via files

Communication via files is in fact the oldest way of exchanging data between programs. Program A writes data to a file and program B reads the data out again. In a system in which only one program can be run at any given time, this does not present any problems.

In a multi-tasking system, however, both programs could be run as processes at least quasi-parallel to each other. Race conditions then usually produce inconsistencies in the file data, which result from one program reading a data area before the other has completed modifying it, or both processes modifying the same area of memory at the same time.

The situation therefore calls for locking mechanisms. The simplest method, of course, would be to lock the whole file. For this LINUX, like other UNIX derivatives, offers a range of facilities. More common and more efficient, however, is the practice of locking file areas. This locking of file access can be either *mandatory* or *advisory*. Advisory locking allows reading and writing to the file to continue after the lock has been set.

However, lockings mutually exclude each other, depending on the semantics determined by their respective types. Mandatory locking blocks read and write operations throughout the entire area. With advisory locking, all processes accessing the file for read or write operations have to set the appropriate lock and release it again. If a process does not keep to this rule, inconsistencies are possible. However, mandatory locking provides no better protection against malfunctions within processes: if processes have write authorization to a file, they can produce inconsistencies by writing to unlocked areas. The problems produced by faulty programs when mandatory locking is employed are extremely critical, because the locked files cannot be modified as long as the process in question is still running. Since version 2.0, LINUX supports mandatory locking, but the corresponding kernel configuration parameter is by default disabled. For the reasons given above and as POSIX 1003.1 does not require mandatory locking, this is perfectly acceptable.

If mandatory locking is supported by a generated LINUX kernel, for each file that is to support mandatory locking the group execution bit must be unset and the SGDI bit set. Mandatory locking does not function with files mapped with `mmap()` and the `MAP_SHARED` flag.

5.2.1 Locking entire files

There are two methods of locking entire files:

(1) In addition to the file to be locked there is an auxiliary file known as a *lock file* which refuses access to the file when it is present. In his book, *Programmieren von* UNIX-*Netzen* (Stevens, 1992b), W. Richard Stevens lists the following procedures:

(a) The first variant of this method exploits the fact that the system call *link* fails if the reference to the file it is instructed to set up already exists. A file with the process number as the filename is set up and then attempts to set up a link to the name of the lock file, which will only be successful if this link does not yet exist. The reference with the process number as its name can then be deleted. After a failure, the process can call the library function sleep() to pause (but only for a short time) and then reattempt the link.

(b) A second approach makes use of a characteristic of the system call *creat*: this aborts with an error code if the process which is being called does not possess the appropriate access rights. When the lock file is set up, all the write access bits are cancelled. This variant, however, also involves active waiting and cannot be used for processes running with the superuser's access rights.

(c) The variant recommended for LINUX programming is based on the use of a combination of the O_CREAT and O_EXCL flags with the system call *open*. The lock file can then only be opened if it does not already exist; otherwise an error message will result. As prescribed by POSIX, *open* cannot be interrupted.

The drawback to all three of these variants, however, is that after a failure the process must repeat its attempt to set up a lock file. Usually, the process will call sleep() to wait for one second and then try again. However, the process which has set up the lock file may be terminated by a SIGKILL, so that the lock file can no longer be deleted. It must now be explicitly deleted. For this reason many programs, such as the mail reader elm, place a restriction on the number of attempts to set up a lock file and abort with an error message once this number is exceeded, to draw the user's attention to this sort of situation.

(2) The second method is to lock the entire file by means of the system call *fcntl*. This is also suitable for locking file areas, which is covered in the next section. Since version 2.0, the library function flock() to lock a complete file, derived from BSD 4.3, is implemented as a separate system call. flock() only supports advisory locking and is based on the same data structures in the kernel as locking with fcntl(). As lock() is not defined by the POSIX standard, programmers are advised against using it.

5.2.2 Locking file areas

Locking file areas is usually referred to as *record locking*; however, this terminology does not help users of UNIX systems a great deal, because the UNIX file concept does not support records.

Under LINUX, advisory locking of file areas can be achieved with the system call `fcntl`.

```
int sys_fcntl(unsigned int fd, unsigned int cmd,
                              unsigned long arg);
```

The parameter `fd` is used to pass a file descriptor. For locking purposes, only the commands `F_GETLK`, `F_SETLK` and `F_SETLKW` are of interest; if one of these commands is used, `arg` must be a pointer to an `flock` structure. The `F_GETLK` command tests whether the lock specified in `flock` would be possible; if not, the attempted lock is returned. `F_SETLK` sets the lock. If it cannot do so, the function returns. `F_SETLKW` locks up if the lock cannot be set. The last two commands can release a lock if the lock type `l_type` is set to `F_UNLCK`.

```
struct flock {
    short l_type;    /* F_RDLCK, F_WRLCK, F_UNLCK, F_SHLCK,
                      * or F_EXLCK */
    short l_whence;  /* SEEK_SET, SEEK_CUR, SEEK_END */
    off_t l_start;   /* offset relative to l_whence */
    off_t l_len;     /* length of area to be locked */
    pid_t l_pid;     /* is returned with F_GETLK */
};
```

The type `F_RDLCK` is used to set up a read lock for the file area, and `F_WRLCK` a write lock. Table 5.2 shows the mutually exclusive nature of the locks. The access mode of files which are being partially locked must allow the process read or write access as appropriate.

A peculiarity of LINUX is that for `l_type`, `F_SHLCK` and `F_EXLCK` are also possible. These were used by an older implementation of the library function `flock()`. Under LINUX, the lock types mentioned above are mapped to `F_RDLCK` and `F_WRLCK` respectively, with the difference that the file to be locked must be

Table 5.2 Semantics of `fcntl` locks.

Existing locks	Set read lock	Set write lock
None	Possible	Possible
More than one read lock	Possible	Not legal
One write lock	Not legal	Not legal

opened for reading and writing. This means that if a *shared lock* is interpreted as a read lock and an *exclusive lock* as a write lock, the semantics are the same as for F_RDLCK and F_WRLCK (*see* Table 5.2). However, the semantics of fcntl() and flock() locks differ in that flock() locks are not associated to processes. For this reason, this *ad hoc* implementation is faulty, but it is still supported in kernel version 2.0 to ensure that old C libraries will run.

The new flock() locks are managed in the kernel using the same data structures as fcntl() locks, but they are marked accordingly to prevent locks of different types being mixed. When an attempt is made to set a lock on a file in which locks of the other type have already been set, an EBUSY error is returned. The two lock types have different handling routines.

Locks can be removed using F_UNLCK, with the starting position given in l_whence and l_start. For the l_whence parameter, the 'seek' parameters familiar from lseek() can be used: SEEK_SET for the start of the file, SEEK_CUR for the current position in the file and SEEK_END for the end of the file. These values are then incremented by l_start. LINUX converts SEEK_END to the current end of file, so that the lock is not set relative to the end of the file. For example, it is not possible to use the same lock, independently of write operations, to inhibit access to the last two bytes at the end of the file.

In this, LINUX behaves in the same way as SVR4 and differs from BSD. The parameter l_len defines the length of the area to be locked; an l_len of 0 is interpreted as indicating that the area stretches to the current end of the file and any future end of file.

If the F_GETLK call finds an existing lock which would exclude locking the area specified, the process number of the process which set up the lock is returned in l_pid. The implementation of these functions centres on the doubly linked list file_lock_table with entries consisting of flock-like file_lock data structures.

```
struct file_lock {
  struct file_lock *fl_next;       /* singly linked list
                                    * for this inode */
  struct file_lock *fl_nextlink;   /* doubly linked list
                                    * of all locks */
  struct file_lock *fl_prevlink;   /* used for simplified
                                    * cancellation of a lock */
  struct file_lock *fl_block;
  struct task_struct *fl_owner;
  struct wait_queue *fl_wait;
  struct file *fl_file;
  char   fl_flags, fl_type;
  off_t  fl_start, fl_end;
};

static struct file_lock *file_lock_table = NULL;
```

The pointer fl_next is used to construct a linear list linking all locks for one file (inode->i_flock).

The component fl_owner stores the process which set up the lock and is used in the command F_GETLCK. The file descriptor for the file locked by the fl_owner process is held in fl_fd.

This parameter is used to distinguish between the fnctl() locks (F_POSIX), the new flock() locks (F_FLOCK) and the old flock() locks (F_BROKEN). The component fl_type holds the type of lock. The remaining parameters specify the locked area in the file and are given as absolute offsets, resulting in the treatment of SEEK_END as in System V Release 4, as mentioned earlier.

These structures determine the implementation of the commands GET_LK, SET_LK and SET_LKW. GET_LK is executed by the function fcntl_getlk() in fs/locks.c and tests whether the file descriptor is open and the values of the flock structure are valid. The flock structure is then copied to a file_lock structure. Running in a loop, fcntl_getlk() calls the posix_lock_conflict() function to check whether there are any existing locks that would exclude the requested lock (file_lock structure).

If so, the function enters the obstructing lock in flock and returns. The commands SET_LK and SET_LKW are executed by fcntl_setlk(). After the validity of the parameters has been checked, this function checks whether the file is opened in the correct mode. All the locks are then tested as to whether they conflict with the current lock, for which fcntl_setlk() also uses the posix_lock_conflict() function.

If such a conflict is found, the function returns EAGAIN if called using SET_LK or blocks if SET_LKW is used. In the latter case, the current process is entered in the wait queue for the lock. When this lock is removed, all the processes in the wait queue are woken up and retest the existing locks for conflicts. If no conflict can be found, the lock is entered in the table.

Let us consider a simple scenario. In Figure 5.1, Process 1 has locked the first byte in the file for read access and Process 2 has locked the second byte. Process 1 then attempts to place a write lock on the second byte, but is blocked by Process 2. Process 2 in turn attempts to lock the first byte and is likewise blocked. Both processes would now wait for the other to release its lock, producing a deadlock situation. The scenarios for deadlocks are generally more complex, as a number of processes may be involved. LINUX tracks down situations of this type and the system call *fcntl* returns the error EDEADLK.

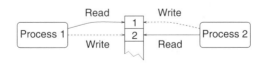

Figure 5.1   A deadlock scenario arising when locking files.

The fcntl() locks are not transferred to the child process by *fork*, but are retained by *execve*. This behaviour conforms to POSIX but is very simple to implement.

The flock() locks are not assigned to individual processes so that locks remain set as long as the file is open. This is not hard to implement either.

5.3 Pipes

Pipes are the classical method of inter-process communication under UNIX. Users of UNIX should not be unfamiliar with a command line such as

```
% ls -l | more
```

Here, the shell runs the processes ls and more, which are linked via a pipe. The first process writes data to the pipe, and the second process then reads it.

Another variant of pipes consists of *named pipes*, also known as FIFOs (pipes also operate on the 'First In, First Out' principle). In the following pages, the terms 'named pipe' and 'FIFO' will be used interchangeably. Unlike pipes, FIFOs are not temporary objects existing only as long as one file descriptor is still open for them. They can be set up in a file system using the command

```
mkfifo pathname
```

or

```
mknod pathname p
```

```
% mkfifo fifo
% ls -l fifo
prw-r--r--   1 kunitz   users         0 Feb 27 22:47 fifo|
```

Linking the standard inputs and outputs of two processes is a little more complicated with FIFOs.

```
% ls -l >fifo & more <fifo
```

There are obviously many similarities between pipes and FIFOs, and these are exploited by the LINUX implementation. The inodes have the same specific components for pipes and FIFOs.

```
struct pipe_inode_info {
   struct wait_queue * wait;   /* a wait queue */
   char * base;                /* address of FIFO buffer */
   unsigned int start;         /* offset for current area */
   unsigned int len;           /* length of current area */
   unsigned int lock;          /* lock */
   unsigned int rd_openers;    /* number of processes
                                * currently opening the
                                * pipe/FIFO for read access */
   unsigned int wr_openers;    /* ditto for write access */
   unsigned int readers;       /* number of processes
                                * reading at this moment */
   unsigned int writers;       /* ditto, writing */
};
```

The system call *pipe* creates a pipe, which involves setting up a temporary inode and allocating a page of memory to base. The call returns one file descriptor for reading and one for writing: this is achieved by the use of separate file operation vectors.

For FIFOs there is an open function which allocates the page in memory and returns a file descriptor that has been assigned an operation vector with read and write operations. Its behaviour is summarized in Table 5.3.

FIFOs and pipes use the same read and write operations, with the memory assigned to the pipe/FIFO interpreted as a circular buffer to which len bytes have been written, starting at start, without yet having been read back. These operations always take into account whether the O_NONBLOCK for the descriptor has been set or not: if it is set, the read and write operations must not block. Unless the number of bytes to be written exceeds the internal buffer size for the pipe (4096 bytes as default), the write operation must be carried out atomically – that is, if a number of processes are writing to the pipe/FIFO, byte sequences for the individual write operations are not interrupted. The semantics implemented in LINUX are shown in Tables 5.4 and 5.5.

Table 5.3 Opening a FIFO.

		Blocking	Non-blocking
To read	No writing processes	Block	Open FIFO with connect operations
	Writing processes	Open FIFO	Open FIFO
To write	No reading processes	Block	ENXIO error
	Reading processes	Open FIFO	Open FIFO
To read and write		Open FIFO	Open FIFO

Table 5.4 Semantics of pipe/FIFO read operation.

	Blocking	Non-blocking
Locked pipe	Block calling process	`EAGAIN` error
Empty pipe	Block calling process if writing processes present, else return 0	`EAGAIN` error if writing processes present, else 0
Else	Read maximum number of characters up to requested position	As for blocking operation

Table 5.5 Semantics of pipe/FIFO write operation.

	Blocking	Non-blocking
No reading process	Send `SIGPIPE` signal to writing process and return `EPIPE` error	As for blocking
Locked pipe	Block calling process	`EAGAIN` error
Atomic write possible, but not enough space in pipe buffer	Block calling process	`EAGAIN` error
Buffer space sufficient for atomic write	Write requested number of bytes to buffer	As for blocking write
Else	Continue blocking until requested number of bytes has been written	Write maximum possible number of bytes

As processes very often block when accessing pipes or FIFOs, it follows that the read and write operations often have to wake up processes in the inode's wait queue. All the processes are managed in a single wait queue although they may be waiting for different events.

5.4 Debugging using *ptrace*

No programmer is capable of writing bug-free programs first time. Any freshly written software needs to be tested. UNIX provides the system call *ptrace*, which gives a process control over another process. The process under its control can be run step by step and its memory can be read and modified. Data can also be read from the process table. Debuggers such as `gdb` are based on the `ptrace()` system call.

Because it is dependent on the process architecture, this call is defined in the file `arch/i386/kernel/ptrace.c`.

```
int sys_ptrace(long request, long pid, long addr,
                              long data);
```

The function processes various requests defined in the parameter `request`. The parameter `pid` specifies the process number of the process to be controlled.

Using `PTRACE_TRACEME`, a process can specify that its parent process controls it via `ptrace()` – in other words, the trace flag (`PF_PTRACED`) for the process is set.

The calling process can use `PTRACE_ATTACH` to make any process its child process and set its `PF_PTRACED` flag. However, the user and group numbers for the calling process must match the effective user and group numbers of the process to be controlled. The new child process is sent a `SIGSTOP` signal, which will usually cause it to stop running. After this request it will be under the control of its new parent process.

With the exception of `PTRACE_KILL`, the following requests are only processed by *ptrace* once the child process has been halted. The requests `PTRACE_PEEKTEXT` and `PTRACE_PEEKDATA` can be used to read 32-bit values from the controlled process's user memory area. LINUX does not make any distinction between the two requests. `PTRACE_PEEKTEXT` will read code, while `PTRACE_PEEKDATA` can be used to read data. The request `PTRACE_PEEKUSR` will cause a long value to be read from the `user` structure for the process. This is where debugging information is stored, such as the process's debug register. They are updated by the processor after a debugging trap and written to the process table by the appropriate handling routine. The `user` structure is virtual. The `sys_ptrace()` function uses the address to be read to decide what information should be returned and provides it. So the registers on the child process's stack and the debug registers stored in the process table will be read by the function.

The requests `PTRACE_POKEDATA` and `PTRACE_POKETEXT` allow the user area for the process under control to be modified. If the area to be modified is write protected, the relevant page is saved by copy-on-write. This is used, for example, to write a special instruction to a particular location in the machine code so that a debugging trap is triggered. In this way, break points can be set by debuggers. The code will be executed until the instruction triggering the trap (`int3` in the case of x86 processors) is processed, at which point the debugging trap handling routine will interrupt the process and inform the parent process.

It is also possible to use `PTRACE_POKEUSR` to modify the virtual `user` structure. The main use for this is modifying the process's registers.

After being interrupted by a signal (in most cases `SIGSTOP`), the child process can be continued by the request `PTRACE_CONT`. The argument `data` can be used to decide what signal the process will handle when it resumes execution.

On receipt of the signal, the child process informs the parent process and halts. The parent process can now continue the child process and decide whether it should handle the signal. If the `data` argument is null, the child process will not process any signal.

The request `PTRACE_SYSCALL` causes the child process to resume in the same way as `PTRACE_CONT`, but only until the next system call. The `sys_ptrace()` function will also set the `PF_TRACESYS` flag. When the child process arrives at the next system call, it halts and receives the `SIGTRAP` signal. The parent process could at this point, for example, inspect the arguments for the system call. If the process is continued with a further `PTRACE_SYSCALL` request, the process will halt on completing the system call; the result and (eventually) the error variable can then be read by the parent process.

The request `PTRACE_SINGLESTEP` differs from `PTRACE_CONT` in setting the processor's trap flag. The process thus executes only one machine code instruction and generates a debug interrupt (No. 1). This sets the `SIGTRAP` signal for the process, which is then interrupted again. In other words, the `PTRACE_SINGLESTEP` request allows the machine code to be processed instruction by instruction. The request `PTRACE_KILL` continues the child process with the signal `SIGKILL` set. The process is then aborted.

The `PTRACE_DETACH` request separates the process under control from the controlling process. The former process is given back its old parent process and the flags `PF_PTRACED` and `PF_TRACESYS` are cancelled along with the processor's trap flag.

A debugger uses *ptrace* in the following way. It executes the system call *fork* and calls the function in the child process with `PTRACE_TRACEME`. There, the program to be inspected is then started by *execve*. As the `PF_PTRACED` flag is set, the *execve* call sends a `SIGTRAP` signal to itself. It will not allow *ptrace* to process programs for which an S bit is set. It is not difficult to imagine the possibilities that would otherwise be open to hackers. On return from *execve* the `SIGTRAP` signal is processed, the process is halted and the parent process is informed by sending it a `SIGCHLD` signal. The debugger will wait for this via the system call *wait*. It can then inspect the child process's memory, modify it and set break points. The simplest way of doing this with x86 processors is to write an `int3` instruction at the appropriate address in the machine code. This instruction is only one byte long.

If the debugger calls `ptrace()` with the request `PTRACE_CONT`, the child process will continue running until it processes the `int3` instruction, at which point the relevant interrupt handling routine sends a `SIGTRAP` signal to the child process, the child process is interrupted and the debugger is again informed. It could then, for example, simply abort the program to be inspected.

There are, of course, other ways of using this system call. The `strace` program provides a report ('trace') on all the system calls that have been carried out. This is illustrated below by the output listing of `strace cat motd`. Naturally, `strace` uses `PTRACE_SYSCALL`.

```
%strace cat motd
uselib("/lib/ld.so")                              = 0
getuid()                                          = 15211
geteuid()                                         = 15211
getgid()                                          = 15200
getegid()                                         = 15200
stat("/etc/ld.so.cache", {st_mode=S_IFREG|0644, st_size=3653,
...}) = 0
open("/etc/ld.so.cache", O_RDONLY)      = 3
mmap(0, 3653, PROT_READ, MAP_SHARED, 3, 0) = 0x40000000
close(3)                                          = 0
uselib("/lib/libc.so.4.6.27")                     = 0
munmap(0x40000000, 3653)                          = 0
munmap(0x62f00000, 24576)                         = 0
brk(0)                                            = 0x3000
brk(0x6000)                                       = 0x6000
brk(0x7000)                                       = 0x7000
stat("/etc/locale/C/libc.cat", 0xbffff1b0) = -1
ENOENT (No such file or directory)
stat("/usr/lib/locale/C/libc.cat", 0xbffff1b0) = -1
ENOENT (No such file or directory)
stat("/usr/lib/locale/libc/C/usr/share/locale/C/libc.cat",
0xbffff1b0) = -1
ENOENT (No such file or directory)
stat("/usr/local/share/locale/C/libc.cat", 0xbffff1b0) = -1
ENOENT (No such file or directory)
fstat(1, {st_mode=S_IFCHR|0622, st_rdev=makedev(4, 195), ...}) = 0
open("motd", O_RDONLY)                  = -1
ENOENT (No such file or directory)
write(2, "cat: ", 5cat: )                         = 5
write(2, "motd", 4motd)                           = 4
write(2, ": No such file or directory", 27:
No such file or directory) = 27
write(2, "\\n", 1)                                = 1
close(1)                                          = 0
_exit(1)                                          = ?
```

The range of functions offered by *ptrace()* is wide enough to debug programs in multi-tasking environments. On the negative side, it should be mentioned that it is very inefficient to use a single system call to read or write a 32-bit value in the address area.

5.5 System V IPC

As long ago as 1970, the classical forms of inter-process communication – semaphores, message queues and shared memory – were implemented in a special variant of UNIX. These were later integrated into System V and are now known as System V IPC. LINUX supports these variants, although they are not included in POSIX. At present, shared memory is the only way of allowing more than one process to access the same area of memory under LINUX. The original LINUX implementation was produced by Krishna Balasubramanian, but it has been modified by Eric Schenk, Bruno Haible and Bjorn Ekwall.

5.5.1 Access permissions, numbers and keys

In System V IPC, objects are created in the kernel. These must be assigned unique identifiers to ensure that operations activated by the user process are carried out on the right objects. The simplest form of identifier is a number: these numbers are dynamically generated and returned to the process generating the object. A process entirely separate from the creator process cannot access the object, as it does not know the number. In a case of this sort, the two processes will have to agree a static key by which they can reference the IPC object. The C library offers the ftok function, which generates a unique key from a filename and a character. A special key is IPC_PRIVATE, which guarantees that no existing IPC object is referenced. Access to objects generated using IPC_PRIVATE is only possible via their object numbers.

As with System V, access permissions are managed by the kernel in the structure ipc_perm.

```
struct ipc_perm
{
    key_t  key;
    ushort uid;    /* owner */
    ushort gid;    /* owner */
    ushort cuid;   /* creator */
    ushort cgid;   /* creator */
    ushort mode;   /* access modes */
    ushort seq;    /* counter, used to calculate the identifier */
};
```

If a process accesses an object, the routine ipcperms() is called, once again using the standard UNIX access flags for the user, the group and others. The superuser, of course, has access at all times. If the uid for the process attempting access matches that of the owner or the creator, the user access permissions are checked. The same applies to checks on group access permissions.

5.5.2 Semaphores

The use of semaphores under System V expands the classical semaphore model. An array of semaphores can be set up using a system call. It is possible to modify a number of semaphores in an array in a single operation. A process can set semaphores to any chosen value, and they can be incremented or decremented in steps greater than one. The programmer can specify that certain operations are reversed at the end of the process.

LINUX provides the following data structure for every reserved semaphore array:

```
struct semid_ds {
    struct ipc_perm  sem_perm;      /* access permissions */
    time_t           sem_otime;     /* time of last semaphore
                                     * operation */
    time_t           sem_ctime;     /* time of last change */
    struct sem       *sem_base;     /* pointer to first semaphore
                                     * in array */
    struct sem_queue *sem_pending;  /* operations pending */
    struct sem_queue **sem_pending_last; /* last pending
                                     * operation */
    struct sem_undo  *undo;         /* pointer to structure
                                     * indicating operations
                                     * to be reversed */
    ushort           sem_nsems;     /* number of semaphores
                                     * in field */
};
```

The semaphores in an array are stored consecutively in the same area of memory, so that any semaphore can be accessed via an offset from `base`. The structure `sem_queue` includes a wait queue in which processes block if their operations cannot be executed.

The structure `sem` manages a single semaphore:

```
struct sem {
    short  semval;   /* current value */
    short  sempid;   /* process number of last operation */
};
```

A more complex situation is presented by the task of undoing individual semaphore operations at the end of a process. The process can require any call to a semaphore operation to be undone when it terminates: for these calls, `sem_undo` structures are generated dynamically.

```
struct sem_undo {
  struct sem_undo *proc_next;   * linear list of all UNDO
                                * structures in a process */
  struct sem_undo *id_next;    /* linear list of all UNDO
                                * structures in a semaphore array */
  int    semid;     .         /* number of semaphore array */
  short * semadj;             /* values to which
                                * semaphores are reset */
};
```

A sem_undo structure stores all the semaphore operations of a process that are to be undone. The kernel sets up a maximum of one sem_undo structure per process. When the process terminates, the system call *exit* attempts to reset the semaphores to the semadj values, a feature often referred to as *adjust on exit*. The process will not block on *exit* if this would produce a value less than zero: the value of the semaphore is simply set to zero. The semaphore operations are implemented with the structures explained.

```
int sys_semget (key_t key, int nsems, int semflg);
int sys_semop (int semid, struct sembuf *sops, unsigned nsops);
int sys_semctl (int semid, int semnum, int cmd, void *arg);
```

Together with other operations in System V IPC, they are called using the system call *ipc*. This in turn calls the appropriate functions by reference to its first argument. The C library must convert all the relevant library calls into system calls. This might be called *system call multiplexing*.

The call sys_semget() is used to find the number of a semaphore array with nsems semaphores. The values which can be used for semflg are listed in Table 5.6.

Table 5.6   Flags for semget().

Flag	
0400	Read permissions for creator
0200	Write permissions for creator
0040	Read permissions for creator group
0020	Write permissions for creator group
0004	Read permissions for all
0002	Write permissions for all
IPC_CREAT	A new object will be created if it is not yet present
IPC_EXCL	If IPC_CREAT is set and such an object already exists, the function will return with the error EEXIST

The semop() call executes a number of operations from the semops table: this number is given by nsops. An operation is described by the structure sembuf.

```
struct sembuf {
    ushort  sem_num;   /* index to semaphore in array */
    short   sem_op;    /* operation */
    short   sem_flg;   /* flags */
};
```

The value in sem_op is added to the semaphore. The operation blocks if the sum would yield a negative value. It must then wait for the semaphore to be incremented. If sem_op is zero, the current process blocks if the value of the semaphore is not zero. It never blocks if sem_op is greater than zero. If the value increases, all the processes waiting for this event for this semaphore array are woken up. Similarly, all the processes waiting for a semaphore in the array to reach zero are woken up if this event occurs.

Two values are possible for sem_flg: IPC_NOWAIT and SEM_UNDO. If IPC_NOWAIT is set, the process will never block. The effect of SEM_UNDO is to cause a sem_undo structure to be set up or updated for all operations in this function call. The negative operation value is entered in the sem_undo structure or added to the old adjust value on updating.

The sys_semctl call can be used to perform a wide range of commands, which must be entered as a parameter. Another parameter for this function is the union semun.

```
union semun {
    int val;                    /* value for SETVAL */
    struct semid_ds *buf;       /* buffer for IPC_STAT and IPC_SET */
    ushort *array;              /* field for GETALL and SETALL */
    struct seminfo *__buf;      /* buffer for IPC_INFO */
    void *__pad;
};
```

IPC_INFO enters values in the seminfo structure (*see* Table 5.7). All the values are specified as fixed values by separate macro definitions.

The ipcs program, which displays information about IPC objects, uses the SEM_INFO variant of this command. This gives the number of semaphore arrays that have been set up in semusz and the total number of semaphores in the system in semaem. This command cannot be called from a user program without special macro definitions.

IPC_STAT returns the semid_ds structure for a semaphore array. For ipcs there is again the SEM_STAT variant, which requires the index in the table of arrays to be specified rather than the number of the semaphore array. The ipcs

Table 5.7 Components in the `sem_undo` structure.

Component	Value	Description
semmni	128	Maximum number of arrays
semmns	4096	Maximum number of semaphores in system
semmsl	32	Maximum number of semaphores per array
semopm	32	Maximum number of operations per `semop` call
semvmx	32767	Maximum value of a semaphore
semmnu	4096	Ignored by LINUX – maximum number of `sem_undo` structures in system
semmap	4096	Ignored by LINUX – number of entries in a 'semaphore map'
semume	32	Ignored by LINUX – maximum number of `sem_undo` entries for a process
semusz	20	Ignored by LINUX – size of `sem_undo` structure (false value)
semaem	16383	Ignored by LINUX – maximum value for a `sem_undo` structure

program can provide information on all the arrays by counting from zero to `seminfo.semmni` in a loop and calling `semctl()` with SEM_STAT and the counter as arguments.

IPC_SET allows the owner and mode of the semaphore array to be set to new values. This command requires the `semid_ds` structure as a parameter, with only the `sem_perm` component actually used. IPC_RMID deletes a semaphore array if the caller is the owner or creator of the array or if the superuser has called `semctl()`. The remaining commands for `sys_semctl` are listed in Table 5.8.

Table 5.8 Commands for `sys_semctl()`.

Command	Value returned and function
GETVAL	Value of semaphore
GETPID	Process number of last process to modify the semaphore
GETNCNT	Number of processes waiting for semaphore to be incremented
GETZCNT	Number of processes waiting for a value of zero
GETALL	Values of all semaphores of the array in the field `semun.array`
SETVAL	Sets value of semaphore
SETALL	Sets values of semaphores

5.5.3 Message queues

Messages consist of a sequence of bytes. In addition, IPC messages in System V include a type code. Processes send messages to the message queues and can receive messages, restricting reception to messages of a specified type if required. Messages are received in the same order in which they are entered in the message queue. The basis of the implementation under LINUX is the structure `msqid_ds`.

```
struct msqid_ds {
    struct ipc_perm msg_perm;    /* access permissions */
    struct msg *msg_first;       /* first message in queue */
    struct msg *msg_last;        /* last message in queue */
    time_t msg_stime;            /* time of last send */
    time_t msg_rtime;            /* time of last receipt */
    time_t msg_ctime;            /* time of last change */
    struct wait_queue *wwait;    /* processes waiting for queue
                                  * to be read */
    struct wait_queue *rwait;    /* processes waiting for queue
                                  * to be sent to */
    ushort msg_cbytes;           /* current number of bytes
                                  * in queue */
    ushort msg_qnum;             /* number of messages in queue */
    ushort msg_qbytes;           /* maximum for bytes in queue */
    ushort msg_lspid;            /* process number of last
                                  * sender */
    ushort msg_lrpid;            /* process number of last
                                  * receiver */
};
```

As well as management information, the structure contains two wait queues of its own, `wwait` and `rwait`. A process enters itself in `wwait` if the message queue is full – that is, when it is no longer possible to send the message without exceeding the maximum number of bytes allowed in the message queue. The queue `rwait` contains processes waiting for messages to be written to the message queue.

The message queue is implemented as a linear list, with its first element referenced by `msg_first` and its last by `msg_last`. The `msg_last` pointer is maintained to assist rapid execution of send operations: using this pointer, a new message can be inserted in the queue without having to scan through all the elements in the queue to find the last one.

A message is stored in the kernel in the `msg` structure.

```
struct msg {
    struct msg *msg_next;    /* next message in queue */
```

```
    long msg_type;          /* message type */
    char *msg_spot;         /* address of text of message */
    time_t msg_time         /* msgsnd time */
    short msg_ts;           /* length of message */
};
```

LINUX stores the message immediately after this structure, which means that the pointer `msg_spot` is in fact unnecessary.

As with semaphores, functions are now required for initialization, for sending and receiving messages, for returning information and for releasing message queues. Although the operations to be performed are relatively simple, access protection and the updating of statistical data make things more complicated. The relevant library functions call the system call *ipc*, which passes on the call to the appropriate kernel functions. The function `sys_msgget()` creates a message queue, using the standard parameters for the IPC get functions.

```
    int sys_msgget (key_t key, int msgflg);
```

The parameter `key` is a mandatory key and `msgflg` is the same as for the flags in `semget()` (*see* Table 5.6). Messages are sent using the function `sys_msgsnd()`.

```
    struct msgbuf {
        long mtype;         /* message type */
        char mtext[1];      /* text of message */
    };

    int sys_msgsnd (int msqid, struct msgbuf *msgp, int msgsz,
                    int msgflg);
```

The parameter `msgsz` is the length of the text in `mtext` and must be no greater than `MSGMAX`. The process blocks if the new number of bytes in the message queue exceeds the value in the component `msg_qbytes`, the permitted maximum. It only resumes processing once other processes have read messages from the queue or when non-blocked signals are sent to the process. Blocking can be prevented by setting the flag `IPC_NOWAIT`.

A message can be read back from the queue by means of `sys_msgrcv()`.

```
    int sys_msgrcv (int msqid, struct msgbuf *msgp, int msgsz,
                    long msgtyp, int msgflg);
```

The messages to be received are specified in `msgtyp`. If the value is zero, the first message in the queue is selected. For a value greater than zero, the first message of the given type in the message queue is read. However, if the `MSG_EXCEPT` flag is set, the first message not matching the message type is received. If `msgtyp` is less than zero, the function selects the first message of the type with the smallest integer value that is smaller than or equal to the absolute value of `msgtyp`. The length of the message must be smaller than `msgsz`, but no error will be returned for longer messages if `MSG_NOERROR` is set: instead, the first `msgsz` bytes of the message will be read. If no message matching the specification is found, the process blocks. This can be prevented by setting the `IPC_NOWAIT` flag.

Another function to manipulate the message queue is `sys_msgctl()`. This function is very similar to `sys_semctl()`.

```
int sys_msgctl() (int msqid, int cmd, struct msqid_ds *buf);
```

The command `IPC_INFO` outputs the maxima for the values relevant to message queues in the structure `msginfo`. These maxima are listed in Table 5.9. As before, LINUX only uses a small number of these values.

The macro for each of the components is defined in `msg.h`. The command `MSG_INFO` is the variant of `IPC_INFO` designed for the `ipcs` program. This gives the number of wait queues used in `msgpool`, the number of messages in `msgmap` and the total number of messages stored by the system in `msgtql`.

`IPC_STAT` copies the `msqid_id` structure of the referenced message queue to the user memory area. Like `SEM_STAT`, the `MSG_STAT` variant allows an index to the system-internal table of the message queue as a parameter. This LINUX feature is also used by the `ipcs` command.

`IPC_SET` enables the owner, mode and maximum possible number of bytes for the message queue to be modified. Processes without superuser rights must not set this value higher than `MSGMNB` (16 384). Without this restriction, a

Table 5.9 Components of the `msginfo` structure.

Component	Value	Description
`msgmni`	128	Maximum number of message queues
`msgmax`	4 056	Maximum size of a message in bytes
`msgmnb`	16 384	Standard value for the maximum size of a message queue in bytes
`msgmap`	16 384	Not used – number of entries in a 'message map'
`msgpool`	2 048	Not used – size of 'message pool'
`msgtql`	16 384	Not used – number of 'system message headers'
`msgssz`	16	Not used – size of message segment
`msgseg`	0xffff	Not used – maximum number of segments

normal process would be in a position, by sending messages to the queue after setting this value high, to allocate kernel memory which cannot be swapped out to secondary memory.

The owner or creator of the message queue as well as the superuser can delete the queue by means of IPC_RMID.

Under Linux 2.0, message queues have the task of communicating with the kerneld daemon. This daemon is responsible for automatic loading of kernel modules requested via messages by kernel routines.

5.5.4 Shared memory

Shared memory is the fastest form of inter-process communication. Processes using a shared section of memory can exchange data by the usual machine code commands for reading and writing data. In all other methods this is only possible by recourse to system calls to copy the data from the memory area of one process to that of the other. The drawback to shared memory is that the processes need to use additional synchronization mechanisms to ensure that race conditions do not arise. Faster communication is only achieved by increased programming effort. Performing the synchronization via other system calls makes for a portable implementation, but reduces the speed advantage. Another possibility would be to exploit the machine code instructions for conditional setting of a bit in the processors for different architectures: these instructions set a bit depending on its value. As this occurs within a machine code instruction, the operation cannot be halted by an interrupt. These instructions provide a very simple and quick way of implementing a system of mutual exclusion. It has already been explained in Section 4.2.2 how complex the shared use of memory areas is. As since version 2.0 it has become possible, with mmap(), to map memory areas that can be written to by several processes, this mechanism too can be used to implement shared memory applications.

As in the other IPC variants of System V, a shared segment of memory is identified by a number, which refers to a shmid_ds data structure. This segment can be mapped to the user segment in the virtual address space by a process with the aid of an attach operation, and the procedure can be reversed with a detach operation. For simplicity, we will refer to the memory managed by the shmid_ds structure as a segment, although this term is already used for the segments of the virtual address space in x86 processors.

```
struct shmid_ds {
    struct  ipc_perm shm_perm;    /* access permissions */
    int     shm_segsz;            /* size of shared segment */
    time_t  shm_atime;            /* last ATTACH time */
    time_t  shm_dtime;            /* last DETACH time */
    time_t  shm_ctime;            /* time of last change */
    unsigned short  shm_cpid;     /* process number of creator */
```

```
      unsigned short   shm_lpid;    /* process number of last process
                                     * to call an operation for the
                                     * shared segment */
      short   shm_nattch;           /* number of current ATTACHes */
      /* new components under Linux */
      unsigned short   shm_npages;  /* number of memory pages */
      unsigned long   *shm_pages;   /* field for page table entries */
      struct vm_area_struct
         *attaches;                 /* ATTACH descriptors*/
   };
```

The modal components in the `ipc_perm` structure are used to store two flags. The flag `SHM_LOCKED` prevents pages in the shared memory segment from being swapped out to secondary devices, while `SHM_DEST` specifies that the segment is released on the last detach operation.

The field `shm_pages` holds the page table entries for the pages of memory comprising the shared segment. After a segment is created, no pages are actually allocated until a page in a segment mapped to virtual address space is accessed. This field may also contain references to pages which have been swapped.

After attach operations, management information is stored in the linear list `attaches`. The entries in this list have the structure of the virtual memory areas. The attach descriptors for a process are held in a circular list via the pointers `vm_next_share` and `vm_prev_share`.

By calling `sys_shmget()` a process can create or set up a reference to a segment.

```
      int sys_shmget (key_t key, int size, int shmflg);
```

The parameter `size` specifies the size of the segment. If the segment has already been set up, the parameter may be smaller than the actual size. The flags listed in Table 5.6 may again be set in the parameter `shmflg`.

This function only initializes the `shmid_ds` data structure. No pages in memory are allocated to the segment at this stage. The `shm_pages` field in the `shmid_ds` data structure contains only blank entries after `sys_shmget()` is called.

By far the most important function when using shared memory is `sys_shmat()`. This maps the segment to the process's user segment.

```
      int sys_shmat (int shmid, char *shmaddr, inst shmflg,
                     ulong *raddr);
```

The parameter `shmaddr` can be used by the process to specify the address at which the segment is to be mapped. If this is zero, the function will find a free

area of memory for itself and the selected address wil'
raddr. This rather complicated procedure using the par
since otherwise addresses over 2 gigabytes would be i
return to the user process.

The flags allowed in shmflg are SHM_RND, SHM_
SHM_RND is set, the address that is passed will be
boundary, as LINUX only allows segments to be m
SHM_RDONLY indicates whether the mapped segmen.
and write.

LINUX's System V IPC was implemented before the iɪɪ.
virtual memory areas, and consequently a very sophisticated methoᴜ
chosen for mapping the shared pages of memory. Special entries based on a
segment's signature are written to the page table for the process during the execution of sys_shmat(). A signature combines a flag for read-only access to a
segment with the number of the segment. In addition, the swap type
SHM_SWP_TYPE is specified. The sys_shmat() function then enters the number of
the page in the segment and enters the resulting value of the signature in a
page table. The presence bit is not set.

If the process attempts to access a page in a newly mapped segment, a
page error exception interrupt is generated. The do_no_page() routine called
during exception handling then calls the shm_swap_in() function, which
inspects the page table entry for the segment and the number of the page in the
segment so that it can write the correct entry from shm_pages to the page table.
The shm_pages field holds the page table entries for the pages in the shared
memory segment. If the page has been swapped out to secondary storage, it is
loaded back.

If no page of memory has yet been allocated for the page in the shared
memory segment, a free page is reserved. Its page table entry is written to the
page table and the shm_pages field in the segment data structure.

The shm_swap() function attempts to swap out memory pages in shared
segments. The number of pages inspected by this process is controlled by the
function's priority argument. For each page in the segment, the page table
entries for the processes that mapped the pages are inspected. Setting the 'age'
attribute in the page table entry prevents the pages most recently accessed from
being swapped. If the age attribute is not set, the value for the page in the
table mem_map is decremented and the page is removed from the address space
for the process.

Once all the processes which had or still have the shared memory page
mapped have been gone through, a check is made on whether the page can be
saved to secondary memory. This is permissible if there is a 1 in the related
mem_map entry. Only then is the page written to a swap area by shm_swap().

The page's swapping number is written to the page table of the segment
(shm_pages). The function then updates the page tables for the processes
sharing the page with the signature of the segment, to which the index for the

as also been added. The swapped page can then be reloaded via the no_page mechanism.

The function sys_shmdt() deletes a mapped page from the user segment of a process.

```
int sys_shmdt (char *shmaddr);
```

The sys_shmctl() function is a counterpart to the functions sys_semctl() and sys_msgctl() mentioned earlier.

```
int sys_shmctl() (int shmid, int cmd, struct shmid_ds *buf);
```

A call to this function using the IPC_INFO command will return the maximum values that apply when using LINUX's implementation of shared memory. The shminfo structure used for this is summarized in Table 5.10.

The related macros (names in upper-case letters) are defined in include/ linux/shm.h. Although a size of 1 is allowed for the segment, LINUX will always allocate a minimum of one page of memory (4096 bytes) for shared use.

The SHM_INFO command fills in the shm_info structure, which is shown in Table 5.11.

The IPC_STAT command can be called to read the segment data structure shmid_ds. The SHM_STAT variant of this command performs the same task, but needs an index to the table of segment data structures as a parameter in place of the segment number.

If sys_shmctl() is called with the command IPC_SET, the owner and access mode for a segment can be modified by the old owner or the process that initialized the shared memory segment.

Unlike the functions sys_semctl() and sys_msgctl(), the IPC_RMID command does not enable the IPC data structure to be released in all cases, as there may still be processes with the segment mapped. To mark the segment

Table 5.10 Components of the shminfo structure for the IPC_INFO command.

Component	Value	Description
shmmni	128	Maximum number of shared memory segments
shmmax	16777216	Maximum size of a segment in bytes
shmmin	1	Minimum size of a segment
shmall	4194304	Maximum number of shared pages of memory in entire system
shmseg	128	Permitted number of segments per process

Table 5.11 Components of the `shminfo` structure for the
`SHM_INFO` command.

Component	Description
`used_ids`	Number of segments used
`shm_rss`	Number of shared pages allocated in main memory
`shm_tot`	Total number of shared pages
`shm_swp`	Number of currently swapped pages
`swap_attempts`	Attempts to swap shared pages
`swap_successes`	Number of shared pages swapped since system start-up

structure as deleted, the `SHM_DEST` flag in the mode field of the `ipc_perm` component is set.

The commands `SHM_LOCK` and `SHM_UNLOCK` allow the superuser to disable and re-enable swapping of pages in a segment. Pages which have already been swapped are not explicitly reloaded by the `SHM_LOCK` command.

5.5.5 The `ipcs` and `ipcrm` commands

One drawback to the System V IPC is that testing and developing programs that make use of it can easily give rise to the problem whereby IPC resources remain present after the test programs have been completed, when this was in no way intended. The `ipcs` command allows the user to investigate the situation and to delete the resources in question using `ipcrm`.

For example, a program may have set up three semaphore arrays. Information can be obtained via `ipcs` on the shared memory segments, semaphore arrays and message queues to which the user has access.

```
% ipcs

------ Shared Memory Segments --------
shmid     owner     perms     bytes     nattch     status


------ Semaphore Arrays --------
semid     owner     perms     nsems     status
1152      kunitz    666       1
1153      kunitz    666       1
1154      kunitz    666       1


------ Message Queues --------
msqid     owner     perms     used-bytes     messages
```

These semaphore arrays can now be deleted (one at a time) using `ipcrm`. The command can also be used analogously for message queues and shared memory segments.

```
% ipcrm sem 1153
resource deleted
% ipcs


------ Shared Memory Segments --------
shmid      owner      perms      bytes      nattch     status


------ Semaphore Arrays --------
semid      owner      perms      nsems      status
1152       kunitz     666        1
1154       kunitz     666        1


------ Message Queues --------
msqid      owner      perms      used-bytes  messages
```

These two commands would be unnecessary if the resources were held as special files in the file system: the system call *select* could then be used to monitor a number of resources at the same time. Integrating the System V IPC resources into the `proc` file system could make for an interesting programming exercise.

5.6 IPC with sockets

So far, we have only looked at forms of inter-process communication supporting communication between processes in one computer. The socket programming interface provides for communication via a network as well as locally on a single computer. The advantage of this interface is that it allows network applications to be programmed using the long-established UNIX concept of file descriptors. A particularly good example of this is the INET daemon. The daemon waits for incoming network service requests and then calls the appropriate service program with the socket descriptor as standard input and output. For very simple services, the program called need not contain a single line of network-relevant code.

In this chapter, we limit ourselves to the use and implementation of UNIX domain sockets. Sockets for the INET domain will be covered in Chapter 8.

5.6.1 A simple example

Similar to FIFOs, UNIX domain sockets enable programs to exchange data the connection-oriented way. The following example illustrates how this works. The same include files are used for both the client and the server program.

```
/* sc.h */

#include <sys/types.h>
#include <stdio.h>
#include <sys/socket.h>
#include <sys/un.h>


#define SERVER "/tmp/server"
```

The job of the client is to send a message to the server along with its process number and to write the server's response to the standard output.

```
/* cli.c - client, connection-oriented model */
#include "sc.h"

int main(void)
{
    int sock_fd;
    struct sockaddr_un unix_addr;
    char buf[2048];
    int n;

    if ((sock_fd = socket(AF_UNIX, SOCK_STREAM, 0)) < 0)
    {
        perror("cli: socket()");
        exit(1);
    }

    unix_addr.sun_family = AF_UNIX;
    strcpy(unix_addr.sun_path, SERVER);

    if (connect(sock_fd, (struct sockaddr*) &unix_addr,
                sizeof(unix_addr.sun_family) +
                strlen(unix_addr.sun_path)) < 0)
    {
        perror("cli: connect()");
        exit(1);
    }
```

```
      sprintf(buf, "Hello Server, this is %d.\n", getpid());
      n = strlen(buf) + 1;

      if (write(sock_fd, buf, n) != n)
      {
         perror("cli: write()");
         exit(1);
      }

      if ((n = read(sock_fd, buf, 2047)) < 0)
      {
         perror("cli: read()");
         exit(1);
      }

      buf[n] = '\0';
      printf("Client received: %s\n", buf);

      exit(0);
}
```

First a socket file descriptor is created with socket(). Then the address of the server is generated; for UNIX domain sockets this consists of a filename – in our example this is /tmp/server. The client then attempts to set up a connection to the server using connect(). If this is successful, it is possible to send data to the server using perfectly standard read and write functions. To be precise, the client does this by sending the message

Hello Server, this is *process number of client.*

To enable the server to reply, we need a few more lines of C program.

```
/* srv.c - server, connection-oriented model */

#include <signal.h>
#include "sc.h"

void stop()
{
   unlink(SERVER);
   exit(0);
}

void server(void)
{
```

```c
int sock_fd, cli_sock_fd;
struct sockaddr_un unix_addr;
char buf[2048];
int n, addr_len;
pid_t pid;
char *pc;

signal(SIGINT, stop);
signal(SIGQUIT, stop);
signal(SIGTERM, stop);

if ((sock_fd = socket(AF_UNIX, SOCK_STREAM, 0)) < 0)
{
   perror("srv: socket()");
   exit(1);
}

unix_addr.sun_family = AF_UNIX;
strcpy(unix_addr.sun_path, SERVER);
addr_len = sizeof(unix_addr.sun_family) +
           strlen(unix_addr.sun_path);

unlink(SERVER);

if (bind(sock_fd, (struct sockaddr *) &unix_addr,
         addr_len) < 0)
{
   perror("srv: bind()");
   exit(1);
}
if (listen(sock_fd, 5) < 0)
{
   perror("srv: client()");
   unlink(SERVER); exit(1);
}

while ((cli_sock_fd =
        accept(sock_fd, (struct sockaddr*) &unix_addr,
               &addr_len)) >= 0)
{
   if ((n = read(cli_sock_fd, buf, 2047)) < 0)
   {
     perror("srv: read()");
     close(cli_sock_fd);
     continue;
   }
```

```
            buf[n] = '\0';
            for (pc = buf; *pc != '\0' && (*pc < '0' || *pc > '9');
                    pc++);

            pid = atol(pc);

            if (pid != 0)
            {
                sprintf(buf, "Hello Client %d, this is the Server.\n",
                        pid);
                n = strlen(buf) + 1;

                if (write(cli_sock_fd, buf, n) != n)
                perror("srv: write()");
            }

            close(cli_sock_fd);
        }

        perror("srv: accept()");
        unlink(SERVER);
        exit(1);
    }

    int main(void)
    {
        int r;
        if ((r = fork()) == 0)
        {
            server();
        }

        if (r < 0)
        {
            perror("srv: fork()");
            exit(1);
        }

        exit(0);
    }
```

The server calls fork() and terminates its run. The child process continues running in the background and installs the handling routine for interrupt signals. Once a socket file descriptor has been opened, the server's own address is bound to this socket and a file is created under the pathname given in the address. By limiting the access rights to this file, the server can reduce the number of users able to communicate with it. A client's `connect` call is only successful if this file exists and the client possesses the necessary access rights. The call to `listen()` is necessary to inform the kernel that the process is now ready to accept connections at this socket. It then calls `accept()` to wait. If a connection is set up by a client using `connect()`, `accept()` will return a new socket file descriptor. This will then be used to receive messages from the client and reply to them. The server simply writes back:

> `Hello Client` *process number of client,* `this is the Server.`

The server then closes the file descriptor for this connection and again calls `accept()` to offer its services to the next client.

The read and write operations usually block on the socket descriptor if either no data are present or there is no more space in the buffer. If the `O_NON-BLOCK` flag has been set with `fcntl()`, these functions do not block.

Since version 2.0 it is possible to use UNIX domain sockets under LINUX in connectionless mode by means of the functions `sendto()` and `recvfrom()`.

5.6.2 The implementation of UNIX domain sockets

A socket is represented in the kernel by the data structure `socket`. Data contained in the sockets is stored in `skbuf` structures. These are described in Chapter 8.

There is a range of socket-specific functions, such as `socket()` and `setsockopt()`. These are all implemented via one system call, *socketcall*, which calls all the necessary functions by reference to the first parameter. The file operations `read()`, `write()`, `select()`, `ioctl()`, `lseek()`, `close()` and `fasync()` are called directly via the file descriptor's file operations.

All socket operations use protocol-specific functions included in the operation vector `proto_ops`, which is contained in the socket structure. The semantics of operations for UNIX domain sockets are briefly described below.

> `int sysk_socket(int family, int type, int protocol);`

This sets up a socket descriptor. The function calls the protocol operation `unix_proto_create()`, sets up the `unix_socket` structure which is identical with the `sock` structure and creates the `skbuf` lists. This function may block. The status of the socket on completion of this operation is `SS_UNCONNECTED`.

> `int sys_bind(int fd, struct sockaddr *umyaddr, int addrlen);`

The address `umyaddr` is bound to the socket. The protocol operation naturally tests whether the address belongs to the UNIX address family and attempts to set up the socket address file and open it for write access. `bind` is only successful if the socket address file has not yet been bound by another program.

```
int sys_connect(int fd, struct sockaddr *uservaddr,
                int addrlen);
```

This operation attempts to bind the socket to the address `uservaddr`. This address must of course be a UNIX address. An attempt is made to open the server's socket address file which, for datagram sockets, is sufficient.

With stream sockets, the protocol operation `unix_proto_connect()` checks whether any connections are being accepted at the server address. The socket switches to `SS_CONNECTING` status, the server is woken up, and the process is blocked. If the process continues but is not connected to the server, this indicates that either the process has been sent a signal or the connection request has been refused by the server. If not, the `sock_connect()` operation has been successful.

```
int sys_listen(int fd, int backlog);
```

With this operation the server informs the kernel that connections are being accepted from now on. The socket flag `SO_ACCEPTCON` is now set, together with the parameter `max_ack_backlog` which is set to the value of the argument.

```
int sys_accept(int fd, struct sockaddr *upeer_sockaddr,
               int *upeer_addrlen);
```

The process can only call this operation if the status of the socket is `SS_CONNECTED` and `listen()` has first been called for this socket. The process blocks if there are no processes which have called a `connect()` for the address of this socket.

```
int sys_getsockname(int fd, struct sockaddr *usockaddr,
                    int *usockaddr_len);
```

The protocol operation `unix_proto_getname()` is the basis of this function. The address bound to the socket is returned.

```
int sys_getpeername(int fd, struct sockaddr *usockaddr,
                    int *usockaddr_len);
```

This function can only be called if the status of the socket is `SS_CONNECTED`. The operation is also based on the `unix_proto_getname()` protocol operation for the socket. However, a parameter for this function specifies that the address of the bound socket (the *peer*) should be returned.

```
int sys_socketpair(int family, int type, int protocol,
                   unsigned long usockvec[2]);
```

Two socket descriptors are generated and bound to each other – that is, the status of the new sockets in usockvec[2] is SS_CONNECTED when the operation is exited.

```
int sys_send(int fd, void * buff, int len, unsigned flags);
int sys_sendto(int fd, void * buff, int len, unsigned flags,
        struct sockaddr *addr, int addr_len);
int sys_sendmsg(int fd, struct msghdr *msg, unsigned int flags);
```

These are the different socket operations for sending messages. They are all based on the unix_sendmsg() protocol operation. The messages are divided across several skbuf structures, if needed, and written into the receive list of the peer socket.

```
int sys_recv(int fd, void * buff, int len, unsigned flags);
int sys_recvfrom(int fd, void * ubuf, int size, unsigned flags,
        struct sockaddr *addr, int *addr_len);
int sys_recvmsg(int fd, struct msghdr *msg, unsigned int flags);
```

These socket operations are realized via the unix_recvmsg() protocol operation. This operation blocks if no data is present.

```
int sys_shutdown(int fd, int how)
```

This socket operation is realized via unix_shutdown(). The socket status is marked as to whether sending and receiving is still allowed. A possibly present peer socket is marked accordingly. The how parameter seems to have different values from the BSD model. Thus, 1 stands for blocking reception, 2 for blocking sending, and 3 for blocking both functions.

```
int sys_getsockopt(int fd, int level, int optname, char *optval,
        int *optlen)
int sys_setsockopt(int fd, int level, int optname, char *optval,
        int optlen)
```

The corresponding protocol operations only allow access on the socket level and call sock_getsock_opt() and sock_setsock_opt() which read or set the corresponding parameters in the sock structure.

As it is intended that processes should be able to use sockets as they would ordinary file descriptors, the functions of nearly all file operations have to be supported. The only operations not to be implemented are mmap(), open() and fsync(). The socket file operation sock_lseek() must be implemented to avoid the standard treatment of the system call lseek(), as sockets do not allow positioning. The sock_readdir() operation sets the error value EBADF instead of ENOTDIR, but otherwise conforms. The remaining operations, as used in the context of UNIX domain sockets, are briefly described below.

```
int sock_read(struct inode *inode, struct file *file,
              char *ubuf, int size);
```

This function calls the protocol operation unix_recvmsg().

```
int sock_write(struct inode *inode, struct file *file,
               char *ubuf, int size);
```

This operation calls the protocol operation unix_sendmsg().

```
int sock_select(struct inode *inode, struct file *file,
                int sel_type, select_table * wait);
```

This function calls the general select routine datagram_select(). With SEL_IN, it checks whether data is present in the receive list, with SEL_OUT whether data is present in the send list, and with SEL_EX whether the socket is in an error condition.

```
int sock_ioctl(struct inode *inode, struct file *file,
               unsigned int cmd, unsigned long arg);
```

The protocol operation ioctl() expects the command TIOCINQ or TIOCOUTQ. TIOCINQ returns the number of bytes which can still be read from the socket, and TIOCOUTQ the size of the buffer area to which data can still be written before a read or write operation blocks the process.

```
void sock_close(struct inode *inode, struct file *file);
```

This operation first calls sock_fasync() so that the socket is deleted from the list for asynchronous input–output of BSD. The operation then sets to SS_DISCONNECTING the status of the socket at which the operation was called, the socket to which this socket may be bound and the sockets wishing to bind to it. The protocol operation unix_release() is then called for the socket. This allows no more operations on the send queue. The data descriptor's data structure and the inode structure are also released.

```
int sock_fasync(struct inode * inode, struct file *filp,
                int on);
```

This routine enters filp in the list for asynchronous input–output of the socket or deletes it from it. Asynchronous input–output in the form implemented here derives from BSD and is used to inform the process via the signal SIGIO that new data are waiting at the socket.

It should also be mentioned that the process can be prevented from blocking while performing this operation by setting the file descriptor's O_NONBLOCK flag. The file set up by bind() can only be opened and closed.

The flag S_IFSOCK in the file's inode structure is set, marking the file as a special socket address file. An ls -l for the socket address file in the example will produce the message:

```
% ls -l server
srwxr-xr-x  1 kunitz   mi89       0 Mar  7 00:09 server=
```

The LINUX file system

*"My dear Watson, coming by good information
is not difficult.
What is far more difficult is finding it again."*

Conan Doyle, The Adventures of Sherlock Holmes

In the PC field, variety in file systems is common; practically every operating system has its own file system, and each of these naturally claims to be 'faster, better and more secure' than its predecessors.

The large number of file systems supported by LINUX is undoubtedly one of the main reasons why LINUX has gained acceptance so quickly in its short history. Not every user is in a position to put in the time and effort to convert his/her old data to a new file system.

The range of file systems supported is made possible by the unified interface to the LINUX kernel. This is the *Virtual File System Switch* (VFS), which will be referred to below simply as the 'Virtual File System', although we are not dealing with a file system so much as an interface providing a clearly defined link between the operating system kernel and the different file systems (as illustrated in Figure 6.1).

The Virtual File System supplies the applications with the system calls for file management (*see* Section A.2), maintains internal structures and passes tasks on to the appropriate actual file system. Another important job of the VFS is performing standard actions. As a rule, for instance, no file system implementation will actually provide an lseek() function, as the functions of lseek() are provided by a standard action of the VFS. We are therefore justified in calling VFS a file system.

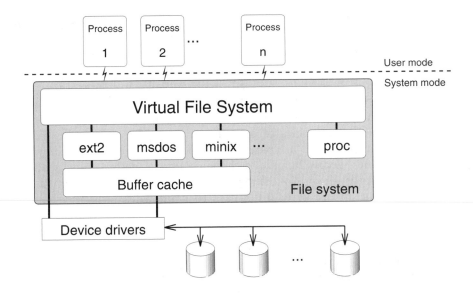

Figure 6.1 The layers in the file system.

In this chapter, we take a closer look at how VFS works and how it interacts with specific file system implementations. As a simple example, the implementation of the *Proc* file system will be considered. In addition, we examine the design and structure of the *Ext2* file system serving as the standard LINUX file system.

6.1 Basic principles

The importance of a good file management system is often underestimated. Where human beings can use their memory or a notebook, a computer has to resort to other means.

A central demand made of a file system is the *purposeful structuring* of data. When selecting a purposeful structure, however, two factors not to be neglected are the *speed* of access to data and a facility for *random access*.

Random access is made possible by block-oriented devices, which are divided into a specific number of equal-sized blocks. When using these, LINUX also has at its disposal the buffer cache described in Section 4.3. Using the functions of the buffer cache, it is possible to access any of the sequentially numbered blocks in a given device. The file system itself must be capable of ensuring unique allocation of the data to the hardware blocks.

In UNIX, the data are stored in a hierarchical file system containing files of different types. These comprise not only regular files and directories but also device files, FIFOs (*named pipes*), symbolic links and sockets. These enable all the resources of the system to be accessed via files.

From a programming point of view, files are simply data flows of unspecified content containing no further structuring. The file system takes on the task of managing these 'data flows' efficiently and allowing the *representation of different file types* (including pseudo-files).

In UNIX, the information required for management is kept strictly apart from the data and collected in a separate inode structure for each file. Figure 6.2 shows the arrangement of a typical UNIX inode. The information contained includes access times, access rights and the allocation of data to blocks on the physical media. As is shown in the figure, the inode already contains a few block numbers to ensure efficient access to small files (which are often encountered under UNIX). Access to larger files is provided via indirect blocks, which also contain block numbers. Every file is represented by just one inode, which means that, within a file system, each inode has a unique number and the file itself can also be accessed using this number.

Directories allow the file system to be given a hierarchical structure. These are also implemented as files, but the kernel assumes them to contain pairs consisting of a filename and its inode number. There is no reason why a file cannot be accessed via a number of names, which can even be held in

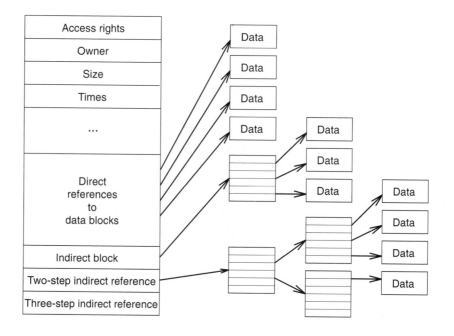

Figure 6.2 Structure of a UNIX inode.

different directories (in the form of a *hard link*). In older versions of UNIX it was still possible to modify directory files using a simple editor, but to ensure consistency this is no longer permitted in recent versions. LINUX file systems will not even allow these to be read with normal system calls.

The basic structure is the same for all the different UNIX file systems (*see* Figure 6.3). Each file system starts with a *boot block*. This block is reserved for the code required to boot the operating system (*see* Appendix D). As file systems should usually be able to exist on any block-oriented device, and on each device, in principle, they will always have the same structure (to ensure uniformity), the boot block will be present whether or not the computer is booted from the device in question.

All the information which is essential for managing the file system is held in the *superblock*. This is followed by a number of *inode blocks* containing the inode structures for the file system. The remaining blocks for the device provide the space for the data. These *data blocks* thus contain ordinary files along with the directory entries and the indirect blocks.

As file systems must be able to be implemented on different devices, the implementation of the file system must also adapt to different device-level characteristics, such as block size, and so on. At the same time, all operating systems aim for *device independence*, which will make it immaterial what media the data have been stored on. In LINUX, this task is handled by the respective file system implementation, enabling the Virtual File System to work with device-independent structures.

In UNIX, the separate file systems are not accessed via device identifiers (such as drive numbers), as is the case for other operating systems, but combined into a hierarchical directory tree.

This arrangement is built up by the action of *mounting* the file system, which adds another file system (of whatever type) to an existing directory tree. A new file system can be mounted onto any directory. This original directory is then known as the *mount point* and is covered up by the root directory of the new file system along with its subdirectories and files. *Unmounting* the file system releases the hidden directory structure again.

A further aspect of major importance to the quality of a file system is *data security*. On the one hand, this comprises facilities to maintain consistency and mechanisms ensuring data protection. On the other hand, the file system should behave robustly in the event of system faults, corruption of data or program crashes.

Figure 6.3   Schematic structure of a UNIX file system.

6.2   The representation of file systems in the kernel

The representation of data on a floppy disk or hard disk may differ considerably from case to case. In the end, however, the actual representation of data in LINUX's memory works out the same. Here, once again, LINUX sticks closely to its 'model', UNIX, because the management structures for the file systems are very similar to the logical structure of a UNIX file system.

These are the responsibility of the VFS, which calls the file-system-specific functions for the various implementations to fill up the structures. These functions are provided by every actual implementation and made known to the VFS via the function `register_filesystem()`.

```
#ifdef CONFIG_MINIX_FS
    register_filesystem(&(struct file_system_type)
        {minix_read_super, "minix", 1, NULL});
#endif
```

By this means the VFS is given the name of the file system ('`minix`'), a function of the implementation and a flag indicating whether a device is strictly necessary to mount the file system from. The function passed, `read_super()`, forms the mount interface: it is only via this function that further functions of the file system implementation will be made known to the VFS.

The function sets up the `file_system_type` structure it has been passed in a singly linked list whose beginning is pointed to by `file_systems`.

```
struct file_system_type {
    struct super_block *(*read_super) (struct super_block *,
                                       void *, int);
    char *name;
    int requires_dev;
    struct file_system_type *next;
}     *file_systems = NULL;
```

In older LINUX kernels (before version 1.1.8) the structures were still managed in a static table, as all the file system implementations were known when the kernel was compiled. With the introduction of modules it became desirable to load new file systems after the LINUX system had started running.

Once a file system implementation has been registered with the VFS, file systems of this type can be administered.

6.2.1   Mounting

Before a file can be accessed, the file system containing the file must be mounted. This can be done using either the system call *mount* or the function `mount_root()`.

The `mount_root()` function takes care of mounting the first file system (the *root file system*). It is called by the system call *setup* (*see* page 378) after all the file system implementations permanently included in the kernel have been registered. The *setup* call itself is called just once,[1] immediately after the init process is created by the kernel function `init()` (file `init/main.c`). This system call is necessary because access to kernel structures is not allowed from user mode (which is the status of the init process).

Every mounted file system is represented by a `super_block` structure. These structures are held in the static table `super_blocks[]` and limited in number to `NR_SUPER`.

The superblock is initialized by the function `read_super()` in the Virtual File System. It interrogates floppy disks and CD-ROM for a change of media, tests whether the superblock is already present and, if so, returns it. If it finds no superblock in existence it searches for a new entry in the superblock table and calls the function to create a superblock which is provided by every file system implementation. This file-system-specific function will have been made known on registering the implementation with the VFS. When called, it will contain:

- a superblock structure in which the elements `s_dev` and `s_flags` are filled in accordance with Table 6.1,

- a character string (in this case `void *`) containing further mount options for the file system, and

- a `silent` flag indicating whether unsuccessful mounting should be reported. This flag is used only by the kernel function `mount_root()`, as this calls all the `read_super()` functions present in the various file system implementations in turn when mounting the root file system, and constant error messages during start-up would be disruptive.

The file-system-specific function `read_super()` reads its data if necessary from the appropriate block device using the LINUX cache functions introduced in Section 4.3. This also provides the reason why a process is required to mount file systems: the process can be halted by the device driver (using the sleep/

---

[1] Nothing would be achieved by calling it a second time, as the system call *setup* returns an error after it has been used once.

Table 6.1 The file-system-independent mount flags in the superblock.

Macro	Value	Remarks
MS_RDONLY	1	File system is read only
MS_NOSUID	2	Ignores S bits
MS_NODEV	4	Inhibits access to device files
MS_NOEXEC	8	Inhibits execution of program
MS_SYNCHRONOUS	16	Immediate write to disk
MS_REMOUNT	32	Changes flags

wake-up mechanism; *see* Section 3.1.5), since it requires time to access the device. The LINUX superblock is structured as follows:

```
struct super_block {
    dev_t s_dev;                      /* device for file system */
    unsigned long s_blocksize;        /* block size             */
    unsigned char s_blocksize_bits;   /* ld (block size)        */
    unsigned char s_lock;             /* superblock lock        */
    unsigned char s_rd_only;          /* not used (= 0)         */
    unsigned char s_dirt;             /* superblock changed     */
    struct file_system_type *s_type;  /* file system type       */
    struct super_operations *s_op;    /* superblock operations  */
    unsigned long s_flags;            /* flags                  */
    unsigned long s_magic;            /* file system identifier */
    unsigned long s_time;             /* time of change         */
    struct inode * s_covered;         /* mount point            */
    struct inode * s_mounted;         /* root inode             */
    struct wait_queue * s_wait;       /* s_lock wait queue      */
    union {
        struct minix_sb_info minix_sb;
            ...
        void *generic_sdp;
    } u;                   /* file-system-specific information */
};
```

The superblock contains information on the entire file system, such as block size, access rights and time of the last change. In addition, the union u at the end of the structure holds special information on the relevant file systems. For file system modules mounted later, there is a pointer generic_sdp.

The components s_lock and s_wait ensure access to the superblock is synchronized. This uses the functions lock_super() and unlock_super(), which are defined in the file <linux/locks.h>.

```
extern inline void lock_super(struct super_block * sb)
{
   if (sb->s_lock)
      __wait_on_super(sb);
   sb->s_lock = 1;
}

extern inline void unlock_super(struct super_block * sb)
{
   sb->s_lock = 0;
   wake_up(&sb->s_wait);
}
```

The superblock also holds references to the file system's *root inode* s_mounted and the mount point s_covered.

Another task performed by the read_super() function in the actual file system implementation involves making the file system's root inode available and entering it in the superblock. This can be carried out using the functions of the VFS, such as the iget() function, which will be described later, provided the components s_dev and s_op are set correctly.

6.2.2   Superblock operations

The superblock structure provides, in the function vector s_op, functions for accessing the file system, and these form the basis for further work on the file system.

```
struct super_operations {
   void (*read_inode) (struct inode *);
   int  (*notify_change) (struct inode *, struct iattr *);
   void (*write_inode) (struct inode *);
   void (*put_inode) (struct inode *);
   void (*put_super) (struct super_block *);
   void (*write_super) (struct super_block *);
   void (*statfs) (struct super_block *, struct statfs *);
   int  (*remount_fs) (struct super_block *, int *, char *);
};
```

The functions in the super_operations structure serve to read and write an individual inode, to write the superblock and to read file system information. This means that the superblock operations contain functions to transfer the specific representation of the superblock and inode on the data media to their general form in memory and vice versa. As a result, this layer completely hides the actual representations. Strictly speaking, the inodes and the superblock do not even have to exist. An example of this is the MS-DOS file system, in which the FAT and the information in the boot block are transferred to the UNIX-internal view consisting of the superblock and inodes. If a superblock operation is not implemented – that is, if the pointer to the operation is NULL – no further action will take place.

- **write_super(sb)**
  The write_super(sb) function is used to save the information of the superblock. This need not necessarily guarantee the consistency of the file system.[2] If the current file system supports a flag indicating inconsistency (*valid flag*), this should be set. In normal cases the function will cause the cache to write back the buffer for the superblock: this is ensured by setting the buffer's b_dirt flag. The function is used in synchronizing the device and is ignored by read-only file systems such as *Isofs*.

- **put_super(sb)**
  The Virtual File System calls this function when unmounting file systems, when it should also release the superblock and other information buffers (*see* brelse() in Section 4.3) and/or restore the consistency of the file system, leaving the valid flag correctly set. In addition, the s_dev entry in the superblock structure must be set to 0 to ensure that the superblock is once again available after unmounting.

- **statfs(sb, statfsbuf)**
  The two system calls *statfs* and *fstatfs* (*see* page 364) call the superblock operation which in fact does no more than fill in the statfs structure. This structure provides information on the file system, the number of free blocks and the preferred block size. Note that the structure is located in the user address space. If the operation fails, the VFS returns the error ENOSYS.

- **remount_fs(sb, flags, options)**
  The remount_fs() function changes the status of a file system (*see* Table 6.1). This generally only involves entering the new attributes for the file system in the superblock and restoring the consistency of the file system.

- **read_inode(inode)**
  This function is responsible for filling in the inode structure it has been passed, in a similar way to read_super(). It is called by the function __iget(), which will already have given the entries i_dev, i_ino, i_sb and i_flags their contents. The main purpose of the read_inode() function is to mark the different file types by entering inode operations in the inode according to the file type. Almost every read_inode function

---

[2] The data and inode blocks need not be written back, nor the lists and bitmaps for the free blocks, which means that the file system may not be consistent.

(the example is taken from the *Ext2* file system) will therefore contain the following lines:

```
if (S_ISREG(inode->i_mode))
    inode->i_op = &ext2_file_inode_operations;
else if (S_ISDIR(inode->i_mode))
    inode->i_op = &ext2_dir_inode_operations;
else if (S_ISLNK(inode->i_mode))
    inode->i_op = &ext2_symlink_inode_operations;
else if (S_ISCHR(inode->i_mode))
    inode->i_op = &chrdev_inode_operations;
else if (S_ISBLK(inode->i_mode))
    inode->i_op = &blkdev_inode_operations;
else if (S_ISFIFO(inode->i_mode))
    init_fifo(inode);
```

- **notify_change(inode, attr)**
  The changes made to the inode via system calls are acknowledged by notify_change(). This operation is missing from a number of file system implementations, but is of interest for the NFS, for example, as this file system has, so to speak, a local and an external inode. All inode changes are carried out on the local inode structure only, which means that the computer exporting the file system needs to be informed. This is done using the structure iattr:

```
struct iattr {
    unsigned int    ia_valid; /* flags for changed components */
    umode_t         ia_mode;  /* new access rights            */
    uid_t           ia_uid;   /* new user                     */
    gid_t           ia_gid;   /* new group                    */
    off_t           ia_size;  /* new size                     */
    time_t          ia_atime; /* time of last access          */
    time_t          ia_mtime; /* time of last modification    */
    time_t          ia_ctime; /* time of creation             */
};
```

  The functions calling notify_change and the flags passed in the component ia_valid are listed in Table 6.2.

- **write_inode(inode)**
  This function saves the inode structure, analogous to write_super().

- **put_inode(inode)**
  This function is called by iput() if the inode is no longer required. Its main task is to delete the file physically and release its blocks if i_nlink is zero.

Table 6.2 The flags for `notify_change`.

Kernel function	ATTR_MODE	ATTR_UID	ATTR_GID	ATTR_SIZE	ATTR_ATIME	ATTR_MTIME	ATTR_CTIME	ATTR_ATIME_SET	ATTR_MTIME_SET
sys_chmod()	×						×		
sys_fchmod()	×						×		
sys_chown()	×	×	×				×		
sys_fchown()	×	×	×				×		
sys_truncate()				×		×	×		
sys_ftruncate()				×		×	×		
sys_write()	×								
open_namei()				×					
sys_utime()					×	×	×	×	×

6.2.3 The inode

When a file system is mounted, the superblock is generated and the root inode for the file system is entered in the component i_mount at the appropriate mount point, that is, in its inode structure. The definition of the inode structure is as follows:

```
struct inode {
    dev_t          i_dev;      /* file device number        */
    unsigned long  i_ino;      /* inode number              */
    umode_t        i_mode;     /* file type and access rights */
    nlink_t        i_nlink;    /* number of hard links      */
    uid_t          i_uid;      /* owner                     */
    gid_t          i_gid;      /* owner                     */
    dev_t          i_rdev;     /* device, if device file    */
    off_t          i_size;     /* size                      */
    time_t         i_atime;    /* time of last access       */
    time_t         i_mtime;    /* time of last modification */
    time_t         i_ctime;    /* time of creation          */
    unsigned long  i_blksize;  /* block size                */
    unsigned long  i_blocks;   /* number of blocks          */
    unsigned long  i_version;  /* DCache version management  */
    struct semaphore i_sem;              /* access control  */
    struct inode_operations * i_op;   /* inode operations   */
    struct super_block * i_sb;        /* superblock          */
```

```
    struct wait_queue * i_wait;      /* wait queue              */
    struct file_lock * i_flock;      /* file locks              */
    struct vm_area_struct * i_mmap;  /* memory areas            */
    struct inode * i_next, * i_prev; /* inode linking           */
    struct inode * i_hash_next, * i_hash_prev;
    struct inode * i_bound_to, * i_bound_by;
    struct inode * i_mount;          /* mounted inode           */
    struct socket * i_socket;   /* socket management            */
    unsigned short i_count;     /* reference counter            */
    unsigned short i_wcount;    /* number authorized to write   */
    unsigned short i_flags;     /* flags (= i_sb->s_flags)      */
    unsigned char i_lock;       /* lock                         */
    unsigned char i_dirt;       /* inode has been modified      */
    unsigned char i_pipe;       /* inode represents pipe        */
    unsigned char i_sock;       /* inode represents socket      */
    unsigned char i_seek;       /* not used                     */
    unsigned char i_update;     /* inode is current             */
    union {
        struct pipe_inode_info pipe_i;
        struct minix_inode_info minix_i;
            ...
        void *generic_ip;
    } u;                    /* file-system-specific information */
};
```

In the first section, this holds information on the file. The remainder contains management information and the file-system-dependent union u.

In memory, the inodes are managed in two ways. First, they are managed in a doubly linked circular list starting with first_inode, which is accessed via the entries i_next and i_prev. The complete list of inodes is scanned through in the following way:

```
struct inode * inode, * next;

next = first_inode;
for(i = nr_inodes ; i > 0 ; i--) {
   inode = next;
   next = inode->i_next;
      ...
}
```

This approach is not particularly efficient, as the complete list of inodes also includes the 'free', unused inodes, for which the components i_count, i_dirt and i_lock should all be zero. The unused inodes are generated via the `grow_inodes()` function, which is called every time that less than a quarter of all the inodes are free but not more than `NR_INODE` are in existence. The number of unused inodes and the count of all available inodes are held in the static variables `nr_free` and `nr_inode` respectively.

For fast access, inodes are also stored in an open hash table `hash_table[]`, where collisions are dealt with via a doubly linked list using the components `i_hash_next` and `i_hash_prev`. Access to any of the `NR_IHASH` entries is made through the device and inode numbers.

The functions for working with inodes are `iget()`, `namei()` and `iput()`.

```
inline struct inode *iget(struct super_block *sb, int nr)
{
    return __iget(sb, nr, 1);
}

struct inode *__iget(struct super_block * sb, int nr,
                     int crossmntp);

void iput(struct inode * inode);
```

The `iget()` function supplies the inode specified by the superblock `sb` and the inode number `nr`. In its turn it calls the `__iget()` function, which is instructed via a further parameter, `crossmntp`, to resolve mount points as well – that is, if the requested inode is a mount point it supplies the corresponding root inode for the mounted file system.

If the required inode is included in the hash table, the `i_count` reference counter is simply incremented. If it is not found, a 'free' inode is selected (`get_empty_inode()`) and the implementation of the relevant file system calls the superblock operation `read_inode()` to fill it with information. The resulting inode is then added to the hash table.

An inode obtained using `iget()` has to be released using the function `iput()`. This decrements the reference counter by 1 and marks the inode structure as 'free' if the former is 0.

Other functions to supply inodes are:

```
int namei(const char * pathname, struct inode ** res_inode);
int lnamei(const char * pathname, struct inode ** res_inode);
```

The filename `pathname` that has been passed is resolved and the address of the inode structure is stored in `res_inode`. The `lnamei()` function differs from `namei()` in that `lnamei()` does not resolve a symbolic link and will continue to supply the inode for the symbolic link. Both functions call `_namei()`. Additional parameters passed to this function are the inode of the base directory for the resolving procedures and a flag indicating whether symbolic links are to be resolved using `follow_link`.

The actual functioning of _namei() derives from `dir_namei()`. This function supplies the inode for the directory that contains the file with the name specified. All functions return an error code smaller than 0 if they are not successful.

6.2.4 Inode operations

The inode structure also has its own operations, which are held in the `inode_operations` structure and mainly provide for file management. These functions are usually called directly from the implementations of the appropriate system calls. Note that in all cases the functions must use `iput()` to release the inodes that have been passed to them, since the inode reference counter is incremented by 1 before the functions are called, to indicate that they are in use. If an inode operation fails, the calling function performs default actions; however, this often comprises the mere generation of an error.

```
struct inode_operations {
    struct file_operations * default_file_ops;
    int (*create) (struct inode *,const char *,int,int,
                    struct inode **);
    int (*lookup) (struct inode *,const char *,int,
                    struct inode **);
    int (*link) (struct inode *,struct inode *,const char *,int);
    int (*unlink) (struct inode *,const char *,int);
    int (*symlink) (struct inode *,const char *,int,const char *);
    int (*mkdir) (struct inode *,const char *,int,int);
    int (*rmdir) (struct inode *,const char *,int);
    int (*mknod) (struct inode *,const char *,int,int,int);
    int (*rename) (struct inode *,const char *,int,struct inode *,
                    const char *,int);
    int (*readlink) (struct inode *,char *,int);
    int (*follow_link) (struct inode *,struct inode *,int,int,
                    struct inode **);
    int (*bmap) (struct inode *,int);
    void (*truncate) (struct inode *);
    int (*permission) (struct inode *, int);
    int (*smap) (struct inode *, int);
};
```

● **create(dir, name, len, mode, res_inode)**
This function is called from within the VFS function `open_namei()`. It performs a number of tasks. First, it extracts a free inode from the complete list of inodes with the aid of the `get_empty_inode()` function.

The inode structure now needs to be filled with file-system-specific data, for which, for example, a free inode on the media is sought out. After this, create() enters the filename name of length len in the directory specified by the inode dir. If create() is not present in a file system implementation, the VFS returns the error EACCESS.

- **lookup(dir, name, len, res_inode)**

  This function is supplied with a filename and its length and returns the inode for the file in the argument res_inode. This is carried out by scanning the directory specified by the inode dir. The lookup() function must be defined for directories, otherwise the VFS will return the error ENOTDIR.

  The calling VFS function lookup() performs a special procedure for the name '..'. If the process is already in its root directory, the root inode is returned. However, if the root inode for a mounted file system is overstepped by '..', the VFS function uses the 'hidden' inode to call the inode operation.

- **link(oldinode, dir, name, len)**

  This function sets up a hard link. The file oldinode will be linked under the stated name and the associated length in the directory specified by the inode dir. Before link() is called, a check is made that the inodes dir and oldinode are on the same device and that the current process is authorized to write to dir. If this function is missing, the calling function in the VFS returns the error EPERM.

- **unlink(dir, name, len)**

  This function deletes the specified file in the directory specified by the inode dir. The calling function first confirms that this operation possesses the relevant permissions. If unlink() is not implemented, the VFS returns the error EPERM.

- **symlink(dir, name, len, symname)**

  This function sets up the symbolic link name in the directory dir, with len giving the length of the name name. The symbolic link points to the path symname. Before this function is called by the VFS, the access permissions will have been checked by a call to permission(). If symlink() is not present in a specific implementation, the VFS returns the error EPERM.

- **mkdir(dir, name, len, mode)**

  This function sets up a subdirectory with the name name and the access rights mode in the directory dir. The mkdir() function first has to check whether further subdirectories are permitted in the directory, then allocate a free inode on the data media and a free block, to which the directory is then written together with its default entries '.' and '..'. The access rights will already have been checked in the calling VFS function. If the mkdir() function is not implemented, the error EPERM is returned.

- **rmdir(dir, name, len)**

  This function deletes the subdirectory name from the directory dir. The function first checks that the directory to be deleted is empty and whether it is currently being used by a process, as well as whether the process is the owner of the subdirectory if the sticky bit is set in the directory dir. As with the functions already described, the access rights are checked beforehand by a VFS function. If rmdir() is not available, the VFS returns the error EPERM.

- **mknod(dir, name, len, mode, rdev)**

  This function sets up a new inode in the mode mode. This inode will be given the name name in the directory dir. If the inode is a device file (in which case either S_ISBLK(mode) or S_ISCHR(mode) applies), the parameter rdev gives the number of the device. If this function is not implemented, the error EPERM is returned.

- **rename(odir, oname, olen, ndir, nname, nlen)**

  This function changes the name of a file. This involves removing the old name oname from the odir directory and entering the new name nname in ndir. The calling function checks the relevant access permissions in the directories beforehand, and a further check is made to ensure that the directories '.' and '..' do not appear as the source or destination of an operation. If the function is missing, an EPERM error is generated by the VFS.

- **readlink(inode, buf, size)**

  This function reads symbolic links and should copy into the buffer in the user address space the pathname for the file to which the link points. If the buffer is too small, the pathname should simply be truncated. If the inode is not a symbolic link, EINVAL should be returned. This function is called directly from sys_readlink() once the write access permission to the buffer buf has been checked and the inode has been found using lnamei(). If the implementation does not exist, the system call returns the error EINVAL.

- **follow_link(dir, inode, flag, mode, res_inode)**

  This function is used to resolve symbolic links. For the inode assigned to a symbolic link, this function returns the inode to which the link points in the argument res_inode. To avoid endless loops,[3] the maximum number of links to be resolved is set at 5 in LINUX. In the implementations, this count is 'hard-wired', and any implementations written should follow this example.

  If follow_link() is missing, the calling function of the same name in the VFS simply returns inode, as if the link were pointing to itself. This behaviour means that the VFS function can always be called

---

[3] A symbolic link can, after all, point to another symbolic link.

without testing whether the current inode describes a file or a symbolic link.

- **bmap(inode, block)**

  This function is called to enable memory mapping of files. In the argument `block` it is given the number of a logical data block in the file. This number must be converted by `bmap()` into the logical number of the block on the media. To do this, `bmap()` searches for the block in the actual implementation of the specified inode and returns its number. This may in some cases involve reading other blocks from the media. A return value of 0 signifies an error and is returned by the Virtual File System's calling function `bmap()` if a file-system-specific `bmap` function is not defined.

  This function is used by `generic_mmap()` to map a block from the file to an address in the user address space. If it cannot be found, executable files must first be loaded into memory completely, as the more efficient demand paging is not then available.

- **truncate(inode)**

  This function is mainly intended to shorten a file, but can also lengthen a file to any length if this is supported by the specific implementation. The only parameter required by `truncate()` is the inode of the file to be amended, with the `i_size` field set to the new length before the function is called. The `truncate()` function is used at a number of places in the kernel, both by the system call `sys_truncate()` and when a file is opened. It will also release the blocks no longer required by a file.

  Thus, the `truncate()` function can be used to delete a file physically if the inode on the media is cleared afterwards. Although the functioning of this function is very simple to describe, it can be very complicated to implement, as problems can arise with synchronization. If this function is not implemented, no error message is generated. In this case, as the `i_size` component has been set beforehand, the length of the file will only appear to have changed.

- **permission(inode, flag)**

  This function checks the inode to confirm the access rights to the file given by the mask. The possible values for the mask are `MAY_READ`, `MAY_WRITE` and `MAY_EXEC`. If the function is not available, the calling function in the Virtual File System checks the standard UNIX permissions, which means that implementation is actually unnecessary, unless additional access mechanisms are to be implemented.

- **smap(inode, sector)**

  This function is intended principally to allow swap files to be created on a UMSDOS file system. Like `bmap()`, this inode operation supplies the logical sector number (not block or cluster) on the media for the sector of the file specified. This means that the operation is only of interest for the UMSDOS file system implementation, but is already provided by the MS-DOS file system in the form of the `msdos_smap()` function, where it is, however, only used internally. In the memory management function `rw_swap_page()`, the `smap()` function is required to prepare to work with a swap file if `bmap()` is not available.

6.2.5   The file structure

In a multi-tasking system the problem often arises that a number of processes wish to access a file at the same time, both to read and to write. Even a single process may be reading *and* writing at different points in the file. To avoid synchronization problems and allow shared access to files by different processes, UNIX has simply introduced an extra structure.

This relatively simple structure, `file`, contains information on a specific file's access rights `f_mode`, the current file position `f_pos`, the type of access `f_flags` and the number of accesses `f_count`.

```
struct file {
    mode_t          f_mode;        /* access type               */
    loff_t          f_pos;         /* file position             */
    unsigned short  f_flags;       /* open() flags              */
    unsigned short  f_count;       /* reference counter         */
    off_t           f_reada;       /* read ahead flag           */
    struct file     *f_next,*f_prev;/* links                    */
    int             f_owner;       /* PID or -PGRP for SIGIO    */
    struct inode    *f_inode;      /* related inode             */
    struct file_operations * f_op; /* file operations           */
    unsigned long   f_version;     /* Dcache version management */
    void            *private_data; /* needed for tty driver     */
};
```

The file structures are managed in a doubly linked circular list via the pointers `f_next` and `f_prev`. This *file table* can be accessed via the pointer `first_file`.

6.2.6   File operations

The `file_operations` structure is the general interface for work on files, and contains the functions to open, close, read and write files. The reason why these functions are not held in `inode_operations` but in a separate structure is that they need to make changes to the `file` structure.

The inode's `inode_operations` structure also includes the component `default_file_ops`, in which the standard file operations are already specified.

```
struct file_operations {
    int (*lseek) (struct inode *, struct file *, off_t, int);
    int (*read) (struct inode *, struct file *, char *, int);
    int (*write) (struct inode *, struct file *, char *, int);
    int (*readdir) (struct inode *, struct file *,
                    struct dirent *, int);
    int (*select) (struct inode *, struct file *, int,
                    select_table *);
    int (*ioctl) (struct inode *, struct file *,
                  unsigned int, unsigned long);
    int (*mmap) (struct inode *, struct file *,
                 struct vm_area_struct *);
    int (*open) (struct inode *, struct file *);
    void (*release) (struct inode *, struct file *);
    int (*fsync) (struct inode *, struct file *);
    int (*fasync) (struct inode *, struct file *, int);
    int (*check_media_change) (dev_t);
    int (*revalidate) (dev_t);
};
```

These functions are also useful for sockets and device drivers, as they contain the actual functions for sockets and devices. The inode operations, on the other hand, only use the representation of the socket or device in the related file system or its copy in memory.

- **lseek(inode, filp, offset, origin)**
  The job of the lseek function is to deal with positioning within the file. If this function is not implemented, the default action simply converts the file position f_pos for the file structure if the positioning is to be carried out from the start or from the current position. If the file is represented by an inode, the default function can also be positioned from the end of the file. If the function is missing, the file position in the file structure is updated by the VFS.

- **read(inode, filp, buf, count)**
  This function copies count bytes from the file into the buffer buf in the user address space. Before calling the function, the Virtual File System first confirms that the entire buffer is located in the user address space and can be written to, and also that the file pointer is valid and the file has been opened to read. If no read function is implemented, the error EINVAL is returned.

- **write(inode, filp, buf, count)**
  The write function operates in an analogous manner to read() and copies data from the user address space to the file.

● **readdir(inode, filp, dirent, count)**
This function returns the next directory entry in the dirent structure or
an ENOTDIR or EBADF error. If this function is not implemented, the
Virtual File System returns ENOTDIR.

● **select(inode, filp, type, wait)**
This function checks whether data can be read from a file or written to
one. An additional test for exception conditions can also be made. This
function only serves a useful purpose for device drivers and sockets. The
main task of the function is taken care of by the Virtual File System;
thus, when interrogating files the VFS always returns the value 1 if it is
a normal file, otherwise 0. Further consideration will be given to the
select function in Section 7.4.6.

● **ioctl(inode, filp, cmd, arg)**
Strictly speaking, the ioctl() function sets device-specific parameters.
However, before the Virtual File System calls the ioctl operation, it
tests the following default arguments:

FIONCLEX	Clears the close-on-exec bit.
FIOCLEX	Sets the close-on-exec bit.
FIONBIO	If the additional argument arg refers to a value not equal to zero, the O_NONBLOCK flag is set; otherwise it is cleared.
FIOASYNC	Sets or clears the O_SYNC flag as for FIONBIO. This flag is not at present evaluated.

If cmd is not among these values, a check is performed on whether filp
refers to a normal file. If so, the function file_ioctl() is called and the
system call terminates. For other files, the VFS tests for the presence of
an ioctl function. If there is none, the EINVAL error is returned,
otherwise the file-specific ioctl function is called.
The following commands are available to the file_ioctl() function:

FIBMAP	Expects in the argument arg a pointer to a block number and returns the logical number of this block in the file on the device if the inode relating to the file has a bmap function. This logical number is written back to the address arg. Absence of the inode operations or bmap() generates an EBADF or EINVAL error respectively.
FIGETBSZ	Returns the block size of the file system in which the file is located. It is written to the address arg if a superblock is assigned to the file. Otherwise, an EBADF error is generated.
FIONREAD	Writes the number of bytes within the file not yet read to the address arg.

As all of these commands write to the user address area, permission for this is always obtained via the function verify_area(), and an access error may be returned. If the command cmd is not among the values described, file_ioctl(), too, calls an existing file-specific ioctl function; otherwise the EINVAL error is returned.

- **map(inode, filp, vm_area)**
  This function maps part of a file to the user address space of the current process. The structure vm_area specified describes all the characteristics of the memory area to be mapped: the components vm_start and vm_end give the start and end addresses of the memory area to which the file is to be mapped and vm_offset the position in the file from which mapping is to be carried out. For a more comprehensive description of the mmap mechanism *see* Section 4.2.2.

- **open(inode, filp)**
  This function only serves a useful purpose for device drivers, as the standard function in the Virtual File System will already have taken care of all the necessary actions on regular files, such as allocating the file structure.

- **release(inode, filp)**
  This function is called when the file structure is released, that is, when its reference counter f_count is zero. This function is primarily intended for device drivers, and its absence will be ignored by the Virtual File System. Updating of the inode is also taken care of automatically by the Virtual File System.

- **fsync(inode, filp)**
  The fsync() function ensures that all buffers for the file have been updated and written back to the device, which means that the function is only relevant for file systems. If a file system has not implemented an fsync() function, EINVAL is returned.

- **fasync(inode, filp, on)**
  This function is called by the VFS when a process uses the system call *fcntl* to log on or off for asynchronous messaging by sending a SIGIO signal. The messaging will take place when data are received and the on flag is set. If on is not set, the process unregisters the file structure from asynchronous messaging. Absence of this function is ignored by the VFS. At present, only terminal drivers and socket handling implement a fasync() function.

- **check_media_change(dev)**
  This function is only relevant to block devices supporting changeable media. It tests whether there has been a change of media since the last operation on it. If so, the function will return a 1, otherwise a zero. The check_media_change() function is called by the VFS function check_disk_change(); if a change of media has taken place, it calls

put_super() to remove any superblock belonging to the device, discards all the buffers belonging to the device dev which are still in the buffer cache, along with all the inodes on this device, and then calls revalidate(). As check_disk_change() requires a considerable amount of time, it is only called when mounting a device. Its return values are the same as for check_media_change(). If it is not available, zero (that is, no change) is always returned.

- **revalidate(dev)**
  This function is called by the VFS after a media change has been recognized, to restore the consistency of a block device. It should establish and record all the necessary parameters of the media, such as the number of blocks, number of tracks and so on. If this function is missing, the VFS takes no further action.

6.2.7 Opening a file

One of the most important operations when accessing data is opening a file with the system call *open*. For this, the system not only has to make the appropriate preparations to ensure access to data without problems, but also has to check the authorizations for the process. This is also where the actual switching function of the Virtual File System is implemented, passing data between the specific file system implementations and the various devices.

Once it has been confirmed that the calling process is entitled to open files in the first place, a new file structure is requested via the function get_empty_filp() and entered in the file descriptor table for the process. In this structure, appropriate contents are entered in the fields f_flags and f_mode, and the open_namei() function is called to obtain the inode for the file to be opened.

Before this function is called, the open() flags are modified, leaving the two lowest bits holding the access permissions – bit 0 for read and bit 1 for write operations. The advantage of representing access to the file in this way is clear: it allows the access authorizations to be checked using a simple bit test.

The open_namei() function calls the function dir_namei() (mentioned earlier) and resolves the filename except for the base name of the file, obtaining the inode for the directory in which the file is located. The open_namei() function then performs a number of tests.

- If a filename ends in a slash (/), the dir_namei() function has already supplied the inode for the directory to be opened. If the process does *not* wish to write, the inode for the directory will be returned after the access authorization test.

- If the O_CREAT flag is set, open_namei() not only calls the VFS function lookup() to obtain the inode for the file, but in the event of an error indicating that the file does not exist, it will generate the file by calling the inode operation `create()`, provided the directory has the appropriate access permissions. The `O_EXCL` flag is also evaluated at this point.

- Once the inode has been obtained using `lookup()`, symbolic links are resolved by calling the `follow_link()` function. As both `lookup()` and `follow_link()` make use of the `iget()` function and therefore also of the `read_inode()` function, the type of file (normal file, device file and so on) is known from this point onwards. Thus, the inode operations contain the file operations specific to the file type in the `default_file_ops` component.

- If the file is a directory and if the process is seeking write permission, `open_namei()` returns the error `EISDIR`.

- The access rights of the inode are now checked. This uses the function `permission()`, which completes its task by reference to those flags shown in Table 6.3 which have been changed. If the file system implementation defines an inode operation `permission()`, it is used instead at this point.

- If access to devices has been prohibited by the mount option `MS_NODEV` and if the file is a device file, the error `EACCES` is returned.

- If the file is not a device file and if the process is attempting to gain write access to a read-only file system, the attempt is aborted with the `EROFS` error.

- If the process is requesting write permission for an 'append only' file for which the `open()` flag `O_APPEND` is not set, `open_namei()` terminates with an `EPERM` error.

- If the `O_TRUNC` flag is set, `open_namei()` calls the function `get_write_access()` to check that the file has not been mapped with `VM_DENYWRITE` set. If this returns successfully, the `notify_change()` function is called to propagate the change in size. Then `open_namei()`

Table 6.3 Conversion of the `open()` flags.

open() flag	Value	Bits 1 and 0 of the open_namei() flag	Permissions required
		00	None (symbolic links)
O_RDONLY	0	01	Read
O_WRONLY	1	10	Write
O_RDWR	2	11	Read and write
O_CREAT	64	1*	Write
O_TRUNC	512	1*	Write

sets the i_size component of the inode to zero and calls the inode operation truncate() and the function put_write_access().

The get_write_access() function is used to announce a write access to a file represented by its inode. If the inode is used a number of times, a check is made for each process to confirm that the file has not been mapped with VM_DENYWRITE set. Also, the inode component i_wcount is incremented. The complementary function put_write_access() simply decrements the value of i_wcount. This makes it a simple matter to test whether processes are currently writing to a file which is about to be executed.

If the file survives all of this, open_namei() enters the inode for the newly opened file in res_inode and returns zero to do_open().

This function calls get_write_access() to request write permission for the file where necessary (if bit 1 is set). In addition, it fills the file structure with default values, so that the current file position is set to 0 and the file operations to the default file operations f_inode->i_op->default_file_ops for the inode. The operation open() is then called if it is defined.

This operation takes care of the actions specific to the file type. If the file that has been opened is a file for a character-oriented device, the function chrdev_open() is called at this point, which in its turn modifies the file operations according to the major number of the device.

```
int chrdev_open(struct inode * inode, struct file * filp)
{
    int i;

    i = MAJOR(inode->i_rdev);
    if (i >= MAX_CHRDEV || !chrdevs[i].fops)
        return -ENODEV;
    filp->f_op = chrdevs[i].fops;
    if (filp->f_op->open)
        return filp->f_op->open(inode,filp);
    return 0;
}
```

The file operations for the device drivers are held in the chrdevs[] table, where they were entered by the function register_chrdev() (*see* Chapter 7) when the driver was initialized. The device driver's open() function is certain to add further file operations according to the minor number of the device. This is described in the next chapter.

If no error is returned by any of these open functions, the file has been successfully opened, and the file descriptor is returned to the process by the functions do_open() or sys_open().

6.2.8 The directory cache

The directory cache originates in the *Ext2* file system. Since LINUX version 1.1.37 it has been part of the VFS and can be used by all file system implementations. This cache maintains directory entries which help to speed up access when reading directories, which is necessary when opening files. The entries in the cache have the following structure:

```
struct dir_cache_entry {
    struct hash_list h;              /* hash list management     */
    unsigned long dev;               /* device number            */
    unsigned long dir;               /* directory inode number   */
    unsigned long version;           /* directory version        */
    unsigned long ino;               /* inode number of file     */
    unsigned char name_len;          /* length of directory entry */
    char name[DCACHE_NAME_LEN];         /* directory entry       */
    struct dir_cache_entry ** lru_head; /* ptr to head of list   */
    struct dir_cache_entry * next_lru,
                        * prev_lru;  /* links in list            */
};
```

Only directory entries up to a length of DCACHE_NAME_LEN (that is, 15) are held in the cache. This is not a severe limitation, however, as the most frequently used files and directories will have short names.

The directory cache is a two-level cache, with both levels operating according to the LRU (*Least Recently Used*) algorithm. Each of the levels consists of a doubly linked circular list, which always contains DCACHE_SIZE entries. The pointers level1_head and level2_head point to the oldest element in each list, which will be the next to be overwritten. The component lru_head in the structure is also a pointer to this, enabling every cache entry to 'know' which level of the cache it is in.

For rapid location of an entry already in the cache, use is made, as regularly occurs in the LINUX kernel, of an open hash list. The hash key is formed from the device number dev, the inode number dir of the directory and a hash function of the name.

To access the directory cache, two functions are exported. The function

```
void dcache_add(struct inode * dir, const char * name,
                int len, unsigned long ino);
```

enters the directory entry name of length len, located in the directory with the inode dir, in the cache. The number ino is the inode number of the directory entry.

If the entry being made is already in the cache, it is revised to make it the youngest in its list, and the function then terminates. A new entry, however, is always inserted in level 1. This involves the oldest element, pointed to by the pointer `level1_head`, being first removed from the hash table and then overwritten with the data for the new directory entry. The pointer `level1_head` is moved on by one entry, so that the newly inserted entry becomes the youngest. Finally, the new entry is added to the hash table.

The function

```
int dcache_lookup(struct inode * dir, const char * name,
                  int len, unsigned long ino);
```

is used to interrogate the cache. If the entry name cannot be found, the function returns zero. If the entry is found in the cache, it is promoted to level 2, where it is entered (or updated, if it was already there). The inode number of the directory entry found is returned in the argument `ino`, and the function itself returns a 1.

Special importance is attached to the component `i_version` in the inode structure. This component is compared with the `version` component in the cache entry, and only if the two match is the cache entry still valid. Every file system implementation must give due attention to the fact that this version is incremented each time the inode of a directory is modified; otherwise it could happen that this function supplies a directory entry which is no longer in the cache. Fortunately, however, this version can be simply updated by the line:

```
dir->i_version = ++event;
```

The variable `event` is defined in `<linux/sched.h>` as an `unsigned long`. This range of values is wide enough to exclude any risk of overlap.

The directory cache thus serves to speed up the `lookup` function specific to a file system, although it is at present used only by the *Ext2* and ISO 9660 file systems. Finally, it should be mentioned that the directory cache is particularly effective in speeding up file access in systems with relatively little memory. On systems with larger memory, this is used for caching block devices anyway, and therefore also maintains directories in memory.

6.3   The *Proc* file system

As an example of how the Virtual File System interacts with a file system implementation, we now take a closer look at the *Proc* file system. The *Proc* file system in this form is peculiar to LINUX. It provides, in a portable way, information on the current status of the LINUX kernel and running processes.

In its general concepts, it resembles the process file system of System V Release 4 and, in some of its approaches, the experimental system Plan 9.[4] Each process in the system which is currently running is assigned a directory /proc/*pid*, where *pid* is the process identification number of the relevant process. This directory contains files holding information on certain characteristics of the process. A detailed breakdown of these files and their contents is given in Appendix C.

Let us now take a look at how this file system is implemented. As in so many other places in this book, we will have to manage without reproducing the algorithms in full and restrict ourselves instead to brief explanations of the most important fragments of the program. A full implementation can be found in the directory fs/proc.

When the *Proc* file system is mounted, the VFS function read_super() is called by do_mount(), and in turn calls the function proc_read_super() for the *Proc* file system in the file_systems list.

```
struct super_block *proc_read_super(struct super_block *s,
                                    void *data, int silent)
{
    lock_super(s);
    s->s_blocksize = 1024;
    s->s_blocksize_bits = 10;
    s->s_magic = PROC_SUPER_MAGIC;
    s->s_op = &proc_sops;
    unlock_super(s);
    if (!(s->s_mounted = iget(s,PROC_ROOT_INO))) {
        s->s_dev = 0;
        printk("get root inode failed\n");
        return NULL;
    }
    parse_options(data, &s->s_mounted->i_uid,
                        &s->s_mounted->i_gid);
    return s;
}
```

Among other things, this initializes the superblock operations (s_op) with the special structure proc_sops:

```
static struct super_operations proc_sops = {
    proc_read_inode,
    NULL,
```

---

[4] Plan 9 has been developed by such notable names as Rob Pike and Ken Thompson at AT&T's Bell Labs, and provides a perspective on what the developers of UNIX are currently doing. A good survey of Plan 9 is given in Pike *et al.* (1991).

```
        proc_write_inode,
        proc_put_inode,
        proc_put_super,
        NULL,
        proc_statfs,
        NULL
    };
```

The following call to `iget()` then uses this structure to generate the inode for the *Proc* root directory, which is entered in the superblock. The `parse_options()` function then processes the mount options `data` that have been provided (for example, 'uid=1701,gid=42') and sets the owner of the root inode.

Let us now take a look at what happens when this file system is accessed. An interesting aspect is that in all cases the relevant data are only generated when they are needed. Accessing the file system is always carried out by accessing the root inode of the file system. The first access is made, as described above, by calling `iget()`. If the inode does not exist, this function then calls the `proc_read_inode()` function entered in the `proc_sops` structure.

```
    void proc_read_inode(struct inode * inode)
    {
        unsigned long ino, pid;
        struct task_struct * p;
        int i;
```

First, the inode is initialized with the default values:

```
        inode->i_op = NULL;
        inode->i_mode = 0;
        inode->i_uid = 0;
        inode->i_gid = 0;
        inode->i_nlink = 1;
        inode->i_size = 0;
        inode->i_mtime = inode->i_atime = inode->i_ctime
                       = CURRENT_TIME;
        inode->i_blocks = 0;
        inode->i_blksize = 1024;
        ino = inode->i_ino;
```

After this, the action depends on the type of inode. We are only interested here in cases in which the inode is the root node of the file system that has been mounted:

```
        if (ino == PROC_ROOT_INO) {
            inode->i_mode = S_IFDIR | S_IRUGO | S_IXUGO;
```

This inode describes a directory (S_IFDIR) with read (S_IRUGO) and execute permissions (S_IXUGO) for all processes. The next step is to calculate the number of references to the directory. As a rule, this will be two plus the number of subdirectories, as each of the subdirectories possesses a reference in the form of '..'. This raises a problem: as the function proc_read_inode() is only called once over the 'lifetime' of the inode in memory, i_link can only be calculated once. This means that the number of processes running at the time when the *Proc* file system was mounted can be taken from the directory listing, especially as the other subdirectories, such as net/, were not taken into account for i_nlink.

All that is required after that is for the inode operations to be set correctly.

```
            inode->i_nlink = 2;
            for (i = 1 ; i < NR_TASKS ; i++)
               if (task[i])
                  inode->i_nlink++;
            inode->i_op = &proc_root_inode_operations;
            return;
      } /* if(ino == PROC_ROOT_INO) */
      ...
   } /* proc_read_inode() */
```

The structure proc_root_inode_operations only provides two functions: the component readdir in the form of the proc_readroot() function and the component lookup as the proc_lookuproot() function.

Both functions operate using the table root_dir[], which contains the invariable entries for the root directory.

```
      static struct proc_dir_entry root_dir[] = {
         { PROC_ROOT_INO, 1, "." },
         { PROC_ROOT_INO, 2, ".." },
         { PROC_LOADAVG,  7, "loadavg" },
         { PROC_UPTIME,   6, "uptime" },
         { PROC_MEMINFO,  7, "meminfo" },
         { PROC_KMSG,     4, "kmsg" },
         { PROC_VERSION,  7, "version" },
   #ifdef CONFIG_PCI
         { PROC_PCI,      3, "pci"  },
   #endif
         { PROC_CPUINFO,  7, "cpuinfo" },
         { PROC_SELF,     4, "self" },    /* changes inode # */
         ...
         { PROC_IOPORTS,  7, "ioports"},
```

```
#ifdef CONFIG_PROFILE
   { PROC_PROFILE,  7, "profile"},
#endif
};
```

The individual structures contain the inode number, the length of the filename and the name itself. When the root directory is read, the `proc_readroot()` function accordingly returns the entries given in the field `root_dir[]` along with one entry per process running. However, these directory entries are only generated once the `proc_readroot()` function is called.

A more interesting function than `proc_readroot()`, however, is `proc_lookuproot()`, which determines the inode of a file by reference to the inode for the directory and the name of a file contained in it. In this procedure, the inode numbers are generated in such a way that they can be used later to identify uniquely the file that has been opened.

```
static int proc_lookuproot(struct inode * dir,
                           const char * name,
                           int len, struct inode ** result)
{
   unsigned int pid, c;
   int i, ino;
```

First, the name of the file to be opened is checked to see if it is a name from the `root_dir[]` table.

```
   ...
i = NR_ROOT_DIRENTRY;
while (i-- > 0 && !proc_match(len,name,root_dir+i))
   /* nothing */;
if (i >= 0) {
   ...
```

If it is, the inode number can be read directly from the table. In this case, the inode number `PROC_SELF` represents the directory `self/` and is replaced by an encoded form of the PID for the current process:

```
if (ino == 7) /* self modifying inode ... */
     ino = (current->pid << 16) + 2;
```

Otherwise, an attempt is made to convert the name into a number, which is then interpreted as the process number. This is followed by a check as to whether a matching process (still) exists; and if not, an error is returned. If it does exist, the process number is stored in the variable `ino`.

```
        ...
      {
          pid = string_to_integer(name);

          for (i = 0 ; i < NR_TASKS ; i++)
             if (task[i] && task[i]->pid == pid)
                break;
          if (!pid || i >= NR_TASKS) {
             iput(dir);
             return -ENOENT;
          }
          ino = (pid << 16) + 2;
      }
```

Now `iget()` is called again, to generate the inode. This function in turn calls the function `proc_read_inode()` described above with the relevant inode number.

```
      if (!(*result = iget(dir->i_sb,ino))) {
          iput(dir);
          return -ENOENT;
      }
      iput(dir);
      return 0;
} /* proc_lookuproot() */
```

If the requested inode is that of a process directory, the function finally returns an inode for which the inode operations are given in the structure `proc_base_inode_operations`. However, this structure in its turn contains only the components `readdir` and `lookup` to describe a directory.

This covers the representation of directories in a *Proc* file system, which only leaves the question of how normal files are created. By means of the function `proc_read_inode()`, the inode for most normal files is assigned the function vector `proc_array_inode_operations`. All that is implemented in this, however, is the function `array_read()` in the standard file operations to read the files.

If a process wishes, for example, to read the file `/proc/uptime`, it allocates a free page of memory to the function `array_read()` by calling `__get_free_page()` and passes it to the function `get_uptime()`. This in turn generates the content of the file by entering the required values in the memory page and returning the size of the buffer (in other words, the file). In the sources, this appears as follows:

```
static int get_uptime(char * buffer)
{
    unsigned long uptime;
    unsigned long idle;

    uptime = jiffies;
    idle = task[0]->utime + task[0]->stime;
#if HZ!=100
    return sprintf(buffer,"%lu.%02lu %lu.%02lu\n",
                uptime / HZ,
                (((uptime % HZ) * 100) / HZ) % 100,
                idle / HZ,
                (((idle % HZ) * 100) / HZ) % 100);
#else
    return sprintf(buffer,"%lu.%02lu %lu.%02lu\n",
                uptime / HZ,
                uptime % HZ,
                idle / HZ,
                idle % HZ);
#endif
}
```

The functions for the individual files are implemented in `fs/proc/array.c` or in the special sources. The function `get_module_list()` for the file `/proc/module`, for example, is located in the file `kernel/module.c` in the implementation of the module.

6.4   The *Ext2* file system

As LINUX was initially developed under MINIX, it is hardly surprising that the first LINUX file system was the MINIX file system. However, this file system restricts partitions to a maximum of 64 Mbytes and filenames to no more than 14 characters, so the search for a better file system was not long in starting. The result, in April 1992, was the *Ext* file system – the first to be designed especially for LINUX. Although this allowed partitions of up to 2 Gbytes and filenames up to 255 characters, it left the LINUX community far from satisfied as it was slower than its MINIX counterpart and the simple implementation of free block administration led to extensive fragmentation of the file system. A file system which is now little used was presented by Frank Xia in January 1993: the *Xia* file system. This is also based on the MINIX file system and permits partitions of up to 2 Gbytes in size along with filenames of up to

248 characters; but its administration of free blocks in bitmaps and optimizing block allocation functions make it faster and more robust than the *Ext* file system.

At about the same time, Rémy Card, Wayne Davidson and others presented the *Ext2* file system as a further development of the *Ext* file system. It can be considered by now to be *the* LINUX file system, as it is used in most LINUX systems and distributions.

6.4.1   The structure of the *Ext2* file system

The design of the *Ext2* file system was very much influenced by BSD's *Fast File System* (BSD FFS). Thus, a partition is divided into a number of *block groups*, corresponding to the cylinder groups in FFS, with each block group holding a copy of the superblock and inode and data blocks, as shown in Figure 6.4. The block groups are employed with the aim of keeping

- data blocks close to their inodes, and
- file inodes close to their directory inode

and thus reducing positioning time to a minimum, thereby speeding up access to data. As well as this, every group contains the superblock, along with information on all the block groups, allowing the file system to be restored in an emergency.

The physical superblock – defined as the structure `ext2_super_block` – is shown in Figure 6.5. It contains the control information on the file system, such as the number of inodes and blocks. The block size used is not held directly, but as the dual logarithm of the block size minus the minimum block size supported by the *Ext2* file system – in a standard case 0. To use this, all that needs to be done is to 'shift' the minimum block size `EXT2_MIN_BLOCK_SIZE` by the value given. In addition, the superblock includes information on the number of inodes and blocks per block group, along with the times of the last mount operation, the last write to the superblock and the last file system test.

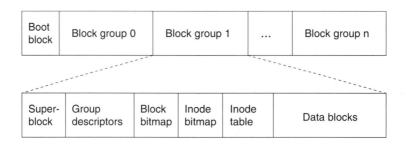

Figure 6.4   Structure of the *Ext2* file system.

	0	1	2	3	4	5	6	7
0	Number of inodes				Number of blocks			
8	Number of reserved blocks				Number of free blocks			
16	Number of free inodes				First data block			
24	Block size				Fragment size			
32	Blocks per group				Fragments per group			
40	Inodes per group				Time of mounting			
48	Time of last write				Status		Max. mount counter	
56	Ext2 signature		Status		Error behaviour		Pad word	
64	Time of last test				Max. test interval			
72	Operating system				File system revision			
80	RESUID		RESGID					

Figure 6.5   The superblock in the *Ext2* file system.

It also holds information on the behaviour of the file system in the event of errors, the maximum time interval to the next file system test, a mount counter and the maximum number of mount operations, which indicates when a mandatory file system test should be carried out. The values *resuid* and *resgid* specify which users or groups are allowed to use the reserved blocks in addition to the superuser.

The superblock is made up to a size of 1024 bytes – the minimum block size `EXT2_MIN_BLOCK_SIZE` – by inserting pad bytes. This makes it a simple matter both to use the space for expansions and to read the superblock using `bread()`.

The superblock is followed in each block group by the *block group descriptors*, which provide information on the block groups. Each block group is described by a 32-byte descriptor (*see* Figure 6.6). This contains the block numbers in the inode bitmap, block bitmap and inode table, the number of free inodes and blocks and the number of directories in this block group. The number of directories is used by the inode allocation algorithm for the directories, which attempts to spread directories as evenly as possible over the block groups – in other words, a new directory will be mounted in the block group with the smallest number of directories.

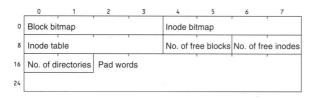

Figure 6.6   The block group descriptors in the *Ext2* file system.

The bitmaps are each the size of one block. This restricts the size of a block group to 8192 blocks for blocks of 1024 bytes.

The inode table for a block group lists consecutive blocks, starting with the one specified, and consists of inodes 128 bytes in size (*see* Figure 6.7). In addition to the data already mentioned, these contain the time when the file was deleted (to use in restoring deleted files), entries for ACLs (*Access Control Lists* to enable access permissions to be differentiated more precisely) and information specific to the operating system used. At present, ACLs are not implemented, which means that the function `ext2_permission()` tests only the UNIX permissions and the `S_IMMUTABLE` flag.

If the inode refers to a device file (that is, if `S_IFCHR` or `S_IFBLK` in `i_mode` is set) the first block number (`i_block[0]`) will give the device number. For a short symbolic link (`S_IFLNK`) the block numbers include the path, so that no additional data block is required and the 'number of blocks' field, `i_blocks`, will contain a value of zero. If the symbolic link is longer than

```
EXT2_N_BLOCKS * sizeof (long)
```

it will be stored in the first block. This limits the maximum length of a reference to the size of a block.

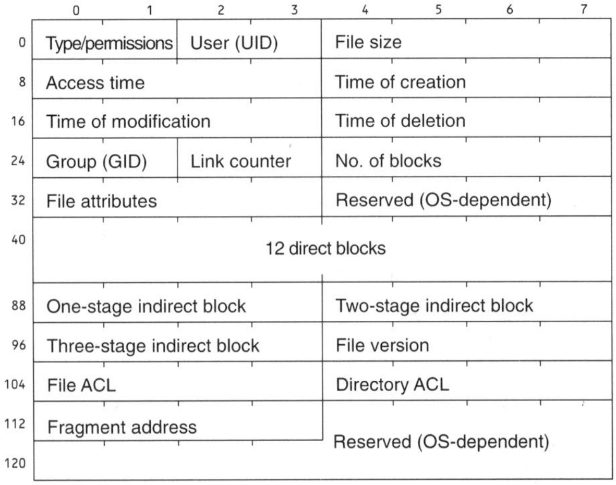

	0	1	2	3	4	5	6	7
0	Type/permissions		User (UID)		File size			
8	Access time				Time of creation			
16	Time of modification				Time of deletion			
24	Group (GID)		Link counter		No. of blocks			
32	File attributes				Reserved (OS-dependent)			
40	12 direct blocks							
88	One-stage indirect block				Two-stage indirect block			
96	Three-stage indirect block				File version			
104	File ACL				Directory ACL			
112	Fragment address				Reserved (OS-dependent)			
120								

Figure 6.7 The inode in the *Ext2* file system.

6.4.2 Directories in the *Ext2* file system

In the *Ext2* file system, directories are administered using a singly linked list. Each entry in this list has the following structure.

Figure 6.8   A directory entry in the *Ext2* file system.

```
struct ext2_dir_entry {
    unsigned long   inode;     /* inode number                */
    unsigned short  rec_len;   /* length of directory entry   */
    unsigned short  name_len;  /* length of filename          */
    char            name[EXT2_NAME_LEN];  /* filename          */
};
```

The field `rec_len` contains the length of the current entry, and is always rounded up to a multiple of 4. This enables the start of the next entry to be calculated. The `name_len` field holds the length of the filename. It is perfectly possible for a directory entry to be longer than is required to store the filename. A possible structure is shown in Figure 6.8.

An entry is deleted by setting the inode number to zero and removing the directory entry from the linked list: that is, the previous entry is simply extended. This eliminates the need for shift operations in the directory, which might otherwise exceed the limits of the buffers. However, the 'lost space' is not wasted, but is reused when a new name is entered, either by overwriting an entry with a value of 0 or by using the additional space provided by removal of the link.

6.4.3   Block allocation in the *Ext2* file system

A problem commonly encountered in all file systems is the fragmentation of files – that is, the 'scattering' of files into small pieces as a result of the constant deleting and creating of new files. This problem is usually solved by the use of 'defragmentation programs', such as `defrag` for LINUX. Some file systems attempt to prevent fragmentation as far as possible by sophisticated systems of block allocation. The *Ext2* file system similarly uses two algorithms to limit the fragmentation of files.

- *Target-oriented allocation*
  This algorithm always looks for space for new data blocks in the area of a 'target block'. If this block is itself free, it is allocated. Otherwise, a free block is sought within 32 blocks of the target block, and if found, is allocated. If this fails, the block allocation routine tries to find a free block which is at least in the same block group as the target block. Only after these avenues have been exhausted are other block groups investigated.

- **Pre-allocation**

  If a free block is found, up to eight following blocks are reserved (if they are free). When the file is closed, the remaining blocks still reserved are released. This also guarantees that as many data blocks as possible are collected into one cluster. Pre-allocation of blocks can be deselected by removing the definition of EXT2_PREALLOCATE from the file <linux/ext2_fs.h>.

How is the target block itself determined? Let n be the relative number in the file of the block to be allocated and ι the logical block number of the last block allocated. The block allocation algorithm then applies the following heuristics in the order given:

- The last block allocated had the relative number n-1. The target block is therefore ι+1.

- All existing blocks in the file, starting at block number n-1, are scanned to confirm that they have been assigned logical blocks (that is, the block is not a 'gap'). The target block is given by the number ι of the first already allocated block found.

- The target block is the first block in the block group in which the inode for the file is located.

6.4.4 Extensions of the *Ext2* file system

The *Ext2* file system has additional file attributes beyond those which exist in standard UNIX file systems (*see* Table 6.4). In version 0.5a, which is current at the time of writing, these are:

EXT2_SECRM_FL

If a file has this attribute, its data blocks are first overwritten with random bytes before they are released via the truncate function. This ensures that the content of the file cannot possibly be restored after it has been deleted.

EXT2_UNRM_FL

This attribute will eventually be used to implement the restoration of deleted files. At present, however, this function is not implemented.

EXT2_COMPR_FL

This attribute will be used to indicate that the file has been compressed. Up to the present, online compression has not yet been implemented.

EXT2_SYNC_FL

If a file has this attribute, all write requests are performed synchronously, that is, not delayed by the buffer cache.

Table 6.4   File attributes in the *Ext2* file system
(n.i. = not yet implemented).

Macro	Value	Description
EXT2_SECRM_FL	1	Secure deletion
EXT2_UNRM_FL	2	Undelete (n.i.)
EXT2_COMPR_FL	4	Compressed file (n.i.)
EXT2_SYNC_FL	8	Synchronous write
EXT2_IMMUTABLE_FL	16	Unmodifiable file
EXT2_APPEND_FL	32	'Append only' file
EXT2_NODUMP_FL	64	Do not archive file

EXT2_IMMUTABLE_FL

Files with this attribute cannot be deleted or amended. Renaming and the setting up of further hard links are also prohibited. Even the superuser cannot modify the file so long as it possesses this attribute. Directories with this attribute cannot be changed – that is, no new files can be created or deleted. Existing files or subdirectories, however, can be modified as desired.

EXT2_APPEND_FL

As for the previous attribute, files with this attribute cannot be deleted, renamed or relinked. However, this attribute does allow a write to the file to add fresh data. Directories with this attribute will only allow new files to be created. These will inherit the EXT2_APPEND_FL attribute when they are created.

EXT2_NODUMP_FL

This attribute is not used by the kernel. It is intended to be used to mark files which are not required in a backup.

However, these attributes can be changed using the `chattr` program. The program `lsattr` displays them.

The development of the *Ext2* file system is not yet complete. The list of planned expansions includes:

- restoration of deleted files,
- ACLs, and
- automatic file compression.

7 Device drivers under LINUX

*A computer terminal is not an old lump of a television
with a typewriter keyboard sitting in front of it.
It is an interface
connecting body and spirit with the universe
and enabling bits of it to be moved around.*

Douglas Adams

There is a wide variety of hardware available for LINUX computers. This means that a wide variety of software is required to operate this hardware. This is the job of device drivers. Without these, an operating system like LINUX would have no means of input or output (such as a keyboard and a monitor) and no file systems. Device drivers are the nuts and bolts of any operating system.

In addition, the computer hardware in UNIX systems is meant to be hidden from the user, without limiting its functions. This is done by having physical devices represented by files, which allows portable programs to be developed that can access both the various devices and the files with the same system calls, for example *read* and *write*. To handle this, device drivers are integrated into the LINUX kernel and given exclusive control of the hardware.

As a result, if a device driver has been properly implemented, the corresponding device can never be used wrongly by the user. This *protective function* of a device driver should not be underestimated.

In this chapter, we shall demonstrate the functioning and the correct implementation of device drivers. The example chosen is the PC speaker driver, which supports the output of sound samples to the internal speaker or a digital–analog converter connected to the parallel interface. It is also designed to be compatible with the sound card driver.

As a number of device drivers have to exist side by side in the LINUX kernel, they are uniquely identified by their *major numbers*. A device driver may be controlling a number of physical and virtual devices, for example a number of hard disks and partitions; thus, the individual device is accessed via its *minor number*, an integer between 0 and 255.

The exception to this rule is the device driver for terminals and serial interfaces, which uses the two major numbers 4 and 5. The devices with the major number 4 are virtual consoles, simple serial interfaces (call-in devices) and *pseudoterminals*.[1] Virtual consoles are given the minor numbers 0 (for tty0) to 63. The special device /dev/tty0 or /dev/console is always the current virtual console.

For every serial interface there are two logical devices, the *dial-in device* ttyS*n* and the *call-out device* cua*n*. When the dial-in device is opened, a process, such as getty, will be blocked until the DTR line at the interface is active. A process opening the call-out device, usually a dial-out program, will be given immediate access to the serial interface if no other process is using it. This will also continue to block a process wishing to open the dial-in device. The serial dial-in devices are given the minor numbers 64 (for ttyS0) to 127.

The remaining minor numbers from 128 to 255 are used for pseudo-terminals. The master terminal pty*n* is given the minor number 128+*n*, while the corresponding slave terminal ttyp*n* has the minor number 192+*n*.

Major number 5 is reserved for the current terminal and for the call-out devices. The device /dev/tty with the minor number 0 is always the terminal belonging to the process. The call-out devices cua*n* have the corresponding minor numbers 64+*n* and thus differ from their 'twins' only in their major numbers.

In the same way as for file systems, device drivers need to be made known to the LINUX kernel. This is done when the system is started up or when the driver modules are initialized, and uses one of the functions

```
int register_chrdev(unsigned int major,
                    const char * name,
                    struct file_operations *fops);
int register_blkdev(unsigned int major,
                    const char * name,
                    struct file_operations *fops);
```

The file operations specified and their symbolic names are entered under the major numbers given in the table chrdevs[] (for character devices) or

---

[1] Pseudoterminals are pairs of master and slave terminals, acting together like one terminal unit. The slave terminal is the interface, acting like a terminal unit as far as the user program is concerned, while the master represents the other end of the link (on a terminal, this is the user) (*see* Stevens (1992b)).

`blkdevs[]` (for block devices). If a driver is already registered under the major number given and if the file operations installed do not match those that have been registered, `register_chrdev()` will return a negative value.

If the major number is 0, the highest available free entry in the table is located and its index returned as the new major number. This allows unused major numbers to be allocated during the development of special drivers. Some of the major numbers which are at present firmly assigned are shown in Table 7.1; a complete list is contained in the file `Documentation/devices.txt`. When a driver is published, it should be registered with the LINUX *Device Registrar*,[2] who will then issue an official major number not used by any other device driver. For example, the PC speaker driver discussed below was given the major number 13 to avoid conflicts with the more recent iBCS2.

7.1 Character and block devices

There are two basic types of device: block-oriented devices and character-oriented devices.[3]

Block devices are those to which there is random access, which means that any block can be read or written to at will. Under LINUX, these read and write accesses are handled transparently by the cache. Random access is an absolute necessity for file systems, which means that they can only be mounted on block devices.

Character devices, on the other hand, are devices which can usually only be processed sequentially and are therefore accessed without a buffer. This class includes the commonest hardware, such as sound cards, scanners, printers and so on, even where their internal operation uses blocks.[4] These blocks, however, are sequential in nature, and cannot be accessed randomly.

Beyond this, LINUX deviates a little from the general UNIX philosophy, as it does not draw such a strict distinction between block and character devices. Thus, in other UNIX systems there are character devices corresponding to each of the block devices – that is, character-oriented interfaces to block devices which are principally used to control[5] the device itself. In LINUX, the interface (VFS) to block and character devices is the same, which means that no additional character devices are required.

---

[2] After a period when this position was without an incumbent, the job has now been taken over by H. Peter Anvin (`Peter.Anvin@linux.org`).

[3] Referred to below simply as 'block devices' and 'character devices'.

[4] If large amounts of data need to be transferred, block transfer, for example DMA, is preferable.

[5] Control programs for block devices in other UNIX systems, such as `mkfs` or `fsck`, operate on the corresponding character-oriented *raw device*.

Table 7.1   Excerpt from the LINUX major numbers list.

Major	Character devices	Block devices
0	*unnamed* for NFS, network and so on	
1	Memory devices (mem)	RAM disk
2		Floppy disks (fd*)
3		IDE hard disks (hd*)
4	Terminals	
5	Terminals & AUX	
6	Parallel interfaces	
7	Virtual consoles (vcs*)	
8		SCSI hard disks (sd*)
9	SCSI tapes (st*)	
10	Bus mice (bm, psaux)	
11		SCSI CD-ROM (scd*)
12	QIC02 tape	
13	PC speaker driver	XT 8-bit hard disks (xd*)
14	Sound cards	BIOS hard disk support
15	Joystick	Cdu31a/33a CD-ROM
16, 17, 18	*not used*	
19	Cyclades drivers	DouBle compressing driver
20	Cyclades drivers	
21	SCSI generic	
22		2nd IDE interface driver
23		Mitsumi CD-ROM (mcd*)
24		Sony 535 CD-ROM
25		Matsushita CD-ROM 1
26		Matsushita CD-ROM 2
27	QIC117 tape	Matsushita CD-ROM 3
28		Matsushita CD-ROM 4
29	Frame buffer drivers	Other CD-ROMs
30	iCBS2	Philips LMS-205 CD-ROM

Each individual device can thus be uniquely identified by the device type (block or character), the major number of the device driver and its minor number. Setting up a device therefore simply requires the command:

```
# mknod /dev/name type major minor
```

with the device type (*type*) set to b or c.

If additional hardware is to be accessed under LINUX, this will generally mean developing a character device driver, as character-oriented hardware makes up the majority.

7.2 Polling and interrupts

Where the synchronization of processor and hardware is concerned, there are a number of requirements. Although the hardware is as a rule very slow compared with the processor, specific access times have to be maintained for some devices. There are essentially two ways of achieving this.

7.2.1 Polling mode

In *polling*, the driver constantly interrogates the hardware. This results in pointless wasting of processor time; but it is sometimes the fastest way of communicating with the hardware.

The device driver for the parallel interface works by polling as the default option (*see* Section 2.3). It thus interrogates the interface (in this case, the interface's status port) until it is ready to accept a further lpchar character, and then passes this character to the interface. In the sources, this procedure looks like this:

```
#define LP_B(minor)    lp_table[(minor)].base    /* IO address  */
#define LP_S(minor)    inb_p(LP_B((minor)) + 1) /* status port */
#define LP_CHAR(minor) lp_table[(minor)].chars  /* busy timeout */

static int lp_char_polled(char lpchar, int minor)
{
   int status, wait = 0;
   unsigned long count = 0;
   struct lp_stats *stats

   do {
      status = LP_S(minor);
      count ++;
      if(need_resched)
         schedule();
   } while(!LP_READY(minor,sta tus) && count < LP_CHAR(minor));

   if (count == LP_CHAR(minor)) {
      return 0;
      /* Timeout, current character not printed */
   }
   outb_p(lpchar, LP_B(minor));
   ...

   return 1;
}
```

The polling count is kept to enable an error in the data terminal device to be detected (in most cases, this will be a printer). It constitutes the timeout and means that the last character has not been sent. The timeout error handling will then result in one of the messages 'lp*n* off-line', 'lp*n* out of paper' or 'lp*n* reported invalid error status (on fire, eh?)'. The LP_CHAR(minor) count is set by default to LP_INIT_CHAR and can be changed by the system call *ioctl*.

7.2.2 Interrupt mode

The use of *interrupts*, on the other hand, is only possible if these are supported by the hardware. Here, the device informs the CPU via an interrupt channel (IRQ) that it has finished an operation. This breaks into the current operation and carries out an interrupt service routine (ISR). Further communication with the device then takes place within the ISR.

Thus, a process attempting to write to the parallel interface in interrupt mode is halted by the device driver by means of the function

```
interruptible_sleep_on(&lp->lp_wait_q);
```

after a character has been written. If the parallel interface is able to accept more characters, it triggers an IRQ. The ISR handling the procedure then wakes up the process and the procedure is repeated. This keeps the ISR very simple.

```
static void lp_interrupt(int irq, void *dev_id
                         struct pr_regs *regs)
{
   struct lp_struct *lp = &lp_table[0];

   while (irq != lp->irq) {
      if (++lp >= &lp_table[LP_NO])
         return;
   }

   wake_up(&lp->lp_wait_q);
}
```

First, the interface that triggered the interrupt is determined, and then the waiting process is brought back to life with wake_up().

A second example is the serial mouse, every movement of which sends data to the serial port, triggering an IRQ. The data from the serial port is read first by the handling ISR, which passes it through to the application program.

IRQs are installed using the function

```
int request_irq(unsigned int irq,
                void (*handler)(int, struct pt_regs *),
                unsigned long irqflags, const char * devname
                void *dev_id)
```

As was mentioned in Section 3.2.4, there are two ways of processing IRQs under LINUX. The argument `irqflags` specifies which type of interrupt is to be used. Slow interrupts run with the interrupt flag set, which means that they can be interrupted in turn by other interrupts. On completion of a slow interrupt the same algorithm is used as on termination of a system call (*see* `ret_from_syscall`). Fast interrupts, however, run with the interrupt flag off. This means that if other interrupts are to be permitted in a fast interrupt routine, this must be achieved by calling the macro `sti()`. As well as this, the only registers saved to the stack are those used as standard in C routines, leaving the programmer of assembler routines responsible for saving registers used in the routine. Fast interrupt routines terminate with an `iret` instruction and return directly to the interrupted process.

Slow IRQs are installed without the `SA_INTERRUPT` flag in the `irqflags` argument; fast IRQs with the `SA_INTERRUPT` flag. The argument `name` has no particular significance for the kernel, but is used by the *Proc* file system to indicate the owner of an IRQ. It should therefore point to the name of the driver using the IRQ. The argument `dec_id` is passed to the interrupt routine unchanged and can thus be used to pass additional data. If the IRQ was found to be free and has been taken, `request_irq()` returns 0.

The handling routine for an IRQ looks like this:

```
void do_irq(int irq, void *dev_id, struct pt_regs * regs);
```

The first argument for any ISR is the number of the IRQ calling the function. This means that, in theory, one ISR can be used for a number of IRQs. The second argument is the `dev_id` pointer described above, while the last argument is a pointer to the structure `pt_regs` and contains all the registers for the process interrupted by the IRQ. This allows the timer interrupt to determine, for example, whether a process has been interrupted in kernel or user mode and to increment the corresponding time for accounting. Fast interrupts are only passed a `NULL`.

An example will demonstrate the installation of a fast interrupt – the `lp_interrupt` described above:

```
ret = request_irq(irq, lp_interrupt, SA_INTERRUPT,
                  "printer", NULL);
```

```
if (ret) {
    ...
    printk("lp%d unable to use interrupt %d, error %d\n", \
                                    minor, irq, ret);
    ...
    return ret;
}
```

It is usually fast interrupts that will be used for communicating with the hardware.

7.2.3 Interrupt sharing

The number of free IRQs in a PC is limited. Thus it can be sensible for various pieces of hardware to share interrupts. For PCI boards, this is mandatory.

The conditions required for such *interrupt sharing* are the possibility of interrogating the hardware as to whether it generated the current interrupt or not, and the capability of the ISR to forward an interrupt not triggered by its hardware.

LINUX version 2.0 supports interrupt sharing by its ability to build chains of interrupt handling routines. When an interrupt occurs, each ISR in the chain is called by the do_IRQ() or the do_fast_IRQ() function.

```
asmlinkage void do_IRQ(int irq, struct pt_regs * regs)
{
    struct irqaction * action = *(irq + irq_action);
    int do_random = 0;

    ...
    while (action) {
        do_random |= action->flags;
        action->handler(irq, action->dev_id, regs);
        action = action->next;
    }
    ...
}
```

If an ISR capable of interrupt sharing is installed, this must be communicated to the request_irq function by setting the SA_SHIRQ flag. If another ISR also capable of interrupt sharing was already installed on this IRQ number, a chain is built. However, it is not possible to mix slow and fast interrupts, that is, an IRQ's handling routines must all be of the same type. As an example, we show a fragment of the DE4x5 Ethernet driver.

```
...
request_irq(dev->irq, (void *)de4x5_interrupt, SA_SHIRQ,
            lp->adapter_name, dev)
...

static void de4x5_interrupt(int irq, void *dev_id,
                struct pt_regs *regs)
{
   ...
   sts = inl(DE4X5_STS);        /* read IRQ status register */
   outl(sts, DE4X5_STS);        /* reset board interrupts   */
   if (!(sts & lp->irq_mask)) break;/* not from board, ready */
   ...
}
```

7.2.4 Bottom halves

However, it frequently happens that not all the functions need to be performed immediately after an interrupt occurs; although 'important' actions need to be taken care of at once, others can be handled later or would take a relatively long time and it is preferable not to block the interrupt. For cases like this, *bottom halves* have been created. After every `ret_from_syscall`, that is, after every slow interrupt, if no further interrupt is running at the time,[6] a list of up to 32 bottom halves is scanned. If they are marked as active, they are each carried out once in turn and then automatically marked as inactive. These bottom halves are atomic, that is, as long as one bottom half is active, none of the others can be performed, so that it is not necessary to use `cli()` to protect them against interruptions.

The function to install a bottom half is `init_bh` which enters the bottom half into the function pointer table `bh_base`.

```
void init_bh(int nr, void (*routine)(void));

enum {
   TIMER_BH = 0,
   CONSOLE_BH,
   TQUEUE_BH,
   DIGI_BH,
   SERIAL_BH,
   RISCOM8_BH,
   BAYCOM_BH,
   NET_BH,
```

---

[6] This can easily happen, for example, if one slow interrupt is interrupted by another.

```
    IMMEDIATE_BH,
    KEYBOARD_BH,
    CYCLADES_BH,
    CM206_BH
};
```

In older Linux versions the bottom halves were entered 'manually' into a `bh_struct` structure; in addition, they could also be passed a pointer to any desired data as an argument. By default, all bottom halves are permitted, but they can be switched off and back on again using the functions

```
void disable_bh(int nr);
void enable_bh(int nr);
```

The function

```
void mark_bh(int nr);
```

marks a bottom half, so that this bottom half is performed at the next available opportunity.

We will now examine how bottom halves are used, taking as an example the keyboard driver.

```
static void keyboard_interrupt(int int_pt_regs)
{
    ...
    mark_bh(KEYBOARD_BH);     /* kbd_bh() is marked */
    ...
}

static void kbd_bh(void * unused)
{
    unsigned char leds = getleds();

    if (leds != ledstate) {
        ledstate = leds;
        ...
    }
}

unsigned long kbd_init(unsigned long kmem_start)
{
    ...
    request_irq(KEYBOARD_IRQ, keyboard_interrupt,
                0, "keyboard", NULL);
    ...
```

```
/* keyboard bottom half is initialized */
/* and immediately marked              */
 init_bh(KEYBOARD_BH, kbd_bh);
 mark_bh(KEYBOARD_BH);
 ...
}
```

The init function of the keyboard driver installs `kbd_bh()` as the bottom half and `keyboard_interrupt()` as a slow interrupt. On every call to the keyboard interrupt, `mark_bh(KEYBOARD_BH)` is called – that is, the bottom half is run at the first opportunity after completion of the keyboard interrupt, in this case immediately after it. The keyboard bottom half, however, only updates the keyboard LEDs.

7.2.5   Task queues

As the previous section shows, direct use of bottom halves is somewhat difficult because their number is limited to only 32, and some tasks are already assigned to fixed numbers. In version 2.0, LINUX therefore offers *task queues* as a dynamic extension of the concept of bottom halves.

Task queues allow an arbitrary number of functions to be entered in a queue and processed one after another at a later time. Chaining of the functions to be executed is carried out by means of the `tq_struct` structure.

```
struct tq_struct {
    struct tq_struct *next;  /* pointer to next entry      */
    int sync;                /* synchronization flag       */
    void (*routine)(void *); /* function to be called      */
    void *data;              /* arbitrary function argument */
};

typedef struct tq_struct * task_queue;
```

Before a function can be entered in a task queue, a `tq_struct` structure must be created and initialized. The `routine` component contains the address of the function to be called, while `data` holds an arbitrary argument to be passed to the function at call time. The `sync` component must be initialized to 0. Insertion into a task queue is carried out by means of one of the following functions:

```
void queue_task(struct tq_struct *bh_pointer, task_queue *bh_list)
{
    if (!set_bit(0,&bh_pointer->sync)) {
        unsigned long flags;
        save_flags(flags);
```

```
        cli();
        bh_pointer->next = *bh_list;
        *bh_list = bh_pointer;
        restore_flags(flags);
    }
}

void queue_task_irq(struct tq_struct *bh_pointer,
                    task_queue *bh_list)
{
    if (!set_bit(0,&bh_pointer->sync)) {
        bh_pointer->next = *bh_list;
        *bh_list = bh_pointer;
    }
}

void queue_task_irq_off(struct tq_struct *bh_pointer,
                    task_queue *bh_list)
{
    if (!(bh_pointer->sync & 1)) {
        bh_pointer->sync = 1;
        bh_pointer->next = *bh_list;
        *bh_list = bh_pointer;
    }
}
```

The application areas of these functions are reflected in their implementation. The `sync` component of the `tq_struct` structure is used for synchronization. It is set when the structure has been insterted into a task queue, thus preventing insertion into a further task queue.

The easiest case occurs when interrupts are disabled. Then it is sufficient to check whether `sync` is already set. Therefore the `queue_task_irq_off()` function may only be called when the interrupt flag is switched off. It is possible that inside an interrupt service routine an additional ISR may be called, but no bottom half handler. Thus it is sufficient to carry out checking and setting of the `sync` flag in an atomic way. This is achieved by the implementation of the `queue_task_irq()` function which must only be called from within interrupt routines or with disabled interrupts. `queue_task()`, on the other hand, can be called at any point because insertion into the task queue is protected by the `cli()` macro.

The function `run_task_queue()` takes care of processing a task queue.

```
void run_task_queue(task_queue *list)
{
    struct tq_struct *p;
```

```
p = xchg(list,NULL);
while (p) {
   void *arg;
   void (*f) (void *);
   struct tq_struct *save_p;
   arg    = p -> data; f = p -> routine;
   save_p = p;
   p      = p -> next;
   save_p -> sync = 0;
   (*f)(arg);
}
}
```

It takes a task queue as argument and processes all `tq_struct` structures inserted in the queue by calling their functions. Before the function is called, the `sync` flag is cancelled, so that within this function it would again be possible to insert the `tq_struct` structure into an arbitrary task queue.

In Linux version 2.0 the following task queues are defined:

- **`tq_timer`**
  is called after each timer interrupt or processed at the next possible point in time after a timer interrupt.

- **`tq_immediate`**
  is called at the next possible point in time after a call of the function `mark_bh(IMMEDIATE_BH)` and thus corresponds to the bottom halves of version 1.x.

- **`tq_scheduler`**
  is called within the scheduler before a task change is carried out.

- **`tq_disk`**
  is used by block devices and called at different points where the VFS must wait for incoming buffers or similar.

`tq_disk` shows that task queues need not necessarily be linked only to bottom halves. Task queues are implemented as pointers to a `tq_struct` structure and should be declared by means of the `DECLARE_TASK_QUEUE()` macro. They can be processed at any point by calling the function `run_task_queue()`. Processing of task queues inside interrupt service routines should, however, be avoided to prevent interrupts from being blocked for an unnecessarily long time.

7.2.6 DMA mode

When particularly large volumes of data are being *continuously* transported to or from a device, DMA mode is an option. In this mode, the *DMA controller* transfers the data directly from memory to a device without involving the processor. The device will generally trigger an IRQ after the transfer, so that the next DMA transfer can be prepared in the ISR handling the procedure. This mode is ideal for multi-tasking, as the CPU can take care of other tasks during the data transfer. Unfortunately, there are a number of devices suitable for DMA operation which do not support IRQs; some hand-held scanners fall into this category. In device drivers written for this class of device, the DMA controller must be polled to check for the end of a transfer.

As well as this, DMA operation of devices throws up quite a different set of problems, deriving in part from compatibility with the 'original' PCs.

- As the DMA controller works independently of the processor, it can only access physical addresses.

- The base address register in the DMA controller is only 16 bits wide, which means that DMA transfers cannot be carried out beyond a 64 Kbyte boundary. As the first controller in the AT performs an 8-bit transfer, no more than 64 Kbytes at a time can be transferred using the first four DMA channels. The second controller in the AT performs a 16-bit transfer – that is, two bytes are transferred in each cycle. As the base register for this is also only 16 bits wide, the second controller attaches a zero, meaning that the transfer must always start at an even address (in other words, the contents of the register are multiplied by 2). This allows the second controller to transfer a maximum of 128 Kbytes, but not to go over any 128 Kbyte boundary.

- In addition to the base address register, there is a DMA page register to take care of address bits from A15 upwards. As this register is only 8 bits wide in the AT, the DMA transfer can only be carried out within the first 16 Mbytes. Although this restriction was removed by the EISA bus and a number of chip sets (but not, unfortunately, in a compatible way), LINUX does not support this.

To overcome this problem, the sound driver of earlier LINUX versions, for example, reserved the buffer for DMA transfer to the sound card by means of a special function.

As the physical addresses required in protected mode interfere with the DMA concept, DMA can only be used by the operating system and device drivers. Accordingly, the sound driver first copies the data to the DMA buffer with the aid of the processor, and then transfers them to the sound card via DMA. Although this procedure is in conflict with the idea of transferring data without involving the processor, it nevertheless makes sense, as it means that attention does not have to be given to timing when transferring data to the sound card or other devices. We take a more detailed look at the use of DMA below.

7.3   The hardware

If we are proposing to write a device driver for the internal loudspeaker, we cannot avoid taking a closer look at the hardware concerned and its control system.

Although it has been part of the package since the earliest days of the PC, the internal speaker is not well suited to reproducing samples. As Figure 7.1 shows, the construction and programming of the speaker are both very simple.

The 8253 timer chip has three internal timers. Timer 2 is designed for use with the speaker, for which the output from timer 2 is connected via an AND gate to bit 1 of the system control latch at I/O address 0x61, with bit 0 used for starting or restarting timer 2. Thus the speaker can only be fully turned on or switched off. The normal procedure is for timer 2 to be programmed as a frequency divider (meaning that both bits are set). This generates square waves, which account for the 'typical' sound of the internal speaker. The frequency is given by dividing the timer's basic frequency of 1.193 MHz (= 4.77 MHz/4) by the timer constant that has been set.

To output an analog signal via the speaker, pulse-length modulation is employed. By rapid variation between on and off phases of different lengths, corresponding to the instantaneous analog value to be output, the mechanical inertia of the speaker can be exploited to give an analog output. However, pulse-length modulation is very sensitive: even one missing sample will produce an annoying click from the speaker.[7]

The central problem in using pulse-length modulation proves to lie in determining and implementing the required time intervals. The first possibility

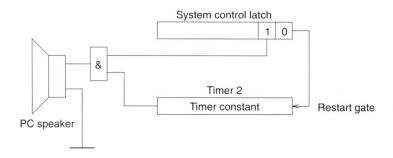

Figure 7.1   Block diagram of PC speaker connections.

---

[7] This also accounts for the extraneous noise sometimes accompanying floppy disk access or even mouse movements. If even a single interrupt fails to be handled, the dynamics of the speaker break down.

is not to use timer 2 at all and control the output entirely with bit 1 of the system control latch. The time intervals can be generated by wait loops. This approach is the simplest to implement, but has two decisive drawbacks:

- The delay loops depend on the processor clock.
- Most of the time during output is spent on *busy waiting*; this is not acceptable in a multi-tasking operating system.

The second approach consists in programming timer 2 as a *retriggerable one-shot*. The timer is started by applying a 1 to the restart gate and produces 0 at the output. Once the timer constant has counted down, 1 is output. After a certain time, corresponding to the maximum sample value, a new constant is transferred to timer 2 and the timer is restarted. This constant time interval can then be generated again using a delay loop or timer 0, which generally runs in divider mode and generates an IRQ of 0 each time the timer constant reaches 0. This frequency generated by timer 0 is also the sampling rate at which the samples can be output. We shall refer to it below as the *real sampling rate*. Timer 2 must then be reinitialized in the interrupt handling routine. This procedure is shown in Figure 7.2.

The timer chip has four I/O ports. Port 0x43 is the mode control register. Data ports 0x40 to 0x42 are assigned to timers 0 to 2. This means that to program a timer, an instruction must be written to 0x43 and the timer constant to the appropriate data port. An instruction is very simple in structure: bits 7 and 6 contain the number of the timer to be programmed, bits 5 and 4 one of the access modes shown in Table 7.2 and bits 3 to 1 the timer mode. For example, to generate a 10 000 Hz tone the following steps are required:

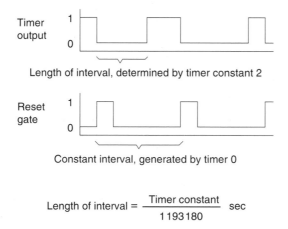

$$\text{Length of interval} = \frac{\text{Timer constant}}{1\,193\,180} \text{ sec}$$

Figure 7.2 Pulse-length modulation using timers 0 and 2.

Table 7.2 Bits 4 and 5 in the timer instruction.

Bits 54	Mode	Description
00	Latch	Counter is transferred to an internal register and can then be read out
01	LSB only	Only the bottom 8 bits of the counter are transferred
10	MSB only	Only the top 8 bits of the counter are transferred
11	LSB/MSB	First the bottom 8 bits of the counter are transferred, then the top 8 bits

```
outb_p (inb_p (0x61) | 3, 0x61);
    /* opens the AND gate and                            */
    /* sets the restart gate to active                   */
tc = 1193180 / 10000;
    /* calculates the timer constant required            */
outb_p (0xb6, 0x43);
    /* corresponds to the instruction:                   */
    /*   timer 2, read/write LSB then MSB, timer mode 3  */
outb_p (tc & 0xff, 0x42); outb ((tc >> 8) & 0xff, 0x42);
    /* writes the time constant to timer 2;              */
    /* from now on the internal loudspeaker will emit a tone */
```

The speaker can be silenced by:

```
outb(inb_p(0x61) & 0xfc, 0x61);
```

This switches off the speaker as well as halting the timer.

Unfortunately, only timer 0 can generate an interrupt in a standard PC, which means that the second possibility described above is not entirely without danger, since the timer interrupt IRQ 0, which is so important under LINUX, is modified. The new interrupt routine must ensure that the original procedure is called again at exactly the same intervals. In addition, interrupt handling in protected mode needs considerably more time than in real mode, so that the larger number of interrupts triggered consumes noticeably more computing time.

Let us now return to pulse-length modulation. As mentioned earlier, the choice of time interval is very important. Tests have shown that the best results are achieved with a real sampling rate between 16 000 and 18 000 Hz. The higher the sampling rate the better, as this specific frequency is audible as a whistling.[8] When using timer 2, these frequencies give possible timer constants between 1 and 74 (a 0 would mean 65 536 and is therefore not admissible); so, as the constants are directly related to the samples, only six bits (1–65) can be output.

The maximum value possible for the real sampling rate is thus 18 357 Hz (or 1.193 MHz/65). However, this is not a very widely used figure; therefore other sampling rates are supported by generating and adding in extra samples (*oversampling*). For considerations of time, a simple algorithm arranges for the data to be 'stretched' by repeating each of the samples.[9] For example, if the output is to be at 10 000 Hz, each sample will need to be repeated on average about 1.8 times.

Compared with this, output via a digital–analog converter (DAC) is very straightforward. This simply connects to a parallel port and converts the incoming 8-bit sequence to an analog signal. As the parallel port buffers the incoming values, the structure of a DAC can be very elementary, and in the most basic version it just consists of a resistor network. The parallel port can also output the data at virtually any speed, so timer 0 can be programmed with the true sampling rate.

This solution also avoids the need to transform the samples into a 6-bit representation; output via a DAC thus makes less demand on processor time than output via the internal speaker. And the final 'plus' is that missing interrupts only make themselves felt as a slow-down in the output sound and are in practice as good as inaudible (within certain limits).

7.3.1 Hardware detection

Although speakers in PCs are always at the same port addresses, this need not be the case for all varieties of add-on hardware. As the design of the ISA bus limits the number of possible port addresses,[10] there can be address overlaps. Probably the most common example is the occupation of the I/O address of the COM4 interface by ISA cards with the S3 chip.

Also, developments in the market have resulted in widely differing hardware using the same I/O address ranges. Usually it is possible to select different base addresses by means of *jumpers*. Although there is often a good reason for this, it confuses less experienced users, as the documentation generally merely

---

[8] The point at which this frequency becomes audible depends on the individual: I start hearing it from about 14 500 Hz onwards, others hear it as far as 17 000 Hz.

[9] Normally, the extra samples would be calculated by interpolation. However, this will not produce any improvement in quality when using the internal speaker for the output.

[10] Only the first 10 bits of a port address lie on the bus. This means that all 65 536 possible port addresses are mapped to the range 0–0x3ff.

notes that 'the default configuration will usually be found to work without problem; if not, jumper XX should be moved to position YY'.

In developing a driver, then, the 'safe option' is always available: all the parameters are fixed before compilation. This is very safe, but not very convenient. Who wants to recompile the kernel every time a jumper has been shifted?

What is needed, therefore, are algorithms that 'detect' the hardware. Ideally, it should be possible to detect the hardware simply by reading the I/O ports, but unfortunately the development of new hardware cuts out this option. There is no choice but to write values at random, read the I/O ports and make a decision on this basis. This generally makes use of certain peculiarities of specific chips (the so-called 'unused features', meaning bugs), which can then result in a failure to detect compatible hardware from another manufacturer.

However, by far the most awkward problem is that this 'test writing' can obstruct the operation of other hardware and ultimately cause the system to crash. The second of these frequently occurs during the development of a driver, as it is only much later that the failure of another device is noticed ....

For this reason, LINUX allows I/O address ranges to be blocked. One way of doing this is to pass a boot parameter to the kernel on start-up containing all the blocked regions. If the system will not run after a new card has been fitted, the first thing to try is to deactivate the address range for this card. A fictional example will help to explain this.

Suppose a scanner card occupies addresses 0x300–0x30f (where there could also be a network card). This area is cut out using the boot parameter

```
reserve=0x300,0x10
```

Thus, if a device driver wishes to test I/O ports, it should first obtain permission for this by calling the function check_region(). To follow this, we will look at a fragment of the skeleton for network drivers.

```
#include <linux/ioport.h>

netcard_probe(struct device *dev)
{
    ...
    for (i = 0; netcard_portlist[i]; i++) {
        int ioaddr = netcard_portlist[i];
        if (check_region(ioaddr, NETCARD_IO_EXTENT))
            continue;
        if (netcard_probe1(dev, ioaddr) == 0)
            return 0;
    }

    return ENODEV;
}
```

If `check_region()` returns a value not equal to 0, at least one port in this region is closed to access and the test should be omitted.

In addition, a driver should block the I/O ports belonging to its hardware, so that they cannot be accessed by other drivers. The corresponding function[11]

```
void request_region(unsigned int from, unsigned int num,
                    const char * name);
```

expects as parameters the number of the first I/O port to be blocked, the number of ports to be blocked and the name of the driver blocking the ports. The name of the driver is only used by the *Proc* file system, enabling the user/programmer to find out which ports are being used by which driver. As modules can also be removed, they must release their I/O ports afterwards, as they would otherwise lock themselves out the next time they attempt to load. Releasing is carried out by the function

```
release_region(unsigned int from, unsigned int num);
```

This still leaves us with the problems of detecting IRQ and DMA channels. The first of these, however, can easily be taken care of under LINUX.

7.3.2   Automatic interrupt detection

On many expansion cards, the IRQ used has to be set by means of jumpers. Only the latest expansions, such as PCI or *Plug-and-Play*, allow the configuration of the expansion card to be set up and read out. As a result, programmers are often faced with the problem of determining the IRQs used during kernel initialization. However, as automatic interrupt detection constitutes a factor of insecurity and can lead to a system crash, it should be avoided during the loading of modules.

The methodology for detecting IRQs used is always the same, and simply involves assigning all possible IRQs and 'forcing' the relevant device or expansion card to trigger an IRQ. If only one of the previously assigned IRQs is triggered, the answer has in all probability been found. All that remains is to release all the other IRQs.

However, LINUX provides functions to simplify this search. Let us first take as an example a section of code from the PLIP driver.

```
unsigned int irqs = probe_irq_on();
                    /* switch on IRQ detection */
```

[11] In older versions of LINUX this function was called `snarf_region()`. It is, however, no longer supported.

```
outb(0x00, PAR_CONTROL(dev));
udelay(1000);
outb(PAR_INTR_OFF, PAR_CONTROL(dev));
outb(PAR_INTR_ON, PAR_CONTROL(dev));
outb(PAR_INTR_OFF, PAR_CONTROL(dev));
udelay(1000);

irq = probe_irq_off(irqs);   /* IRQ detection terminated */

if (irq > 0) {
   dev->irq = irq;
   printk("using probed IRQ %d.\n", dev->irq);
} else
   printk("failed to detect IRQ(%d) --"
          " Please set IRQ by ifconfig.\n", irq);
```

IRQ detection is selected by a call to the function `probe_irq_on()`. This returns in `irqs` a bit mask in which all those IRQ numbers currently free and used for detection are encoded, and then triggers an IRQ at the parallel interface. The `udelay()` function introduces a delay of 1000 microseconds in each case.[12] The call to `probe_irq_off()` then terminates IRQ detection. This call must be given as an argument the bit mask supplied by `probe_irq_on()` and will return the number of the IRQ which has occurred. If this number is less than zero, more than one IRQ has occurred. This may indicate a wrongly configured card or some other hardware conflict. The detection could now be tried once again or, as in the example, the assignment of IRQs can be left to the user. A value of 0 indicates that no IRQ has occurred, for example because no IRQ jumper has been set. In this case, too, the user will have to intervene. Only a positive return value indicates that an IRQ has been clearly detected.

The operation of the pair of functions `probe_irq_on()` and `probe_irq_off()` is very simple to describe and essentially follows the outline given above. The first, `probe_irq_on()`, uses the function `request_irq()` to activate all IRQs not yet taken, which while they were not yet allocated were marked neither as slow nor as fast interrupts, but as BAD. The handling routine for a BAD interrupt simply switches the interrupt off again in the interrupt controller. Then the function `probe_irq_on()` waits another 100 ms, thus intercepting interrupts which might occur without having been requested and returns the mask of all still legal IRQs. Thus, the `probe_irq_off()` function only needs to test for which IRQs allocated by `probe_irq_on()` have since been switched off again. This test is done by comparing the argument `irqs` with the bit masks for all currently active IRQs. If the two masks differ by

---

[12] For this, `udelay()` uses the BogoMips calculated at kernel start-up.

only one bit, only one BAD interrupt has been triggered and its number is easily determined. If there are several mismatches, or none, an error is returned.

Detecting DMA channels is more tricky. Fortunately, most cards only support a few DMA channels, or enable them to be selected via configuration registers. If this facility is not available, the DMA channel should be set using setup parameters. An alternative approach is simply to allocate all possible channels and trigger a DMA transfer. However, this will only work if the hardware provides a facility for checking whether the transfer is successful.

Finally, the way the PC speaker driver detects Stereo-on-Ones should be mentioned. As this was taken into account at the design stage (and the three possible parallel ports are fortunately at fixed addresses), this is very simple. Data bit 7 is connected to the control input BUSY. As this control signal is read inverted, the following function can be derived:

```
/* tests whether there is a Stereo-on-One at lp(port) */
inline static int stereo1_detect(unsigned port)
{
    outb(0, LP_B(port));
    if (LP_S(port) & 0x80) {
        outb(0xFF, LP_B(port));
        return (LP_S(port) & 0x80) ? 0 : 1;
    } return 0;
}
```

7.4   Implementing a driver

Now that the internal speaker's hardware has been discussed in detail, the question arises as to why a special device driver is required to take care of writing and reading at some I/O ports.

To generate 'noises' we could write a program auplay,[13] which would release the relevant ports by means of the system call *ioperm*:

```
if (ioperm(0x61,1,1) || ioperm(0x42,1,1) || ioperm(0x43,1,1)) {
  printf("can't get I/O permissions for internal speaker\n");
  exit(-1);
}
```

and then output the samples itself. However, this would have the following drawbacks:

---

[13] Rick Miller's auplay program provided the initial impetus for implementing a PC speaker driver.

- The *ioperm* system call only works successfully with privileged authorizations. The program thus requires the set UID rights assigned to `root`. As a rule, no programs with the `root` set UID rights should exist in UNIX systems, as they would present a major security problem. This can normally be guaranteed by setting up special users and groups (for example, the group `kmem` to use the device `/dev/kmem`), but it is difficult to avoid in our example.

  A device driver, on the other hand, operates with kernel authorizations and thus has free access to all resources – a fact which should always be borne in mind when implementing a driver, as errors in a driver could have more serious consequences than errors in a program.[14]

- Probably the main problem is precise time determination for a program in a multi-tasking system. The only way of doing this is to use wait loops of the type:

  ```
  for ( j = 1; j < DELAY; j++);
  ```

  This *busy waiting* is not acceptable, as no precise determination of the sampling rate is possible. Use of the timer interrupt is a distinctly more elegant variant, but can only be done in the kernel.

- Another problem is control of the PC speaker. Who guarantees that no other process will access the I/O ports at the same time and corrupt the sample? Using System V IPC here (in this case semaphores) is like using a sledgehammer to crack a nut, especially as there is no way of knowing whether other programs may be accessing the same ports.

  Compared with this, access restriction for devices is relatively simple and will be described below.

Writing an 'audio daemon' which will read the sampled data from a *named pipe* and be run via the file `rc.local` when the system is booted is only of limited help. The problem of coordinating the timing remains.

This makes a device driver the best option. The actual implementation of the PC speaker driver involves filling in the structure `file_operations` described in the previous chapter, although the programmer will not need to complete all the functions, depending on the type of device. A further procedure to initialize the driver must also be provided.

The names of these C functions should all be formed on the same principle to avoid conflicts with existing functions. The safest approach is to place an abbreviation for the name of the driver in front of the function name. This gives for the PC speaker driver, or 'pcsp' in short, the functions `pcsp_init()`, `pcsp_read()` and so on, which will be explained in detail below. The same principle should be applied for external and static C variables.

---

[14] This is only true up to a point, as incorrect use of the mode control register for I/O address 0x43 by the `auplay` program could confuse the timer interrupt and cause the computer to crash.

7.4.1 The setup function

Sometimes it is desirable to pass parameters to a device driver or to the LINUX kernel in general. This may be necessary where automatic detection of hardware is not possible or may result in conflicts with other hardware, and can be done using the LINUX boot parameters, which can be passed to the kernel during the boot process. As a rule, these parameters will come in the form of a command line from the LINUX loader LILO (*see* Section D.2.5).

This command line will be analysed into its component parts by the function parse_options(), which is located in init/main.c. The checksetup() function is called for each of the parameters and compares the beginning of the parameter with the string stored in the bootsetups[] field, calling the corresponding setup() function whenever these match. The structure of the parameter should be:

name=param1,...,paramn

The checksetup() function will attempt to convert the first ten parameters into integer numbers. If this is successful, they will be stored in a field. Index 0 in this field contains the number of converted parameters. The remainder of the line is simply passed on as a string. The setup function for the PC speaker driver will serve as an example here.

```
void pcsp_setup(char *s, int *p)
{
    if (!strcmp(s, "off")) {
        pcsp_enabled = 0;
        return;
    }
    if (p[0] > 0)
        pcsp.maxrate = p[1];
    pcsp_enabled = 1;
}
```

As this shows, the function first tests for the presence of the word 'off', and thus the boot parameter 'pcsp=off' switches the PC driver off. Otherwise, if the number of numerical parameters is not 0, the first parameter, p[1], is used to initialize a global variable in the PC speaker driver.

This function now needs to be registered. This involves entering it in the field bootsetups[], as the following lines illustrate.

```
struct {
    char *str;
    void (*setup_func)(char *, int *);
} bootsetups[] = {
    ...
```

```
#ifdef CONFIG_PCSP
    { "pcsp=", pcsp_setup },
#endif
    { 0, 0 }
};
```

When a `setup` function is used, it should always be called before the device driver is initialized using its `init()` function. This means that the `setup` function should only set global variables, which can then be evaluated by the `init` function.

7.4.2 `init`

The `init()` function is only called during kernel initialization, but is responsible for important tasks. This function tests for the presence of a device, generates internal device driver structures and registers the device.

The call to the `init` function must be carried out in one of the following functions,[15] depending on the type of device driver:

drivers/char/mem.c
> The initialization of the device drivers (for example terminals, parallel interfaces, first initialization of sound cards and so on) is handled by `chr_dev_init()`.

drivers/block/ll_rw_bl.c
> The initialization of the block drivers is handled by the function `blk_dev_init()`.

drivers/scsi/scsi.c
> The initialization of the SCSI devices is handled by `scsi_dev_init()`.

drivers/net/net_init.c
> The initialization of special 'exotic' network devices takes place in `net_dev_init()`.

Accordingly, the function `pcsp_init()` is called by the function `chr_dev_init` in the case we are considering.

```
void pcsp_init(void)
{
```

Before LINUX can make use of the driver, it must be registered using the function `register_chrdrv()`, which contains:

- the major number of the device driver,

---

[15] The functions are called in `device_setup()` (file `drivers/block/genhd.c`) in the order shown.

- the symbolic name of the device driver, and
- the address of the `file_operation` structure (in this case, `pcsp_fops`).

If a zero is returned, the new driver is registered. If the major number has already been taken by another device driver, `register_chrdrv()` returns the error `EBUSY`.

```
if (register_chrdev(PCSP_MAJOR, "pcsp", &pcsp_fops))
    printk("unable to get major %d for pcsp devices\n",PCSP_MAJOR);
else {
    printk("PCSP-device 1.0 init:\n");
    ...
```

In this case, an attempt can be made to allocate a free major number by giving the `register_chrdrv()` function a 0 as the major number. The function then scans the list of all major numbers, starting at `MAX_CHRDEV-1`, and registers the driver under the first free number, returning this number. If no free number can be found, `register_chrdrv()` returns the `EBUSY` error.

```
if (!register_chrdev(DEFAULT_MAJOR, "device", &device_ops))
    printk("Device registered.\n");
else {
    major = register_chrdev(0, "device", &device_ops));
    if (major > 0)
        printk("Device registered using major %d.\n", major);
    else {
        printk("Cannot register device!\n");
        ...
    }
}
```

The `init()` function is also the right place to test whether a device supported by the driver is present at all. This applies especially for devices which cannot be connected or changed during operation, such as hard disks. If no device can be found, *this is the time* for the driver to say so (failure to detect a device could also indicate a hardware fault, after all) and make sure that the device is not accessed later.

For example, if a CD-ROM driver is unable to find a CD drive, there is no point in the driver taking up memory for a buffer, as the drive cannot be added during the running of the program. For devices which can be connected at a later stage, the situation is different: if the PC speaker driver fails to detect a Stereo-on-One,[16] it will still permit it to be included afterwards.

---

[16] A Stereo-on-One is a simple stereo digital–analog converter designed by Mark J. Cox, which only occupies one parallel port and can be detected by software.

If one or more devices are detected, these should be initialized within the init function if necessary.

Prior to version 2.0, the highest address used by the kernel so far was passed as a parameter to the init function. This could be used to allocate memory for buffers quite easily, by just noting the address, increasing it by the required number of bytes and passing it back as a return value to the init() function. However, the area of memory allocated in this way was permanently occupied and also not paged out. This means that it could be used for interrupt buffers, but was otherwise unavailable for processes to use. Another disadvantage of this method was that it was incompatible with the module init function. Since version 2.0, init() is called without parameters, so that the same function can also be used as a module during loading of the driver. Because of the change in memory allocation possibilities since version 1.2, it is also no longer necessary to allocate buffers for DMA and non-swappable memory areas permanently.

7.4.3 open and release

The open function is responsible for administering all the devices and is called as soon as a process opens a device file. If only one process can work with a given device (as in the example we are following), -EBUSY should be returned. If a device can be used by a number of processes at the same time, open() should set up the necessary wait queues where these cannot be set up in read() or write(). If no device exists (for example, if a driver supports a number of devices but only one is present), it should return -ENODEV. The open() function is also the right place to initialize the standard settings needed by the driver. The PC speaker driver uses the open function to set the audio format according to the minor number of the opened device, to allocate two buffers to receive the samples, to set both buffers to a length of 0 and to lock the driver against later access by another process. If the file has been opened successfully, a 0 should be returned.

```
static int pcsp_open(struct inode *inode, struct file *file)
{
    if (pcsp_active)
        return -EBUSY;

    switch (minor) {
        case PCSP_DSP_MINOR:
            pcsp_set_format(AFMT_U8);
        break;
        case PCSP_AUD_MINOR:
            pcsp_set_format(AFMT_MU_LAW);    /* ULAW-Format */
        break;
        ...
    }
```

```
    if (! (pcsp.buf[0] = vmalloc(pcsp.ablk_size)))
        return -ENOMEM;
    if (! (pcsp.buf[1] = vmalloc(pcsp.ablk_size))) {
        vfree(pcsp.buf[0]);
        return -ENOMEM;
    }

    pcsp.buffer    = pcsp.end    = pcsp.buf[0];
    pcsp.in[0]     = pcsp.in[1] = 0;
    pcsp.timer_on = 0;
    pcsp.timer_on =
    pcsp.frag_size =
    pcsp.frag_cnt  = 0;

    ...

    pcsp_active   = 1;
    MOD_INC_USE_COUNT;
    return 0;
}
```

The release function, as opposed to open(), is only called when the file
descriptor for the device is released (*see* Section 6.2.6). The tasks of this function comprise cleaning-up activities global in nature, such as clearing wait
queues. For some devices it can also be useful to pass through to the device all
the data still in the buffers. In the case of the PC speaker driver, this could
mean that the device file can be closed before all the data in the output buffers
have been played out. The function pcsp_sync() therefore waits until both
buffers have been emptied and then releases them.

```
static void pcsp_release(struct inode *inode,
                         struct file *file)
{
    pcsp_sync();
    pcsp_stop_timer();
    outb_p(0xb6,0x43);      /* binary, mode 2, LSB/MSB, ch 2 */

    vfree(pcsp.buf[0]);
    vfree(pcsp.buf[1]);

    pcsp_active   = 0;
    MOD_DEC_USE_COUNT;
}
```

The release function is optional; however, configurations where it might be
omitted are difficult to imagine.

7.4.4   **read and write**

In principle, the `read()` and `write()` functions are a symmetrical pair. As no data can be read from the internal loudspeaker, only `write()` is implemented in the PC speaker driver. However, for the sake of simplicity, we will start by considering the structure of a `write` function for drivers in polling mode, taking the printer driver as an example.

```
static int lp_write_polled(unsigned int minor,
                           char *onst char * buf, int count)
{
    int  retval, status;
    char c;
    const char *temp;

    temp = buf;
    while (count > 0) {
        c = get_user(temp);
        retval = lp_char_polled(c, minor);
        if (retval) {
            count--; temp++;
        lp_table[minor].runchars++;
        } else { /* error handling */
            ...
        }
    }
    return temp-buf;
}
```

Note that the buffer `buf` is located in the user address space and bytes therefore have to be read using `get_user()`.

If a data byte cannot be transferred for a certain period, the driver should abandon the attempt (timeout) or else reattempt it after a further delay. The following mechanism can be used for this.

```
if (current->signal & ~current->blocked) {
    if (temp != buf)
        return temp-buf;
    else
        return -EINTR;
}

current->state = TASK_INTERRUPTIBLE;
current->timeout = jiffies + LP_TIME(minor);
schedule();
```

This first tests whether the current process has received signals. If so, the function terminates and returns the number of bytes transferred. Then the process is switched to TASK_INTERRUPTIBLE mode and the 'waking up' time is determined by adding the minimum waiting time in ticks to the current value of jiffies. A call to schedule() holds up the process for this period or until a signal is received. The program then returns to schedule(); current->timeout will be 0 if a timeout has occurred.

We now take the PC speaker driver's simplified write function as an example of an interrupt operation.

```
static int pcsp_write(struct inode *inode, struct file *file,
                      char *buffer, int count)
{
   unsigned long copy_size;
   unsigned long max_copy_size;
   unsigned long total_bytes_written = 0;
   unsigned bytes_written;
   int i;

   ...

   max_copy_size = pcsp.frag_size \
                        ? pcsp.frag_size : pcsp.ablk_size;
   do {
      bytes_written = 0;
      copy_size = (count <= max_copy_size) \
                        ? count : max_copy_size;
      i = pcsp.in[0] ? 1 : 0;
      if (copy_size && !pcsp.in[i]) {
         memcpy_fromfs(pcsp.buf[i], buffer, copy_size);
         pcsp.in[i] = copy_size;
         if (! pcsp.timer_on)
            pcsp_start_timer();
         bytes_written += copy_size;
         buffer += copy_size;
      }

      if (pcsp.in[0] && pcsp.in[1]) {
         interruptible_sleep_on(&pcsp_sleep);
         if (current->signal & ~current->blocked) {
            if (total_bytes_written + bytes_written)
               return total_bytes_written + bytes_written;
            else
               return -EINTR;
         }
      }
```

```
                total_bytes_written += bytes_written;
                count -= bytes_written;

            } while (count > 0);
            return total_bytes_written;
        }
```

Data from the user area are first transferred to the first free buffer by means of a call to `memcpy_fromfs()`. This is always necessary, as the interrupt may occur independently of the current process, with the result that the data cannot be fetched from the user area during the interrupt, since the pointer `buffer` would be pointing to the user address space for the current process. If the corresponding interrupt is not yet initialized, it is now switched on (`pcsp_start_timer()`). As the transfer of data to the device takes place in the ISR, `write()` can begin filling the next buffer.

If all the buffers are full, the process must be halted until at least one buffer becomes free. This makes use of the `interruptible_sleep_on()` function (*see* Section 3.1.5). If the process has been woken up by a signal, `write()` terminates; otherwise the transfer of data to the newly released buffer continues.

Let us take a look at the basic structure of the ISR.

```
int pcsp_do_timer(void)
{
    if (pcsp.index < pcsp.in[pcsp.actual]) {
        /* output of one byte */
        ...
    }
    if (pcsp.index >= pcsp.in[pcsp.actual]) {
        pcsp.xfer = pcsp.index = 0;
        pcsp.in[pcsp.actual] = 0;
        pcsp.actual ^= 1;
        pcsp.buffer = pcsp.buf[pcsp.actual];
        if (pcsp_sleep)
            wake_up_interruptible(&pcsp_sleep);
        if (pcsp.in[pcsp.actual] == 0)
            pcsp_stop_timer();
    }
    ...
}
```

As long as there are still data in the current buffer, these are output. If the buffer is empty, the ISR switches to the second buffer and calls `wake_up_interruptible()` to wake up the process. If the second buffer is empty too, the interrupt is disabled. The `if` before the call to the function is not in fact necessary, as `wake_up_interruptible()` carries out this test itself. It is included here for reasons of timing only.

As the example shows, this ISR does not fit the framework of fast and slow interrupts explained earlier. This is because the timer interrupt in LINUX is a slow interrupt, but for reasons of speed the PC speaker driver requires a fast interrupt. The PC speaker driver therefore contains a 'third' type, with features of both fast and slow interrupts. The routine `pcsp_do_timer()` is called like a fast interrupt (but with the interrupt flag set, meaning it is interruptible); if it returns 0, the interrupt is terminated. Otherwise, the original timer interrupt is started as a slow interrupt. As the original timer interrupt needs to be called far less often, this approach gives a major speed advantage.

7.4.5   IOCTL

Although a device driver aims to keep the operation of devices as transparent as possible, each device has its own characteristics, which may consist in different operation modes and certain basic settings. It may also be that device parameters such as IRQs, I/O addresses and so on need to be set at run-time.

The parameters passed to the `ioctl` function are an instruction and an argument. Since, under LINUX, the following holds:

```
sizeof(unsigned long) == sizeof(void *)
```

a pointer to data in the user address space can also be passed as the argument. For this reason, the `ioctl` function usually consists of a long `switch` instruction, with an appropriate type conversion occurring for the argument. Calls to `ioctl` usually only change variables global to the driver or global device settings.

Let us consider a fragment of the PC speaker driver's `ioctl` function.

```
static int pcsp_ioctl(struct inode *inode, struct file *file,
                      unsigned int cmd, unsigned long arg)
{
    unsigned long ret;
    unsigned long *ptr = (unsigned long *)arg;
    int i, error;

    switch (cmd) {
       case SNDCTL_DSP_SPEED:
          error = verify_area(VERIFY_READ, ptr, 4);
          if (error)
             return (error);
    arg = pcsp_set_speed(get_user(ptr));
    arg = pcsp_calc_srate(arg);
    return 0pcsp_ioctl_out(ptr, arg);
```

```
        ...
    case SNDCTL_DSP_SYNC:
        pcsp_sync();
        pcsp_stop_timer();
        return (0);
        ...
    }
}
```

The command SNDCTL_DSP_SPEED converts the argument arg to a pointer and uses it to read the new sampling rate. The function pcsp_calc_srate() then simply calculates a number of time constants depending on the new sampling rate. SNDCTL_DSP_SYNC, on the other hand, completely ignores the argument and calls the function pcsp_sync(), which suspends the process until all the data still in the buffer have been played out. This synchronization procedure becomes necessary if, for example, the sampling rate or the play mode (mono or stereo) is changed during the playback of audio data or if the output of audio data needs to be synchronized with events in another process.

Thus, the ioctl function can also be used to execute other functions within the driver which are not included in the Virtual File System. Another example of this behaviour is contained in the driver for the serial interface: the TIOCSERCONFIG command initiates automatic detection of the UART chip and of the IRQs used for the interfaces.

In developing a custom driver, the coding of the IOCTL commands should conform to a standard. The file <linux/ioctl.h> contains macros which should be used to code the individual commands. If these macros are used, the various IOCTL commands can easily be decoded.

As illustrated in Figure 7.3, bits 8–15 of the command contain a unique identifier for the device driver. This ensures that if the IOCTL command is erroneously used on the wrong device, an error will be returned, instead of possibly incorrectly configuring this device driver. The unique identifier recommended for the device driver is its major number.

The macros to encode the IOCTL commands are given the driver identifier as the first argument and the command number as the second:

_IO(*c,d*)   for commands with no argument,

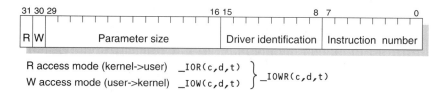

Figure 7.3   Coding of IOCTL commands.

_IOW(*c*,*d*,*t*)   for commands which write back to the user address space a value of the C type **t**,

_IOR(*c*,*d*,*t*)   for commands which read a value of the C type **t** from the user address space,

_IOWR(*c*,*d*,*t*)   for commands which both read and write.

In conclusion, let us take as an example the definitions for some IOCTLs for the sound driver.

```
#define SNDCTL_DSP_RESET    _IO  ('P', 0)
#define SNDCTL_DSP_SYNC     _IO  ('P', 1)
#define SNDCTL_DSP_SPEED    _IOWR('P', 2, int)
#define SNDCTL_DSP_STEREO   _IOWR('P', 3, int)
```

Thus, while the `SNDCTL_DSP_RESET` command, for example, needs no arguments, `SNDCTL_DSP_SPEED` reads an argument of the `int` type from the user address space and writes one back. Of course, the file `<linux/ioctl.h>` also contains macros to simplify the decoding of the IOCTL commands:

_IOC_DIR(*cmd*)   returns whether it is an input or output command,

_IOC_TYPE(*cmd*)   returns the device identifier,

_IOC_NR(*cmd*)   returns the command without type information,

_IOC_SIZE(*cmd*)   returns the size of the argument received in bytes.

The file `Documentation/ioctl-number.txt` holds information on device identifiers already in use.

7.4.6   `select`

Although `select()` is not implemented, its operation will be described here since this function is particularly useful for character devices. As an example, we shall take the implementation of `select()` for the ATI bus mouse driver:

```
static int mouse_select(struct inode *inode, struct file *file,
                        int sel_type, select_table * wait)
{
    if (sel_type != SEL_IN)
        return 0;
    if (mouse.ready)
        return 1;
    select_wait(&mouse.wait,wait);
    return 0;
}
```

The task of the `select` function is to check whether data can be read from the device (`sel_type == SEL_IN`) or written to it (`SEL_OUT`). `SEL_EX` can also be used to wait for the occurrence of an exception condition. As almost the entire complexity of this is handled by the Virtual File System, the task of the `select` function is simple to describe.

If the argument `wait` is `NULL`, the device will only be interrogated. If it is ready for the function concerned, `select()` will return a 1, otherwise a 0. If `wait` is not `NULL`, the process must be held up until the device becomes available. However, `sleep_on()` is not used; instead, the task is taken care of by the function

```
void select_wait(struct wait_queue **wait_address,select_table *p)
```

The function expects as arguments a wait queue and the last argument given to the select function. As `select_wait()` immediately returns if this latter argument is `NULL`, the interrogation can be dispensed with, giving a structure for the function as shown in the example above.

If the device becomes available (usually indicated by an interrupt), the process is woken up by a `wake_up_interruptible(wait_address)`. This is indicated by the driver's mouse interrupt.

```
void mouse_interrupt(int unused)
{
    ...
    if (dx != 0 || dy != 0 || buttons != mouse.latch_buttons) {
        mouse.latch_buttons |= buttons;
        mouse.dx += dx;
        mouse.dy += dy;
        mouse.ready = 1;
        wake_up_interruptible(&mouse.wait);
    }
    ...
}
```

7.4.7 lseek

This function is not implemented in the PC speaker driver. It is also only of limited relevance to character devices, as these cannot position. However, as the Virtual File System's standard function `lseek()` does not return an error message, an `lseek` function must be explicitly defined if the driver is required to react to `lseek()` with an error message.

7.4.8 mmap

The `mmap` function is used to map the device to the user address space. This function is not relevant to character devices, as it assumes the 'addressing' of data within the device. This means that `mmap()` is only for use by file systems and at best by block devices. An exception to this rule is the device /dev/mem, as this (of course) does not represent an infinite data stream, but the finite and addressable memory.

7.4.9   `readdir`, `fsync` and `fasync`

These functions are primarily intended for file systems and are not implemented in the PC speaker driver. As the `file_operations` structure is not just used for devices, specifically character devices, it includes functions not used by device drivers. The functions `readdir()` and `fasync()`, for example, are meaningless for devices. Although block devices may have an `fsync` function, they will then be using the `block_fsync()` function in the cache.

7.4.10   `check_media_change` and `revalidate`

These functions are not implemented in the PC speaker driver and are not relevant to character devices. Block devices supporting exchangeable media should implement at least `check_media_change()`. This function tests whether a media change has taken place and if so returns a 1. If `check_media_change()` has detected a change, `revalidate()` is called by the VFS. This function must be defined by block device drivers supporting media of different formats, such as floppy disks or exchangeable hard disks. It should read the parameters for the new media and configure the driver accordingly. For hard disk drivers, for example, this will include reading in the partition table.

7.5   An example of DMA operation

To examine DMA in more detail, we need to start by considering how the DMA controller is programmed. However, the following is only intended as a brief introduction: for more detailed information the reader is referred to Messmer (1997).

As mentioned earlier, the DMA has a base register which holds the lower 16 bits of the address of the area of memory to be transferred. A second 16-bit register, the base count register, contains the number of data transfers to be carried out. This register is decremented on each data transfer, and the point at which a value of 0xFFFF is reached is called *terminal count* (TC). Every DMA controller possesses four channels, with a base register and a base count register assigned to each channel. An input signal DREQx and an output signal DACKx are likewise assigned to each channel. A device requests a DMA transfer by activating the DREQ signal. When the DMA controller has obtained control over the bus, it indicates this by means of the DACK signal. At any given time, however, only a maximum of one DACK can be active, and the individual DREQ signals are therefore given different priorities. Usually it is DREQ0 which has the highest and DREQ3 the lowest priority. By modifying the request register, DMA transfer can also be activated 'by hand', as if the relevant DREQ signal had been received. However, this facility is not normally used; it is provided in the PC/XT and other machines to allow a memory-to-memory transfer, but this is not possible on an AT, as DMA channel 0 of the master controller, which is required for this mode, is used to cascade the slave controller.

In all, each DMA controller possesses 12 different registers governing its operation. However, the functions in the LINUX kernel fully encapsulate these registers, so any further explanation is unnecessary here.

The DMA controller also supports a number of different transfer modes, which must be set in the mode register for each channel. These include the following operation modes:

- *Demand transfer*
  In this mode, the DMA controller continues transferring data until the terminal count is reached or the device deactivates the DREQ. The transfer is then suspended until the device reactivates the DREQ.

- *Single transfer*
  In this mode, the DMA controller transfers one value at a time and then returns the bus to the processor. Each further transfer must be requested by the DREQ signal or an access to the request register. This mode is used for slow devices, such as floppy disks and scanners.

- *Block transfer*
  In this mode, the DMA controller carries out a block transfer without relinquishing the bus. The transfer is initiated by a DREQ.

- *Cascade*
  Cascading of another DMA controller: in this mode the DMA controller passes on the DMA requests it receives and thus enables more than one controller to be used. By default, DMA channel 0 of the second controller (or DMA channel 4 in consecutive numbering), which is the master in the AT, is in this mode.

These basic modes may be used in both read and write transfers. The DMA controller can both increment and decrement the memory addresses, enabling a transfer to start with the highest address. In addition, auto-initialization can be selected and deselected. If it is selected, the relevant DMA channel will automatically be reinitialized to the starting value when the terminal count is reached. This allows constant amounts of data to be transferred to or from a fixed buffer in memory.

Let us take as an example of DMA operation the implementation of a driver for a hand-held scanner. In the same way as the IRQs to be used, the DMA channel must first be allocated.

```
if ( (err = request_dma(AC4096_DMA, AC4096_SCANNER_NAME)) ) {
    printk("AC 4096: unable to get DMA%d\n", AC4096_DMA);
    return err;
}
```

The functions `request_dma()` and `free_dma()` work in a similar way to `request_irq()` and `free_irq()` described earlier. The `request_dma()` function expects to be given the number of the DMA channel and the name of the driver wishing to use this channel. However, this name is only inspected by the *Proc* file system. As with IRQs, DMA channels should only be allocated if they are about to be used: as a rule, this will be done in a device driver's `open` function. If a driver is using both IRQ and DMA channels, the interrupt should be allocated first, followed by the DMA channel.

The allocation of buffers can also be carried out in the `open` function, but also as late as the `read()` or `write()` stage, as memory is a far less critical resource. Since LINUX version 1.2 it is no longer necessary to assign permanent buffers for DMA transfer when booting the kernel. This means that device drivers can now also be implemented as modules using DMA transfer. The LINUX memory administration routines themselves ensure that memory allocated for DMA buffers is below the 16 Mbytes limit and no 64 Kbyte boundary is crossed. To use this facility, memory must be allocated using the `kmalloc()` function and the additional flag `GFP_DMA` must be passed to it.

```
tmp = kmalloc(blksize + HEADERSIZE, GFP_DMA | GFP_KERNEL);
```

The DMA transfer can now be initiated. As mentioned above, the functions for this encapsulate the hardware to an extreme degree, so that the DMA transfer is easy to program. As a general rule, it will even conform in all cases to the sequence shown in the following example.

```
static void start_dma_xfer(char *buf)
{
    cli();
        disable_dma(AC4096_DMA);
        clear_dma_ff(AC4096_DMA);
        set_dma_mode(AC4096_DMA, DMA_MODE_READ);
        set_dma_addr(AC4096_DMA, (unsigned int) buf);
        set_dma_count(AC4096_DMA, hw_modeinfo.bpl);
        enable_dma(AC4096_DMA);
    sti();
}
```

The function `disable_dma()` disables the DMA transfer on the channel given to the function as an argument. The programming of the DMA controller can now be carried out. The `clear_dma_ff()` function deletes the *DMA pointer flip-flop*. As the DMA controller only has 8-bit data ports, accesses to internal 16-bit registers have to be broken up. The DMA pointer flip-flop indicates whether the next value is to be interpreted as LSB (least significant bit) or MSB (most significant bit). Each time it is deleted, the DMA controller expects the LSB as the next value. As the calls to `set_dma_addr()` and `set_dma_count()` rely on this, `clear_dma_ff()` should be called once before these functions are used. The function `set_dma_mode()` sets the mode of the DMA channel. The modes supported by LINUX via pre-defined macros are:

- **DMA_MODE_READ**
  Single transfer from device to memory without auto-initialization, addresses incremented.

- **DMA_MODE_WRITE**
  Single transfer from memory to device without auto-initialization, addresses incremented.

- **DMA_MODE_CASCADE**
  Cascading of another controller.

However, these modes are adequate for most cases.

All that remains is to set the address of the buffer area by a call to `set_dma_addr()` and the number of bytes to be transferred via `set_dma_count()`. Both functions take care of the proper conversion of the values they are given for the DMA controller and therefore expect even addresses and an even number of bytes if a DMA channel for the second controller is used.

If the device generates an interrupt after the transfer is completed, an ISR should be implemented matching the one for pure interrupt operation. After testing, if necessary, whether the interrupt really has been triggered by the device concerned, the waiting process must be woken up by a call to `wake_up_interruptible()` and – if there is still data to be transferred – the next DMA transfer must be initiated.

If, as in our example, the device does not trigger an interrupt, the DMA controller must be interrogated as to whether the end of the DMA transfer has been reached. This involves interrogating the status register in the relevant DMA controller. The lower four bits of the register indicate whether the corresponding channel has reached a terminal count. If the bit is set, the TC has been reached and the transfer is complete. Every time the status register is read, however, these bits are cleared. The following function can be used for the interrogation procedure.

```
int dma_tc_reached(int channel)
{
    if (channel < 4)
```

```
            return ( inb(DMA1_STAT_REG) & (1 << channel) );
        else
            return ( inb(DMA2_STAT_REG) & (1 << (channel & 3)) );
    }
```

This can be used in a polling routine, for example as follows:

```
int dma_polled(void)
{
    unsigned long count  = 0;
    do {
        count ++;
        if(need_resched)
            schedule();
    } while(!dma_tc_reached(dma_channel) && count < TIMEOUT );
    ...
}
```

However, depending on the device concerned, this may still result in a loss of data, as the time before the process is next activated (that is, before the process returns from schedule()) cannot be predicted. When using a scanner, this may mean the loss of scan lines if the device has no buffer or only a very small one. Our example therefore uses a different option: the DMA controller is interrogated in a timer routine which is called 50 times per second. This routine operates just like the corresponding ISR, but instead of testing whether the device has triggered the interrupt, it tests whether the DMA transfer has been completed.

```
static inline void start_snooping(void)
{
    timer.expires = 2;
    timer.function = test_dma_rdy;
    add_timer(&timer);
}

static void test_dma_rdy(unsigned long dummy)
{
    static int needed_bytes;
    char cmd;

    if (! xfer_going) return;
    start_snooping(); /* restart timer */

    if ( dma_tc_reached(AC4096_DMA) ) {

        ...
```

```
        stop_scanner(); /* halt scanner */

        /* if a sufficiently large buffer is still free */
        if (WR_BUFSPC >= hw_modeinfo.bpl) {
            ...
            /* initiate next DMA transfer */
            start_dma_xfer(WR_ADDR);
        }
        else xfer_going = 0;
    }
}
```

8 Network implementation

Then a voice spoke out of the chaos and said,
'Be quiet, it could get worse'.
And I kept quiet, and it got worse.

Unknown network administrator

Nowadays, support for network communication is one of the basic demands made of an operating system. For LINUX, this requirement existed from the start. Such communication lays the foundations for a range of network services, including services familiar to most users such as ftp (file transfer), telnet and rlogin (remote log-in). In addition, there are facilities to use file systems on other computers (NFS), receive *e-mail* and *NetNews* and much more. The type of network used (OSI, IPX, UUCP and so on) is a secondary consideration as far as the user is concerned.

In the UNIX world, the dominating protocols are those collected under the name of TCP/IP. LINUX is modelled on UNIX and so, as might be expected, an implementation of TCP/IP is provided which concentrates mainly on communication via Ethernet. But LINUX can do more than this. Using SLIP (*Serial Line Interface Protocol*) or PLIP (*Parallel Line Interface Protocol*) it is possible to link computers together via their serial or parallel interfaces. The capabilities of the SLIP protocol are particularly impressive, as it can use modems and telephone lines to set up network links to anywhere in the world.

In its AX.25 protocol, LINUX even provides a way of communicating between computers by radio. Communication via IPX, a protocol developed by

Novell, has also been realized. The world of Apple data is accessible through an adaptation of the AppleTalk protocol. Both for AppleTalk and IPX, software packages have been developed that allow file access and printing.

In this chapter, we deal with the characteristics of the LINUX implementation of TCP/IP. It is not the authors' intention to provide a description of how TCP/IP works,[1] but rather to look at the design of its implementation under LINUX. The chapter therefore assumes that the reader is familiar with the basics of TCP/IP.

8.1 Introductory summary

For the 'normal' programmer, access to network services is available via sockets. Under LINUX, these have an extended functionality. The interface consists of the following C library routines:

```
int socket(int addr_family,int type,int protocol);
int bind(int s,struct sockaddr *address,int address_len);
int listen(int s,int backlog);
int connect(int s,struct sockaddr *address,int address_len);
int accept(int s,struct sockaddr *address,int *address_len);
int send(int s,char *msg,int len,int flags);
int sendto(int s,char *msg,int len,int flags,
          struct sockaddr *to, int tolen);
int recv(int s,char *buf,int len,int flags);
int recvfrom(int s,char *buf,int len,int flags,
            struct sockaddr *from,int *fromlen);
int getsockopt(int s,int level,int oname,char *ovalue,
              int *olen);
int setsockopt(int s,int level,int oname,char *ovalue,
              int *olen);
```

All of these functions are based on the system call *socketcall* (*see* page 371). In addition, the system call *ioctl* to socket file descriptors enables network-specific configurations to be changed.

As the C library routine `socket()` returns a file descriptor, the usual I/O system calls, such as *read* and *write*, are of course also applicable.

A computer can be connected to a network via a great variety of hardware including, for example, Ethernet cards and D-Link adaptors. The

---

[1] For more detailed reading on the subject of TCP/IP, we recommend Comer (1991), Comer and Stevens (1991), Stevens (1994) and Washburn and Evans (1993).

differences between these are hidden behind a unified interface, namely the network devices. The network devices assigned to Ethernet cards have the names `eth0`, `eth1` and so forth. They also include the D-Link adaptors. The names for the devices handling SLIP and PLIP links are `sl0`, `sl1`, ... and `plip0`, `plip1`, ... respectively.

There is no representation in the file system for these network devices. They cannot be set up in the `/dev/` directory using the `mknod` command like 'normal' devices. A network device can only be accessed if the initialization function has identified the corresponding hardware.

8.1.1 The layer model of the network implementation

As communication with network components presents a fairly complex task, it uses a layer structure like the file system. The individual layers correspond to levels of abstraction, with the level of abstraction increasing from layer to layer, starting with the hardware.

When a process communicates via the network, it uses the functions provided by the BSD socket layer. This takes care of a range of tasks similar to those handled by the Virtual File System and administers a general data structure for sockets which we shall call BSD sockets. The BSD socket interface has been selected by virtue of its widespread use, which simplifies the porting of network applications, most of which are already quite complex.

Below this layer is the INET socket layer. This manages the communication end points for the IP-based protocols TCP and UDP. These are represented by the data structure `sock`, which we shall call INET sockets.

In the layers we have mentioned so far, no type distinction is as yet made between the sockets in the `AF_INET` address family. The layer that underlies the INET socket layer, on the other hand, is determined by the type of socket, and may be the UDP or TCP layer or the IP layer directly. The UDP layer implements the *User Datagram Protocol* on the basis of IP, and the TCP layer similarly implements the *Transmission Control Protocol* for reliable communication links. The IP layer contains the code for the *Internet Protocol*. This is where all the communication streams from the higher layers come together.

Sockets of the `SOCK_PACKET` type are not included in this survey. Below the IP layer are the network devices, to which the IP passes the final packets. These then take care of the physical transport of the information.

True communication always takes place between two sides, producing a two-way flow of information. For this reason, the various layers are also connected together in the opposite direction. This means that when IP packets are received, they are passed to the IP layer by the network devices and processed. The interaction between the different layers is illustrated in Figure 8.1.

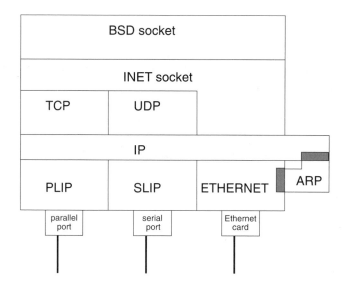

Figure 8.1 The layer structure of a network.

8.1.2 Getting the data from A to B

To understand better the interaction between the various parts of the network implementation, we shall follow the data which are sent through the network by process A to process B.

We assume that both processes have already created a socket and are connected to each other via `connect()` and `accept()`, and will restrict our survey to one TCP connection under LINUX. Data are to be sent from process A to process B. They are stored in a buffer of length `length` pointed to by the `data` pointer. Process A contains the following fragment of code:

```
write(socket,data,length);
```

which it uses to call the kernel function `sys_write()` (*see* Section 6.2.6 and page 335), which is a component of the Virtual File System.

This tests for a number of conditions, including whether a read access may be made to the area of memory referenced by `data` (*see* `verify_area()` in Section 4.2.5) and whether a write operation is entered in the descriptor's file operation vector. To use the Virtual File System, a socket provides the classical file operations in a vector.

The write operation for the BSD sockets is `sock_write()`, which only takes care of administrative functions. This searches for the socket structure associated with the inode structure. Then, the parameters of the write operation are transferred into a message structure. As the socket we are concerned with belongs to the AF_INET address family, sock_write() calls the send function inet_sendmsg(), to which it passes as parameters the pointer to the BSD socket data structure, the pointer to the message structure, the length of the data, and an indication of whether it is permissible to block the function, plus several additional flags.

From the data component of the BSD socket passed to it, the function inet_sendmsg() extracts a pointer to the INET socket structure sock. In the present example, this structure contains the essential data used in the TCP and IP layers. The prot pointer in this structure refers to the operation vector of the TCP implementation. The inet_sendmsg() function calls this vector's send operation, tcp_sendmsg(), passing to it parameters consisting of the pointer to the INET socket, the pointer to the message structure, the length of the data, the blocking flag and the additional flags. The flags are used to indicate data to be given priority transfer 'out of band'. In the present example, however, this is not the case.

Up to now, the data have only passed through the different abstraction levels. In tcp_sendmsg(), the actual handling of communication aspects proper begins. After tests for a number of error conditions, such as the socket not being ready to send, the work itself is carried out by the function do_tcp_sendmsg(). Memory, which will later contain an sk_buff structure, the header and the TCP segment, is requested via a call to the TCP protocol operation wmalloc. The do_tcp_sendmsg() function initializes the sk_buff structure by calling the protocol operation build_header() to complete the packet header. In the present example, do_tcp_sendmsg() calls the ip_build_header() operation. Once the headers for the lower-layer protocols have been initialized, the TCP protocol header is added by means of a call to tcp_build_header().

The TCP send operation now copies the data from the process address space to the TCP segment for the almost complete packet (*see* memcpy_fromfs() in Section 4.1.2). Usually, after this, the checksum is calculated. To optimize this process, a function csum_partial_copy_fromuser() is available which carries out both actions in one step. If the length of the data exceeds the maximum segment size (MSS) they are divided into a number of packets. However, it is also possible for short data blocks from a number of send operations to be collected together in one TCP segment. A feature of LINUX is that all the headers are written to memory in a linear sequence. In other TCP/IP implementations, the packet is stored as a vector of separate fragments.

The packet stored in the sk_buff structure is transferred by a call to tcp_send_skb(). This adds a variety of protocol-specific information to the header – for example, the checksum is calculated on the TCP segment. A call to the protocol operation queue_xmit() (in the present case, the ip_queue_xmit() function) then slots the packet into the wait queue of packets ready for transfer.

Now, the ip_queue_xmit() function adds to the IP protocol header values which can only now be established, such as the checksum for the IP header. It then passes the packet to the function `dev_queue_xmit()`. The discussion below assumes that the device is an Ethernet card of type WD8013.

The `dev_queue_xmit()` function finally calls `do_dev_queue_xmit()` which uses the pointer `hard_start_xmit`. For the WD8013 card, this points to the function `ei_start_xmit()`, which passes the data to the network adaptor, which in turn sends it to the Ethernet.

We could say at this point that the data are halfway there. The data, embedded in an Ethernet packet, are received by a network card in the destination computer. As before, we assume here that the adaptor is a WD8013 card.

After receiving the Ethernet packet the network card triggers an interrupt. This is handled by the `ei_interrupt()` function. If the transfer via the Ethernet was completed without error, the `ei_receive()` function will be called with a reference to the network device. This uses the `block_input` operation to write the packet to a newly set-up buffer, using, in our example, the `wd_block_input()` function. As for the send operation, this buffer includes space for the `sk_buff` structure, which is appropriately initialized in `ei_receive()` after the call to `wd_block_input()`.

Once this has been done, the function `netif_rx()` is called with the packet as argument. This adds it to the `backlog` list. There is only one list of this type in the entire system, which contains all the packets received by the system. All the functions so far described for receiving packets are executed within the interrupt. The `netif_rx()` function then marks the network implementation's bottom-half routine in the bottom-half mask `bh_mask`.

The `net_bh()` function is now called by `do_bottom_half()` with the mask marker set. The `do_bottom_half()` function is called after system calls and slow (normal) interrupts. The call is not made if an interrupt has interrupted another interrupt or `do_bottom_half()` itself. Further information on the bottom-half mechanism is given in Section 3.3.1.

The `net_bh()` function sets the `raw` pointer of union `h` in the `sk_buff` structure to the beginning of the protocol packet, after the Ethernet header. The packet type in the Ethernet header then decides which receive function for the protocol is called. In the SLIP and PLIP protocols the type is not held in the packet header but is implicit, as these protocols only support IP packets.

In the case considered here, an IP packet has been received, and the receive function `ip_rcv()` is called. This demonstrates the advantages of the union `h`. In the bottom-half routine, the `raw` pointer was set to the header of the protocol packet. The IP header can now be accessed via the `iph` pointer provided by the union `h` without the need to initialize it specially, as it is identical to the `raw` pointer.

In `ip_rcv()`, the header is checked for correctness and the handling routines for the IP options are executed if necessary. Packets addressed to other hosts are sent on by the function `ip_forward()` and fragmented packets are reassembled by `ip_defrag()`.

Let us assume that the packet has not been fragmented. The raw pointer in the union h in the sk_buff structure is now set to the end of the IP header and thus points to the start of the header for the next protocol. This protocol is specified in the protocol field of the IP header; in the present case, it is TCP. The appropriate protocol receive function for this protocol is now called. For TCP, this is tcp_rcv().

This calls the get_tcp_sock() function to determine, by reference to the sender and destination addresses and the sender and destination port numbers, the INET socket to which the TCP segment is addressed. After a number of consistency tests, tcp_data() enters the buffer sk_buff in the list of data received for the socket. If fresh data have been received in the sequence of the data flow, the appropriate acknowledge packets are sent after a delay and the INET socket's data_ready operation is called. This wakes up all the processes waiting for an event at the socket. The delay with which the acknowledgements are sent is necessary to avoid sending superfluous packets over the network. Up to this point, all the actions related to receiving a packet have been carried out in the kernel, outside the program flow of any process. The processor time used for this cannot be assigned to any process.

Process B wishes to receive the data sent by process A. To do so, it executes a read operation with the socket file descriptor.

```
read(socket,data,length);
```

This call is passed to a C library function via different abstraction levels and calls to sys_read(), sock_read(), inet_rcvmsg() and tcp_rcvmsg(). If the INET socket's receive buffer is empty, the process is forced to block. However, blocking can be prevented by setting the O_NONBLOCK flag using *fcntl*. As mentioned in the previous paragraph, the process is woken up once data are received. After the process has been woken up, or if data are already present in the buffer on the read call, these are copied to the data address in the user area of the process's memory.

This completes the data's travels from process A to process B, which have led us through various layers of the operating system. The data have been copied only four times: from the user area of process A to kernel memory, from there to the network card, from the network card in the second computer to kernel memory and from there to the user area of process B. In the LINUX implementation of the TCP/IP code, a great deal of care has been taken to avoid unnecessary copy operations.

The network implementation is very tightly interwoven: there is a wealth of mutually dependent functions, and it is not always easy to say to which layer any of these belong. A glance at the sources shows that many of these functions are very long (more than 200 lines of source text), making them far from easy to follow. To be sure, the complexity of the C sources is a function of the subject matter; but it is also a clear indication of the importance of good design in a network implementation. In LINUX version 1.2, the interfaces between the layers were tailored to IP, but several improvements have been integrated into version 2.0.

It is widely believed that a network implementation is a balancing act between speed of operation and tidy structuring. The authors, however, do not consider these two aspects to be necessarily exclusive. Other areas of the kernel (such as the Virtual File System) are proof of this.

8.2 Important structures

One way of achieving tidy structuring is correct definition of the data structures forming the basis of any function in a network. This section therefore provides an introduction to the many different data structures in the LINUX network implementation.

8.2.1 The socket structure

The `socket` structure forms the basis for the implementation of the BSD socket interface. It is set up and initialized with the system call *socket*. This section only deals with the characteristics of sockets in the AF_INET address family.

```
struct socket {
    short                type;
```

Valid entries for type are SOCK_STREAM, SOCK_DGRAM and SOCK_RAW. Sockets of the type SOCK_STREAM are used for TCP connections, SOCK_DGRAM for the UDP protocol and SOCK_RAW for sending and receiving IP packets.

```
    socket_state         state;
```

In `state`, the current state of the socket is stored. The most important states are SS_CONNECTED and SS_UNCONNECTED.

```
    long                 flags;
    struct proto_ops     *ops;
```

For a socket in the INET address family, the `ops` pointer points to the operation `vector inet_proto_ops`, where the specific operations for this address family are entered.

```
    void                 *data;
```

Socket

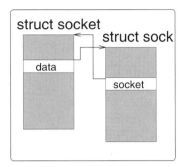

Figure 8.2   Relationships between the substructures within a socket.

The `data` pointer points to the substructure of the socket corresponding to the address family. For `AF_INET`, this is the INET socket (*see* Figure 8.2).

```
        struct socket        *conn;
        struct socket        *iconn;
        struct socket        *next;
        struct wait_queue    **wait;
        struct inode         *inode;
        struct fasync_struct *fasync_list;
        struct file          *file;
    };
```

The pointers `conn`, `iconn` and `wait` are not used by sockets in the `AF_INET` address family. In LINUX, each file is described by an inode. There is also an inode for each BSD socket, so that there is one-to-one mapping between the BSD sockets and their respective inodes. A reference to the corresponding inode is stored in `inode`, whereas `file` holds a reference to the primary file structure associated with this node.

However, this can give rise to certain problems during asynchronous processing of files. Different file structures can refer to one and the same inode and as a result to the same BSD socket. If processes have selected asynchronous handling of this file, all the processes need to be informed of events. For this reason, they are held in `fasync_list`. The relationship between inodes and file structure is described in more detail in Sections 3.1.1 and 6.2.6.

8.2.2   The `sk_buff` structure – buffer management in the network

The task of `sk_buff` buffers is to manage individual communication packets (*see* Figure 8.3).

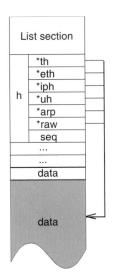

Figure 8.3 Normal use of the `sk_buff` structure.

```
struct sk_buff {
    struct sk_buff          *next, *prev;
    struct sk_buff_head     *list;
    unsigned long            magic_debug_cookie;
```

To support fault-tracing, the type of list including the buffer is entered here.

```
    struct sk_buff          *link3;
```

Exactly as for the first two pointers in the structure, this pointer is required for linking in a circular list and various other lists.

```
    struct sock             *sk;
```

The pointer `sk` points to the socket to which the buffer belongs (*see* Figure 8.4).

```
    volatile unsigned long   when;
    struct timeval           stamp;
```

The variable `when` indicates when the packet was last transferred. The time unit used is 1/100 of a second. The value is simply taken over from the kernel variable `jiffies` (*see* Section 3.2.4) at the time of transfer.

However, the buffers are used not only when sending packets but also when receiving them. When a packet is forwarded by the network devices to the higher layers of the network implementation, the function `netif_rx()` enters the current time in the structure `stamp`, using the kernel variable `xtime`, which is also updated by the timer interrupt.

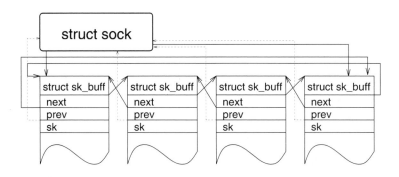

Figure 8.4   The normal localization of `sk_buff` structures.

```
struct device          *dev;
```

In the administration of network buffers, the identity of the network device by or via which a packet is sent or received is of great importance. A pointer to the device is therefore entered in `dev`.

```
union {
    struct tcphdr   *th;
    struct ethhdr   *eth;
    struct iphdr    *iph;
    struct udphdr   *uh;
    unsigned char   *raw;
    void            *filp;
} h;
```

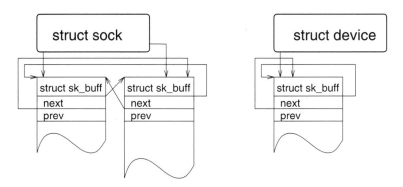

Figure 8.5   Transfer of a packet before calling the `xmit` function
(the buffer is in the socket).

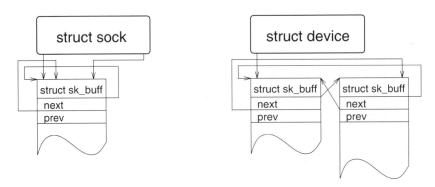

Figure 8.6 Transfer of a packet after calling the `xmit` function
(the buffer is now in the device, for example, `eth0`).

```
union {
  unsigned char          *raw;
  struct ethhdr          *ethernet;
} mac;
struct iphdr             *ip_hdr;
```

This union, mentioned earlier, serves in general as a pointer to various header structures within the packet. The additional pointer to the IP header is used by sockets working directly with the IP.

```
unsigned long            len, csum;
```

The variable `len` gives the length of the packet; `csum` holds the checksum if it has been calculated.

```
__u32                    saddr, daddr, raddr;
```

The source and destination address respectively are held in `saddr` and `daddr`, while `raddr` holds the next address to which the packet is to be sent.

```
__u32                    seq, end_seq, ack_seq;
unsigned char            proto_priv[16];
volatile char            acked, used, free, arp;
unsigned char            tries, lock, localroute,
                         pkt_type, pkt_bridged,
                         ip_summed;
unsigned short           users, protocol,
                         truesize;
```

These are some variables used by different parts of the network implementation.

```
atomic_t                    count;
struct sk_buff              *data_skb;
unsigned char               *head, *data, tail, *end;
void (*destructor)(struct sk_buff *);
```

These elements are concerned with the management of the memory belonging to the structure. Unlike in implementations up to version 1.2, data need not necessarily be located directly behind the sk_buff structure, but can also be stored in a separate sk_buff structure. This makes the cloning function work very fast. It copies the sk_buff structure, sets the reference counter to 1 and increments the reference counter of the sk_buff structure that holds the data.

```
        __u16                   redirport;
};
```

redirport contains a redirection port. This field is only used when the kernel has been configured with the 'IP: transparent proxy support' option.

The administration of the sk_buff structures normally uses double linked lists, so there is also a structure to implement a list header.

```
struct sk_buff_head {
    struct sk_buff          *next, *prev;
    __u32                   qlen;
    int                     magic_debug_cookie;
};
```

8.2.3   The INET socket – a special part of a socket

It is in the INET structure that the network-specific parts of the sockets are administered. This is required for TCP, UDP and RAW sockets.

```
struct sock {
    struct options          *opt;
    atomic_t                wmem_alloc, rmem_alloc;
    unsigned long           allocation;
```

The opt pointer points to a structure containing the individual IP options to be used for this socket. These have to be taken into account when setting up an IP protocol header. The two variables wmem_alloc and rmem_alloc indicate how much memory has already been requested by this socket for writing and reading respectively. During creation of the socket, allocation is assigned the priority with which memory is requested for this socket (*see* Figure 4.3).

```
        __u32                   write_seq, send_seq, acked_seq,
                                copied_seq, rcv_ack_seq;
```

```
unsigned short              rcv_ack_cnt;
__u32                       window_seq, fin_seq, urg_seq,
                            urg_data;
```

The sequence numbers required by the TCP protocol are stored in these variables. They are used to ensure that reliable transfer takes place. As TCP is connection-oriented, these sequence numbers need to be administered separately for each socket.

```
int                         users;
volatile char               dead, urginline, intr, blog,
                            done, reuse, keepopen, linger,
                            delay_acks, destroy, ack_timed,
                            no_check, zapped, broadcast,
                            nonagle, bsdism;
unsigned long               lingertime;
```

These variables contain various flags and values which can be set for a socket.

```
int                         proc;
```

The `proc` variable is used to store a process or process group which will be sent a signal on receipt of out-of-band data.

```
struct sock                 *next,*prev;
```

The `next` component links sockets with the same hash value in the socket hash table. This table speeds up the assignment of IP packets to specific sockets using open hashing.

```
struct sock                 *pair;
```

The INET socket's protocol operation `accept()` sets up a new `sock` structure. The `pair` pointer then points to the newly generated structure.

```
struct sk_buff              *volatile send_head,
                            *volatile send_next;
                            *volatile send_tail;
struct sk_buff_head         back_log;
struct sk_buff              *partial;
struct timer_list           partial_timer;
long                        retransmits;
struct sk_buff_head         write_queue,
                            receive_queue;
```

All the above pointers are used in the management of buffers associated with the INET socket. Circular lists are defined via the sk_buff_head structures for both the sending and the receiving TCP segments (*see* Figure 8.4).

```
struct proto          *prot;
```

This contains the operation vector for the protocol with which the socket is associated. In most cases, this will be the address of one of the following structures: tcp_prot, udp_prot or raw_prot.

```
struct wait_queue     **sleep;
```

The sleep pointer points to a wait queue containing processes which have blocked during actions on this socket.

```
__u32                 daddr, saddr, rcv_saddr;
```

The source and destination addresses must be entered in each IP packet; rcv_saddr specifies the address to which the socket has been bound.

```
unsigned short          max_unacked, window;
__u32                   lastwin_seq, high_seq;
volatile unsigned long  ato, lrcvtime, idletime;
unsigned short          bytes_rcv;
unsigned short          mtu;
volatile unsigned short mss, user_mss, max_window;
unsigned long           window_clamp;
unsigned int            ssthresh;
unsigned short          num;
volatile unsigned short cong_window, cong_count,
                        packets_out, shutdown;
volatile unsigned long  rtt, mdev, rto;
volatile unsigned short backoff;
```

These fields in the structure are also for the use of TCP and contain other protocol-related data.

```
int                     err, err_soft;
unsigned char           protocol;
volatile unsigned char  state;
unsigned char           ack_backlog, max_ack_backlog,
                        priority, debug;
unsigned short          rcvbuf, sndbuf;
```

The `err` variable is an error indicator very similar to the `errno` variable in C. The state of the socket is given in `state`. The two `buf` quantities indicate the maximum amount of memory which can be requested for this socket when sending or receiving packets.

```
unsigned short          type;
unsigned char           localroute;
```

The socket type specification `type` is taken over from the associated BSD `socket` structure; `localroute` is used to indicate that the packets should only be routed locally.

```
union {
    struct unix_opt         af_unix;
    struct inet_packet_opt af_packet;
} protinfo;
```

Private data for each address family.

```
int                     ip_ttl, ip_tos;
```

These values are used when generating an IP header and are entered in the corresponding fields in the header.

```
struct tcphdr           dummy_th;
```

Once a TCP connection has been set up, the basic framework of a TCP header is entered here.

```
struct timer_list       keepalive_timer, retransmit_timer;
                        delack_timer;
int                     ip_xmit_timeout;
struct rtable           *ip_route_cache;
unsigned char           ip_hdrincl;
int                     timeout;
struct timer_list       timer;
struct timeval          stamp;
```

These two components of the structure are used in the administration of timers required for the implementation of TCP. As `stamp` is updated on receipt of each packet, this enables the time when the last packet was received to be precisely determined.

```
struct socket           *socket;
```

This pointer points to the associated BSD socket.

```
void                    (*state_change)(struct sock *sk);
void                    (*data_ready)(struct sock *sk,int bytes);
void                    (*write_space)(struct sock *sk);
void                    (*error_report)(struct sock *sk);
};
```

The `state_change()` function is executed every time the status of the socket has changed. Similarly, `data_ready()` is called when data have been received, `write_space()` when the free memory available for writing has increased, and `error_report()` when an error occurs. In the present implementation, these operations only wake up those processes that have blocked during operations on the socket.

In the following description, the term 'socket' is used to refer to the combination of a BSD socket and an INET socket (*see* Figure 8.2).

8.2.4   Protocol operations in the proto structure

In LINUX, protocols such as TCP and UDP are accessed via an abstract interface. This consists of a number of operations and means that functions whose actions are the same for all protocols only need to be programmed once. This helps to avoid implementation errors and keep the code as compact as possible.

```
struct proto {
    void                    (*close)(struct sock *sk, int timeout);
```

The `close()` function initiates the actions required to close a socket. For a TCP socket, for example, a packet with the necessary ACK and a FIN is sent.

```
int                     (*build_header)(struct sk_buff *skb,
                        __u32 saddr, __u32 daddr,
                        struct device **dev, int type,
                        struct options *opt, int len,
                        int tos, int ttl, struct rtable **rp);
```

At present, the `ip_build_header()` function, which initializes the IP protocol header, is assigned to this pointer in all cases. It is not entirely clear, however, why this function pointer is defined in this way, as its arguments are tailored to `ip_build_header()`. Therefore, it does not represent an abstraction of different protocols.

```
int                     (*connect)(struct sock *sk,
                        struct sockaddr_in *usin, int addr_len);
struct sock         *(*accept) (struct sock *sk, int flags);
```

The connect() function requires implementation for all protocols, whereas accept() is not necessary for connectionless protocols. The semantics of connect() are different for connectionless and connection-oriented protocols. For connectionless protocols, it specifies an address to be used as the destination address for write calls, whereas for TCP, connect() sets up the connection.

```
void                (*queue_xmit)(struct sock *sk,
                    struct device *dev, struct sk_buff *skb,
                    int free);
void                (*retransmit)(struct sock *sk, int all);
```

Here again no functions are to be found for the protocols mentioned so far except those of IP (ip_queue_xmit() and ip_retransmit()). The function of queue_xmit is to send the packet in the skb buffer. This action is illustrated in Figure 8.5.

The retransmit function is responsible for a repeat send of the packets still located at the socket. This is only meaningful for TCP, however. The behaviour of this function is controlled by the parameter all, which specifies whether all packets are to be retransmitted or only the first.

This is another case where the authors feel that inclusion in the abstract interface is questionable, especially as ip_retransmit() is called directly by the TCP implementation.

```
void                (*write_wakeup)(struct sock *sk);
void                (*read_wakeup)(struct sock *sk);
```

The wakeup functions are only used and implemented by TCP, and are used to maintain a TCP connection. As a general rule, no packets are sent over a TCP connection if no data are sent by the user. Therefore, it is not easy to determine whether the communication partner has quit or whether the connection is already closed. If the SO_KEEPALIVE option is set for a socket, an old sequence number is sent by write_wakeup() at specified intervals, which is then acknowledged by the receiver by means of read_wakeup(). If such an acknowledgement is no longer received, the user is informed by a signal or an appropriate error message.

```
int                 (*rcv)(struct sk_buff *buff, struct device *dev,
                    struct options *opt, __u32 daddr,
                    unsigned short len, __u32 saddr,
                    int redo, struct inet_protocol *protocol);
```

Every protocol must provide an rcv function, to which the packets received by the lower layers are passed. This function is entered in the associated inet_protocol structure for each of the IP-based protocols.

```
int                 (*select)(struct sock *sk, int which,
                            select_table *wait);
```

The return value of `select()` is 1 if the condition specified in the parameters is met, otherwise 0 (*see* Section 6.2.6). In the network implementation there are two functions which implement `select()`: `datagram_select()` for UDP and `tcp_select()` for TCP.

```
int                 (*ioctl)(struct sock *sk, int cmd,
                            unsigned long arg);
```

A call to the `ioctl` function can be used, among other things, to find out the quantity of data at a TCP or UDP socket yet to be read or sent and to select and deselect debugging output.

```
int                 (*init)(struct sock *sk);
```

A call to the `init` function of the protocol in use executes the initialization procedures required by the protocol unit. As TCP and UDP each have only one unit, the initialization is carried out statically during LINUX start-up.

```
void                (*shutdown)(struct sock *sk, int how);
int                 (*setsockopt)(struct sock *sk, int level,
                            int optname, char *optval,
                            int optlen);
int                 (*getsockopt)(struct sock *sk, int level,
                            int optname, char *optval,
                            int *optlen);
```

The first of these functions is at present used only by TCP connections, and can be used to abort a TCP connection. The other two functions implement `setsockopt()` and `getsockopt()` for the associated protocol. Strictly speaking, the protocols should call the corresponding functions of the lower-layer protocol via the protocol structure, but this is not yet implemented.

```
int                 (*sendmsg)(struct sock *sk, struct msghdr *msg,
                            int len, int noblock, int flags);
int                 (*recvmsg)(struct sock *sk, struct msghdr *msg,
                            int len, int noblock, int flags,
                            int *addr_len);
int                 (*bind)(struct sock *sk,
                            struct sockaddr *uaddr, int addr_len);
```

During the development of LINUX (1.2–2.0) substantial changes have been made to the protocol interfaces. Thus, all send and receive functions were replaced by `sendmsg` and `recvmsg`. Specific parameters are passed in the `msghdr` structure. In addition, in version 2.0, the functions `readv()` and `writev()` can now be applied to sockets. With the `bind()` function, a socket is bound to a determined address.

```
unsigned short    max_header;
```

The value of `max_header` specifies the maximum size of the protocol header which is possible using this protocol implementation. The value also includes headers for the lower-layer protocols.

```
unsigned long     retransmits;
```

This variable counts the repeat sends required by a protocol.

```
    char        name[80];
    int         inuse, highestinuse;
};
```

For fault-tracing purposes, `name` holds the name of the associated protocol (for example, TCP). The other values are statistical in nature and are required for the SNMP.

```
struct sock       *sock_array[SOCK_ARRAY_SIZE];
```

By reference to the destination of a packet and this field, the INET socket to which the packet is directed can be determined. This is the precise function of `get_sock()`.

The `proto` structure which has just been described can be regarded as an interface for protocols in the `AF_INET` family. A very similar structure describes the interface to the next higher layer, the BSD socket layer. The name of this structure is `proto_ops`, and it is provided for each of the protocol families implemented. In version 1.2 of LINUX, this means `AF_INET`, `AF_IPX` and `AF_UNIX`.

8.2.5 The general structure of a socket address

As sockets have to support different address formats for different address families, there is a general address structure containing the address family, the port number and a field for addresses of different sizes. For Internet addresses, a special structure `sockaddr_in` is defined, which matches the general structure `sockaddr`.

```
    struct sockaddr {
        unsigned short sa_family;   /* address family AF_xxx    */
        char           sa_data[14]; /* start of protocol address    */
    };
```

```
struct sockaddr_in {
    short int    sin_family;    /* address family                */
    unsigned short int sin_port; /* port number                  */
    struct in_addr  sin_addr;   /* Internet address              */

    /* pad bytes for sockaddr structure                          */
    unsigned char __pad[__SOCK_SIZE__ - sizeof(short int)
                        - sizeof(unsigned short int)
                        - sizeof(struct in_addr)];
};
```

8.3 Network devices under LINUX

As we have already seen, there is a great variety of hardware that can be used to connect computers. As a result, this hardware is controlled in many different ways. To hide this from the upper layers, an abstract interface to the network hardware was introduced to enable the upper network layers to be implemented independently of the hardware used. This, of course, embodies a polymorphic approach to programming the operating system.

The data structure device controls an abstract network device. This is often referred to as a *network interface*, meaning the interface to the network rather than to the hardware.

```
struct device {
    char                *name;
```

In LINUX, every network device has a unique name. A reference to this name is held in name.

```
    unsigned long       rmem_end;
    unsigned long       rmem_start;
    unsigned long       mem_end;
    unsigned long       mem_start;
    unsigned short      base_addr;
    unsigned char       irq;
```

These elements describe the hardware of the device. The I/O address, which is important to PC architecture, and the number of the interrupt associated with the device, are held in base_addr and irq respectively. The ranges rmem_start to rmem_end and mem_start to mem_end describe the device's receive and send memories. However, these parameters are tailored to Ethernet cards; for other devices some of these fields in the structure are employed with different semantics. For a SLIP device, base_addr holds the index to the corresponding SLIP structure.

```
volatile unsigned char    start, interrupt;
unsigend long             tbusy;
struct device             *next;
```

The variables `start`, `interrupt` and `tbusy` are used as flags, `start` indicating whether the network device is running and `interrupt` being set when the interrupt is triggered. This enables nested calls to the interrupt handling function to be avoided. The function of `tbusy` is to indicate that the hardware has initiated the transfer of a packet.

Under LINUX, the network devices are managed in a list. The kernel variable `dev_base` points to the first element in this list, with `next` used to link the elements. A network device can be accessed in the kernel using its unique name and the function `dev_get()`.

```
int       (*init)(struct device *dev);
```

This function detects whether the necessary hardware is present for this device and initializes the `device` structure.

As described in Section 2.3, before the kernel is compiled it can be specified which devices are to be tested for their presence. This includes network devices, and a static list of structures of the `device` type is therefore held in `drivers/net/Space.c`. This list contains elements consisting only of the public section of the `device` structure, which runs from the start of the structure to the `init` component. The pointer `dev_base` points to the start of this list. By modifying this list it can now be determined which devices are tested for their presence during booting and which initialization functions are used. This is especially important for the different types of Ethernet card, as the separate card types are tested in sequence in the `ethif_probe` function.

If we turn once again to the sequence of actions when the kernel is started up, as described in Section 3.2.3, we see that this involves a call to `sock_init()`. The task of this function is to initialize the entire network part of the kernel. As part of this, the BSD sockets are set to their default settings, after which the `dev_init()` function is called. This `init` function initializes all the configured network devices by iteration through the list of network devices pointed to by `dev_base()`. The `init` function is called for each entry and fills the entire `device` structure with correct values, including the function pointers.

```
unsigned char             if_port;
unsigned char             dma;
```

The hardware of some network devices uses DMA and communication with I/O ports for input and output. In version 1.2 of LINUX, the `device` structure therefore had to be expanded by appropriate fields.

```
struct enet_statistics* (*get_stats)(struct device *dev);
```

This is the statistics function for the current device. It is used whenever statistical information is requested about the network device by another part of the kernel.

```
unsigned long               trans_start, last_rx;
```

These two fields are used to note the last time something was sent (`trans_start`) or received (`last_rx`). The time units used are hundredths of a second, taken from the variable `jiffies`.

```
unsigned short              flags;
unsigned short              family;
unsigned short              metric;
unsigned short              mtu;
```

These variables are used by the IP protocol. They can be modified using the system command `ifconfig` (*see* Appendix B.8). The maximum size of a packet that can be transferred by this device is given in `mtu`, and is the size excluding the hardware header (for example, the header for Ethernet packets). The `family` is the address family to which the device belongs. The possible values for `flags`, which allows the behaviour of the device to be modified, are shown in Table 8.1. The `metric` value is not used and appears to be included for historical reasons only.

```
unsigned short              type;
unsigned short              hard_header_len;
void                        *priv;
```

The device type, which in effect means the hardware, is entered in `type`. At the present stage of development, however, all protocols use the type ARPHRD_ETHER, including SLIP and PLIP. The variable `hard_header_len` specifies the length of the protocol header at hardware level. The `priv` variable can hold a pointer to a structure specially adapted to the device type.

```
unsigned char               broadcast[MAX_ADDR_LEN], pad;
unsigned char               dev_addr[MAX_ADDR_LEN];
unsigned char               addr_len;
```

The field `dev_addr[]` contains the hardware address for the device. The broadcast[] field also holds an address, which could be termed the broadcast address. Packets with this destination address are received by all computers

Table 8.1 Flags for network devices.

Flag	Description
IFF_UP	The network device can receive and send packets
IFF_BROADCAST	The broadcast address in `struct device` is valid and may be used
IFF_DEBUG	Debugging is selected (at present not used)
IFF_LOOPBACK	This device returns all packets received to its own computer
IFF_POINTOPOINT	Point-to-point connection, with the protocol address of the remote station (SLIP, PLIP) held in `pa_dstaddr`
IFF_NOTRAILERS	Is always switched off, but was used in BSD systems for the alternative positioning of the header at the end of a packet
IFF_RUNNING	Operational resources are in use
IFF_NOARP	ARP is not used by this network device
IFF_PROMISC	The network device will receive all packets on the network, even those addressed to other devices
IFF_ALLMULTI	The network device will receive all IP multicast packets
IFF_MASTER	Master–slave mode is activated: there is a slave for the device
IFF_SLAVE	This device is being used as a slave for another network device
IFF_MULTICAST	The hardware is capable of receiving IP multicast packets

connected to the network. As the addresses are implemented as byte fields, they are type-independent. The variable `addr_len` details the length of the addresses, which is, of course, limited by `MAX_ADDR_LEN`. The values in these fields are entered on initializing the device and cannot be changed.

```
unsigned long          pa_addr;
unsigned long          pa_brdaddr;
unsigned long          pa_dstaddr;
unsigned long          pa_mask;
unsigned short         pa_alen;
```

These are the addresses of the protocol used to access the device, with `pa_addr` holding the protocol address for the network device and `pa_brdaddr` the broadcast address at protocol level. An important part is played by the network mask `pa_mask`, which is interpreted by the IP as a bit mask. The bits in an address which are set in the mask belong to the network address, and the remainder to the host. In point-to-point connections this mask is not relevant, as there is only one communication partner, and its protocol address is then held in `pa_dstaddr`. The data type `unsigned long` indicates that only IP addresses are supported. This makes it all the more surprising to see the field `pa_alen` here, as it only makes sense for variable-length addresses.

```
struct dev_mc_list      *mc_list;
int                      mc_count;
struct ip_mc_list        ip_mc_list;
__u32                    tx_queue_len;
unsigned long            pkt_queue;
struct device           *slave;
```

These elements were added for versions 1.2 and 2.0 of LINUX. The components `mc_list` and `mc_count` are used in implementing multicasting on hardware level and `ip_mc_list` on IP level. The list holds the IP multicast addresses and `mc_count` the number of entries. Each element in the list describes exactly one IP multicast address; these addresses are already supported by the hardware in a number of Ethernet cards.

The other two entries are no longer used in the current version, but were previously used to distribute the packet load between two network devices.

```
struct net_alias_info   *alias_info;
strcut net_alias        *my_alias;
```

These two elements are used for network devices with several protocol addresses.

```
struct sk_buff *volatile buffs[DEV_NUMBUFFS];
```

As shown in Figure 8.5, network devices administer the packets waiting to be processed in lists. More of these are held in `buffs[]`, where the index in `buffs[]` indicates the priority assigned to the packets in the list. Three priorities are allowed for: `SOPRI_INTERACTIVE`, `SOPRI_NORMAL` and `SOPRI_BACKGROUND`. `SOPRI_INTERACTIVE`, with a value of 0, is the highest priority.

```
int        (*open)(struct device *dev);
int        (*stop)(struct device *dev);
```

The operations `open()` and `stop()` should really be called `start()` and `close()`, which would describe their interaction more precisely. After `open()` is called, packets can be sent via the network device, but the function does not initialize the addresses. The `stop()` function ends the transfer of packets and sets the addresses to `NULL`.

```
int       (*hard_start_xmit) (struct sk_buff *skb,
                               struct device *dev);
int       (*hard_header)     (struct sk_buff *skb,
                               struct device *dev,
                               unsigned short type,
                               void *daddr, void *saddr,
                               unsigned len);
int       (*rebuild_header)  (void *eth,
                               struct device *dev,
                               unsigned long raddr,
                               struct sk_buff *skb);
```

The function `hard_start_xmit()` is hardware-dependent. Its parameters are set to the appropriate values when a particular card is detected. It is charged with sending the packet waiting in the indicated buffer. The global function `dev_queue_xmit()` can be regarded as the buffered variant of `hard_start_xmit()`. If the device is not busy, `dev_queue_xmit()` calls `hard_start_xmit()` and attempts to transfer the packet immediately. Otherwise, the packet is added to one of the lists for packets waiting to be sent, according to its priority. The `hard_header()` function writes the hardware protocol header to the buffer indicated, while `rebuild_header()` updates the buffer according to the data in the `device` structure pointed to by `dev`.

```
unsigned short (*type_trans) (struct sk_buff *skb,
                               struct device *dev);
void       (*add_arp)        (unsigned long addr,
                               struct sk_buff *skb,
                               struct device *dev);
```

The function `add_arp()` associates the protocol address `addr` with the hardware address contained in the protocol header of the packet (*see* Section 8.4). The type of packet it is passed is indicated by `type_trans()`.

```
#define HAVE_MULTICAST
    void    (*set_multicast_list)(struct device *dev);
#define HAVE_SET_MAC_ADDR
    void    (*set_mac_address)(struct device *dev, void *addr);
#define HAVE_PRIVATE_IOCTL
    void    (*do_ioctl)(struct device *dev, struct ifreq *ifr,
                        int cmd);
#define HAVE_SET_CONFIG
    void    (*set_config)(struct device *dev, struct ifmap *map);
```

`set_multicast_list()` is a function which supports recent developments in the Internet. It enables a network device to receive packets not sent to the protocol address. The implementation for Ethernet cards uses their 'promiscuous' mode, in which the cards receive all packets sent to the network.

```
#define HAVE_SET_MAC_ADDR
    int       (*set_mac_address) (struct device *dev,
                                  void *addr);
#define HAVE_PRIVATE_IOCTL
    int       (*do_ioctl)        (struct device *dev,
                                  void *addr);
#define HAVE_SET_CONFIG
    int       (*set_config)      (struct device *dev,
                                  struct ifmap *map);
};
```

The `set_mac_address()` function has only been implemented for SLIP, to set the hardware address. Using the `do_ioctl` function, network devices can enable special configurations to be set from outside – with PLIP, for example, the value of the timeout can be set or read. More general settings of the hardware are possible using the `set_config()` function. This, for example, allows the number of the interrupt to be set.

```
#define HAVE_HEADER_CACHE
    void      (*header_cache_bind)(struct hh_cache **hhp,
                                   struct device *dev,
                                   unsigned short htype,
                                   __u32 daddr);
    void      (*header_cache_update)(struct hh_cache *hh,
                                     struct device *dev,
                                     unsigned char *haddr);
#define HAVE_CHANGE_MTU
    void      (*change_mtu)(struct device *dev, int new_mtu);
};
```

The two `header_cache` functions are needed for the implementation of the routing cache. This has been added in Linux version 2.0 in order to achieve an improved network throughput. The `change_mtu` function is called when a user program changes the MTU of a network device.

The `device` structure we have described represents a mixture of elements from the higher levels of the kernel and hardware-level data, and is not an example of good programming style. It is also noticeable that a range of IP-specific components are included in this abstract device description. This does not exclude the use of other protocols on this device.

8.3.1   Ethernet

LINUX supports two groups of adaptors for Ethernet. These include on the one hand the classic Ethernet cards connected to the PC bus, and on the other adaptors linked to the PC via the parallel interface or the PCMCIA bus.

The network devices for Ethernet cards are named 'eth0', ..., 'eth3'. This also applies for pocket adaptors operated via the PCMCIA bus, which are included as a module. LINUX assigns cards to devices in the sequence in which the hardware is detected. On start-up, the kernel outputs a message on the cards detected and their allocation to the network devices. For modules, of course, this output only takes place at the time of loading.

Information on which cards and/or adaptors LINUX supports can be found in the 'Ethernet HOWTO'.[2] As cards compatible with the WD8013 and NE2000 cards are supported, a large number of inexpensive Ethernet adaptors are available.

Let us take a close look at the Ethernet network devices. The Ethernet address of the associated network card is held in the field dev_addr[]. Every Ethernet adaptor has a completely unique address. These addresses are 6 bytes long; an example, represented as text, would be 0:0:c0:9b:13:29. After the network device has been configured with an IP address, an entry in the ARP table is generated when the card is selected (*see* ifconfig in Appendix B.8).

A field in the hardware header of an Ethernet packet allows various types of Ethernet packet to be differentiated. There are types for IP, ARP, IPX and other protocols. The type determines which receive function the packet is passed to.

The allocation of packet types is carried out with the aid of a list. It is thus possible to carry out dynamic modifications on the known packet types. For IP, for example, there is a list element as follows:

```
static struct packet_type ip_packet_type = {
  htons(ETH_P_IP),
  0,
  ip_rcv,
  NULL,
  NULL
};
```

This entry contains both the Ethernet packet type and the associated receive function. The first zero indicates that no copies need to be made of packets of this type. At the position of the NULL pointer, there may be a pointer to special data. The final pointer links the elements in the list of all packet types.

---

[2] The 'Ethernet HOWTO' is located in the file docs/HOWTO/Ethernet-HOWTO on the CD-ROM accompanying this book.

This list thus represents the interface between the network devices and the separate protocols as far as the devices are concerned. Packets which do not match any of the types registered in the list are discarded.

8.3.2 SLIP and PLIP

Now let us turn to some more 'exotic-looking' devices. The only significant difference between SLIP and PLIP is that the one protocol uses the computer's serial interface for data transfer while the other transfers data via the parallel port. When we speak of the parallel interface here, we do not mean Ethernet pocket adaptors but the 'bare' interface.

PLIP enables a very powerful link to be set up between two computers. SLIP is the simplest way of connecting a computer or a local network to the Internet via a serial link (a modem connection to a telephone network). SLIP and PLIP differ from Ethernet in that they can only transmit IP packets. For simplicity, SLIP does not even use a hardware header. Nor does PLIP make great demands: it simply sets the hardware address to 'fd:fd' plus the IP address and then uses the Ethernet functions for the protocol header (*see* Figure 8.7).

8.3.3 The loopback device

The loopback device provides communication facilities to applications on the local computer using sockets in the INET address family. It can be implemented with little effort, as it immediately returns to the upper layers the packets to be sent. It can also be used to test network applications on a computer: this excludes the possibility of faults in the network hardware. The loopback device 'lo' is generally assigned to the IP address 127.0.0.1.

8.3.4 The dummy device

In the dummy device we encounter a rather exotic representative of network devices. It behaves in fact like any other device, except that no real data transfer takes place.

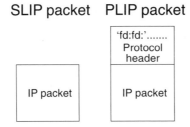

Figure 8.7   The relationship of SLIP and PLIP packets to IP packets.

It might well be asked what use a network device of this sort is. It is mostly used to present a functioning network device to the higher-level areas of the network implementation when there is not actually one present. By the higher-level areas of the network implementation we also mean user processes.

8.4 ARP – the Address Resolution Protocol

As the name implies, the task of the ARP is to convert the abstract IP addresses into real hardware addresses. This conversion is required because a hardware network cannot do anything with IP addresses. The ARP is not restricted to one hardware type, but can resolve addresses for a number of types of network (for example, FDDI, Ethernet and so on). The only condition made on the hardware is a facility to send a packet to all the other stations on the network (in other words, to broadcast). The LINUX ARP is capable of mapping Ethernet addresses, arcnet addresses and AX.25 addresses to the corresponding IP addresses. This is the reason for the rather odd position in which the ARP is drawn in Figure 8.1: it does not belong directly to the IP, although up to now only IP addresses have been considered as protocol addresses.

The reverse function is handled by RARP (reverse ARP). Unlike ARP, the RARP in LINUX can at present only convert Ethernet addresses into IP addresses.

A further facility offered by LINUX is 'proxy' ARP. This enables sub-networks which should really be directly interconnected by hardware to be separated. The separate parts are then usually provided with gateways to communicate with each other. The gateway in each subnetwork responds to ARP requests from local computers with its own hardware address. If packets for a remote computer are received at the gateway, it forwards these to the appropriate gateway.

The central element in address resolution is the ARP table, which consists of a field of pointers to structures of the type `arp_table`. The size of the table is `ARP_TABLE_SIZE`, which is defined in `net/inet/arp.h`. It must always be a power of 2, as this is assumed by the hash function. In LINUX, there is only one such table and not, as might be expected, one for each network interface. This makes the ARP entries easier to administer.

```
struct arp_table {
    struct arp_table        *next;
    volatile unsigned long  last_used;
    volatile unsigned long  last_updated;
    unsigned int            flags;
    u32                     ip;
    u32                     mask;
```

Table 8.2 Flags for entries in the ARP table.

Flag	Description
ATF_COM	The entry is complete
ATF_PERM	There is no time limit on this element
ATF_PUBL	This is a proxy entry
ATF_USETRAILERS	The network devices uses packet trailers
ATF_NETMASK	The value in netmask is to be used: this is a proxy entry for an entire subnetwork

```
    unsigned char           ha[MAX_ADDR_LEN];
    struct device           *dev;
    struct hh_cache         *hh;
    struct timer_list        timer;
    int                      retries;
    struct sk_buff_head      skb;
};
```

Apart from the elements necessary for linking the entries, an entry in the ARP table contains the protocol address and, if present, a reference to the list of hardware headers. The use of an entry is largely determined by flags. If ATF_COM remains unset, this means it has not yet been possible to determine the hardware address. As the ARP is hardware-dependent information, each element is assigned to a network device. The device to be used can be determined via the protocol's routing function; also all queries are then sent via this device. To resolve hardware addresses, it is sometimes necessary to send the query several times. When an query is generated, the timer (timer) is set. If it has expired and no further repeat is indicated, the query is considered not to have been answered. To make it simple to generate individual repeats, the buffer that contains the packet at the entry that has not yet been given a reply is marked.

Proxy entries are marked with an ATF_PUBL flag and are of course permanent. With 'proxy' ARP it is also possible to use subnetwork entries, which are then given an ATF_NETMASK flag. In mask we also find the netmask belonging to the subnetwork.

The following tasks are assigned to the ARP software:

- Address resolution for its own IP layer.
- Address resolution for queries from other hosts in the network.
  If the resolution of the machine's own IP address is required by another host, a reply packet is sent to the remote enquirer.
- Query generation for IP addresses not contained in the table.

- Removal of time-expired entries from the table.
- Removal of invalid entries from the table.
  If a network device is closed down, all associated entries are deleted, including the proxy entries.

Access to the address resolution procedure is provided by ARP by means of the function arp_find(), which either fetches the desired information direct from the table or sends an ARP query to the network. It follows from this that the quality of the ARP is primarily dependent on the ratio of 'hits' when accessing the ARP table. LINUX's ARP therefore includes a facility to optimize this: if an ARP query is received from the network, the information about the enquirer's hardware address already held in the network is included in the ARP table. This saves a further query to the network the next time a local query is received.

The ARP packets are passed by the central function net_bh() (*see* Section 8.1.2) to the arp_rcv() function appropriate to their protocol types, which also handles the optimization procedure described above. If the query concerns our own machine, the reply is generated and sent to the enquirer.

The deletion of obsolete entries is governed by timers. If an entry is filled with valid values, the timer is started and on expiry calls the function arp_check_expire(). This tests whether the entry has been used since the timer was reset: if not, the entry can be deleted.

Another element which can initiate the deletion of entries is the network timer, where the entries for the communication partner of a recently closed connection are deleted. This may seem pointless at first glance, but it should be borne in mind that if the IP hardware address allocations change, the packets could be sent to the wrong hardware and consequently to the wrong host.

```
struct rarp_table
{
    struct rarp_table        *next;
    unsigned long            ip;
    unsigned char            ha[MAX_ADDR_LEN];
    unsigned char            hlen
    unsigned char            htype;
    struct device            *dev;
};
```

Most elements in the RARP data structure should be self-explanatory, as they match those in the ARP table. The hardware address is entered when the structure is generated, and the IP address is added when the reply to an RARP query is received.

8.5   IP

The IP layer is the most important section of all the communication software, as all of the network traffic is carried by this layer. What are the tasks assigned to it?

8.5.1   IP – general introduction

The IP layer provides a packet transfer service – that is, it can be given a packet and the addressees and it will take care of the transfer. IP, however, does not guarantee safe and correct arrival of the packet at its intended destination: secure transfer of packets is ensured by the TCP, which is dependent in turn on the services of the IP layer.

In principle, the packets being transferred can be divided into two categories. Those in one category are generated by the local host and have to be sent to others. The other category of packets are generated by other hosts, and the local host is merely a link in the transmission chain. This process is known as *IP forwarding*.

The following much simplified picture describes the tasks of the IP layer. This description does not include any true error handling, but is sufficient for a general understanding.

The schematic flow of the outgoing packet stream of IP is as follows:

- Receipt of a packet.
- Option handling.
- Routing to the destination address.
- Generating the hardware header.
  During the routing process, the device through which the packet has to be sent is determined. A header for the hardware type of this device is then constructed, containing the hardware address of the next recipient.
- Creating the IP packet.
  This involves generating an IP header, which is simply added to the hardware header along with the data packet.
- Fragmenting the IP packet.
  If the IP packet is too large for the device, it will need to be broken down into smaller packets.
- Passing the IP packet to the appropriate network device.

The schematic flow of the incoming packet stream of IP is:

- Checking the IP header.

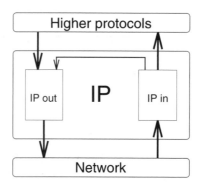

Figure 8.8 Incoming and outgoing packet streams.

- Decrementing the ttl field.
  If this results in the value reaching zero, the packet has to be discarded; an appropriate ICMP message is sent to the sender.

- Comparing destination address with local address.
  If the IP packet is not for the local computer, it is subsequently processed as an outgoing packet.

- Defragmenting the IP packet.
  If the packet is fragmented, it is reconstructed using fragments already received. If this is not yet possible, the fragment is stored in the fragment list.

- Forwarding the packet to the next protocol.
  Packets are demultiplexed according to the value of the protocol field in the IP header.

8.5.2   IP functions

The following section deals with the essential functions of the IP layer. For details of their operation the reader is recommended to consult the implementation. We will consider first the functions used by the other protocols, as shown in Table 8.3.

As mentioned above in the description of the data structures for the proto structure in Section 8.2.4, some of the other protocols do not implement their own functions and use the IP functions.

The two socket option functions are, of course, used by the higher protocols. If we look again at the layer model in Figure 8.1, it is clear that the layer in which the options are located is specified by the level parameter in setsockopt(). In each layer, the strategy followed is: 'If it is not for me, it must be for the layer below me'.

Table 8.3 Exported functions of the IP layer.

Function	AF_INET/ (R)ARP	Packet	UDP RAW	TCP	ICMP	IGMP
ip_chk_addr()	×		×	×	×	
ip_setsockopt()			×	×		
ip_getsockopt()			×	×		
ip_build_header()		×	×	×	×	×
ip_queue_xmit()		×	×	×	×	×
ip_build_xmit			×		×	
ip_send_check()				×		
ip_check_route()				×		

Probably one of the most frequently used functions in the implementation of IP and the protocols based on it is `ip_chk_addr()`. This is given an IP address as a parameter and returns a value classifying this address. There are four groups of addresses:

- addresses for a local network device,
- broadcast addresses,
- multicast addresses,
- all other addresses.

An important element throughout the network implementation is `ip_build_header()`, which is used by all the layers above the IP. Its job is to write the header for the packet to a buffer. 'Header' here does not mean the IP protocol header only, but all the header data needed by the corresponding network device. Consecutive calls to each of the header routines are the only way linear memory organization in the buffers can be achieved. However, this linearity also has its disadvantages: for example, the maximum possible amount of memory must be reserved for each packet.

For TCP, the checksum is calculated by calling the `ip_send_check()` function. The `ip_check_route()` function checks whether the computer to which the packet is next to be sent is still reachable.

The `ip_queue_xmit()` function is also already familiar to us. Like the last function described, it is also used by the other protocols. This is particularly surprising in the case of sockets of the SOCK_PACKET type, as these packets are sent direct to a network device and the IP function is not really concerned with them. However, this is just one of the minor inconsistencies we have found in the LINUX network implementation. If the packet to be transferred is too large, that is, larger than the MTU of the network device, the packet is split up into

ragments. The transfer is then initiated by a call to the
) function, with the network device determined in the routing
as a parameter.

UX version 2.0 is the function `ip_build_xmit()`. Its task is to
t, calculate the checksum and send the packet off.

d in Section 8.1.2, the link to the lower layers is implemented
`ip_rcv()`. This function is the only point of access to the IP for
the lower layers, and only goes into action for IP packets, expecting as parameters pointers to the packet, the receiving device and the packet type. Once
the protocol header has been checked for correctness, the options held in it are
processed. Next, the function checks whether the packet is addressed to the
local computer. If the packet is not for the local host, and if the computer has
not been configured as a router,[3] the packet is discarded; otherwise it is forwarded using `ip_forward()`. If any of the above conditions is not met, the
packet is similarly discarded. This may also occur if the computer no longer
has enough memory for the incoming packets. When a packet is discarded, an
error message is always sent to the sender. This is taken care of by the ICMP
protocol. To avoid a snowball effect, error messages are never generated for
faulty ICMP packets.

All that remains is to deal with fragmentation. If the packet is a fragment, we try to use it to build up a complete packet with the aid of any other
fragments that may have been received. This function is carried out in
`ip_defrag()`. If we are successful or if we have received a complete packet, we
forward the packet to the protocols above the IP.

In the function `ip_forward()` we check whether the packet's 'time to
live' has been exceeded.[4] We then work out the route to be taken by the packet
when it leaves us. A new packet is now constructed, consisting of the contents
of the old one, including the IP header. The hardware header now holds the
address of the next computer on the packet's route to its destination. If necessary, the packet must again be split up into a number of fragments. This,
however, is the task of `ip_fragment()`. Finally, all that is left is the transmission itself, which is handled by the appropriate network device.

As we have already seen in Section 8.3, it is perfectly possible that the
different networks (for example SLIP and Ethernet) have different maximum
packet sizes. This makes it necessary to divide oversize packets into a number
of smaller ones. However, this type of fragmentation can clearly only be
carried out in computers functioning as routers.

A case of this sort is handled by `ip_fragment`. The function splits the
packet into as many parts as are required to enable each of the parts to fit into
a fragment along with the protocol header. The size of the fragment must, of
course, be smaller than the maximum packet size for the receiving network.

---

[3] In which case 'IP: forwarding/gatewaying' has to be selected when configuring the LINUX kernel.
[4] This field is in the IP protocol header, and is decremented before the packet is forwarded.

The fragments, which are no more than specially marked packets, are then delivered to the network device.

In this process, special attention is required by packets which are themselves already fragments. An additional facility provided by the IP protocol prohibits the fragmentation of packets by setting an option in the protocol header. In this case, a special ICMP error message is sent to the sender of the packet if a case arises where fragmentation is necessary.

As the higher protocols should not be concerned with the details of fragmentation, this process is kept transparent to them. Accordingly, when fragments of an IP packet are received by the IP layer, nothing is delivered until all the fragments belonging to the packet have been received. They are then recombined into a single packet, which can then be passed through to the higher protocols. This procedure, the opposite of fragmentation, is known as defragmentation. For IP, it is carried out by the function `ip_defrag()`.

The `ip_defrag()` function is based on a number of utility routines (`ip_expire()`, `ip_glue()`, `ip_done()`, `ip_find()` and `ip_frag_create()`). A central role in fragmentation is played by the `ipq` structure and the timers it contains. In the `ipq` structure, all the fragments of an IP packet are collected together. The timer is restarted whenever a further fragment is received. If all the fragments arrive before the timer expires, they are joined up and from then on treated as a newly received packet. If the timer expires, the fragments are discarded and the sender informed via the ICMP.

8.5.3 Routing

A route must be established by the IP for every packet that is sent. The decision on whom the packet is sent to, and via which network device, is made by reference to the *Forwarding Information Base* (FIB). Earlier versions of LINUX used the routing table, but this became hopelessly slow for bigger tables. Therefore, a new structure based on a two-step hash method was designed. On the higher step, we find structures of the `struct fib_zone` type. These are responsible for one zone each. A zone denotes all routes that have the same route mask. Thus, all host routes are in the same zone.

The zones manage all associated routes in a list or a hash table. Hash tables are only used when a greater number of routes must be dealt with. The list or hash table contains structures of the `struct fib_node` type. Together with the corresponding `struct fib_info` they hold all information for a determined route. The information is divided into two structures because much of the information for different routes is identical.

For continuous fast access, there is yet another hash table of the `struct rtable` type. This is automatically extended with the necessary entries, while obsolete entries are deleted. As the routing cache entries are of the original type `struct rtable`, nothing has changed for the other parts of IP.

The routing cache is located in the field `ip_rt_hash_table[]`. The index is a hash value calculated from the destination address. The method used is open hashing because, with limited table size, several destination addresses are assigned the same hash value. The cache is also used to realize dynamic routes which are valid only for a limited period of time.

```
struct rtable {
    struct rtable          *rt_next;
```

The element `rt_next` points to the next entry in the list mentioned above.

```
    __u32                  rt_dst;
    __u32                  rt_mask;
```

The variable `rt_dst` holds the destination address for the route, which can of course be an entire network or subnetwork. The so-called *default route*, represented numerically by '0.0.0.0', is a special case: it is used for all packets not covered by the other routes. The mask gives the network part of the address. This enables a working *subnetting* to be run on routers. Practically all commercial products could do worse than emulate LINUX in this respect.

```
    __u32                  rt_gateway;
```

Without a gateway, even the best route is useless. We need to know the address of the host which is acting as a gateway.

```
    atomic_t               rt_refcnt;
    atomic_t               rt_use;
    unsigned long          rt_window;
    atomic_t               rt_lastuse;
    struct hh_cache        *rt_hh;
    struct device          *rt_dev;
    unsigned shart         rt_flags, rt_mtu, rt_irtt;
    unsigned char          rt_tos;
};
```

The flags provide information on the status of the route (How should the route be used? Is it only used for one host? Is the destination a gateway? Is it a dynamic route? and so on). The metric indicates the assessed costs for this route: this parameter is used for the various routing protocols.

So much for the basic structure by which the separate routing functions operate. We are not concerned here with the internal administration functions. We shall only describe the routines used by other parts of the network implementation.

Table 8.4 Routing functions used externally.

Function	INET socket	TCP, UDP and IP protocol/(R)ARP	ICMP protocol
ip_rt_ioctl()	×		
ip_rt_route()		×	×
ip_rt_redirect()			×
ip_rt_flush()		×	
ip_rt_put()		×	

One of the most important functions for routing is ip_rt_ioctl(), which enables the routing table to be manipulated. For reasons of compatibility, the function also reacts to ioctl commands of the old style. The contents of the table can only be read via the *Proc* file system (/proc/net/route); there is no ioctl command to do this. In addition, the contents of the routing cache are also represented in the *Proc* file system (/proc/net/rt_cache).

The correct processing of ICMP redirect messages also includes entering the corresponding routes in the routing table. For this, ICMP uses the function ip_rt_add(). The routes generated or modified by this are always marked as dynamic routes.

The central function in routing is ip_rt_route(). It evaluates the information held in the cache or in the FIB and determines the route to be taken by the packet. This function is used at least once for each IP packet, which means that the overall speed of the TCP/IP implementation depends to a large degree on ip_rt_route().

The routes supplied by the ip_rt_route() function are marked as 'in use' and cannot be changed. After using the routing information, the route must therefore be released by means of ip_rt_put(). Once released, the route must no longer be accessed.

When a network device is deactivated, the transfer of packets via this device is no longer possible. This means that routes in the table which refer to this device are no longer operable, and they are therefore automatically deleted from the table when a device is taken off the network. This task is handled by ip_rt_flush(). The function is given a pointer to a network device as a parameter and removes all relevant entries from the routing table.

8.5.4 IP multicasting and IGPM

One of the central innovations in communication using TCP/IP is IP multicasting. Until now there were really only two modes of communication under IP:

1-to-1 The packets are sent from one computer to just one other. The best example of this is a TCP connection.

1-to-N When packets are sent, all the computers in a network or subnetwork are potential recipients. This type of communication is mostly used to find the remote station for a following *1-to-1* communication. An example of this is the BOOTP protocol.

For a number of reasons, it is desirable to be able to operate *N-to-M* communication. This kind of communication mode greatly facilitates the implementation of programs like IRC, as it already supplies the majority of the necessary functions.

To use IP multicasting, two conditions must be met: first, the computer on which the relevant program is to run must support IP multicasting. Second, if the host group also includes computers in other subnetworks, there must be a chain of IP multicasting routers to allow packets to be forwarded.

The changes necessary to the computer are described in Deering (1989). These comprise on the one hand an implementation of IGMP as a component of the IP. On the other, changes need to be carried out on the network devices.

For the Ethernet cards, the changes are relatively generic. The IP multicast addresses are mapped to corresponding Ethernet addresses. However, receiving IP multicast addresses is only possible with the support of the hardware. Packets not addressed to the local hardware address must now also be received; this is handled by multicast support provided by the Ethernet cards. However, this support normally relates only to a very limited number of addresses. If this number is exceeded, or no multicast support is present, it is still possible to receive all packets. These are then filtered out afterwards by the network device or forwarded directly to the IP. The IP will then in any case discard packets which are not required.

The location is not exactly as shown in Figure 8.9. As with all the other protocols using the IP's transfer mechanism, the packets are passed to IGMP by a call to a receive function (`igmp_rcv()`). The rest of the IGMP implementation is equally unproblematical.

The IGMP in version 1 described here supports two types of packet:

- *Host membership query*
  These queries are sent by the IP multicast routers to find out the membership of the IP multicast addresses for all hosts in a subnetwork. Once it has this information, a router is then able to forward the IP multicast packets efficiently.

- *Host membership report*
  These packets are sent by the individual computers in reply to packets of the type above. The router only requires one reply for each IP multicast address.

As we do not want all the hosts in a subnetwork to create a reply packet to a query at the same time, it has been specified in Deering (1989) that each of the

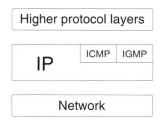

Figure 8.9 Location of the IGMP protocol module.

computers is to wait for a random interval before sending a reply packet. If, during this waiting state, a computer receives a reply with the same content as the one it would have sent, it is no longer necessary to do so. In the best case, this will reduce the packet traffic on the Ethernet to one reply packet per IP multicast address.

A further aspect of IP multicasting in LINUX is its configuration. When the kernel is generated, it must be told whether or not the code necessary for the use of IP multicasting is to be generated. This is done by the configuration parameter `CONFIG_IP_MULTICAST`.

8.5.5   IP packet filters

With IP packet filters, a very powerful tool has been placed in the hands of network administrators. Using these filters, they can specify very precisely which IP packets are to be forwarded or recorded. Figure 8.10 shows the logical location of the IP packet filters.

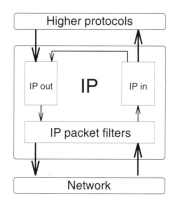

Figure 8.10 Location of the packet filters.

A filter consists of a list of packet patterns. If a packet matches a pattern in the list it will be recognized by the corresponding filter. The semantics of a filter must however be specified externally.

Users are provided with a variety of ways of specifying a packet pattern. For example, exactly one connection may be specified. In this case, the source and destination addresses will be given. The associated masks indicate the entire address range (0xffffffff). The user may specify in addition whether all packet types are to be included. However, this can also be restricted to TCP and/or UDP. For the UDP and TCP types, the port numbers of the protocol can also be specified. For each matching packet, the packet counter and byte counters are incremented by the appropriate values.

```
struct ip_fw {
    struct ip_fw    *fw_next;              /* linking              */
    struct in_addr  fw_src, fw_dst;        /* source and destination */
    struct in_addr  fw_smsk, fw_dmsk;
    struct in_addr  fw_via;
    struct device   *fw_viadev;
    unsigned short  fw_flg;                           /* TCP/UDP */
    unsigned short  fw_nsp, fw_ndp;
    unsigned short  fw_pts[IP_FW_MAX_PORTS];
    unsigned long   fw_pcnt, fw_bcnt;
    unsigned char   fw_tosand, fw_tosxor;
    char            fw_vianame[IFNAMSIZ];
}
```

But this is not all a pattern can do. Taking the source and destination addresses together with the masks, whole networks can be used as patterns. Also, the ports for TCP and UDP can be omitted.

8.5.6   IP accounting and IP firewalling

Having familiarized ourselves with the basic technology, we will now look at the use of the IP packet filters.

The characteristics of IP packet filters we have described make them suitable for use in two areas. Firstly, it is possible using the filters to find out exactly which computer in the local network has sent a packet to the Internet. This is the basis for IP accounting, which can also be used, of course, to monitor network traffic from the local computer to other networks and hosts.

The necessary conditions for precise accounting, however, do not usually exist. Unfortunately, the IP packet filters presented here do not allow network traffic to be broken down to individual users, as this requires a *one-to-one* relation of IP addresses to users.

IP accounting is normally not present in the LINUX kernel. If it is required, it must be included by setting the configuration parameter CONFIG_IP_ACCT when the kernel is generated.

However, the demands made by IP firewalling are well within the capabilities of the IP packet filters. As an IP firewall machine is always located at a gateway, the checking mechanisms can be implemented relatively easily. The function `call_fw_firewall()` is concerned with forwarding IP packets received. This makes it the obvious place for the control mechanism which is to be implemented by IP firewalling. `call_in_firewall()` and `call_out_firewall()` restrict receiving and sending of IP packets, respectively.

There are two IP packet filters for the administration of IP firewalling. This allows the restrictions for the IP packet to be applied in stages. The first filter is located directly in the IP receive function. If a packet matches a pattern in this blocking filter, it is subsequently ignored by the IP.

Firewalling too is normally not present in the LINUX kernel and must be included by setting the configuration parameter `CONFIG_IP_FIREWALL` when the kernel is generated.

8.6 UDP

Before we turn to the complexities of TCP, we will provide an 'introduction' by describing UDP. It has only a few functional expansions as compared with IP.

8.6.1 Functions of UDP

As with the IP protocol, a `rcv` function again plays a decisive role. The `udp_rcv` function is charged with processing packets received. As Figure 8.11 shows, the function has to find the destination socket for the packet. For this, it falls back on the services of `get_sock()`. It then has the INET socket and the IP packet as a basis from which to work.

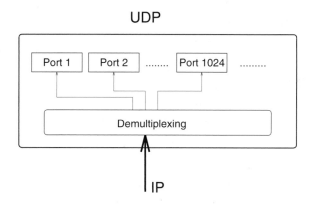

Figure 8.11 Demultiplexing in UDP.

Table 8.5 Functions exported from the UDP layer.

Function	struct inet_protocol udp_protocol	struct proto udp_prot	RAW protocol
udp_err()	×		
udp_rcv()	×	×	
udp_connect()		×	×
udp_close()		×	
udp_sendmsg()		×	
udp_recvmsg()		×	
udp_ioctl()		×	

If we have not been able to find a socket matching the destination port for the packet, we send the sender an error message. This again uses ICMP. We then analyse the checksum, if one is provided. The UDP protocol does not make the use of a checksum mandatory; however, if there is one and it is not correct, the packet is rejected. Now the socket, the receiving network device, the packet length and the source and destination addresses are entered in the buffer containing the packet. As each of the sockets only has a limited amount of memory available to it, a test is carried out to see whether the new packet will exceed the limit. If there is sufficient memory, the buffer is entered in the list of packets received for the socket. After this, the process to which this socket belongs must be notified, for which we use the socket's `__sock_queue_rcv_skb` and `data_ready` functions. This wakes up all the processes sleeping on the socket.

The data are now assigned to the socket, and the process can fetch them using the library functions `recvfrom()` or `read()`. Here, both the `read()` and the `recvfrom()` functions are mapped to the protocol operation `recvmsg()`. This is followed by the standard procedures for a read system call: first test the area of memory where the results will be written; calculate the results (which in this case means checking whether a packet is there); finally, output the results, that is, copy the contents of the packet to the process's buffer and the address into the address structure provided. That is all there is to it. However, if there is no packet there, and the `noblock` flag tells us that the process should not wait, we return the appropriate error message. Otherwise the process blocks at the socket and only wakes up if a change is made to the socket. The sleep/wake-up mechanism is described more fully in Section 3.1.5.

The data flow in the opposite direction is equally uncomplicated. All this involves is determining the correct address using `udp_sendto()`. The actual work is done by `udp_sendmsg()`, which reserves memory for the buffer including the packet. We now use the address received by `udp_sendto()` to make IP generate a protocol header. After this header, the UDP writes its own protocol header into the buffer. All that remains is to copy the contents into the buffer and pass the packet to the IP, which takes care of everything else. Finally, it should be mentioned as before that `udp_write()` is an alias of `udp_sendmsg()`. However, no destination is given, which assumes that the socket has been assigned to a destination address by means of the system call *connect*.

Finally, let us look at a few less interesting functions. The user can call `udp_ioctl()` to find the size of the data to be read or written. The function `udp_err()` is concerned with the error messages received from ICMP that are relevant to UDP. These primarily comprise `ICMP_SOURCE_QUENCH` messages, telling us to stop sending data so quickly. The `udp_connect()` function in effect simply sets the destination address for the socket, as mentioned above, and `udp_close()` initiates the release of the socket because a direct communication partner to be informed does not exist.

8.6.2   Other functions

For reasons connected with the implementation, some functions included in the UDP protocol have been located in the 'datagram' section. These functions also include the `select` function used in UDP.

Its name is therefore `datagram_select()`. It checks whether the condition passed to it is met. The write condition is met if the memory space which can still be requested by this socket for writing is above the minimum value. Only an error event constitutes an exception condition. The `select` function (*see* Section 6.2.6) returns 1 if the relevant condition is true, otherwise 0.

8.7   TCP

Now that we are familiar with the basic approach to a protocol in UDP, we will explore the mysteries of the LINUX network implementation more deeply. We should bear in mind that the transition from the connectionless, insecure UDP to the connection-oriented, secure TCP represents not only a quantitative difference. Rather, we are dealing with a new quality of service.

8.7.1   General notes on TCP

First, a few preliminary remarks on TCP. To guarantee secure data transfer (TCP) on the basis of insecure data transfer (IP), we need timers. It is only these that enable the TCP protocol to be implemented with correct timing behaviour. In LINUX we have timers which are used by calling the functions `add_timer()` and `del_timer()` in the kernel. This facility is not used in the network implementation. A new interface for network timers has been written, which includes the functions `reset_timer()` and `delete_timer()` as well as the timer for the network, `net_timer()`, which is mainly concerned with the requirements of TCP. This interface has simplified the use of timers in the network code: users do not have to implement their own timeout functions everywhere and the handling is carried out centrally in the `net_timer()` function, controlled via the states of the INET socket and the timings of the timers. It is not only in the functions belonging directly to TCP that state transitions take place in a finite state machine, but also here in the network timer.

8.7.2 The TCP communication end-point – a finite state machine

The behaviour of TCP connections is specified in Postel (1981). The following description outlines the specification for the finite state machine for the TCP end points. In this description, the paragraph numbering matches the numbers in Figure 8.12.

First we look at the server side of communication set-up.

(1)   The transition to the LISTEN state is initiated by the process itself by a call to the function `listen()`. With this, the process then blocks, informing the kernel that it should handle incoming communication requests.

(2)   A segment containing a SYN has been received and one containing a SYN/ACK returned to the sender. The process is now waiting for the concluding ACK from the communication partner.

(3)   The ACK has been received, and the connection is now established.

We now look at the client side of communication set-up.

(4)   The client uses the function `connect()` to set up a connection to the server. The function sends a segment containing a set SYN to the server and then goes over to the SYN_SENT state. The process now remains blocked until it receives the SYN/ACK from the server.

(5)   When the SYN/ACK has been received from the server, the client sends back the concluding ACK. As far as the client is concerned, connection set-up is now completed.

When breaking the connection we cannot speak of a server and client as in the set-up phase. We must now distinguish between the initiator and its counterpart.

(6)   By calling `close()` or a similar termination, one side of the TCP connection initiates the release of the connection. This sends a FIN to the opposite communication end-point. Note that further segments may continue to arrive from the other side.

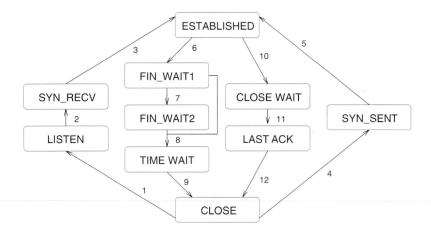

Figure 8.12 State transition diagram for TCP end-points.

(7) An ACK has been received, but no FIN. Here again, further data may still arrive from the other station.

(8) The FIN/ACK has now been received. However, to ensure proper handling of segments still in the network, we wait for a further specified interval (twice the maximum lifetime of a TCP segment). If a FIN/ACK is received during the FIN_WAIT1 state, FIN_WAIT2 is skipped.

(9) The connection is now terminated. All information related to it is deleted. The communication end-point can be reused.

(10) We have received a FIN from the remote station. We send the buffered data and report the start of connection release to the program.

(11) The program has been informed of the release of the connection. A FIN is sent. Now we are only waiting for the ACK from the other side, which acknowledges our FIN.

(12) The other communication end-point informs us via an ACK that it has also released the connection. We can now initiate a new connection set-up for this end-point.

8.7.3 Functions of TCP

As can be seen in the layer implementation of LINUX, the `tcp_rcv()` function is at the centre of the processing of incoming packets. This is hardly surprising, as the description of the TCP protocol for the lower layers consists only of the `tcp_protocol` structure, where only the `rcv` function is listed.

We will now follow the operation of the `tcp_rcv()` function. As in the other protocols, it first obtains an INET socket. Then the checksum for the

Table 8.6 Functions exported by the TCP layer.

Function	INET socket	struct inet_protocol tcp_protocol	struct proto tcp_prot
`tcp_dequeue_partial()`	×		
`tcp_connected()`	×		
`tcp_err()`		×	
`tcp_rcv()`		×	×
`tcp_close()`			×
`tcp_sendmsg()`			×
`tcp_recvmsg()`			×
`tcp_connect()`			×
`tcp_accept()`			×
`tcp_retransmit()`			×
`tcp_write_wakeup()`			×
`tcp_read_wakeup()`			×
`tcp_select()`			×
`tcp_ioctl()`			×
`tcp_shutdown()`			×
`tcp_setsockopt()`			×
`tcp_getsockopt()`			×

segment is checked for correctness. If an error occurs, we simply release the buffer memory and ignore the segment. The fields in the `sk_buff` structure used by TCP are now initialized to 0. The buffer memory is considered to belong to the socket, so is included in the memory reserved for reading. After this, various `if` instructions are used to simulate the finite state machine, with the behaviour for the separate states described in the various branches. The behaviour of almost the entire protocol is described here. The processing of the data held in the segment is carried out by the `tcp_data()` function; for out-of-band data this task is taken over by `tcp_urg()` (for 'urgent'). Here, the 'receive acknowledgements' central to the operation of TCP are extracted and entered in the INET socket.

In the TCP protocol, the data are not necessarily returned immediately when they are written to the socket by the process. To keep the protocol overhead as small as possible, the protocol first waits for half a second to check that no further data are incoming from the process before sending off the TCP segment. If the quantity of data has by now become greater than the maximum segment size, a segment is sent to the remote station at once. This mechanism is implemented in the functions `tcp_enqueue_partial()`, `tcp_send_partial()` and `tcp_dequeue_partial()`.

The `tcp_connected()` function divides the states which can be adopted by the INET socket into two classes. If `tcp_connected()` returns with a value other than 0, this means that the socket is connected to another. A return value of 0 indicates that the socket is not connected.

If the ICMP receives an error message of the type `ICMP_...UNREACH` or `ICMP_SOURCE_QUENCH`, the error handling routine for the next higher protocol is called. This uses `tcp_err()`. As each ICMP error message must contain the first 80 bytes of the packet causing the error, TCP can precisely determine the related INET socket. By accessing the field `icmp_err_convert[]`, the function then fetches the error code for the socket and can then establish whether the error should cause the connection to be terminated. The error code is then entered in the INET socket. Only `ICMP_QUENCH` messages are processed by reducing the protocol window: these do not result in an error entry in the socket.

A call to `tcp_close()` initiates the active phase of connection release (*see* Section 8.7.2 and Figure 8.12) on the local host. All packets yet to be read are discarded and the remaining data are sent to the remote station with a FIN. We then switch from the current state to the next state. Normally this will be FIN_WAIT1 or FIN_WAIT2.

`tcp_sendmsg()` and `tcp_recvmsg()` receive the address information from the INET socket. The system calls `read()` and `write()` are already converted to the corresponding protocol operations in the BSD socket layer.

But now let us look at the two central communication functions in TCP. Specifying the flag `MSG_OOB` can cause the `tcp_recvmsg()` function to read only out-of-band data, and this will then be carried out by the `tcp_rcv_urg()` function. The buffers present at the INET socket are then examined. Here, particular attention is given to the out-of-band data: the processing of these data can be modified by the socket option `SO_OOBINLINE`. If this option is set, the out-of-band data are regarded as forming part of the standard data stream and handled as such. If the option has not been set, these data are simply skipped when read without a `MSG_OOB`. If data have already been found, and then out-of-band data arrive, the read process is terminated at the stage reached. The data in all valid buffers are then copied to the process address space. We then go on to the next buffer. If no data have been received at the INET socket, the process blocks at the socket, and is woken up when fresh data arrive.

Data transfer in the opposite direction is handled by `tcp_sendmsg()`. This first carries out a number of tests required by the TCP protocol, and then checks whether the INET socket is in a state (*see* Figure 8.12) which permits data exchange. We now investigate whether a packet which has already been started on is waiting at the socket. If so, we fill the packet using the data we have received. If we reach the maximum segment size, or if we have to deal with out-of-band data, the packet is sent off immediately. Otherwise, the packet will wait at the socket, but for no more than half a second. If there is not yet a packet at the INET socket, we allocate memory using the socket's `walloc` function. The `struct sk_buff` included in memory is initialized and a protocol header is written to the buffer using the protocol's `build_header` function (in this case `ip_build_header()`). Now our own `build_header` function – `tcp_build_header()` – is called. From this point, the procedure continues as if we had a packet which had already been started on. However, it is possible that we have already taken up the maximum memory for the socket. The process will in that case go to sleep at the socket. When memory is released for the socket it will be woken up.

To be able to set up a TCP connection in the first place, the active phase of connection set-up must be carried out. This task is assigned to the function `tcp_connect()`, where the address to which a connection is to be set up is checked for correctness. It is then entered in the INET socket structure. We now create a TCP packet for the connection set-up. For this, the sequence numbers for the INET socket are set to random starting values. We then use the protocol's `build_header()` function to write a protocol header to the buffer we have requested by calling `walloc()`. To this we add our own protocol header, with the SYN flag set. As well as this, the packet also contains the initial window size for our protocol unit. The INET socket then goes over to the SYN_SENT state and waits for a reply from the other communication end-point.

The `tcp_accept()` function implements the passive phase of connection set-up. At least, this is how it appears to the process. However, all the function does is fetch the INET socket which has already been created and which has been entered in the `sk_buff` structure of the connection set-up packet, and returns this to the higher protocol layer. The actual work is done while processing the incoming TCP packets and cannot be assigned to any process. If a packet is received there for connection set-up, an INET socket structure is generated for it (*see* the `tcp_conn_request()` function in `net/ipv4/tcp_input.c`).

In the case of `tcp_retransmit` it is probably safer to call it an alias rather than a true function. This simply reduces the size of the transmission window; the actual work is done by `tcp_do_retransmit()`.

We now come to the function which could be called the heart of 'secure' data transfer: `tcp_do_retransmit()`. The parameter `all` allows the function to be controlled in respect of whether all packets waiting at the INET socket are to be retransmitted, or only the first one. Here, `tcp_do_retransmit()` checks every packet to see whether the network device for the following transfer is known. If necessary, the protocol header is recreated. The current time is entered in the buffer containing the packet and the `dev_queue_xmit` function is then called. In the socket and in its related `proto` structure, this action is recorded by incrementing the counters (`retransmits`) for statistical purposes. Where necessary, these steps are repeated for each packet.

If the `ack_backlog` field in the INET socket structure is set, `tcp_read_wakeup()` returns to the communication partner an otherwise empty segment with a receive acknowledgement for the segments so far received. The `tcp_write_wakeup()` function sends a similar packet, but with the acknowledged sequence number one smaller. The two wakeup functions are mainly used by the network timer.

The `select()` function in TCP is almost the same as in UDP. In TCP, however, the receipt of out-of-band data is treated as a trigger for the exception conditions.

In addition to the functions mentioned in Section 8.2.4, the `tcp_ioctl()` function can also be used to check whether the current read position is on out-of-band data or not. This calls for the use of the symbolic value `SIOCATMARK`.

The `tcp_shutdown()` function terminates an existing connection 'slowly'. This function generates a segment that includes a FIN, which is added to the end of the list of packets waiting to be transferred. This means that all the unacknowledged data are first transferred before the release of the connection is initiated.

The functions `tcp_getsockopt()` and `tcp_setsockopt()` enable the maximum segment size and character buffering to be read or set, respectively. The character buffering (maximum half a second) is deselected by interactive programs such as `telnet` and `rlogin` in order to achieve acceptable response times, while `ftp` and `lpd` derive an advantage from this buffering.

8.8   The packet interface – an alternative?

LINUX has also introduced new approaches to network implementation. An interface has been created, for example, which can operate on network devices directly. This, of course, is only possible if the general layer model is circumvented, and we will therefore take a closer look at the sequence of actions involved in creating an interface of this type. Although there exists a separate stack for the Apple network protocol, an alternative approach will be considered. A process to implement the network communication functions of 'AppleTalk' on the basis of Ethernet could look like the following.

```
#include <sys/socket.h>
#define ETH_P_APPLETALK    0x809B
#define MAX_PACKET_SIZE    2048

extern void do_appletalk(unsigned char *, int);

main()
{ int fd, len;
  unsigned char buf[MAX_PACKET_SIZE];
```

```
        fd = socket(AF_INET, SOCK_PACKET, ETH_P_APPLETALK);
        if (fd < 0) exit(1);

        for(;;) {
          if ((len = read(fd, buf, MAX_PACKET_SIZE)) < 0) exit(2);
          do_appletalk(buf, len);
        }
    }
```

The section of principal interest to us is carried out in the call to socket. As we have already mentioned, this takes us into the kernel via the system call *socketcall*. This is given SYS_SOCKET as a call parameter, while args points to the original parameters passed to socket(). Processing then continues with the function sock_socket(), which looks almost the same as our original socket call. This sets up the BSD socket structure. By reference to the protocol family, this function recognizes which lower protocol needs to be brought in to handle the function. We now leave the BSD socket layer and reach the INET socket via the INET protocol. The protocol's create function – in this case, inet_create() – is then called. We can now set up the INET socket structure. The functions for a packet socket are entered in the INET socket in accordance with the type parameters provided to socket(), and finally the protocol's init function is called with the protocol parameter. This will be the packet_init() function.

The packet_init() function creates a new packet-type structure (*see* Section 8.3.1). The rcv function used is packet_rcv(), and our INET socket is entered in the data pointer. The gist of the packet interface is that the type for the Ethernet packets to be received is passed as the protocol number. The type is now entered in the packet_type structure. We then report the new packet type to the network devices using the function dev_add_pack(). From now on, packets of this type will no longer be discarded but will be forwarded to our socket. The packet_rcv() function in the packet driver has nothing else to do but take each packet from the queue of incoming packets and pass it to the process, which then takes care of interpreting the packet data.

The packet_sendmsg() function is also simple in construction. In the address structure we pass it the name of the network device, via which the packet contained in the data will be sent. Now we simply request a buffer, initialize the sk_buff structure and copy the data to the buffer. Finally, it is simply a matter of calling the network device's queue_xmit() function, and the packet is on its way.

This is how simple it is to implement another communications protocol under LINUX. The method has the additional crowning advantage that the implementation of the protocol is carried out in a user process, so that the system is safe from unpleasant crashes during development.

Modules and debugging

'Good luck guys,' chirped the computer,
'impact minus thirty seconds...'

Douglas Adams

The LINUX kernel is increasing in size as version follows version. This is a result of both the continuous improvement and expansion of kernel functions and the addition of new device drivers, file systems and emulations such as iBCS2. As LINUX is a monolithic system, however, all the device drivers and file systems used are permanently incorporated into the kernel. This means on the one hand that when the configuration is changed the kernel has to be recompiled, and on the other hand that drivers and file systems occupy permanent space in memory even if they are only used very rarely. Another disadvantage makes itself felt to developers of new kernel code: however trivial the modification, it means that a new kernel has to be created and installed and the computer rebooted. These and many other reasons have led to the development of modules. To begin with, this raises the question: what are modules?

9.1 What are modules?

From the point of view of the kernel, modules consist of object code linkable and removable at run-time, usually comprising a number of functions (at least two). This object code is integrated into the already running kernel with equal

279

rights, which means that it runs in system mode. The monolithic structure of the kernel is not changed: unlike the microkernel, the newly added functions do not run as processes in their own right. One advantage of implementing device drivers or file systems as modules is that only the documented interfaces can be used.

For the user, modules enable a small and compact kernel to be used, with other functions only being added as and when required. With the kernel daemon support of version 2.0, it is even possible to load modules automatically, without the user having to attend to this him/herself. As a further example we can mention the *PCMCIA* card manager.

The structure of the source text for the LINUX kernel is described in Section 2.1. The C files are organized in directories comprising functional groupings of various kinds. On compilation, the functional sub-units are collected into an object file, so that when the kernel is subsequently loaded as a whole there is no need to access every object file individually. These functional units can often be used as modules.

9.2   Implementation in the kernel

Now that we have seen the advantages of using modules, we will consider their implementation. For this, LINUX provides three system calls: `create_module`, `init_module` and `delete_module`. A further system call is used by the user process to obtain a copy of the kernel's symbol table.

The administration of modules under LINUX makes use of a list in which all the modules loaded are included. The form of the entries is shown on page 299. This list also administers the modules' symbol tables and references.

As far as the kernel is concerned, modules are loaded in two steps corresponding to the system calls `create_module` and `init_module`. For the user process, this procedure divides into four phases.

(1)   The process fetches the content of the object file into its own address space. In a normal object file the code and the data are arranged as if they started from address 0 after loading. To get the code and data into a form in which they can actually be executed, the actual load address must be added at various points. This process is known as *relocating*. References to the required points are included in the object file. There may also be unresolved references in the object file. When the object file is analysed, the size of the object module is also obtained (*see* Figure 9.1a).[1]

---

[1] Further details on the structure and use of object files can be found in Gircys (1990) and *ELF (executable and linkable format)*.

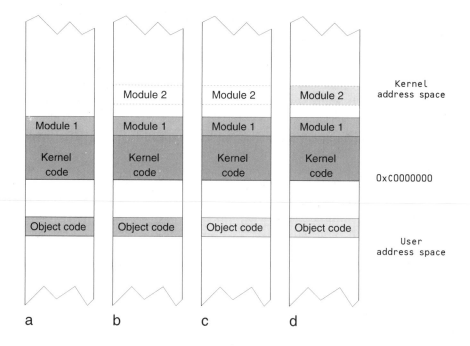

Figure 9.1   The address space on loading a module.

(2)   The system call *create_module* is now used, firstly to obtain the final address of the object module and secondly to reserve memory for it. To do this, a structure module is entered for the module in the list of modules and the memory is allocated. The return value gives us the address to which the module will later be copied (*see* Figure 9.1b).

(3)   The load address received by *create_module* is used to relocate the object file. This procedure takes place in a memory area belonging to the process – that is, at this point the object module is still not at the right address, but is relocated for the load address of the module in the kernel segment.

Unresolved references can be solved using the kernel symbols, for which LINUX provides the system call *get_kernel_syms*. When the function is called, LINUX makes a distinction between two different cases. If the null pointer NULL is passed as a parameter, it is possible to find out the size of the kernel's symbol table. If other parameters are used, the location indicated will provide memory for a copy of the symbol table. This enables a process first to determine the table's size and then request a corresponding amount of memory and use the get_kernel_syms() system call again. Note that there is no type information of any sort in the table, only addresses. Care must therefore be taken during the development of a module to ensure that the correct header files are included.

To achieve the greatest possible degree of flexibility, the modules themselves can add symbols to the kernel's symbol table. This allows another module to use functions from one loaded earlier. This mechanism is known as *module stacking*. All the symbols exported by a module are collected in a separate symbol table (*see* Figure 9.1c).

(4)   Once the preliminary work is complete, we can load the object module. This uses the system call *init_module*, which is given among its parameters pointers to a structure mod_routines and the module's symbol table. The module's administration functions are entered in the mod_routines structure, and LINUX now copies the object module into the kernel address space. The administration function init() is called once the code and data have been installed, and within this the relevant register function should also be called.

The return value determines whether or not the installation procedure is judged to have been successful. The second administration function cleanup() is called when the module is deinstalled, and initiates the relevant unregister function.

The symbol table for the kernel is defined in the file kernel/ksyms.c. Each exported function has an entry in the table symbol_table. The name of the function or variable in each case is transferred to symbol_table by the macro X().

The module's own symbol table lists not only the symbols to be exported, but also references to symbols in the kernel which have been used by the module. This enables the mutual dependence of the modules to be gauged. As a result, a module which is still being used by another module will not be deinstalled.

An additional aid in avoiding problems when deinstalling modules after use is the USE_COUNT mechanism. If, for example, we have implemented a device driver as a module and it has been loaded, the use counter will be incremented every time the module is opened and decremented every time it is closed. This means that when deinstalling the module we can find out whether it is still in use. It should be mentioned that the locations where the use counter is changed are in some cases difficult or impossible to find.

As a final recourse in particularly difficult cases, it is of course possible to increment the use counter as a one-off operation during the init() function. This means that the module can never be removed.

The flexibility of modules does not only lie in the fact that they can be loaded dynamically. By using the system call *delete_module*, a module that has been loaded can be removed again. Two preconditions need to be met for this: there must be no references to the module and the module's use counter must hold a value of zero. Before the module is released, the cleanup() function registered during installation is called. In this function, dynamic resources requested during operation and in the `init()` function can be released.

9.2.1   Signatures of symbols

A common problem in module implementation is the module's dependence on the version of the kernel. Because of the continued rapid development of the LINUX kernel, exported structures and functions are also in continuous change. For every new version of the kernel, therefore, all the modules should be recompiled to make sure that symbols are being used in accordance with their definitions. A way out of this dilemma is offered by symbol names containing a signature to the associated C object (the function or elements of the structure). A similar mechanism is used in C++: for example, for functions and name spaces, where it is unequivocal.

In the LINUX kernel a different model is used, in which the symbols to be exported are expanded to their full definitions and 32-bit checksums are calculated on the results, which are then added to the original symbol. Although this procedure is not unequivocal, the likelihood of a clash is sufficiently small. However, this mechanism must be included when configuring the kernel. This is achieved by answering 'yes' to the question

```
Set version information on all symbols for modules
```

The creation of this special symbol information is handled by the `genksyms` program, which is included in the module tools.

The `insmod` program included in this automatically tests for matching checksums when a module with signature information is loaded. This avoids the situation in which a module is loaded that is liable to call a function with the wrong parameters or access a structure for which the definition has changed.

9.3   What can be implemented as a module?

As a basic rule, the aim should always be to use as few symbols or functions from the kernel or other modules as possible. In addition, the facility to register and unregister the module dynamically should be retained. It can be taken as a general rule of thumb that there should be a registering and unregistering function for the functions implemented by a module. This condition is met by a number of kernel elements; the best-known example of this is offered by file system implementations, for which there are the `register_filesystem()` and `unregister_filesystem()` functions. These satisfy all the conditions, including suitable points where the use counter can be

Table 9.1   Functional units which can be implemented as modules.

File system	`register_filesystem()`
	 `unregister_filesystem()`
	 `read_super` function
	 `put_super` function

Block device drivers	`register_blkdev()`
	 `unregister_blkdev()`
	 open function
	 `release` function

Character device drivers	`register_chrdev()`
	 `unregister_chrdev()`
	 open function
	 `release` function

Network device drivers	`register_netdev()`
	 `unregister_netdev()`
	 open function
	 `close` function

Exec domain	`register_exec_domain()`
	 `unregister_exec_domain()`
	 `load_binary` function, *fork* system call
	 `load_binary` function, *exit* and *personality* system calls

Binary format	`register_binfmt()`
	 `unregister_binfmt()`
	 `load_binary` function, *fork* system call
	 `load_binary` function, *exit* system call

PCMCIA Ethernet card	`register_pcmcia_driver()`
	 `unregister_pcmcia_driver()`
	 open function
	 `close` function

administered. As described in Section 9.2, modules must be prevented from being removed while they are still in use. In file system implementations, this is relatively simple: a file system implementation is in use if a file system of this type is mounted. During the mount procedure, the `read_super` function of the file system implementation is called, and in this the counter can be incremented before successful termination. The counterpart to the mount procedure is unmounting, for which the function is `put_super()`.

Table 9.1 lists the functional units which can be implemented as modules. The registration and unregistration functions are given for each, as well as the functions in which the administration of the use counter must take place. This is already implemented in the system calls.

9.4   Parameter passing

At module start, it is sometimes necessary to pass parameters, such as the I/O address or the interrupt used by an ISA device, because modules normally should not carry out automatic recognition of hardware resources on the ISA bus.[2] Therefore, modules can be passed numeric or string parameters. Inside the module, variables of `int`, `int[]` or `char *` type bearing the parameter name must be defined. During loading of the module, the variables are initialized with the specified numeric parameters; string parameters are first allocated, then the pointer is adjusted, as shown in the following example.

```
static int io[MAX_IO] = { 0, };
static char *name = NULL;

int init_module(void)
{
    int dev;

    for (dev = 0; dev < MAX_IO; ++dev) {
        if (io[dev]) {
            /* address was passed */
            ...
        }
        if (name) {
            /* name was passed */
            ...
        }
    }
}
```

A call to `insmod module io=0x300,0x308 name="test"` initializes the `io` array with the values `0x300` and `0x308` and the `name` pointer with the passed string.

9.5   The kernel daemon

One of the novelties of Linux kernel version 2.0 is the kernel daemon. This is a process which automatically carries out loading and removing of modules without the system user noticing it. But how does the kernel daemon know that modules need to be loaded?

---

[2] As devices cannot be uniquely distinguished on the ISA bus, this might lead to erroneous programming and crashes of other devices.

Communication between the Linux kernel and the kernel daemon is carried out by means of IPC. The kernel daemon opens a message queue with the new flag `IPC_KERNELD`. This queue is then automatically used by the kernel as a message queue for the kernel daemon. For this purpose, the existing IPC implementation was extended with the function

```
int kerneld_send(int msgtype, int return_size, int msgsz,
                 const char *text, const char *return_value);
```

which is responsible for sending messages to the kernel daemon. The following structure is transmitted:

```
struct kerneld_msg {
   long mtype;
   long id;
   short version;
   short pid;
   char text[1];
};
```

The `mtype` component contains the message; `id` indicates whether the kernel expects an answer. If `id` is not equal to zero, then after termination of the requested operation, the kernel daemon sends a message with the contents of `id` as `mtype` and passes the return value of the executed command as the new `id` value. The `pid` component holds the PID of the process that triggered the kernel request. The kernel daemon passes this PID to all programs it starts by entering it into the environment variable `KERNELD_TRIGGER`. This could be a way to call a just-in-time debugger automatically, when a process triggers an exception.

Responsibility for loading and releasing modules lies with the functions

```
int request_module (const char *name);
int release_module (const char *name, int wait_flag);
int delayed_release_module (const char *name);
int cancel_release_module (const char *name);
```

With `request_module()` the kernel requests the loading of a module and waits until the operation has been carried out. The function `release_module()` removes a module, with the `wait_flag` specifying whether the termination of the operation should be waited for. The `delayed_release_module()` function allows a module to be removed with a specified delay. This function marks a module, which is automatically removed after 60 seconds if the operation has not been aborted by means of `cancel_release_module()`. If, for example, a file system type cannot be found when mounting a data resource, the kernel executes the following code:

```
for (fs = file_systems; fs && strcmp(fs->name, name);
     fs = fs->next) ;
#ifdef CONFIG_KERNELD
if (!fs && (request_module(name) == 0)) {
    for (fs = file_systems; fs && strcmp(fs->name, name);
         fs = fs->next) ;
}
#endif
```

In this way, unknown file systems are always loaded when the module name is identical with the file system name. For device drivers, generic requests are generated following the `char-major`-*major* or `block-major`-*major* pattern. The kernel daemon converts requests for loading and releasing modules into calls to `modprobe -k`. This system program can assign the names of the modules to be loaded from the generic requests. It already possesses the names of all modules used in the LINUX kernel, so that only new modules must be registered with an entry in the file `/etc/modules.conf` or `/etc/conf.modules`. In order, for example, to load the PC speaker driver automatically, the entry

```
alias char-major-13 pcsnd
```

is needed. The `-k` parameter ensures that the modules are marked with the *autoclean* attribute. Modules with this attribute are automatically removed after 60 seconds when their reference counter has reached zero.

9.6   An example module

An interesting modular application is the PCMCIA card manager, which combines the dynamic characteristics of modules with those of the PCMCIA system. Just as a PCMCIA card is only slotted into the computer if its services are required, the PCMCIA card manager ensures that the modules for the card are loaded.

As a basis for this service a PCMCIA device is implemented. With its help, the PCMCIA card manager is informed of every status change in the PCMCIA hardware. In addition, this device provides for the card identifier to be read. Using this identifier and the information in its database, the PCMCIA card manager is now able to load and remove modules.

Modules have also been chosen to implement the necessary basic functions in the kernel. There is a central module which contains the general standard for PCMCIA. A second module drives the PCMCIA controller chip. As there are two different types of the latter, there are also two different modules for this task. Finally, there is a module in which the interfaces are

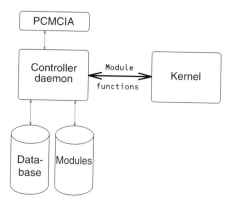

Figure 9.2 The daemon for dynamic loading and removal of modules.

implemented: these include the character device driver for the PCMCIA device and the functions for the device drivers based on this system.

The function of the PCMCIA card manager can be described relatively simply. It opens the character devices associated with the individual sockets (PCMCIA inserts). By accessing these devices, the PCMCIA card manager can keep itself informed of status changes at the sockets. It can also obtain detailed information on the inserted cards.

The information that decides its behaviour is taken from the database, which is usually located in the file /etc/pcmcia/config and holds definitions for various devices. The definitions comprise the modules to be loaded and programs to be executed for the addition and removal of cards.

```
device "de650_cs"
    module "net/8390", "de650_cs"
    start "/etc/pcmcia/network start %d%"
    stop  "/etc/pcmcia/network stop %d%"
```

The other part of the data is concerned with detecting various cards. Each of the PCMCIA cards contains an ASCII character string with its name. By reference to this information, the various cards are assigned to the devices.

```
card "Accton EN2212 EtherCard"
    version "ACCTON", "EN2212", "ETHERNET", "*"
    bind "de650_cs"

card "D-Link DE-650 Ethernet Card"
    version "D-Link", "DE-650", "*", "*"
    bind "de650_cs"
```

```
card "GVC NIC-2000P Ethernet Card"
    version "GVC", "NIC-2000p", "*", "*"
    bind "de650_cs"
```

The drivers produced up to version 2.5.0 comprise Ethernet cards, memory cards, serial cards, modem cards, SCSI cards and many others.

Furnished with all this information, the PCMCIA card manager does not have a great deal more to do. By means of `select()`, it waits for a change at any of the devices. If one occurs, it fetches the corresponding data from the device, then refers to the database to determine the appropriate actions, which it then carries out. This takes care of all the events and the manager can return to waiting with `select()` until its services are required again.

9.7   Debugging

Only in vanishingly few cases will a section of program code be free of bugs as soon as it is written. Usually the program will need debugging, for which it will be loaded into a debugger such as `gdb` and run step by step until the error has been found. Unfortunately, software exists which cannot be debugged so easily. This includes real-time applications, (quasi-) parallel processes and software which runs without a host operating system. Unfortunately, the LINUX kernel (like all operating system kernels) matches all three of these conditions. It hardly needs stressing that changes to an operating system kernel are equally – and particularly – liable to error. This section suggests ways out of the dilemma.

9.7.1   Changes are the beginning of the end

A useful general tip is: Try not to change the kernel, because if you don't amend the LINUX kernel, you will not have to debug it and you will save yourself lots of problems. Simple though this statement is, it is not without meaning for the kernel programmer.

We have no wish to prevent people carrying out creative work on the LINUX kernel. However, anyone contemplating this should seriously ask him/herself whether the expansion that is planned really has any business in the kernel. It is often possible to implement it wholly or partly as an external program, or at least to divert some of the functions to an external process. A privileged process (that is, one with a UID of 0) can do practically anything a driver in the kernel can do. As often as not, communication with the hardware is only carried out via I/O ports, and a privileged process can do that too. This approach is used in the `svgalib` library, which takes care of controlling the graphic modes for various SVGA cards. Of course, there are also cases where this approach does not achieve the desired result.

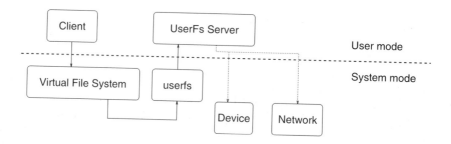

Figure 9.3 Operation of the *User* file system.

Device drivers communicating with the hardware via interrupts need, at the very least, purposeful support by the LINUX kernel, as this alone has the right to handle interrupts. Only the really necessary functions are implemented in the kernel; the actual work should be handled by a normal process. The *User* file system is a rather good example of this approach. However, it is not a part of the standard kernel: it can be found in the directory src/extensions/userfs-0.8.1 on the CD-ROM accompanying this book.

The logical grouping of data on a physical device is traditionally carried out in the operating system kernel, although strictly speaking this is not where it belongs. The *User* file system enables this set of functions to be located in an ordinary process. The kernel merely contains an interface for the queries, which are then forwarded to the process. One advantage is immediately obvious: the greater part of the code is in a normal process, which means that it can be debugged using the standard tools. A further advantage becomes apparent when we consider why the file system implementation always has to access a hard disk or similar. The process can make any data it likes available as a file system. Thus, in the current implementation of the *User* file system there is also an FTP file system, which accesses the data via the FTP protocol. This enables any FTP server to be made available to the user as if he/she were accessing it via NFS. There is one disadvantage of the *User* file system architecture that should not be ignored, however: access to data is not particularly fast.

9.7.2 The best debugger – `printk()`

A test printout at a strategic point can save hours of debugging. Unfortunately, a little experience is required to find the right points ....

For this reason, test printouts from a driver should be planned for even at the design stage: these are short but highly informative. When debugging the kernel, break points can only be included if major changes are made to the kernel itself. Instead, we can make do with suitable test printouts at these points, for example by means of the `printk()` function (*see* Appendix E).

Once again, an expansion of the GNU C compiler will serve excellently here. This permits C preprocessor macros to be used with a variable number of arguments. A debugging macro can thus be defined along the following lines:

```
#ifdef DEBUG
#define MY_PRINTK(format, a...)    printk(format, ## a)
#else
#define MY_PRINTK(format, a...)
#endif /* DEBUG */
```

Defined in this way, MY_PRINTK can be used in exactly the same way as the function printk(). However, it allows a decision on whether or not test printouts should be produced to be made at compile-time. A second advantage is that it saves a lot of writing in comparison with ordinary C macros. If, in addition, the printouts are made dependent on a flag in the kernel, the process becomes even more dynamic. The flag then needs to be set by an external event: for this we can fall back on a system call of our own or an ioctl command.

As described in Appendix E, only printouts with a level lower than the kernel variable console_loglevel are also displayed on the console. As it is sometimes useful to have the information there as well, because the kernel crashes immediately afterwards or for some similar reason, the value of console_loglevel will need to be changed appropriately. There are a number of ways of doing this:

- using the system call *syslog* or
- by direct modification of the variable.

When serious problems (traps) occur, the kernel automatically sets the level to the highest value, so that all messages appear at the console.

The user of modules should also be aware that direct manipulation of the variable console_loglevel is only possible in quite a roundabout way, as the associated symbol is not included in the global symbol table. This means that this external reference must be resolved using the map file system.map in the kernel, or else the symbol must be entered in the file kernel/ksyms.c.

9.7.3 Debugging with gdb

Finally, the LINUX kernel can also be debugged with ease using the GNU debugger gdb. However, a number of conditions need to be satisfied first. The kernel, or at least the area of the kernel to be debugged, must be compiled with debugging information. This calls for nothing more than replacing the line in the kernel's central makefile

```
CFLAGS = -Wall -Wstrict-prototypes -O2 -fomit-frame-pointer
```

with

```
CFLAGS = -Wall -Wstrict-prototypes -O2 -g
```

The relevant area can then be compiled and the kernel relinked. Memory requirements should not be underestimated, and the computer used should have adequate memory for the task. For example, if the entire kernel has been compiled with debugging information, gdb alone will need some 9 Mbytes of memory.

We can now run the debugger via

```
# gdb /usr/src/linux/vmlinux /proc/kcore
```

As is evident from the command line, /proc/kcore is read in by the debugger as the core file for the kernel. This enables all the structures in the kernel to be read, but no local variables. Unfortunately, it is not possible to change values or call kernel functions: the functions are restricted to simple reading of values. Despite this, many errors can be tracked down. Unlike the use of standard core files, gdb reads the values from memory, which means that it is always the current, updated value that is given.

10 Multi-processing

Even though ever more advanced and faster processors are entering the market, there will always be applications that require still more processor power. In multi-tasking systems, a solution to this problem is to employ several processors in order to achieve true parallel processing of tasks. As in all truly parallel systems, performance does not increase linearly with the number of processors employed. Rather, it is the operating system that bears an increased responsibility to distribute all tasks among the processors in such a way that as few processors as possible hamper each other. This chapter deals with *Symmetric Multi Processing* (SMP) which is supported by LINUX version 2.0.

10.1 The Intel multi-processor specification

Most of the currently available multi-processor main boards for PCs use i486, Pentium or Pentium Pro processors. The Pentium already has some internal functions which support multi-processor operation, such as cache synchronization, inter-processor interrupt handling and atomic operations for checking, setting and exchanging values in main memory. Cache synchronization in particular greatly facilitates SMP implementation in the kernel.

Intel's multi-processor specification Version 1.4 (Intel, 1997) defines the interaction between hardware and software in order to facilitate the development of SMP-capable operating systems and to create the possibility of making these systems run on new hardware. The aim of the specification is to create a multi-processor platform which remains 100% compatible with the PC/AT. It defines a highly symmetrical architecture in terms of:

- *Memory symmetry*
  All processors share the same main memory; in particular, all physical addresses are the same. This means that all processors execute the same operating system, all data and applications are visible to all processors and can be used or executed on every processor.

- *I/O symmetry*
  All processors share the same I/O subsystem (including the I/O port and the interrupt controller). I/O symmetry allows reduction of a possible I/O bottleneck. However, some MP systems assign all interrupts to one single processor.

Figure 10.1 shows the hardware overview of a typical SMP system with two processors. Both are connected via the ICC (*Interrupt Controller Communications*) bus with one or more I/O APICs (*Advanced Programmable Interrupt Controller*). Pentium processors have their own integrated local APIC. These

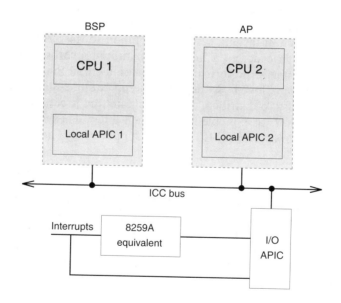

Figure 10.1   A typical **SMP** system with two Pentium processors.

local APICs, together with the I/O APICs, constitute a unit which deals with the distribution of incoming interrupts.

One processor is chosen by the BIOS; it is called the boot processor (BSP) and is used for system initialization. All other processors are called application processors (AP) and are initially halted by the BIOS. The MP specification defines a configuration structure which is filled in by the BIOS and informs the operating system about the existing MP system. The BIOS initially forwards all interrupts only to the boot processor, so that single-processor systems see no difference and run only on the BSP.

10.2 Problems with multi-processor systems

For the correct functioning of a multi-tasking system it is important that data in the kernel can only be changed by one processor so that identical resources cannot be allocated twice. In UNIX-like systems, there are two approaches to the solution of this problem. Traditional UNIX systems use a relatively coarse-grained locking; sometimes even the whole kernel is locked so that only one process can be present in the kernel. Some more advanced systems implement a finer grained locking which, however, entails high additional expenditure and is normally used only for multi-processor and real-time operating systems. In the latter, fine-grained locking reduces the time that a lock must be kept, thus allowing a reduction of the particularly critical latency time.

In the LINUX kernel implementation, various rules were established. One of them is that no process running in kernel mode is interrupted by another process running in kernel mode, except when it releases control and sleeps. This rule ensures that large areas of the kernel code are atomic with respect to other processes and thus simplifies many functions in the LINUX kernel.

A further rule establishes that interrupt handling can interrupt a process running in kernel mode, but that in the end control is returned back to this same process. A process can block interrupts and thus make sure that it will not be interrupted.

The last rule that is important for us states that interrupt handling cannot be interrupted by a process running in kernel mode. This means that the interrupt handling will be processed completely, or at most be interrupted by another interrupt of higher priority.

In the development of the multi-processor LINUX kernel a decision was made to maintain these three basic rules, on the one hand to facilitate the first implementation, on the other to allow a simple integration of already existing code. One single semaphore is used by all processes to monitor the transition to kernel mode. Each processor that owns this lock can always enter kernel mode, for example for interrupt handling. As soon as the process no longer owns the lock, it is no longer allowed to change to kernel mode.

This semaphore is used to ensure that no process running in kernel mode can be interrupted by another process. Furthermore, it guarantees that only a process running in kernel mode can block the interrupts without another process taking over the interrupt handling.

This design decision results, however, in low performance of I/O-intensive applications because the CPU time in kernel mode becomes a bottleneck. At a later point in the development, it will become necessary to change over to a finer grained locking. Only this can ensure a higher parallelism and consequently a higher system performance. The transition can be carried out hierarchically, by substituting one semaphore with several others which cover an increasingly smaller area of the LINUX kernel. The current LINUX multiprocessor implementation achieves good performance for CPU-intensive processes which are in user mode most of the time, whereas processes with a large amount of I/O cause the system to degenerate into a single-processor system.

10.3   Changes to the kernel

In order to implement SMP in the LINUX kernel, changes have to be made to both the portable part and the processor-specific implementations.

10.3.1   Kernel initialization

The first problem with the implementation of multi-processor operation arises when starting the kernel. All processors must be started because the BIOS has halted all APs and initially only the boot processor is running. Only this processor enters the kernel starting function start_kernel(). After it has executed the normal LINUX initialization, smp_init() is called. This function activates all other processors by calling smp_boot_cpus().

Each processor receives its own stack in which initially the trampoline code is entered. When starting up, the processor executes this code and then also jumps into the start_kernel function. There, however, once exception handling and interrupt handling have been initialized, the processors are again trapped by smp_callin() inside the start_secondary() function.

```
asmlinkage void start_secondary(void)
{
    trap_init();
    init_IRQ();
    smp_callin();
    cpu_idle(NULL);
}
```

```
void smp_callin(void)
{
   ...
   /* determine the processor's BogoMips */
   calibrate_delay();
   /* save processor parameters */
   smp_store_cpu_info(cpuid);
   ...
   while(!smp_commenced);
   ...
}
```

But how can a halted processor be started? This purpose is served by the APIC. It allows each processor to send other processors a so-called inter-processor interrupt (IPI). Furthermore, it is possible to send each processor an INIT (INIT IPI). On a Pentium processor, an INIT signal works like a reset, but the cache, FPU and write buffer are reset as well. Then, via its reset vector, the processor jumps into the BIOS. If previously the warm start flag was set in CMOS, and the warm start vector (0040:0067) was set to a real-mode routine, the processor will then jump into that routine. Furthermore, it is possible to send Pentium processors a STARTUP IPI. With this, the processor begins to execute a real mode routine at the address VV00:0000.[1]

Let us now go back to the `smp_init()`function. After all remaining processors have been started, the variable `smp_num_cpus` contains the number of all currently running processors. Now, a separate idle task is created for each processor. This is necessary because in SMP operation the idle task must run in user mode in order not to block the kernel mode for all other processors.

After termination of `smp_init()` the boot processor generates the init task which finally calls `smp_commence()`. This function sets the `smp_commenced` flag, at which point all APs can quit the `smp_callin()` function and process their individual idle tasks.

10.3.2   Scheduling

The LINUX scheduler shows only slight changes. First of all, the task structure now has a `processor` component which contains the number of the running processor or the constant `NO_PROC_ID` if no processor has been assigned as yet. The `last_processor` component contains the number of the processor which processed the task last.

Each processor works through the schedule and is assigned a new task which is executable and has not yet been assigned to any other processor. Furthermore, those tasks are preferred that last ran on the currently available

---

[1] The MP specification defines the precise algorithm of how to start APs. Amongst others, Pentiums are sent one INIT IPI and two STARTUP IPIs.

processor. This can lead to an improvement in system performance when the internal processor caches still contain the data valid for the selected process.

Also, since now each processor possesses its own active process, the current symbol which normally points to the current process expands to

```
current_set[smp_processor_id()];
```

where the smp_processor_id() function supplies the number of the currently running processor.

10.3.3   Message exchange between processors

Messages in the form of inter-processor interrupts are handled via interrupts 13 and 16. In 386 processors, interrupt 13 had the task of informing the system about FPU errors. Since the 486, which is the smallest processor supported by the Intel MP specification, this is now carried out by exception 16 which is the only one used in SMP mode. Interrupt 13 is defined as a fast interrupt which, however, does not need the kernel lock and can thus always be processed. This interrupt cannot be used to trigger the scheduler, but only to distribute messages. Interrupt 16, on the contrary, is a slow interrupt which waits for the kernel lock and can trigger scheduling. It is used to start the schedulers on the other processors.

10.3.4   Entering kernel mode

As already described, the kernel is protected by a single semaphore. All interrupt handlers, syscall routines and exception handlers need this semaphore and wait in a processor loop until the semaphore is free. This could lead to a deadlock problem when the processor that is running in kernel mode changes the memory mapping and wants to inform all other processors about this fact. It triggers an IPI and waits until all processors have carried out a TLB flush.[2] Processors that wait for the kernel lock with deactivated interrupts do not handle the IPI. For this reason, while waiting for the kernel lock, each processor checks its own bit in the variable smp_invalidate_needed and carries out a TLB flush when it is set. If at a later stage the IPI is handled, the handling routine sees that the flush has already been carried out and does nothing.

The enter code for the kernel is defined in the ENTER_KERNEL assembler macro and the lock_kernel() function.

---

[2]   Since Intel processors possess a cache (Translation Lockaside Buffer) for paging, this cache must be adjusted when the paging is changed. On the 386 this was only possible by emptying the entire cache (TLB flush). Since the 486, it is also possible to change individual cache entries.

```
void lock_kernel(void)
{
    unsigned long flags;
    int proc = smp_processor_id();

    save_flags(flags);
    cli();
    /* set_bit is an atomic operation under SMP */
    while(set_bit(0, (void *)&kernel_flag)) {
        /*
         * if the processor already owns the kernel lock
         */
        if (proc == active_kernel_processor)
            break;
        do {
            if (test_bit(proc, (void *)&smp_invalidate_needed))
                if (clear_bit(proc, (void *)&smp_invalidate_needed))
                    local_flush_tlb();
        } while(test_bit(0, (void *)&kernel_flag));
    }
    /*
     * now we have our kernel lock
     */
    active_kernel_processor = proc;
    kernel_counter++;
    restore_flags(flags);
}
```

This macro is used for all assembler entry points in the kernel, whereas the
lock_kernel function must be called at the beginning by all kernel daemons,
such as kswapd.

10.3.5 Interrupt handling

Interrupts are distributed to the processors by the I/O APIC. At system start,
however, all interrupts are forwarded only to the BSP. Each SMP operating
system must therefore switch the APIC into SMP mode, so that other processors too can handle interrupts (exception: IPI).

Currently, however, LINUX does not use this operating mode, that is,
during the whole time the system is operating, interrupts are only delivered to
the BSP. This compromises the latency time, since incoming interrupts can
only be handled when no processor or the BSP is in the kernel. However, if
there is an AP in the kernel, the interrupt handling routine must wait until the

AP has left the kernel. In order to be able to use the APIC's SMP mode, changes must be made to the current interrupt handling.

10.4 Compiling LINUX SMP

In order to compile an SMP-capable kernel, it is necessary to edit the topmost Makefile and remove the comment character from the following line:

```
SMP = 1
```

In addition, it is sensible to activate the SMP profiling in order to view some statistics:

```
SMP_PROF = 1
```

Then, the smp file in the *Proc* file system supplies information on the current system:

```
CPUS:            2
                SUM        P0         P1
   0:        599296     599296          0    timer
   1:         20113      20113          0    keyboard
   2:             0          0          0    cascade
   4:          2413       2413          0 +  serial
   8:             0          0          0 +  rtc
   9:         13497      13497          0    3c590 Vortex 10Mbps
  13:          8573       1110       7463 +  IPI
  14:         97091      97091          0 +  ide0
 LCK:      12153103    8328361    3824742    spins from int
 LCK:             0          0          0    spins from syscall
 LCK:             0          0          0    spins from sysidle
 IDLE       1140565     569172     571393    idle ticks
 IPI:          8573    received
```

As can be clearly seen, interrupts are only handled by the first processor. The spins lines supply information on how often each processor has cycled through the waiting loop while waiting for the kernel lock. Currently, however, no distinction is made between individual cases, so that the line spins from int displays the sum of all waiting times.

APPENDIX A

System calls

Call unto me, and I will answer thee,
and show thee great and mighty things
which thou knowest not.

Jeremiah 33:3

This appendix describes the implementation of all system calls in LINUX. With regard to architecture-dependent implementations, the emphasis[1] is on the LINUX system running on the Intel PC. A description of the other architectures is not possible for several reasons (including time and the lack of documentation). A basic knowedge is given in the previous chapters. We also recommend having a look at the corresponding source files of the kernel.

A precise distinction has to be made between the system call[2] and its corresponding kernel function. A system call is the transition of a process from user mode to system mode. In LINUX this is done by calling the interrupt 0x80, together with the actual register values. The kernel (in system mode) calls a kernel function out of the _sys_call_table table. These functions, which in the source text begin with 'sys_', are described in the following sections.

The conversion from a function used by a program to the system call is carried out in the C library. This allows, for example, several functions to be handled with one single kernel function, as is shown rather nicely by sys_socketcall(). Such functions have a typical characteristic: parameters whose structure can vary are passed to the kernel function as unsigned long, which is then used as an address. In LINUX it is common to provide generally known system calls as library functions – which blurs the borderline between system calls and C library functions.

---

[1] It is, however, explicitly mentioned when a system call is not available for a different architecture.
[2] The discussion *'What is a system call?'* kept us busy for quite a while!

The kernel functions are divided into six groups: process management, file system, inter-process communication, memory management, initialization and the rest (not or not yet implemented system calls). The division can be roughly expressed as follows: system calls whose source files can be found in the same subdirectory are described together in a group.

The description of a kernel function is structured similarly to a UNIX manual page: top left we find the name of the kernel function, top right the origin of the corresponding system call (POSIX, BSD, SVR4). Below there is the name of the file in which the kernel function is implemented. If special header files are needed for the corresponding system call, these are also listed. The prototype of the function and the description follow. The interface provided by the C library and any peculiarities are described in the *implementation* section. The description finishes with a list of errors that can occur during execution of the kernel function.

A.1 Process management

The following calls access the kernel of each and every UNIX system, the scheduler and the process management. The foundations for this are described in Chapters 3 and 4.

System call	adjtimex	4.3+BSD

File: kernel/time.c

```
#include <sys/timex.h>

int sys_adjtimex(struct timex *txc_p);
```

The sys_adjtimex() call allows reading and setting of the kernel's time structures, or more precisely, of the variables beginning with 'time_'. As these control the timer, the system's time behaviour can be controlled.[3] The timex structure is an extension of the timeval structure:

```
struct timex {
   unsigned int modes;      /* function                    */
   long offset;             /* time offset (usec)          */
   long freq;               /* frequency offset (scaled ppm) */
```

---

[3] The commented source code calls it 'to discipline the kernel clock oscillator'.

```
        long maxerror;           /* max. error (usec)                 */
        long esterror;           /* estimated error (usec)            */
        int status;              /* clock status                      */
        long constant;           /* PLL time constant                 */
        long precision;          /* clock precision (usec) (ro)       */
        long tolerance;          /* frequency variations (ppm) (ro)   */
        struct timeval time;     /* system time (read only)           */
        long tick;               /* microseconds between two ticks    */

        long ppsfreq;            /* PPS frequency (scaled ppm) (ro)   */
        long jitter;             /* PPS jitter (us) (ro)              */
        int shift;               /* interval duration (s) (shift) (ro) */
        long stabil;             /* PPS stability (scaled ppm) (ro)   */
        long jitcnt;             /* jitter limit exceeded (ro)        */
        long calcnt;             /* calibration intervals (ro)        */
        long errcnt;             /* calibration errors (ro)           */
        long stbcnt;             /* stability limit exceeded (ro)     */

        int :32; int :32; int :32; int :32; int :32; int :32;
        int :32; int :32; int :32; int :32; int :32; int :32;
    };
```

If `mode` is zero, the values are read, otherwise they are written. The following values are possible (also in combination):

ADJ_STATUS – `time_status` is set.

ADJ_FREQUENCY – `time_freq` derives from `txc.frequency`.

ADJ_MAXERROR – `time_maxerror` is set.

ADJ_ESTERROR – `time_esterror` is set.

ADJ_TIMECONST – `time_constant` is set.

ADJ_OFFSET – If, in addition, `ADJ_OFFSET_SINGLESHOT` is set, the `time_adjust` value derives from `txc.offset`. Otherwise, `time_offset` is set to the value `txc.offset` `<<` `SHIFT_UPDATE` and `time_reftime` to `xtime.tv.sec`, and `time_freq` is recalculated.

ADJ_TICK – `tick` is set to `txc.tick`. For reasons of stability, the value `txc.tick` must not deviate more than 10 per cent from the normal value (1000).

ADJ_OFFSET_SINGLESHOT – allows, together with `ADJ_OFFSET`, emulation of the well-known system call *adjtime*.

As the timer interrupt would disturb the settings, interrupts are disabled while copying. After copying, the `txc` structure is filled with the currently valid `time_` values (`offset` contains the previously stored `time_adjust` value) and returned.

Implementation

The system call is converted with the syscall macro. Furthermore, the well-known system call *adjtime* is based on the function `adjtimex()`, as shown in the following (abridged) source text.

```
int adjtime(struct timeval * itv, struct timeval * otv)
{ struct timex tntx;

  if (itv) { struct timeval tmp;

    tmp.tv_sec = itv->tv_sec + itv->tv_usec / 1000000L;
    tmp.tv_usec = itv->tv_usec % 1000000L;

    tntx.offset = tmp.tv_usec + tmp.tv_sec * 1000000L;
    tntx.mode = ADJ_OFFSET_SINGLESHOT;
  }
  else tntx.mode = 0;
  if (adjtimex(&tntx) < 0) return -1;
  return 0;
}
```

Errors

EPERM – a write access was attempted without superuser privileges.

EINVAL – a value in the `txc` structure is not valid.

System call	alarm	POSIX

File: kernel/sched.c

```
int sys_alarm(long seconds);
```

`sys_alarm()` sets a timer to the value `seconds`. After the timer's expiry, the SIGALRM signal is triggered. When `seconds` equals zero, the timer is restarted.

If a previous alarm is still running, its remaining time (in seconds) is returned and the timer is restarted. The execution of the alarm is described in Section 3.2.1.

Implementation

The conversion is carried out through the syscall macro. This function is not available on Alpha machines.

System call   brk

File: kernel/sys.c

```
int sys_brk(unsigned long new_brk);
```

sys_brk() changes the size of the unused area of the data segment. It sets the value mm->brk of the task structure to new_brk, after rounding up brk to the beginning of the next memory page.

The value new_brk must be bigger than the text segment and lie 4 memory pages before the end of the stack in order to leave it enough space. If this cannot be achieved, the segment is not changed.

The do_mmap() function (*see* Section 4.2.2) organizes the necessary memory (vma zones) and sets the flags PROT_READ, PROT_WRITE, PROT_EXEC, MAP_FIXED and MAP_PRIVATE. The new brk value is returned.

Implementation

In Intel systems, the system call does not use the syscall macro, but jumps directly via assembler code into the interrupt 0x80.

This system call is used in malloc() to allocate memory. The memory requested by malloc() is added to the current brk value and claimed.[4]

Errors

ENOMEM – no memory available for a bigger brk value.

System call   _exit   POSIX

File: kernel/exit.c

```
int sys_exit(int status);
```

When a process is terminated, it calls (explicitly or implicitly) _exit(). The kernel function sys_exit() releases all resources used by the process in the kernel and informs the processes concerned.

The status value is returned to the parent process. The function is described in Section 3.3.3.

Implementation

The system call is converted into the kernel function with no modification of the parameters.

---

[4] The function used for this has the typical name morecore(), but is only a pointer to brk().

| System call | fork | POSIX |
| | clone | LINUX |

File: kernel/fork.c

```
int sys_fork(struct pt_regs regs);
int sys_clone(struct pt_regs regs);
```

sys_fork() generates a new process (child process) as a copy of the current process (parent process). In order to be able to distinguish between parent and child process, the PID of the child process is returned in the parent process, while a 0 is returned in the child process. In LINUX, *copy-on-write* is used, so that only the page tables and the task structure are duplicated. The maximum number of processes is limited to the value specified in NR_TASKS. The termination signal of the child process is SIGCHLD.

In order to extend the semantics of the *fork* system call, LINUX provides a system call *clone*. By means of the regs registers, two parameters are passed: in regs.ebx this is a pointer used as the stack pointer of the child. If it is zero, the stack pointer of the parent process is used. The register regs.ecx contains the flags and the signal. The signal is located in the lower two bytes and is passed to the parent process upon termination of the child. Interestingly enough, the signal is later masked out with 0xff, which would allow for up to 255 signals. The flags control the 'nursery' of the new process:

CLONE_VM – Parent and child process share the same memory pages. If this flag is not specified, the memory pages of the child are generated via *copy-on-write*.

CLONE_FILES – Parent and child process use the same descriptors. Otherwise, the file descriptors are copied.

CLONE_FS – Parent and child process use the same file system structure (with the counter being incremented). Otherwise, the structure is copied.

CLONE_SIGHAND – Parent and child process share the same signal handling routines. Otherwise, these structures are copied.

Thus, the calls sys_fork() and sys_clone(0, SIGCHLD|COPYVM) have the same effect. The implementation of the system calls is described in Section 3.3.3.

Implementation

The conversion of fork() is carried out via the syscall macro. The pt_regs structure of <asm/ptrace.h> contains exactly those registers in their correct order which a system call puts on the stack. Thus, the kernel function can

access them, although the call itself is parameterless. The cl█
converted via the syscall macro.

Errors

EAGAIN – if sys_fork() cannot allocate memory for the page table and █
structure.

System call	getpid	getuid	geteuid	POSIX
	getgid	geteuid	getegid	4.3+BSD
	getppid	getpgid	getpgrp	
	setuid	setgid	setreuid	
	setregid	setfsuid	setfsgid	

File: kernel/sched.c
kernel/sys.c

```
int sys_getpid(void);
int sys_getuid(void);
int sys_geteuid(void);
int sys_getgid(void);
int sys_getegid(void);
int sys_getppid(void);
int sys_getpgid(pid_t pid);
int sys_getpgrp(void);
int sys_setuid(uid_t uid);
int sys_setgid(gid_t gid);
int sys_setreuid(uid_t ruid, uid_t euid);
int sys_setregid(uid_t rgid, uid_t egid);
int sys_setpgid(pid_t pid,pid_t pgid);
int sys_setsid(void);
int sys_setfsuid(uid_t uid);
int sys_setfsgid(gid_t gid);
```

sys_getpid() and sys_getpgrp() determine the process identification (PID)
and the process group (PGRP)[5] of the current process. sys_getpgid() returns
the process group of an arbitrary process pid; if pid is zero, it returns its own
group. The sys_getppid() function returns the process identification of the
parent process (PPID).

The sys_getuid() function returns the user identification (UID) and the
sys_getgid() function the group identification (GID) of the calling process.

---

[5] You may also find PGID as the denomination of the process group (for example, in *ps*).

roup (EGID) identifications are determined by
) and `sys_getegid()`.
ad the task structure of the calling process.

ɔid)

id

id for the current process or one of
..ıe values of the calling process will be
ıı one of the following conditions is met: the
̗ leader, the indicated child process belongs to a dif-
̣ already exists a process with the requested PGRP, but it
..ierent session. The call checks all current processes.

.. functions `sys_setreuid()` and `sys_setregid()` manipulate the UIDs
.. GIDs of a process. Provided that the parameter (`ruid` or `euid`) is not equal
to –1, the following occurs: if the calling process has privileges in `setreuid()`,
the UID is set to `ruid`. Privileges in this case means: the process has superuser
rights or UID equals `ruid` (the value is already set) or the EUID equals `ruid`.
Otherwise, an error is returned. In order to set the EUID to `euid`, one of the
following conditions must be met: superuser rights; UID, EUID or SUID
equal `euid`. Here, too, the function returns an error otherwise. If `ruid` or `euid`
are equal to –1, the SUID of the process is given the value of the EUID. If no
error has occurred until then, the function finally sets FSUID to EUID and
returns zero.

Thus, a user with no superuser privileges can only exchange effective
and normal (real) IDs. `setreuid(geteuid(),getuid())` performs the exchange;
if the call is repeated, the original values are restored. The superuser has free
access.

`sys_setuid()` sets the UIDs of a process to `uid`. For the superuser, these
are UID, EUID, SUID and FSUID. For normal users, only FSUID and
EUID are set, provided that `uid` is equal to the UID or the SUID. As an
equivalent for the setting of the process GIDs, there is the `sys_setgid()` function. The functions are the SVR4 counterpart to the above `set` calls, which
originate from the world of BSD. It has to be borne in mind that there is no
possibility of resetting a EUID once it has been changed, as is possible with
`sys_setreuid()`. The return value is zero upon successful execution and a negative value in the event of an error.

The functions `sys_setfsuid()` and `sys_setfsgid()` set the FSUID and
FSGID, that is, the IDs with which the file system is accessed. These functions
are used in `access()` and in the NFS daemon. The return value is the old ID.

`sys_setsid()` makes the calling process the process session leader. It sets
SESSION and PGRP to PID, the `leader` component of the task structure to 1

and deletes its controlling terminal. If the process is already the session leader, an error is returned. The return value is the new PGRP.

Implementation

Owing to the simplicity of the functions, the conversion of the system calls is carried out via the syscall macro. The `get*id()` functions are not available on Alpha machines.

The well-known system calls *seteuid*, *setegid* and *setpgrp* are provided by LINUX as library functions. The conversion is shown taking `seteuid()` and `setpgrp()` as examples.

```
int seteuid(uid_t uid)
{
    return setreuid(-1, uid);
}
```

Errors

EINVAL – if an invalid PID, PGID and so on is passed to a function.

EPERM – if the function used is not allowed. Generally, only the superuser may change all process data. Normal users can only change their group and user IDs.

ESRCH – if no processes are found by `sys_setpgid()`.

| System call | getpriority | 4.3+BSD |
| | setpriority | |

File: kernel/sys.c

```
#include <sys/time.h>
#include <sys/resource.h>

int sys_getpriority(int which, int who);
int sys_setpriority(int which, int who, int niceval);
```

The kernel functions `sys_getpriority()` and `sys_setpriority()` administer the priorities for scheduling.

`sys_getpriority()` is used for interrogation. The `which` parameter specifies whether the priority of a process, a process group or a user is requested. In `who`, the value is specified. The following values are allowed for `which`:

PRIO_PROCESS – the value in who specifies a PID.

PRIO_PGRP – the value in who specifies a PGRP.

PRIO_USER – the value in who specifies a UID.

If zero is specified for who, the kernel uses the value of the calling process.

All processes are searched to find out whether they match the specified values (proc_sel()). The return value is the highest value found, if more than one entry has been found (process group).

The sys_setpriority() function sets the priority for the processes selected via which and who, where niceval must lie between [–20,20]. The priority is scaled to time slice units and assigned to all processes found. Only the superuser is allowed to increase the priority of a process.

Implementation

While setpriority() simply uses the syscall macro, the getpriority() call assembles the interrupt 0x80 by hand and calculates the mirroring at PZERO back in order to make the return value of getpriority() match the value passed to sys_setpriority().

This constitutes a *dangerous exception*! It is possible that the library function getpriority() returns –1 without an error having occurred. In this case, for the purpose of error checking, not only the return value, as is normally done in UNIX, but also errno should be tested.

Errors

ESRCH – if no matching process could be found for which and who.

EINVAL – if an invalid value is specified for which.

EPERM – if in sys_setpriority() the EUID of the specified process is not equal to the EUID of the calling process.

EACCES – if a non-privileged user wants to increase the priority.

System call	ioperm	iopl	LINUX

File: arch/i386/kernel/ioport.c

```
int sys_ioperm(unsigned long from,
    unsigned long num, int turn_on);
int sys_iopl(int level);
```

These calls can only be used with superuser privileges. The bits of the port access rights are set by sys_ioperm(), that is, num bits beginning with the address from are set to the value turn_on. The value 1 means full access to the port (read and write) and 0 no access. Only the first 1023 (32×IO_BITMAP_SIZE) ports can be set.

In order to access all 65 536 ports under LINUX, for example for the X server, the system call *iopl* is provided. The corresponding kernel function sys_iopl() sets the I/O privilege level of the process. Normally, only two of the four possible levels are used: level 0 and level 3.

Implementation

Both system calls work with the syscall macro.

Errors

EINVAL – if a negative value has been specified for num, from+num is greater than 1023 or level is greater than 3.

EPERM – if the calling process has no superuser rights.

System call	kill	POSIX

File: kernel/exit.c

```
#include <signal.h>

int sys_kill(int pid, int sig);
```

sys_kill() sends the signal sig to a process or a process group. If pid is greater than zero, the signal is sent to the process with the PID pid. If pid is zero, the signal is sent to the process group of the current process. If pid is less than –1, the signal is sent to all processes of the process group –pid.

In POSIX, the behaviour of kill(-1,sig) is not defined. In LINUX, the signal is sent to all processes with a PID greater than 1 (except the current one).

Implementation

The system call is converted via the syscall macro.

Errors

EINVAL – if sig is not valid.

ESRCH – if the process or the process group pid does not exist.

EPERM – the privileges of the calling process do not allow the signal to be sent.

System call	modify_ldt	LINUX

File: arch/i386/kernel/ldt.c

```
#include <linux/ldt.h>

int sys_modify_ldt(int func, void *ptr, unsigned long count);
```

In the course of the implementation of WINE it became necessary to emulate the internal functions of MS-Windows. These include manipulation of the local descriptor table. This is precisely the task of the system call modify_ldt. Being a part of the task structure, this table can be manipulated quite easily.

If func equals zero, the local descriptor table of the current process is read. If it does not yet possess a table, the default table {0,0} is provided. The required size can be set with the count parameter. If the table is smaller, only the table of size LDT_ENTRIES*LDT_ENTRY_SIZE is read. The return value is the actual size of the table; ptr is a pointer to the structure desc_struct:

```
typedef struct desc_struct {
    unsigned long a,b;
} desc_table[256];
```

In order to change an entry in this table, func must be 1. Then ptr is a pointer to the structure modify_ldt_ldt_s:

```
struct modify_ldt_ldt_s {
    unsigned int  entry_number; /* index of the required entry */
    unsigned long base_addr;
    unsigned int  limit;
    unsigned int  seg_32bit:1;
    unsigned int  contents:2;
    unsigned int  read_exec_only:1;
    unsigned int  limit_in_pages:1;
    unsigned int  seg_not_present:1;
};
```

count must indicate exactly the size of the structure. The specified structure is described in the table of the current process. If this does not yet possess a local descriptor table, a table is initialized. It is also possible to delete an entry (by entering 0).

Implementation

The C library does not provide an interface to this system call. Users must proceed in the same way as specified for sys_sysinfo() (*see* page 332).

Errors

ENOSYS – `func` is invalid.

EINVAL – `ptr` is 0 (for reading) or incorrectly set (for writing).

System call	create_module	delete_module	LINUX
	init_module	get_kernel_syms	

File: kernel/module.c

```
unsigned long sys_create_module(char *name, unsigned long size);
int sys_init_module(char *name, char *code, unsigned codesize,
    struct mod_routines *routines, struct symbol_table *symtab);
int sys_delete_module(char *name);
int sys_get_kernel_syms(struct kernel_sym *table);
```

The `sys_create_module()` function allocates memory for a module. The size of the required memory is specified by `size`. The call generates an instance of the `module` structure, where `name` is the name of the module. The following values of the structure are set: the name, the size (number of pages), the start address of the memory allocated for the module and the status (to `MOD_UNINITIALIZED`). All other values are initialized with `NULL`.

```
struct module {
    struct module *next;             /* the next module           */
    struct module_ref *ref;          /* list of modules that      */
                                     /* point to myself           */
    struct symbol_table *symtab;     /* symbol table              */
    char *name;                      /* name of the module        */
    int size;                        /* module size in pages      */
    void* addr;                      /* address of the module     */
    int state;                       /* status flags of the module */
    void (*cleanup)(void);           /* cleanup routine           */
};
```

If a module of the same name already exists, an error is returned, otherwise the return value is the address of the memory allocated in the kernel address space. `sys_init_module()` loads the module and activates it. `code` is the address where the module is loaded, `codesize` its size in bytes. This must not exceed the value stored in `module->size`. If the loaded module does not end on a page address, the remainder is initialized with 0. The pointer `routines` to the structure `mod_routines` is the interface for the administration of the module. It consists of two function pointers, one to an initialization, the other to a delete function for the module.

```
struct mod_routines {
   int (*init)(void);        /* initialization */
   void (*cleanup)(void);    /* cleanup        */
};
```

The `symtab` pointer points to the symbol table. This is loaded and its pointer is recalculated by adding the address of the table (in the module). In addition, references to other modules are entered in their reference lists.

After the module has been loaded, its own initialization routine `init()` is called and the status is set to `MOD_RUNNING`; now the module is activated. `sys_delete_module()` removes modules. If `name` is specified, that particular module is released. There must be no references to the module, and its usage counter must be 0. If the module is running [`MOD_RUNNING`], its own `cleanup` function is called and the status set to `MOD_DELETED`. Then the module can be removed by a call to `free_modules()`. If no name is specified, the function searches the list of all modules and tries to release all modules that are no longer in use.

`sys_get_kernel_syms()` allows access to the symbol table. It copies the symbol table to the location referenced by `table` and returns the number of known symbols. First, the call checks whether there is enough memory for writing following the address. Therefore, the size of the table is normally determined by means of a call to `get_kernel_syms(0)`, then the necessary memory is allocated, after which `get_kernel_syms()` is called again. Except for the system call *get_kernel_syms*, these system calls are reserved for use by the superuser.

Errors

EPERM – if a non-privileged user uses one of these system calls.

ENOENT – if the module `name` does not exist. This error message is possible with `sys_init_module()` and `sys_delete_module()`.

EEXIST – if the module `name` already exists. This error can be returned by `sys_create_module()`.

ENOMEM – if with `sys_create_module()` there is not enough free memory.

EBUSY – if the initialization routine fails or an attempt is made to remove a module that is still in use.

System call	nanosleep	LINUX

File: kernel/sched.c

```
int sys_nanosleep(struct timespec *rqtp, struct timespec *rmtp);
```

The increased clock frequency of today's CPUs allows (or necessitates) more precise time structures. This kernel function allows halting of the current process on nanosecond level. The required period of time is specified in `rqtp`:

```
struct timespec {
        long    tv_sec;   /* seconds     */
        long    tv_nsec;  /* nanoseconds */
};
```

Provided that `SCHED_OTHER` is not set, a period of up to 2 ms is delayed by the process itself in a short `for` loop. Otherwise, the pause is converted into `jiffies` and entered as the process's `timeout`, after which the scheduler is called. If the timeout has not yet expired after re-entering the function, the remaining time is returned in `rmtp`.

Errors

EINVAL – if a negative period of time or more than 1 000 000 000 nanoseconds were specified.

EINTR – if a period of time remains.

System call	nice	4.3+BSD

File: kernel/sched.c

```
int sys_nice(long inc);
```

`sys_nice()` sets the priority of the current process. As priorities are measured in time slices, some conversions are needed. The new priority is (approximately) obtained by subtracting `inc` from the old priority. This means that the higher the value of `inc`, the lower the priority of the process after the execution of the call. Only the superuser is allowed to specify negative values for `inc` and thus increment the priority. First, however, the new priority is set to inc and limited to a maximum of 40, then it is scaled to one time slice (DEF_PRIORITY). Then the new priority is subtracted from the old one, the resulting value is limited to the interval [1, DEF_PRIORITY*2] and assigned to the process. `sys_nice()` does not use `sys_setpriority()`. The reason for this is probably that `sys_nice()` has simply been implemented earlier.

Implementation

The system call is converted via the syscall macro.

Errors

EPERM – if a non-privileged user specifies a negative value for `inc`.

> | System call | pause | POSIX |
> | --- | --- | --- |

File: kernel/sched.c

```
int sys_pause(void);
```

The `sys_pause()` function is a very simple system call. It sets the status of the current process to `TASK_INTERRUPTIBLE` and calls the scheduler. With this, the process voluntarily relinquishes control. It can only continue to work if it is woken up by a signal. The function returns `-ERESTARTNOHAND`; this error message is changed into `-EINTR` by the routine `ret_from_sys_call`.

Implementation

The system call is converted via the syscall macro. This function is not available on Alpha machines.

> | System call | personality | LINUX |
> | --- | --- | --- |

File: kernel/exec_domain.c

```
#include <personality.h>

int sys_personality(unsigned long personality);
```

The LINUX kernel supports several execution environments, called *exec-domains*. During booting, the kernel generates the first exec-domain (filled with LINUX-specific data); all others can be loaded at a later stage via modules. A domain has the following structure:

```
struct exec_domain {
  char *name;
  lcall7_func handler;
  unsigned char pers_low, pers_high;
  unsigned long * signal_map;
  unsigned long * signal_invmap;
  int *use_count;
  struct exec_domain *next;
};
```

The values `pers_low` and `pers_high` are not, as one might think, the higher and lower byte values of `personality`; they represent, instead, a (numerical) upper and lower limit for the operating system located in `personality`. The `personality` parameter is divided into two areas. The upper word contains flags for known bugs,[6] the lower word contains the operating system. The values can be found in the header file `<linux/personality.h>`.

By means of `sys_personality()`, a certain domain can now be set or the current domain can be interrogated. If in the call all bits in `personality` are set (`0xffffffff`), the current value is returned. Otherwise a domain that matches `personality` is sought. For this, the lower 2 bytes of `personality` must lie between the `low` and the `high` value.

This domain is entered, together with `personality`, in the task structure of the current process. The counter of the old domain (`use_count`) is decremented, that of the new domain is incremented. The return value is the old value of `personality`.

Errors

EINVAL – There is no domain that matches `personality`.

System call	`ptrace`

File: arch/i396/kernel/ptrace.c

```
#include <sys/ptrace.h>

int sys_ptrace(long request, long pid, long addr, long data);
```

By means of the system call *ptrace* a process can monitor the execution of another process. This system call is used, for example, in the implementation of debug algorithms. A process in whose task structure the `PF_PTRACED` flag is set, is stopped upon a signal. It halts and its parent process is informed via the system call *wait*. The memory of the halted process can then be read and written to. The parent process can make the child process continue.

In `pid`, the PID of the required process is specified. Obviously, not every arbitrary process can be monitored: one should generally keep one's hands off `init`; further conditions depend on the desired `request`. The value in `request` determines the exact meaning of the call:

PTRACE_TRACEME – The process sets the flag `PF_TRACED`. The parent process is requested to monitor the process. If this flag is already set, an error occurs.

---

[6] It would be more correct to refer to them not as bugs, but as features of the operating systems concerned. One example is the flag `STICKY_TIMEOUTS`; *see also* Appendix A.2.

PTRACE_ATTACH – Sets the PF_PTRACED flag in the process specified by pid. For this, one of the following conditions must be met: the UID (GID) of the current process must match the UID, EUID or SUID (GID, EGID or SGID) of the desired process, the child is 'willing' (dumpable) or the user is the superuser. Furthermore, the flag must not be set yet. If all these obstacles have been surmounted, the flag is set, the current process becomes the father of the child and sends it the SIGSTOP signal.

PTRACE_PEEKTEXT, **PTRACE_PEEKDATA** – Reads a word (32 bits) from the address addr. The value is stored in data and returned. As yet, there is no distinction between text and data segment.

PTRACE_PEEKUSR – Reads a word from the address addr out of the user structure of the process. The value is stored in data and returned.

PTRACE_POKETEXT, **PTRACE_POKEDATA** – Writes the value contained in data to the address addr.

PTRACE_POKEUSR – Writes the value contained in data to the address addr of the user structure. Great care is taken to ensure that no register or task structure information is overwritten. Only a few debug registers are allowed.

PTRACE_SYSCALL, **PTRACE_CONT** – Continues processing the child process. With PTRACE_SYSCALL, the PF_TRACESYS flag is set. This causes processing to stop after the return of the next system call. With PTRACE_CONT, this flag is deleted. Then the contents of data are entered into the exit code of the child and it is woken up. Finally, the *trap* flag[7] is deleted.

PTRACE_KILL – Sends a SIGKILL signal to the child process. In addition, the trap flag is deleted.

PTRACE_SINGLESTEP – The PF_TRACESYS flag is deleted. The trap flag is set instead and data is entered as the exit code.

PTRACE_DETACH – Releases the process stopped by PTRACE_ATTACH. The PF_TRACED and PF_TRACESYS flags of the task structure are deleted, the process is woken up, data is entered as the exit code, the original father is re-entered as the parent process, and finally the trap bit in the EFlags register is deleted.

Implementation

Since in the peek calls the value of the data parameter is not used but is nevertheless placed on the stack (for the interrupt), the C library provides a secure pointer by placing a dummy value on the stack.

---

[7] This flag (also known as single step) is located in the processor's EFlags register. If it is set and a SIGTRAP is sent to the monitored process, the process executes exactly one instruction.

```
int ptrace(int request, int pid, int addr, int data)
{
    long ret; long res;
    if (request > 0 && request < 4) (long *)data = &ret;
        __asm__ volatile ("int $0x80"
                    :"=a" (res)
                    :"0" (SYS_ptrace),"b" (request), "c" (pid),
                    "d" (addr), "S" (data));
    if (res >= 0) {
        if (request > 0 && request < 4) {
            errno = 0; return (ret);
        }
        return (int) res;
    }
    errno = -res; return -1;
}
```

Errors

EPERM – if no sys_ptrace() can be executed for the process specified by pid or there is one already running.

ESRCH – if the process specified by pid does not exist.

EIO – if an invalid value is specified for request.

System call	reboot	LINUX

File: kernel/sys.c

```
int sys_reboot(int magic, int magic_too, int flag);
```

sys_reboot() boots the system or enables booting via the key combination Ctrl+Alt+Del. The parameters magic and magic_too are fixed. They must be set to 0xfee1dead and 672274793;[8] the function depends on flag. If flag equals

0x1234567   the system reboots,

0x89abcdef   booting via Ctrl+Alt+Del is enabled,

0   booting via Ctrl+Alt+Del is disabled or

---

[8] If you find this number somewhat strange, look at it in hexadecimal.

0xCDEF0123 the system is merely shut down. The message 'System halted' is displayed on the console and all running processes are terminated (sys_kill(-1, SIGKILL)). If *Power off shutdown* and *APM BIOS* were configured during compilation of the kernel, the apm_set_power_state() function of the BIOS is activated as well.

It should be noted that sys_reboot() does *not* call sys_sync()!

Implementation

The system call is converted via the syscall macro.

Errors

EINVAL – if an invalid value is specified for one of the parameters.

EPERM – if a non-privileged user calls the function.

System call	sched_getparam	sched_getscheduler	LINUX
	sched_setparam	sched_setscheduler	

File: kernel/sched.c

```
int sys_sched_getparam(pid_t pid, struct sched_param *param);
int sys_sched_setparam(pid_t pid, struct sched_param *param);
int sys_sched_getscheduler(pid_t pid);
int sys_sched_setscheduler(pid_t pid, int policy,
        struct sched_param *param);
```

A process can control its handling by the scheduler. The parameters (only one up to now) are combined in a structure:

```
struct sched_param { int sched_priority; };
```

The function sys_sched_getparam() returns the basic priority of real-time processes (rt_priority) of the process pid in the param structure.

sys_sched_setparam() enters the passed value as the rt_priority of the process pid and calls the scheduler. The value must lie between 0 and 99. A non-privileged user may only change his/her own processes.

The function sys_sched_getscheduler() returns the scheduler tactics for the process. The scheduler knows three tactics:

SCHED_OTHER – The rt_priority of these processes is 0. Thus they receive a normal value when the priority is recalculated.

SCHED_FIFO – Small, time-critical processes. They get a priority bonus of 1000.

SCHED_RR – Big, time-critical processes. When their `counter` has expired, they are inserted at the very back of the scheduler's process list.

With `sys_sched_setscheduler()`, a process can change its tactics and its `rt_priority` value. If `policy` is negative, the old value is maintained. The priority must also correspond to the tactics; only the superuser is allowed to assign time-critical tactics.

Errors

EPERM – if a normal user attempts to change another process.

ESRCH – if the process `pid` could not be found.

EINVAL – if an invalid parameter is passed.

System call	`sched_get_priority_min` `sched_get_priority_min`	LINUX

File: kernel/sched.c

```
int sys_sched_get_priority_min(int policy);
int sys_sched_get_priority_max(int policy);
int sys_sched_yield(void);
int sys_sched_rr_get_interval(pid_t pid,
        struct timespec *interval)
```

The first two functions return the lower and upper limit of the `rt_priority` values of the individual scheduler tactics.

With `sys_sched_yield()`, a process can acquiesce in its fate. It is inserted at the end of the list of running processes and treated by the scheduler accordingly.

The function `sys_sched_rr_get_interval()` is not yet implemented; it returns `-ENOSYS`.

Errors

EINVAL – if incorrect tactics were passed.

System call	`setdomainname`

File: kernel/sys.c

```
int sys_setdomainname(const char *name, int len);
```

The sys_setdomainname() function overwrites the domain name with the name specified in name. The name does not have to terminate with a null byte: this is entered by the function itself.

Implementation

The system call setdomainname is converted via the syscall macro. The system call *getdomainname* is implemented in the C library. A call to __uname() is made and the domain name read. The return value (upon success) is 0.

```
int getdomainname(char *name, size_t len)
{
    struct utsname uts;

    if (name == NULL) {
        errno = EINVAL; return -1;
    }
    if (__uname(&uts) == -1) return -1;

    if (strlen(uts.domainname)+1 > len) {
        errno = EINVAL; return -1;
    }
    strcpy(name, uts.domainname);
    return 0;
}
```

Errors

EINVAL – if in getdomainname() the string supplied by sys_uname() points to NULL or is greater than len.
If in sys_setdomainname() len is too big.

EPERM – if a non-privileged user calls sys_setdomainname().

System call	getgroups	POSIX
	setgroups	

File: kernel/sys.c

```
#include <sys/types.h>

int sys_getgroups(int len, gid_t *groups);
int sys_setgroups(int len, gid_t *groups);
```

The functions `sys_getgroups()` and `sys_setgroups()` allow several group privileges for a process to be read and set. `sys_getgroups()` provides the groups, where `len` is the maximum number required. If this is specified as zero, the call just returns the number of groups. The groups are part of the task structure (*see* Section 3.3.1). `sys_setgroups()` sets the group privileges. It is only possible to set all groups at once, as the old groups are overwritten. The number of groups is given by `len`. Only the superuser can execute this call.

Implementation

Both system calls are converted via the syscall macro.

Errors

EINVAL – if in `sys_setgroups()` the value `len` is greater than NGROUPS.

EPERM – if a non-privileged user calls `sys_setgroups()`.

System call	sethostname	4.3+BSD
	gethostname	

File: kernel/sys.c

```
int sys_sethostname(char *name, int len);
```

This function allows a write access to the computer name. It works analogously to `set_setdomainname()`. `sys_sethostname()` can only be executed by the superuser. Upon success, 0 is returned.

Implementation

The system call *sethostname* is converted via the syscall macro. The system call *gethostname* is implemented in the C library and makes use of `__uname()`.

```
int gethostname(char *name, size_t len)
{
    struct utsname uts;

    if (name == NULL) {
        errno = EINVAL; return -1;
    }
    if (__uname(&uts) == -1) return -1;
    if (strlen(uts.nodename)+1 > len) {
        errno = EINVAL; return -1;
    }
```

```
        strcpy(name, uts.nodename);
        return 0;
    }
```

Errors

EINVAL – if in `sys_sethostname()` the name string points to NULL or the size
specified in `len` exceeds `__NEW_UTS_LEN`. The value is defined as 64 in
`<linux/utsname.h>`.

EPERM – if a non-privileged user calls `sys_sethostname()`.

System call	getitimer
	setitimer

File: kernel/itimer.c

```
#include <sys/time.h>

int sys_getitimer(int which, struct itimerval *value);
int sys_setitimer(int which, const  struct  itimerval  *value,
                struct itimerval *ovalue);
```

These functions allow better time monitoring of a process than does
`sys_alarm()`. Three special timers can be programmed for the current process,
specified by `which`:

ITIMER_REAL – refers to real time. The alarm is updated each time a process is
triggered in the scheduler and, on expiry, provides a `SIGALRM`.

ITIMER_VIRTUAL – is the time during which the process is active but is not in a
system call (system mode). The alarm is updated by the `do_timer()`
routine and, on expiry, provides a `SIGVTALRM`.

ITIMER_PROF – indicates the total time the process is running. After expiry of
the alarm, a `SIGPROF` is sent. Together with `ITIMER_VIRTUAL`, this makes
it possible to distinguish between the time consumed in system mode and
in user mode.

The times are indicated in the following structure:

```
struct itimerval {
    struct timeval it_interval; /* interval       */
    struct timeval it_value;    /* starting value */
};
```

```
struct timeval {
    long tv_sec;
    long tv_usec;
};
```

sys_getitimer() returns the current value for the alarm set in which. sys_setitimer() sets the alarm specified in which to value. The old value is returned in ovalue. At its first start, the timer is set to the value it_value. When the timer has expired, a signal is generated and the alarm reset, from now on to the value it_interval, as described in Section 3.2.4. The alarm may be triggered slightly later than the specified time: this depends on the system clock. Generally, the delay is 10 milliseconds.

Under LINUX, generation and sending of signals are separate. Thus it is possible that under *pathologically* heavy load a SIGALRM is sent before the process has received the signal of the previous cycle. Then the second signal is ignored.

Implementation

Both system calls are converted via the syscall macro.

Errors

EFAULT – if value or ovalue are invalid pointers.
EINVAL – if which is invalid.

System call	getrlimit	4.3+BSD
	setrlimit	
	getrusage	

File: kernel/sys.c

```
#include <sys/resource.h>

int sys_getrlimit(unsigned int resource, struct rlimit *rlim);
int sys_setrlimit(unsigned int resource, struct rlimit *rlim);
int sys_getrusage(int who, struct rusage *usage);
```

sys_getrlimit() reads the size of a resource of the current process and stores it in rlim. Setting is possible by means of the function setrlimit(). The following values are defined in <linux/resource.h> as resource:

RLIMIT_CPU – maximum CPU time (sum of `utime` and `stime` of the process) in milliseconds.

RLIMIT_FSIZE – maximum file size.

RLIMIT_DATA – maximum size of the data segment used.

RLIMIT_STACK – maximum stack size.

RLIMIT_CORE – maximum size of a `core` file.

RLIMIT_RSS – maximum memory size for arguments and environment (RSS).

RLIMIT_NPROC – maximum number of child processes.

RLIMIT_NOFILE – maximum number of open files.

RLIMIT_MEMLOCK – maximum memory size a process can block.

RLIMIT_AS – maximum address space.

The `rlimit` structure is defined in the same file:

```
struct rlimit {
    int  rlim_cur; /* soft limit  */
    int  rlim_max; /* hard limit  */
};
```

There are two limits for a process: the *soft limit* (current limit) and the *hard limit* (upper limit). A non-privileged process can set the soft limit to an arbitrary value between zero and the hard limit, and it can lower the hard limit down to the soft limit. Lowering the hard limit cannot be undone. If the value of a resource is `RLIM_INFINITY`, there is no restriction. For `RLIMIT_NOFILE`, `NR_OPEN` is the maximum upper limit, both for `rlim_cur` and `rlim_max`. A process that exceeds its current soft limit is aborted. Both calls return 0 upon successful execution.

While the above functions administer the environment of a process, the `sys_getrusage()` function provides information about the process itself. The individual values are defined in the `rusage` structure:

```
struct    rusage {
    struct timeval ru_utime; /* user time            */
    struct timeval ru_stime; /* system time          */
    long ru_maxrss;          /* max. RSS             */
    long ru_ixrss;        /* size of shared RSS      */
    long ru_idrss;        /* size of unshared RSS    */
    long ru_isrss;        /* stack size              */
    long ru_minflt;       /* number of minor faults  */
    long ru_majflt;       /* number of major faults  */
    long ru_nswap;        /* swap operations         */
```

```
    long ru_inblock;       /* block input operations      */
    long ru_oublock;       /* block output operations     */
    long ru_msgsnd;        /* messages sent               */
    long ru_msgrcv;        /* messages received           */
    long ru_nsignals;      /* signals received            */
    long ru_nvcsw;         /* voluntary context changes   */
    long ru_nivcsw;        /* involuntary context changes */
};
```

The function does not, however, fill the complete structure. Only the values for ru_utime and ru_stime, together with the indication for the memory pages (minor faults and major faults), are filled in. If the value RUSAGE_SELF is specified for who, the information refers to the process itself. Data about child processes are obtained by specifying RUSAGE_CHILDREN. All other values for who supply the sum of both.

Implementation

Both system calls are converted via the syscall macro.

Errors

EINVAL – if sys_getrlimit() and sys_setrlimit() are called with an invalid resource value or if the who value in sys_getrusage() is invalid.

EPERM – if a non-privileged user calls sys_setrlimit().

System call	signal	sigaction	POSIX
	sigpending	sigsuspend	
	sgetmask	ssetmask	
	sigprocmask	sigreturn	

File: kernel/signal.c
        arch/i386/kernel/signal.c

```
#include <signal.h>

unsigned long sys_signal(int signum, void (*handler)(int)):
int sys_sigaction(int signum, const struct sigaction *new,
                  struct sigaction *old);
int sys_sgetmask(void);
int sys_ssetmask(int newmask);
int sys_sigpending(sigset_t *buf);
```

```
int sys_sigsuspend(int restart, unsigned long oldmask,
                   unsigned long set);
int sys_sigprocmask (int how, const sigset_t *set,
                     sigset_t *old_set);
int sys_sigreturn(unsigned long __unused);
```

The sys_signal() function sets the handling routine for the signum signal. The handler routine can be a user-defined function or a macro taken from <signal.h>. The following are possible:

SIG_DFL – standard handling of the signal is carried out.

SIG_IGN – the signal is ignored.

The handling routine is entered in the sigaction structure of the current process. The flags SA_ONESHOT and SA_NOMASK are set and all other values are initialized with 0. Upon success, the address of the old routine is returned, otherwise a negative value (–1) is returned. For the SIGKILL and SIGSTOP signals no new handlers can be implemented, and the signal number must be lower than 32 (set in the source text).

According to POSIX 3.3.1.3 the following holds: if SIG_IGN is specified as a routine, any signal still pending is deleted (except for SIGCHLD). If the routine is SIG_DFL, the signal is deleted if it is not one of SIGCONT, SIGCHLD or SIGWINCH. In both cases, it does not matter whether the signal is blocked or not. This is handled by the check_pending() function.

The sys_sigaction() function is the up-to-date and extended version of sys_signal(). It is used to specify the routine for the signal more precisely. In new, the new routine is defined. If old is different from NULL, the old routine is returned. The sigaction structure is defined as follows:

```
struct sigaction {
   void (*sa_handler)(int);
   sigset_t sa_mask;
   int sa_flags;
   void (*sa_restorer)(void);
};
```

If in sa_flags the value SA_NOMASK is not set, the signal is entered in the signal mask. Again, the final call is to check_pending(). Please note that SIGKILL and SIGSTOP cannot be blocked.

For simply setting and interrogating the signal mask of blocked signals the functions are sys_sgetmask() and sys_ssetmask(). Whereas the first function simply returns current->blocked, the second deletes SIGKILL and SIGSTOP from the passed mask and enters them in the task structure.

sys_sigpending() checks whether there are blocked signals pending for the process. The signals are stored in buf; the return value is 0.

With the functions `sys_sgetmask()` and `sys_ssetmask()`, blocking of signals can be toggled. `sys_sigsuspend()` makes it possible to set a signal mask and stop the process in a single action. The process is set to sleep until a non-blocked signal arrives.

If only the mask for blocking signals has to be set, the `sys_sigprocmask()` function can be used. The **how** parameter specifies how the new signal mask should be used:

SIG_BLOCK – the signals set in the signal mask are blocked. The new mask is superimposed on the old mask using |=.

SIG_UNBLOCK – the signals set in the signal mask are deleted. The new mask is superimposed on the old mask using &= ~.

SIG_SETMASK – the signal mask is taken over as the signal mask for the current process.

The call first deletes the signal bits for SIGKILL and SIGSTOP from the passed mask. If old_set is different from NULL, the old mask is returned.

The `sys_sigreturn()` function organizes the return from a signal interrupt. It is called internally in order to return to system mode after a signal handling routine. To do this, for each signal to be handled, a frame is generated on the stack of the process which ensures that the system call *sigreturn* is triggered.[9]

Implementation

The functions `sys_signal()`, `sys_sigprocmask()`, `sys_sgetmask()` and `sys_ssetmask` are not available on Alpha machines. Curiously enough, the library function `signal()` does not work with the system call *signal*, but is based on *sigaction*.

```
__sighandler_t signal (int sig, __sighandler_t handler)
{
    int ret;
    struct sigaction action, oaction;
    action.sa_handler = handler;
    __sigemptyset (&action.sa_mask);
    action.sa_flags = SA_ONESHOT | SA_NOMASK | SA_INTERRUPT;
    action.sa_flags &= ~SA_RESTART;
    ret = __sigaction (sig, &action, &oaction);
    return (ret == -1) ? SIG_ERR : oaction.sa_handler;
}
```

[9] For this purpose, all important registers and the machine code (!) that triggers *sigreturn* are put on the stack as a frame.

The remaining calls work with the syscall macro, whereas for `sys_sigreturn()` there is no external interface.

Errors

EINVAL – if an invalid signal number is used.

EFAULT – if the handling routine is bigger than the permitted process size (`TASK_SIZE`).

EINTR – if the process returns from `sys_sigsuspend()`.

System call	`sysctl`

File: kernel/sysctl.c

```
int sys_sysctl(struct __sysctl_args *args);
```

This function allows extensive administration of system-relevant information. This information is held in internal tables and mapped onto /proc/sys. The precise effect of the function is controlled via the __sysctl_args structure.

```
struct __sysctl_args {
        int *name;        /* name of information   */
        int nlen;         /* extent of information */
        void *oldval;     /* pointer to old value  */
        size_t *oldlenp;  /* length of old value   */
        void *newval;     /* pointer to new value  */
        size_t newlen;    /* length of new value   */
        unsigned long __unused[4];
};
```

The information results from `name` and `nlen`. These components are, however, not yet completely implemented. The second parameter specifies which area the information refers to:

CTL_KERN – kernel and control structures

CTL_VM – VM managment

CTL_NET – network

CTL_PROC – process information

CTL_FS – file systems

CTL_DEBUG – debugging

CTL_DEV – devices

The first parameter contains the required information. The following values are implemented as a standard; they are listed together with their type:

KERN_OSTYPE – a string: the operating system

KERN_OSRELEASE – a string: the version

KERN_VERSION – a string: the compile information

KERN_NODENAME – a string: the host name

KERN_DOMAINNAME – a string: the domain name

KERN_NRINODE – two numbers: the current inode number and the number of free inodes

KERN_MAXINODE – a number: the maximum number of inodes

KERN_NRFILE – a number: the number of open files

KERN_MAXFILE – a number: the maximum number of open files

KERN_SECURELVL – a number: the security level

KERN_PANIC – a number: timeout in case of a `panic` message

KERN_REALROOTDEV – device which actually holds the root (only with configured `CONFIG_BLK_DEV_INITRD`)

KERN_NFSRNAME – a string: name of the root file system (only with configured `ROOT_NFS`)

KERN_NFSRADDRS – a string: the address of the root file system (only with configured `ROOT_NFS`)

KERN_JAVA_INTERPRETER – a string: the path of the Java interpreter

KERN_JAVA_APPLETVIEWER – a string: the path of the Java applet viewer

VM_SWAPCTL – a structure: the parameters of the swap process

VM_KSWAPD – a structure: the parameters of the kswap daemon

VM_FREEPG – three numbers: the values of free page grades

VM_BDFLUSH – a structure: the parameters of the `bd_flush()` process

In order to read a value, `name` and `nlen` must be entered, and the required value and its size are returned in `oldval` and `oldlenp`. If `newval` and `newlen` are not equal to 0, the memory area of size `newlen` addressed by `newval` is entered.

Implementation

The C library does not provide an interface. Also, the kernel function does not yet check for superuser privileges!

Errors

ENOTDIR – if `nlen` or `name` are invalid.

EFAULT – If `oldlenp` equals 0.

System call	sysinfo	LINUX

File: kernel/info.c

```
#include <linux/sys.h>
#include <linux/kernel.h>


int sys_sysinfo(struct sysinfo *info);
```

sys_sysinfo() provides information about the system load. The data are returned in the following structure:

```
struct sysinfo {
    long uptime;                /* seconds since start              */
    unsigned long loads[3];     /* load 1, 5 and 15 min. ago        */
    unsigned long totalram;     /* size of RAM memory               */
    unsigned long freeram;      /* free RAM memory                  */
    unsigned long sharedram;    /* size of shared memory            */
    unsigned long bufferram;    /* size of buffer memory            */
    unsigned long totalswap;    /* size of swap memory              */
    unsigned long freeswap;     /* free swap memory                 */
    unsigned short procs;       /* number of running processes      */
    char _f[22];                /* dummy, rounds up to 64 bytes     */
};
```

sys_sysinfo provides a generally accessible method for obtaining system information. This is simpler and less risky than reading /dev/kmem.

Implementation

This system call is not supported by the C library. In order to use it, a file sysinfo.c with the following contents should be created.

```
#include <unistd.h>

_syscall1(int, sysinfo, struct sysinfo *, s)
```

This corresponds to the process of implementing a system call as described in Section 3.3.4.

Errors

EFAULT – if the pointer to info is invalid.

System call	syslog

File: kernel/printk.c

```
int sys_syslog(int type, char *buf, int len);
```

sys_syslog() administers the *log book* of the system and sets the *log level*. The log book is a memory area in the kernel 8 Kbytes in size and is filled by the printk() function (*see* Appendix E). The log level is the priority level for the behaviour of the printk() function. Only messages whose priority is higher than the log level are displayed by printk() on the console.

```
#define LOG_BUF_LEN    8192
static char log_buf[LOG_BUF_LEN];
```

There are three variables for the access:

```
unsigned long log_size = 0;
static unsigned long log_start = 0;
static unsigned long logged_chars = 0;
```

The first variable describes the size of the log book, which can vary between 0 and LOG_BUF_LEN, the second gives the beginning of the current message. With the access operation

```
(log_start+log_size) & (LOG_BUF_LEN-1)
```

we thus arrive at the last position of the current entry. The overall number of characters in the log book is stored in logged_chars.

The precise functioning of syslog can be specified in type, using the following values:

0   Closes the log book. This is not implemented. The return value is 0.

1   Opens the log book. This is not implemented. The return value is 0.

2   Reads len characters from the log book. For this, the variable log_size is evaluated. If the book is empty (log_size equals 0) this call blocks until a process has left an entry and then reads it. log_size is decremented by the number of characters actually read.

3   Reads entries from the log book into the buffer buf of length len. This function does not block. len is first checked against the values LOG_BUF_LEN and logged_chars and (if greater) set to this value.

4   As 3; in addition, the call clears the log book by setting logged_chars to 0.

5 The call clears the log book.

6 Sets the log level for the `printk()` function to 1. Only messages of the highest priority are displayed on the console.

7 Sets the log level for the `printk()` function to the default value (7).

8 Sets the log level for the `printk()` function to the value of `len`, which in this case must lie between 0 and 9.

The return value is the number of characters actually read (in cases 2, 3 and 4) or 0.

Implementation

There is no conversion in the C library. Linking is possible with the following file:

```
#include <unistd.h>

_syscall1(int, syslog, int, type, char *, buf, int, len)
```

Errors

EPERM – if a non-privileged user calls `sys_syslog()` with a type other than 3.

EINVAL – if `buf` is NULL or `len` is negative.

System call	time	stime	POSIX
	gettimeofday	settimeofday	SVR4
			4.3+BSD

File: kernel/time.c

```
#include <time.h>

int sys_time(long *t);
int sys_stime(const time_t *t);
int sys_gettimeofday(struct timeval *tv,
                     struct timezone *tz);
int sys_settimeofday(struct timeval *tv,
                     struct timezone *tz);
```

`sys_time()` stores in `t` the time passed since 1 January 1970, 0.00 am, in seconds, and returns it using the macro `CURRENT_TIME`.

`sys_stime()` sets the system time, more precisely `xtime.tv_sec`, to the value specified in `t`. Only the superuser may execute this function. It returns 0 upon success and a negative number in the event of an error.

sys_gettimeofday() and sys_settimeofday() allow a more exact time management. tv is the same structure as the one specified in sys_setitimer():

```
struct timeval {
    long tv_sec;    /* seconds      */
    long tv_usec;   /* microseconds */
};
```

and tz is a time zone:

```
struct timezone {
    int  tz_minuteswest;
    /* minutes west of Greenwich */
    int  tz_dsttime;
    /* uses summer time */
};
```

The file <sys/time.h> defines the values for the specification of summer time, for example DST_NONE for no summer time, DST_USA for USA summer time and DST_MET for mid-European summer time. The header file also defines some macros for the handling of timeval values. The timerisset(tvp) macro checks whether the time tvp is 0, while timercmp(tvp, uvp, cmp) compares two times using cmp.

The sys_settimeofday() function, like sys_stime(), can only be executed by the superuser. If tv or tz are set to NULL, the corresponding system value does not change. At the first call[10] with tz set, the CMOS clock is changed to UTC. The data are transferred into the address space of the kernel and the system values updated. For the setting of the tv values, the interrupts are disabled and time_status is set to TIME_BAD. The system call returns 0 upon success. The functioning of the underlying timer is described in Section 3.1.6.

Implementation

All four system calls are converted via the syscall macro. The first two functions are not available on Alpha machines.

Errors

EPERM – if the process calling sys_stime() or settimeofday does not have superuser privileges.

EINVAL – if an invalid value (time zone, and so on) is specified.

---

[10] This should happen as early as possible in order not to confuse other possibly running programs. Usually, a script in /etc/rc is used.

System call	times	POSIX

File: kernel/sys.c

```
#include <sys/times.h>

long sys_times(struct tms *buf);
```

sys_times() writes the time used by the current process and its children into the structure buf. The structure tms is defined in <linux/times.h> as follows:

```
struct  tms  {
   time_t tms_utime;  /* user time                */
   time_t tms_stime;  /* system time              */
   time_t tms_cutime; /* user time of children    */
   time_t tms_cstime; /* system time of children */
};
```

sys_times() returns the jiffies of the system.

Implementation

The system call is converted via the syscall macro.

System call	uname	POSIX

File: kernel/sys.c

```
#include <sys/utsname.h>

int sys_newuname(struct new_utsname *buf);
```

sys_uname() returns information about the system. The information can then be found in buf. The structure utsname appears as follows:

```
struct utsname {
   char sysname[65];     /* operating system name   */
   char nodename[65];    /* computer name           */
   char release[65];     /* operating system release */
   char version[65];     /* operating system version */
   char machine[65];     /* processor type          */
   char domainname[65];  /* computer domain         */
};
```

Release is the current state of development of the system (e.g. 1.2.0). Version is the number of hitherto existing kernel configurations together with the time of the most recent compilation (e.g. #95 Sat Apr 1 05:08:15 MET DST 1995).

For reasons of compatibility, there are another two simplified versions: the first one (old_utsname) lacks the domain; the second one (oldold_utsname) additionally limits the entry lengths to 9 bytes (POSIX defines entries for the structure that are only 8 bytes long (plus the space for the null byte)).

Implementation

The system call is converted via the syscall macro.

Errors

EFAULT – if buf is NULL.

System call	vm86	LINUX

File: arch/i386/kernel/vm86.c

```
#include <sys/vm86.h>

int sys_vm86(struct vm86_struct * info);
```

The sys_vm86() function sets the process into virtual 8086 mode. To control this, the register set of the 8086, regs, can be used.

```
struct vm86_struct {
    struct vm86_regs regs;
    unsigned long flags;
    unsigned long screen_bitmap;
};
```

The registers DS, ES, FS and GS are set to 0. In addition, the EFlags register is controlled. The function stores the current stack of the kernel and then jumps into virtual mode. The call is used by the DOS emulator.

Implementation

The system call is converted via the syscall macro.

Errors

EPERM – if the stack has already been stored.

System call	wait4	4.3+BSD
	waitpid	POSIX

File: kernel/exit.c

```
int sys_waitpid(pid_t pid, unsigned long *stat_addr,
                int options);

int sys_wait4(pid_t pid, unsigned long *stat_addr,
              int options, struct rusage *ru);
```

sys_wait4() waits for the process pid to terminate. In addition, the function writes the exit code to the address stat_addr and information about resources used by the process into the structure ru. Possible options are the values:

__WCLONE – only processes generated with clone() are waited for.

WUNTRACED – also those stopped processes are considered in which PF_TRACE is not set.

WNOHANG – sys_wait4() does not block.

The function interrogates all child processes in a loop to check whether one of them is in the ZOMBIE or STOPPED state. If pid is

>0   wait4() waits for the child process with PID equal to pid.

0   wait4() waits for each child process whose PGRP matches the PGRP of the calling process.

−1   wait4() waits for all child processes.

<−1   wait4() waits for each child process whose PGRP equals −pid.

If no process was found, sys_wait4() returns if WNOHANG was set. Otherwise, the scheduler is called and the loop entered again.

sys_wait4() returns when the process (that is being waited for) terminates or is a zombie, if WNOHANG is set or a non-blocking signal was received. Return values are a negative number in the event of an error, the PID of the terminated process or 0 (with WNOHANG).

sys_waitpid() waits for the process pid with the specified options options. The sys_waitpid() function is only still provided for compatibility reasons and could well be implemented in the C library in future versions.

```
asmlinkage int sys_waitpid(pid_t pid, unsigned long * stat_addr,
                           int options)
{
    return sys_wait4(pid, stat_addr, options, NULL);
}
```

The exact interplay of `sys_wait4()`, `sys_exit()` and the scheduler is described in Section 3.3.3.

Implementation

The system calls *wait4* and *waitpid* are converted via the syscall macro. The function `waitpid()` is not available on Alpha machines. `wait()` is no longer provided as a system call, but only as a library function (in `unistd.h`).

```
static inline pid_t wait(int *wait_stat)
{
    return waitpid(-1, wait_stat, 0);
}
```

Errors

ERESTARTSYS – if WNOHANG is not set and the process receives a non-blocking signal or a SIGCHLD.

ECHILD – if the child process `pid` does not exist.

A.2   The file system

The following system calls establish connection with the file system. Because of the existence of a virtual file system in LINUX the transition from the user to the kernel is just an intermediate step of the real work involved.

Nearly all system calls execute a parameter check first and then call the corresponding inode or file operation of the file system implementation. All system calls that possess a `path` parameter use the `namei()` function. This function determines the inode belonging to the name and is described in detail in Section 6.2.3.

System call	access	POSIX

File: fs/open.c

```
#include <unistd.h>

int sys_access(const char *filename, int mode);
```

The `sys_access()` function checks whether a user has the access rights `mode` for the file `filename`. Possible values for `mode` are:

F_OK – if the file exists.

R_OK – if the file can be read.

W_OK – if the file can be written to.

X_OK – if the file can be executed.

For the access to the file system, `sys_access()` does not use the effective UID (EUID), but only the normal ones, which for the access test are copied into the FSUID. If the inode operations provide a `permission` component, this function is used to determine the access rights. Otherwise the decision is made with `inode->i_mode` according to the UNIX rights.

Implementation

The conversion is simply carried out via the syscall macro.

Errors

EINVAL – if the rights specified in `mode` do not coincide with the rights of the file or if the file `filename` does not exist.

EACCES – if access with the specified rights is not permitted.

System call   bdflush

File: fs/buffer.c

```
int sys_bdflush(int func, long data);
```

The kernel function `sys_bdflush()` organizes the swapping out of the blocks marked as 'dirty' in the buffer cache.

The LINUX kernel administers the buffer cache by means of two tables (among other things).

```
#define NR_LIST 6

static struct buffer_head * lru_list[NR_LIST] = {NULL, };
int nr_buffers_type[NR_LIST] = {0,};
```

The first table contains pointers to doubly linked lists each of which contains a class of blocks. A class can be, for example, `BUF_SHARED` or `BUF_LOCKED`. The second table contains the number of blocks in the corresponding list.

The pointer `lru_list[BUF_DIRTY]` points to the list administered by `bdflush()`, which contains the blocks not yet swapped out to the storage media.

The number of blocks in this list is contained in nr_buffers_type[BUF_DIRTY]. A block is administered by means of the structure buffer_head and appears as follows:

```
struct buffer_head {
    char * b_data;                         /* pointer to data block  */
    unsigned long b_size;                  /* block size             */
    unsigned long b_blocknr;               /* block number           */
    dev_t b_dev;                           /* device                 */
    unsigned short b_count;                /* number of users        */
    unsigned char b_uptodate;              /* read flag              */
    unsigned char b_dirt;                  /* 0 clean, 1 dirty       */
    unsigned char b_lock;                  /* 0 ok,    1 locked      */
    unsigned char b_req;                   /* operations flag        */
    unsigned char b_list;
    unsigned char b_retain;
    unsigned long b_flushtime;             /* write time             */
    unsigned long b_lru_time;              /* last time used         */
    struct wait_queue * b_wait;
    struct buffer_head * b_prev;           /* list of hash tables    */
    struct buffer_head * b_next;
    struct buffer_head * b_prev_free;      /* list of buffers        */
    struct buffer_head * b_next_free;
    struct buffer_head * b_this_page;      /* buffer of current page */
    struct buffer_head * b_reqnext;
};
```

In order to control swapping, there is a structure that contains the neccessary parameters.

```
static union bdflush_param {
    struct {
        int nfract;    /* activation threshold in per cent     */
        int ndirty;    /* max. number of blocks to be swapped  */
                       /* out in one cycle                     */
        int nrefill;   /* number of free blocks that are       */
                       /* loaded by means of refill_freelist   */
        int nref_dirt;
        int clu_nfract; /* percentage of buffer cache to be    */
                       /* searched for free clusters           */
        int age_buffer; /* ageing time for data blocks         */
        int age_super; /* ageing time for metablocks           */
                       /* (directories and so on)              */
        int lav_const; /* load constant for calculating        */
                       /* the buffer size                      */
```

```
        int lav_ratio;  /* load minimum for recalculating    */
                        /* the buffer size                    */
    } b_un;
    unsigned int data[N_PARAM];
} bdf_prm = {{25, 500, 64, 256, 15, 30*HZ, 50*HZ, 1884, 2}};
```

Apart from the default values, the kernel also sets the minimum and maximum values.

```
static int bdflush_min[N_PARAM] =
          {  0,   10,    5,   25,   0,   100,   100,    1, 1};
static int bdflush_max[N_PARAM] =
          {100, 5000, 2000, 2000, 100, 60000, 60000, 2047, 5};
```

If the argument func is 1, all marked blocks are swapped out. If func is greater than 1, a parameter is modified, where (func-2)>>1 is the number of the parameter. An even value of func means that the parameter is filled with the word contained in data, whereas an odd value yields the reading of the parameter.[11] During writing a check is made as to whether data lies between minimum and maximum.

Formerly, with func equal 0, the daemon itself was activated. Now, this is carried out by init() in main.c. In this case, the kernel function returns 0.

Implementation

The C library does not provide an interface for converting the system call into the kernel function.

Errors

EPERM – Only the superuser may execute this function.

EINVAL – The value for func or data is invalid.

System call	chdir	POSIX
	fchdir	

File: fs/open.c

```
int sys_chdir(const char *path);
int sys_fchdir(unsigned int fd);
```

---

[11] For example, 2 means 'write parameter 0', 3 'read parameter 0', 4 'write parameter 1' and so on.

sys_chdir() sets the current working directory to the directory specified in path. It determines the inode belonging to path and enters it in the fs.pwd component of the task structure. sys_fchdir() works in the same way, except that by using the file descriptor passed, the function can determine the inode somewhat more easily.

Implementation

Both system calls use the syscall macro.

Errors

ENOTDIR – if path is not a directory.

EBADF – if fd is invalid.

ENOENT – if there exists no inode for path.

EACCES – if no execution rights are set for the directory.

System call	chmod	fchmod	POSIX
	chown	fchown	

File: fs/open.c

```
#include <sys/types.h>
#include <sys/stat.h>

int sys_chmod(const char *filename, mode_t mode);
int sys_fchmod(unsigned int fildes, mode_t mode);
int sys_chown(const char *filename, uid_t owner, gid_t group);
int sys_fchown(unsigned int fd, uid_t owner, gid_t group);
```

sys_chmod() sets the rights of the file filename to the rights specified in mode. Bits that are higher than S_ISUID (for example S_IFIFO) are first masked out in order to prevent manipulation. If mode is set to −1, the current access rights remain unchanged; only ctime is reset. In sys_fchmod(), a file descriptor is specified instead of the name.

sys_chown() changes the owner and group of a file in owner and group. The call sys_fchown() has the same function, except that a descriptor is specified. If the UID or GID of the file is changed, the corresponding set s bit (S_ISGID only if S_IXGRP is not set) is deleted. In both functions, the quotas are updated (transferred) according to the new users.

All four calls update their inode information using the notify_change() function. Only the owner of the file or the superuser can execute these system calls.

Implementation

All four system calls work with the syscall macro.

Errors

EACCES – if the EUID of the process is different from the UID of the file or other than 0.

ENOENT – if the file does not exist.

EROFS – if the file system is read-only.

EDQUOT – if the quotas of the new owner do not allow the operation.

System call	chroot

File: fs/open.c

```
int sys_chroot(const char * filename);
```

sys_chroot() sets the directory filename as root directory for the calling process. The call determines the inode belonging to filename, checks whether it is a directory and enters it as fs.root in the task structure. The FSUID of the process must be 0.

Implementation

The conversion is carried out via the syscall macro.

Errors

EPERM – if a non-privileged user executes the call.

EROFS – if the directory lies on a read-only file system.

ENAMETOOLONG – if the specified name is too long.

ENOENT – if the directory does not exist.

ENOTDIR – if a part of the path is not a directory, but a file.

System call	dup	dup2	POSIX

File: fs/fcntl.c

```
int sys_dup(unsigned int oldfd);
int sys_dup2(unsigned int oldfd, unsigned int newfd);
```

`sys_dup()` and `sys_dup2()` generate a copy of the file descriptor. Afterwards, both descriptors point to the same file structure. A set `close_on_exec` flag is deleted. `sys_dup()` returns the first free descriptor for the copy; `sys_dup2()` uses `newfd` as a copy. If `newfd` is not yet free, the corresponding file is closed. Both system calls are mapped onto the `dupfd()` function.

Implementation

The conversion of both system calls is carried out via the syscall macro.

Errors

EBADF – if an invalid file descriptor is used.

EMFILE – if there is no free file descriptor in `sys_dup()`.

System call	**execve**	POSIX

File: fs/exec.c
      arch/i386/kernel/process.c

```
int sys_execve(struct pt_regs regs);
```

This function is passed the register stack `pt_regs` as arguments in the kernel. As these arguments are obviously different for the individual architectures, the function (which is an interface to the actual `do_execve()` function) is located in the architecture directory.

`sys_execve()` executes a new program. The necessary parameters can be found in the register structure. Thus `regs.ebx` contains a pointer to the file name of the program, `filename`, `regs.ecx` a pointer to the arguments to be passed to the specified program and `regs.edx` the address of the environment in which the process should be running.

The file `filename` must be a binary file whose format is known to LINUX, or a script. The script must begin with the characters '#!' and the first line must not exceed a length of 127 characters.

The program called with `sys_execve()` completely overlays the calling process, which means that text and data segments plus stack and BBS are overwritten with those of the loaded program. The program takes over the PID of the calling process and its opened file descriptors. Pending signals are deleted. In the event of an error, a negative number is returned; there is no return value upon success. The implementation of the call is described in Section 3.3.3.

If the current process is executed with `ptrace()`, the system call *execve* returns a **SIGTRAP** signal after successful completion. In addition, UID and

GID are set to EUID and EGID of the current process in order to prevent programs with set SUID or SGID bits from being modified by `ptrace()`.

`sys_execve()` analyses the file `filename`, searches the list of known binary formats (plus `kerneld`, if configured) and tries to load the file by means of the `load_binary` fucntion.

Implementation

The structure `pt_regs` in `<asm/ptrace.h>` contains exactly one image of the registers on the stack which are deposited there during a system call before the kernel function is called. LINUX supports several binary formats, and each format carries along its own function for loading binaries. To this function, the name of the program (which might be an interpreter with a script as an argument) is passed together with the registers (*see* Section 3.3.3).

The normal system calls, such as *execl* or *execv*, are implemented as library functions. In `execv()` the current environment is passed to the actual system call, whereas in `execvp()` the command name is sought in the current path and a new argument assembled. In argument list functions, such as `execl()`, the passed argument list is, in addition, copied into a vector.

Errors

EACCES – if `filename` is not a normal file.

EPERM – if the file system has been mounted with `MS_NOEXEC`.

ENOEXEC – if no file identification (*magic number*) or no shell could be found after #!.

E2BIG – if there is no memory free in the kernel.

System call	fcntl	POSIX

File: fs/fcntl.c
         net/inet/sock.c

```
#include <fcntl.h>

int sys_fcntl(unsigned int fd, unsigned int cmd,
              unsigned long arg);
```

The system call `sys_fcntl()` modifies the characteristics of an opened file `fd`. The corresponding operation is specified by `cmd`:

F_DUPFD – the file descriptor `fd` is duplicated in `arg`. This corresponds to the functioning of `sys_dup2()`. The error messages, however, are different. Upon success, the new file descriptor is returned.

F_GETFD – reads the `close-on-exec` flag of the specified file descriptor. If the lowest bit of the return value is 0, the file remains opened during the system call *execve*, otherwise it is closed.

F_SETFD – sets or deletes, depending on `arg`, the `close-on-exec` flag of the specified file descriptor. Only the lowest bit of `arg` is evaluated.

F_GETFL – returns the flags of the descriptor. The flags are the same as described in `sys_open()`.

F_SETFL – sets the flags to the value specified in `arg`. Internally, only `O_APPEND`, `FASYNC` and `O_NONBLOCK` are set. The flags and their semantics are the same as in `sys_open()`. If the file has been created as an append-only file and `O_APPEND` is not specified in the flags (that is, it has to be deleted), the function reacts with an error message. Upon modification of the `FASYNC` flag, the file operation `fasync()` is called.

F_GETLK, **F_SETLK** and **F_SETLKW** – sets or reads the locks of a file. Functioning and use of file locking is described in detail in Section 5.2.2.

F_GETOWN – returns the PID (PGRP) of the process that uses the socket `fd`. Process groups are returned as negative values! The value can be found in `f_owner` of the file structure.

F_SETOWN – sets the PID (PGRP) for the specified file descriptor. The process is identified by `arg`, values greater than 0 indicate a PID, values less than 0 a PGRP. If this value does not match the current process, the first matching process in the process table is used.

If the file descriptor `fd` is connected to a socket, the call is mapped to the corresponding function for sockets.

Implementation

The conversion is carried out via the syscall macro.

Errors

EBADF – if `fd` is not a descriptor of an opened file.

EINVAL – if with `F_DUPFD` a negative or excessively large value has been specified for `arg`, or if the process has already reached its maximum number of open files, or if an invalid value has been specified for `cmd`.

EPERM – no privileges for `F_SETOWN`.

System call	flock	POSIX

File: fs/locks.c

```
int sys_flock(unsigned int fd, unsigned int cmd);
```

This function is used to administrate locks on files. If several locks exist for one file, they are administrated in a list. For this purpose, each inode contains a reference to a file_lock structure:

```
struct file_lock {
  struct file_lock *fl_next;
  struct file_lock *fl_nextlink;
  struct file_lock *fl_prevlink;
  struct file_lock *fl_block;
  struct task_struct *fl_owner;
  struct wait_queue *fl_wait;
  struct file *fl_file;
  char fl_flags;
  char fl_type;
  off_t fl_start;
  off_t fl_end;
};
```

The function always affects the entire file. Subordinate functions allow more precise locking by means of specifying file areas. The following values are permitted for cmd:

LOCK_SH – the file is locked for read access.

LOCK_EX – the file is locked for write access.

LOCK_UN – all locks are removed. All processes that entered a waiting loop by accessing the lock are woken up.

Implementation

Implementation is carried out in two steps. First, the kernel function is called via the syscall macro. If this fails, an attempt is made to use sys_fcntl().

Errors

EBADF – the descriptor is invalid.

EINVAL – the cmd value is invalid.

ENOLCK – no further entry can be made in the list.

EBUSY – the `F_POSIX` flag is set.

System call	ioctl	4.3+BSD

File: fs/ioctl.c

```
#include <fs/ioctl.h>

int sys_ioctl(unsigned int fd, unsigned int cmd,
              unsigned long arg);
```

The `sys_ioctl()` function manipulates the parameters of a device. This function is mainly used to control device drivers. The first parameter is an opened descriptor of the corresponding file.

The required function is specified in the argument `cmd`. Macros and definitions for the use of this call are to be found in `<linux/ioctl.h>`. Some functions are permitted for all file descriptors:

FIOCLEX – the `close_on_exec` flag is set.

FIONCLEX – the `close_on_exec` flag is deleted.

FIONBIO – if the value specified by the address `arg` equals 0, the `O_NONBLOCK` flag is deleted, otherwise it is set.

FIOASYNC – as with `FIONBIO` the `O_SYNC` flag is set or deleted. The synchronization flag has not yet been implemented, but is dealt with for reasons of completeness.

These four functions are handled by the call itself. All others are passed on to the `ioctl` functions of the file system, either to the function `file_ioctl()` if `fd` refers to a regular file, or to the file operation `ioctl()` (*see* Section 6.2.6).

Implementation

The system call is converted via the syscall macro.

Errors

EBADF – if `fd` is invalid.

ENOTTY – if `fd` does not refer to a character-oriented device or the `cmd` used is not supported by the device `fd`.

EINVAL – if `cmd` or `arg` are invalid.

System call	link	unlink	POSIX
	rename	rmdir	
	symlink		

File: fs/namei.c

```
int sys_link(const char *oldname, const char *newname);
int sys_rename(const char *oldname, const char *newname);
int sys_rmdir(const char *name);
int sys_symlink(const char *oldname, const char *newname);
int sys_unlink(const char *name);
```

sys_link() and sys_symlink() create references (hard links) and symbolic references (soft links) with the name newname which refer to oldname. sys_link() first checks the file oldname using the function namei(), copies newname to the kernel segment (for reasons of runtime performance) and then calls the function do_link() with the inode obtained.

sys_symlink() copies oldname and newname and then calls the function do_symlink(). In addition, the quota structure of the directory in which the reference is created is initialized.

sys_rename() recreates the file under the name newname and deletes the old file. Here too, the quota structure of the directory in which the reference is created is initialized.

The sys_unlink() function deletes, with the appropriate rights, the file name. sys_rmdir() works similarly to sys_unlink(), but removes the directory.

These kernel functions are internally converted into the corresponding inode operations after the necessary rights have been tested.

Implementation

The system calls are converted via the syscall macro.

Errors

EACCES – if the directory has no execution rights.

ENOENT – if oldname does not exist or the path name is invalid.

ENOTDIR – if name in sys_rmdir() is not a directory.

EPERM – if the inode of the file does not permit the link, newname is invalid or the file system does not support the operation.

EXDEV – if in sys_link() oldname and newname lie on different file systems.

System call	lseek	POSIX
	llseek	

File: fs/read_write.c

```
#include <sys/types.h>

long sys_lseek(unsigned int fd, off_t offset, unsigned int origin)
int sys_llseek(unsigned int fd, unsigned long offset_high,
               unsigned long offset_low, loff_t * result,
               unsigned int origin);
```

sys_lseek() sets a new current position in the file relative to offset and origin. LINUX first tries to use the sys_lseek() function of the file system to which the file belongs. If this does not possess an lseek function, the kernel calculates the new position itself. The following values are permitted for origin:

SEEK_SET – offset indicates the absolute position.

SEEK_CUR – the new position is the sum of offset and the current position.

SEEK_END – sys_lseek() positions relative to the end of the file.

The new absolute address is returned. Current position and file size can then be easily determined:

```
pos  = lseek(fd, 0, SEEK_CUR); size = lseek(fd, -1, SEEK_END);
```

The sys_llseek() function is used to position in larger files. To do this, a new offset of type long long is assembled from offset_high and offset_low.

```
offset = (loff_t) (((unsigned long long) offset_high << 32)
         | offset_low);
```

If the file system supports an lseek() inode operation, this is called. Then, however, the offset values are limited to the long value range; higher values return an error! Otherwise, the function tries to calculate the new position itself. This function returns 0 upon success. The new position is stored in result.

Implementation

While the system call *lseek* is converted, as usual, via the syscall macro, there exists only a restricted implementation in the C library for sys_llseek() on Intel computers.

```
loff_t __lseek(int fd, loff_t offset, int origin)
```

Errors

EBADF – if fd is invalid.

EINVAL – if offset is greater than 2 or the new position cannot be calculated.

ESPIPE – if fd points to a pipe.

System call	mount	SVR4
	umount	

File: fs/super.c

```
int sys_mount(char * dev_name, char * dir_name, char * type,
              unsigned long new_flags, void * data);
int sys_umount(const char *devname);
```

sys_mount() mounts the file system located on the block device devname in the directory dirname. type contains the type of the file system, for example ext2. The new_flags control the mounting process and the properties of the mounted file system.

MS_RDONLY – the file system is read-only.

MS_NOSUID – SUID and SGID bits are ignored.

MS_NODEV – access to device files is prohibited.

MS_NOEXEC – execution of files is prohibited.

MS_SYNCHRONOUS – write accesses are immediately executed on disk.

MS_REMOUNT – the flags of an already mounted file system are modified (*remount*).

S_WRITE – when deleting an inode, its quota structure is released.

S_APPEND– the O_APPEND flag must be set when opening files for writing.

S_IMMUTABLE – the files and their inodes must not be modified.

MS_MGC_VAL – indicates the more recent version of the system call *mount*. Without this signature in bits 16–31, only the first 4 options are evaluated.

data is a pointer to an arbitrary structure of maximum size PAGE_SIZE-1 that may contain file-system-specific information.[12]

With MS_REMOUNT, no type and device have to be indicated. In this case, the call just updates the information contained in new_flags and data. The functioning is described in Section 6.2.1.

---

[12] These data are stored in the u union of the superblock, *see* Section 6.2.1.

`sys_umount()` removes the file system. It writes the superblock back and releases the file system's device. If `dev_name` holds the root directory, the quotas are disabled, a `sync_dev()` is called and the device is remounted `MS_RDONLY`. This decreases the risk of file system inconsistencies. Both system calls are reserved for use by the superuser.

Implementation

Both system calls are converted via the syscall macro.

Errors

EPERM – no superuser privileges.

ENODEV – no file system is known for `type`.

EACCES – `dev_name` is not a device.

ENOTBLK – `dev_name` is not a block device or does not provide file operations.

ENXIO – the major number of the device is invalid.

EBUSY – a process is running in the directory or the directory is already mounted.

ENOTDIR – `dir_name` is not a directory.

EINVAL – `read_super()` has failed or `dev_name` is not mounted.

System call	creat	open	POSIX
	mkdir	mknod	4.3+BSD
	close		SVR4

File: fs/open.c
      fs/namei.c

```
#include <sys/types.h>

int sys_close(unsigned int fd);
int sys_creat(const char *file_name, int mode)
int sys_mkdir(const char *file_name, int mode);
int sys_mknod(const char *file_name, int mode, dev_t dev);
int sys_open(const char *file_name, int flag, int mode);
```

`sys_open()` opens a file indicated by `file_name` for the operations specified by `flag`. The possible values for `flag` are:

O_RDONLY – the file is opened for reading only.

O_WRONLY – the file is opened for writing only.

O_RDWR – both reading and writing are possible.

O_CREAT – the file is created if it does not exist. The third parameter, mode, must be specified. mode is then combined with umask (~umask & mode).

O_EXCL – an error is returned if O_CREAT is specified and the file already exists. With this, a simple lock mechanism can be implemented.

O_NOCTTY – the terminal specified in file_name becomes the *controlling terminal*. This flag is not implemented.

O_TRUNC – if the file exists and is writeable, it is set to size 0.

O_APPEND – data of subsequent write operations are appended to the file.

O_NONBLOCK – operations on the file do not block.

O_NDELAY – is mapped to O_NONBLOCK.

O_SYNC – changes to the file in (buffer) memory are immediately written to the device. This operation is only implemented for block devices and files of the *Ext2* file system.

sys_creat() does exist as a system call, but the kernel calls sys_open() with the corresponding flags.

```
asmlinkage int sys_creat(const char * pathname, int mode)
{
    return sys_open(pathname, O_CREAT | O_WRONLY | O_TRUNC, mode);
}
```

The sys_close() function closes the file descriptor fd. Any existing file locks (i_flock) are deleted and a release is executed.

sys_mkdir(), after checking the rights, creates the directory file_name by using the inode operation mkdir(). sys_mknod() creates a pseudofile, with mode specifying the type and access rights of the pseudofile to be created. For device files, dev contains the device number. Creation of FIFOs is permitted to all users. For all other file types, superuser privileges are required.

Implementation

All five system calls work with the syscall macro. The sys_creat() function is not available on Alpha maschines. The system call *mkfifo* is implemented in the C library by means of mknod():

```
int mkfifo(const char path, mode_t mode)
{
    return mknod (path, mode | S_IFIFO, 0);
}
```

Errors

EMFILE – if too many files are open.

EACCES – if the directory has no execution rights.

ENFILE – if no free file descriptors are available to the system or the process. Both values are defined in `<linux/fs.h>`.

EEXIST – if a file is to be created that already exists as a directory.

EISDIR – if a directory is to be opened that cannot be read or if with `sys_open()` the flags `O_CREATE` or `O_TRUNC` are set.

ENOENT – if the path name is invalid.

EPERM – if the inode of the file does not permit the requested operation.

System call	pipe	POSIX

File: arch/i386/kernel/sys_i386.c

```
int sys_pipe(unsigned long * fildes);
```

`sys_pipe()` creates two descriptors and writes them into a field addressed by `fildes`. `fildes[0]` is opened for read operations and `fildes[1]` for write operations, provided that the process has two free descriptors available.

Implementation

The system call is converted via the syscall macro. As other architectures use the stack registers as arguments for the kernel functions, it has been moved to the architecture-dependent directory.

Errors

EMFILE – if there are no free descriptors in the system.

ENFILE – if there are no free descriptors for the process.

EINVAL – if `fildes` is invalid.

System call	quotactl	LINUX

File: kernel/sched.c

```
#include <linux/sys.h>
#include <linux/quota.h>
```

```
int sys_quotactl(int cmdo, const char *special,
                 int id, caddr_t addr);
```

This kernel function represents the entry point of the quota program. Currently, only disk quotas are considered; for process quotas, use of rlimits is probably the most suitable way.

The quotas look as follows:

```
struct dquot {
    unsigned int dq_id;         /* for which ID (uid, gid) */
    short dq_type;              /* type                    */
    kdev_t dq_dev;             /* device                  */
    short dq_flags;            /* flags                   */
    short dq_count;            /* reference counter       */
    struct vfsmount *dq_mnt;   /* VFS mount point         */
    struct dqblk dq_dqb;       /* usage                   */
    struct wait_queue *dq_wait; /* processes waiting for  */
                               /* a quota change          */
    struct dquot *dq_prev;
    struct dquot *dq_next;
    struct dquot *dq_hash_prev;
    struct dquot *dq_hash_next;
};

struct dqblk {
    __u32 dqb_bhardlimit; /* hard limit of usable blocks */
    __u32 dqb_bsoftlimit; /* soft limit of usable blocks */
    __u32 dqb_curblocks;  /* current number of blocks    */
    __u32 dqb_ihardlimit; /* hard limit of usable inodes */
    __u32 dqb_isoftlimit; /* soft limit of usable inodes */
    __u32 dqb_curinodes;  /* current number of inodes    */
    time_t dqb_btime;     /* time limit for a soft       */
                          /* excess (blocks)             */
    time_t dqb_itime;     /* time limit for a soft       */
                          /* excess (inodes)             */
};
```

Time limits have their meaning. Usually, for example in response to interrogations, the expiration time of the limit is supplied in seconds. Limits are set by entering the value in the vfsmount structure of the device. The value is used as the interval for updating the limit (new expiration = current time + interval).

In addition, the following structure is used for administration:

```
struct dqstats {
    __u32 lookups;
```

```
    __u32 drops;
    __u32 reads;           /* number of quotas read     */
    __u32 writes;          /* number of quotas written  */
    __u32 cache_hits;
    __u32 pages_allocated; /* number of pages occupied  */
    __u32 allocated_dquots; /* quotas used .            */
    __u32 free_dquots;     /* quotas free              */
    __u32 syncs;           /* number of sync operations */
};
```

The cmdo parameter contains the command and type of the call. It can be assembled via the QCMD(cmd, type) macro.[13] The function disassembles cmdo again. If no cmd is given, QUOTA_SYSCALL is entered. The next three parameters have the following meaning (if not specified otherwise):

special – the required device

type – specification whether id is a UID or GID or the index of the dq_mnt array.

id – ID that the quotas shall refer to.

The following values are permitted as commands:

Q_GETQUOTA – supplies the quotas and their current usage. A non-privileged process may only call its own quotas.

Q_SYNC – a sync on the list of quotas is executed.

Q_GETSTATS – addr is a pointer to a dqstats structure. However, only the number of used and free quotas is entered.

The remaining commands are only permitted if the FSUID of the current process equals 0.

Q_QUOTAON – enables the quotas for a file. addr holds the name of the file, type is used as an index for the mnt_quotas array.

Q_QUOTAOFF – disables the quotas. With type=-1, all mnt_quotas quotas are disabled for the device.

For the next four functions, a new inode is created first, then dev, id and type are entered, and the inode is entered in the list and hash table. addr is a pointer to a dqblk structure.

Q_SETQLIM – if id==0, the time limits are reset; if id>0, all limits are set to the values passed.

---

[13] It is defined as (((cmd) << SUBCMDSHIFT) | ((type) & SUBCMDMASK)).

Q_SETUSE – the curinodes and curblocks values are set and if the soft limit is exceeded, the time limits are updated. If id==0, all time limits are reset at the end.

Q_SETQUOTA – combines the effects of the last two flags.

Q_SYSCALL – if id==0, the time limits are reset.

Implementation

The C library does not provide a syscall macro; the quota package must be used instead.

Errors

EINVAL – type is greater than MAXQUOTAS.

EPERM – a non-privileged process attempts to change other quotas or call a privileged command.

ENOTBLK – special is not a block device.

ESRCH – if no matching quota structure could be found.

System call	write	POSIX
	read	

File: fs/read_write.c

```
#include <sys/types.h>

int sys_read(unsigned int fd, char * buf,unsigned int count);
int sys_write(unsigned int fd, char * buf,unsigned int count);
```

sys_read() tries to read count bytes from the file fd. The bytes are stored in the buffer buf. The system call sys_write() works with the same parameters, except that the bytes are written to the descriptor. Previously, a check is made as to whether the corresponding area was blocked by an FLOCK. In addition, the S_ISUID and IS_ISGID bits are deleted (the latter only if S_IXGRP is set).

The return value is the number of bytes actually read or written, 0 upon EOF and a negative number in the event of an error. In the last analysis, it is the corresponding file operations that are actually called.

Implementation

Both system calls work via the syscall macro.

Errors

EBADF – if `fd` is invalid or the file has been opened incorrectly.

EINVAL – if there are no read or write rights set for the file.

System call	`readv`	POSIX
	`writev`	

File: fs/read_write.c

```
#include <sys/types.h>
#include <sys/uio.h>

int sys_readv(unsigned long fd, const struct iovec * vector,
        long count)
int sys_writev(unsigned long fd, const struct iovec * vector,
        long count)
```

Both functions read (or write) data via a file descriptor. The difference from the known read/write functions lies in the type of buffers passed. The `iovec` structure looks as follows:

```
struct iovec
{
        void *iov_base; /* pointer to a memory area */
        int iov_len;    /* size of memory area      */
};
```

The number of buffers is held in `count`, the upper limit being `UIO_MAXIOV=16`.

The areas are checked one after the other for readability or writeability, their lengths are added, and the resulting area of the file is checked for an `FLOCK`.

If `fd` refers to a socket, the socket operations are used, otherwise the file operations are used. In `sys_readv()` the buffers are filled one after the other by reading from the descriptor; in `sys_write()` they are written one after the other into the descriptor.

The return value is the number of bytes actually read or written, 0 upon EOF and a negative number in the event of an error.

Implementation

Both system calls work via the syscall macro.

Errors

EBADF – if fd is invalid or the file has been opened incorrectly.

EINVAL – if an invalid parameter has been passed.

System call	readdir	POSIX
	getdents	LINUX

File: fs/read_write.c
        fs/readdir.c

```
int sys_readdir(unsigned int fd, struct dirent *dirent,
                unsigned int count);
int sys_getdents(unsigned int fd, void * dirent,
                unsigned int count)
```

The sys_readdir() function fills the dirent structure with the data of the fd directory. count specifies the maximum space to be filled with dirent structures. The dirent structure looks as follows:

```
struct dirent {
  long           d_ino;
  off_t          d_off;
  unsigned short d_reclen;
  char           d_name[NAME_MAX+1];
};
```

LINUX forwards the call to the operations of the Virtual File System by calling the corresponding file operation (*see* Section 6.2.6).

In the meantime, the new improved sys_getdents() function has become available. It also comprises two new structures:

```
struct linux_dirent {
        unsigned long  d_ino;
        unsigned long  d_off;
        unsigned short d_reclen;
        char           d_name[1];
};

struct getdents_callback {
        struct linux_dirent * current_dir;
        struct linux_dirent * previous;
        int count;
        int error;
};
```

The function reads several entries, as long as the sum of their sizes (calculated from the offset of the current name and its length) does not exceed the value `count`. The return value is the difference between `count` and the size of the entries actually read.

Implementation

Both system calls are used by the library function `readdir()`. The old `sys_readdir()` call is called when no `sys_getdents()` is available. Both kernel functions are directly jumped into via the 0x80 interrupt.

Errors

EBADF – if `fd` is invalid.

ENOTDIR – if no `sys_readdir()` file operation exists.

System call	readlink	POSIX

File: fs/stat.c

```
int sys_readlink(const char *path, char *buf, int bufsize);
```

The `sys_readlink()` function reads the path to which a symbolic link refers. A maximum of `bufsize` characters are stored in the buffer `buf` by the corresponding inode operation. No null byte is appended to the end of `buf`. The function, however, returns the length of the path.

Implementation

The system call is converted via the syscall macro.

Errors

EINVAL – if `bufsize` is negative, the call is not supported by the file system or `path` is not a reference.

ENOENT – if `path` does not exist.

System call	select	4.3+BSD

File: fs/select.c

```
#include <sys/time.h>
#include <sys/types.h>

int sys_selectt(int n, fd_set *inp, fd_set *outp,
                fd_set *exp, struct timeval *tvp)
```

The sys_select() function allows multiplexing of input and output operations. The time interval is converted to jiffies and entered as the timeout of the process. The process sleeps after the call, until one of the descriptors in inp, outp or exp is available or the time span tvp has elapsed.

The function returns the number of available descriptors. If the flag STICKY_TIMEOUTS is set in personality, tvp is updated as well. Several macros are defined for their use:

FD_ZERO(*fdset*) – deletes all bits in *fdset*.

FD_CLR(*fd*, *fdset*) – deletes the descriptor *fd* in *fdset*.

FD_SET(*fd*, *fdset*) – sets the descriptor *fd* in *fdset*.

FD_ISSET(*fd*, *fdset*) – checks the descriptor *fd* in *fdset*. Returns a value other than 0 if *fd* is set.

Implementation

The system call is converted via the syscall macro.

Errors

EBADF – if there is an invalid descriptor in one of the fields.

EINTR – if a non-blocking signal has been received.

EINVAL – if fd is negative.

ENOMEM – if there is not enough memory for internal tables in the kernel.

System call	stat	newstat
	fstat	newlstat
	lstat	newfstat

File: fs/stat.c

```
#include <sys/stat.h>

int sys_stat(const char *file_name, struct old_stat *buf);
int sys_fstat(unsigned int fd, struct old_stat *buf);
int sys_lstat(const char *file_name, struct old_stat *buf);
```

sys_stat(), sys_fstat() and sys_lstat() return a filled data structure that is defined in <asm/stat.h>:

```
struct old_stat {
    unsigned short    st_dev;      /* device                             */
    unsigned short    st_ino;      /* inode                              */
    unsigned short    st_mode;     /* access privileges                  */
    unsigned short    st_nlink;    /* number of hard links               */
    unsigned short    st_uid;      /* UID of owner                       */
    unsigned short    st_gid;      /* GID of owner                       */
    unsigned short    st_rdev;     /* device type                        */
    unsigned short    st_size;     /* size in bytes                      */
    unsigned long     st_atime;    /* time of last access                */
    unsigned long     st_mtime;    /* time of last change (file)         */
    unsigned long     st_ctime;    /* time of last change (inode)        */
};
```

For the future, there is an extended structure (new_stat) which contains two new items of information and is extended by pad data to a size of 64 bytes. This structure is used by functions beginning with 'new_'.

```
struct new_stat {
    unsigned short st_dev;        unsigned short __pad1;
    unsigned long st_ino;
    unsigned short st_mode;
    unsigned short st_nlink;
    unsigned short st_uid;
    unsigned short st_gid;
    unsigned short st_rdev;       unsigned short __pad2;
    unsigned long st_size;
    unsigned long st_blksize;     /* block size           */
    unsigned long st_blocks;      /* file size in blocks  */
    unsigned long st_atime;       unsigned long __unused1;
    unsigned long st_mtime;       unsigned long __unused2;
    unsigned long st_ctime;       unsigned long __unused3;
    unsigned long __unused4;      unsigned long __unused5;
};
```

sys_stat() returns the data for the file file_name. For references, there is sys_lstat(), which returns the data for the symbolic link itself. sys_fstat() is identical to sys_stat(), but uses a descriptor fd instead of the name.

All three calls determine the inode of the object passed and call the kernel function cp_old_stat(). This simply reads most of the data from the inode. The new functions use cp_new_stat(). If the file system does not support st_blocks and st_blksize, these are determined by means of a simple algorithm.

Implementation

The system calls are converted via the syscall macro.

Errors

EBADF – if fd is invalid.

ENOENT – if file_name does not exist.

System call	statfs	SVR4
	fstatfs	

File: fs/open.c

```
#include <sys/vfs.h>


int sys_statfs(const char *path, struct statfs *buf);
int sys_fstatfs(unsigned int fd, struct statfs *buf);
```

The sys_statfs() function returns the information about the file system on which the file path is located. In sys_fstatfs() a descriptor is specified instead of the name. The structure buf is defined in <linux/vfs.h>:

```
struct statfs {
    long    f_type;     /* type of file system        */
    long    f_bsize;    /* optimum block size         */
    long    f_blocks;   /* number of blocks           */
    long    f_bfree;    /* total number of free blocks */
    long    f_bavail;   /* free blocks for user       */
    long    f_files;    /* number of inodes           */
    long    f_ffree;    /* number of free inodes      */
    fsid_t  f_fsid;     /* file system ID             */
    long    f_namelen;  /* max. file name length      */
    long    f_spare[6]; /* not used                   */
};
```

Fields which are not defined in the file system are set to –1. The data are read using the superblock operations (*see* Section 6.2.2).

```
asmlinkage int sys_statfs(const char * path, struct statfs * buf)
{
  error=namei(path,&inode); if (error) return error;
```

```
        inode->i_sb->s_op->statfs(inode->i_sb, buf,
                               sizeof(struct statfs));
        return 0;
}
```

Implementation

The system call is converted via the syscall macro.

Errors

EBADF – if fd is not a valid descriptor.

EFAULT – if buf points to an invalid address.

System call	sync		SVR4
	fsync	fdatacync	4.3BSD

File: fs/buffer.c

```
        int sys_sync(void);
        int sys_fsync(unsigned int fd);
        int sys_fdatasync(unsigned int fd);
```

sys_sync() writes all information stored in memory, such as buffers, super-blocks and inodes, to the disk. The function always returns 0.

```
        void sync_dev(dev_t dev)
        {
            sync_buffers(dev, 0);    sync_supers(dev);
            sync_inodes(dev);        sync_buffers(dev, 0);
        }

        asmlinkage int sys_sync(void)
        {
            sync_dev(0);
            return 0;
        }
```

The function works via sync_dev(). The specification 0 as device means that all block devices are to be synchronized. The parameter 0 in sync_buffers() means that waiting for successful execution of write operations is not required.

The sys_fsync() function writes the data stored in memory of the file fd. To do this, it calls fsync(). The default implementation works in the same way as sync_dev(), but is passed the number of the device on which the file is located and waits at the second sync_buffers() call until the write operations have executed successfully. The sys_fdatasync() function is (yet) another call to sys_fsync().

Implementation

Both system calls are converted via the syscall macro.

System call	sysfs	SVR4

File: fs/super.c

```
int sys_sysfs(int option, ...);
```

The sys_sysfs() function returns information about the file systems known to the kernel by reading the file_systems list. The option argument specifies the required function.

(1)   The call returns the index of the specified file system. It has the following form:

```
sysfs(int option, char *name);
```

(2)   The name of the specified (index[th]) file system is returned. The call has the following form:

```
sysfs(int option, int index, char *name);
```

(3)   The call returns the number of known file systems. No further parameter is required.

Implementation

There is as yet no interface in the C library.

Errors

EINVAL − if index or name are invalid.

System call	truncate	4.3+BSD
	ftruncate	

File: fs/open.c

```
int sys_truncate(const char *path, unsigned int len);
int sys_ftruncate(unsigned int fd, unsigned int len);
```

sys_truncate() shortens or lengthens the file path to the size of len bytes. sys_ftruncate() carries out the same operation for the file behind fd.

The conditions are that it is not a directory and that the inode flags allow modification (shortening). Furthermore, there must be no lock on the area to be changed.

The quotas of the inode are updated, the corresponding inode operation is carried out and ctime and mtime are updated. If the file is mapped into memory, the corresponding memory area is modified as well.

Implementation

Both system calls are converted via the syscall macro.

Errors

EACCES – if the file path has no write access or is a directory.

EROFS – if the file is located in an IS_RDOLY file system.

EPERM – if the file is located in an IS_IMMUTABLE or IS_APPEND file system.

EBADF – if an invalid descriptor is used in sys_ftruncate().

ENOTDIR – if a part of path is not a directory.

ENOENT – if the file does not exist.

ETXTBSY – if the file is just being executed.

System call	uselib	LINUX

File: fs/exec.c

```
int sys_uselib(const char *library);
```

sys_uselib() selects a *shared library* for the current process. The file is opened with sys_open(), after which an attempt is made to execute the load_shlib()

operation for each registered binary format. The first successful attempt terminates the call. It is important that both read and execution rights are set for the library file.

Implementation

The system call is converted via the syscall macro.

Errors

ENOEXEC – if no matching binary format could be found for library.

EACCES – if library cannot be read.

System call	umask	POSIX

File: kernel/sys.c

```
int sys_umask(int mask);
```

sys_umask() sets the mask for the access rights of a file. The value mask & S_IRWXUGO (0777) is used as the new mask. The old mask is returned. This mask is used in open_namei() when creating a file. The mode specified there is overlaid with umask:

```
mode &= S_IALLUGO & ~current->fs->umask;
```

Implementation

The system call is converted via the syscall macro.

System call	utime	POSIX

File: fs/open.c

```
#include <utime.h>

int sys_utime(char *filename, struct utimbuf *buf);
```

sys_utime() sets the time stamps for the file filename to the values specified in buf. The structure buf is defined as follows:

```
struct utimbuf {
    time_t actime; time_t modtime;
};
```

Both time specifications are in UNIX seconds, corresponding to `sys_time()`. The time of last change (`i_ctime`) is set to `CURRENT_TIME` upon execution of `sys_utime()`. If `buf` is NULL, the values are set to `CURRENT_TIME`.

Implementation

The system call is converted via the syscall macro. This function is not available on Alpha machines.

Errors

ENOENT – if the file `filename` does not exist.

EACCES – if the inode of the file cannot be changed.

System call	vhangup	LINUX

File: fs/open.c

```
int sys_vhangup(void);
```

`sys_vhangup()` executes a *hangup* for the current terminal. The call is, for example, used by `init` in order to provide users with a clean login terminal on which no processes are active. Upon success, the call returns 0.

The called function `tty_vhangup()` is implemented in `drivers/tty_io.c`. In it all processes that work with the terminal are woken up, the current session is closed and the corresponding `tty` value of all processes set to –1. The function is only carried out if the current process actually possesses a terminal (`current->tty`).

The 'v' in the name of the system call stands for *virtual*. This does not mean, however, that a hangup is only simulated, but that this call is used for the virtual terminals.

Implementation

The system call is converted via the syscall macro.

Errors

EPERM – if a non-privileged user calls `sys_vhangup()`.

A.3 Communication

There are only two system calls for communication. This may, at first sight, seem somewhat strange, but nevertheless, the entire gamut of commonly used system calls is available in the form of library functions.

This concentration has made the implementation a lot simpler, because the required functionality can be easily defined in `sys_ipc()`, for example. However, when it comes to putting the right parameters on the stack, things quickly become unfathomable. The usual system calls, such as *semget*, are therefore provided as library functions.

System call	ipc	LINUX

File: ipc/util.c

```
#include <sys/ipc.h>

Int sys_ipc (uint call, int first, int second,
            int third, void *ptr, long fifth);
```

`sys_ipc()` allows full use of the System V inter-process communication by means of one call.

All system calls that work with message queues, shared memory or semaphores are mapped to this system call. The parameter `call` specifies the exact function; in addition, the `IPCCALL(version,call)` macro can be used to pass a version. The `call` values are defined in `<linux/ipc.h>`:

SEMOP − function corresponds to `semop()`.

SEMGET − function corresponds to `semget()`.

SEMCTL − function corresponds to `semctl()`.

MSGGET − function corresponds to `msgget()`.

MSGSND − function corresponds to `msgsnd()`.

MSGRCV − function corresponds to `msgrcv()`. With `version` equal to 0, an old `msgbuf` is assumed and the parameters are converted.

MSGCTL − function corresponds to `msgctl()`.

SHMGET − function corresponds to `shmget()`.

SHMAT − function corresponds to `shmat()`. With `version` equal to 1, iBCS2 is assumed and the parameter `raddr` is passed (not newly created and copied upon return).

SHMDT – function corresponds to shmct().

SHMCTL – function corresponds to shmget().

The remaining parameters must be set according to the specification of call. If during kernel compilation no CONFIG_SYSVIPC has been set, this call returns -ENOSYS.

Implementation

The library naturally provides the usual functions for inter-process communication. They are mapped onto the library function ipc() which is defined via the syscall macro. The example below illustrates the implementation of the system call semget():

```
int semget (key_t key, int nsems, int semflg)
{
    return ipc (SEMGET, key, nsems, semflg, NULL);
}
```

Errors

EINVAL – if an invalid value is specified for call.

System call	socketcall	LINUX

File: net/socket.c

```
#include <sys/socketcall.h>

int sys_socketcall(int call, unsigned long *args);
```

Just as there is exactly one system call for the SVR4 IPC, there is a call that allows the entire programming of the sockets. The sys_socketcall() function makes it possible, by specifying a parameter, to implement all usual calls as library functions.

The parameter call specifies the exact functionality. The following macros are defined in <linux/net.h>:

SYS_SOCKET – function corresponds to socket().

SYS_BIND – function corresponds to bind().

SYS_CONNECT – function corresponds to connect().

SYS_LISTEN – function corresponds to listen().

SYS_ACCEPT – function corresponds to accept().

SYS_GETSOCKNAME – function corresponds to getsockname().

SYS_GETPEERNAME – function corresponds to getpeername().

SYS_SOCKETPAIR – function corresponds to socketpair().

SYS_SEND – function corresponds to send().

SYS_RECV – function corresponds to recv().

SYS_SENDTO – function corresponds to sendto().

SYS_RECVFROM – function corresponds to recvfrom().

SYS_SHUTDOWN – function corresponds to shutdown().

SYS_SETSOCKOPT – function corresponds to setsockopt().

SYS_GETSOCKOPT – function corresponds to getsockopt().

SYS_SENDMSG – function corresponds to sendmsg().

SYS_RECVMSG – function corresponds to recvmsg().

The remaining parameters must be set according to the specification of call.

Implementation

As with the IPC calls, the well-known socket functions are also called via the C library. As an example, we present socket(); the other functions are implemented in practically the same way.

```
static inline
_syscall2(long,socketcall,int,call,unsigned long *,args);

int sys_socket(int family, int type, int protocol)
{
    unsigned long args[3];
    args[0] = family;
    args[1] = type;
    args[2] = protocol;
    return socketcall(SYS_SOCKET, args);
}
```

Errors

EINVAL – if an invalid value is specified for call.

A.4   Memory management

The next group describes the system calls for memory management. There are only a few calls, although this area is one of the most important in multi-tasking systems. On the other hand, the work connected with administration of memory is far from trivial, and the less (disturbing) influences there are, the safer the system runs.

System call	mmap	4.3+BSD
	munmap	

File: arch/i386/kernel/sys_i386.c
mm/mmap.c

```
#include <sys/types.h>
#include <sys/mman.h>

int old_mmap(unsigned long *buffer);
int sys_munmap(unsigned long addr, size_t len);
```

old_mmap() is used to map a file into memory; the reason for the old prefix is probably the way of parameter passing and seems to indicate a coming revision. The parameter passed to the function is the address buffer of an array of values, where:

buffer[0] – corresponds to the address in main memory,

buffer[1] – the size of the area,

buffer[2] – the access rights of the mapped data,

buffer[3] – the flags,

buffer[4] – the file descriptor, and

buffer[5] – the offset in the file that is to be mapped.

The following values are possible as access rights:

PROT_EXEC – pages can be executed.

PROT_READ – pages can be read.

PROT_WRITE – pages can be written to.

The parameter flags specifies the type and treatment of memory pages; the last four flags are LINUX specific:

MAP_FIXED – the precise address must be used, and `addr` must be a multiple of the page size.

MAP_PRIVATE – changes affect only the memory.

MAP_SHARED – changes in memory also affect the file.

MAP_ANONYMOUS – no file is mapped.

MAP_GROWSDOWN – the memory area is oriented towards the bottom (stack).

MAP_DENYWRITE – direct write access to the file yields -EXTTBSY.

MAP_EXECUTABLE – the mapped memory area is marked as library.

MAP_LOCKED – the memory area is locked.

In Intel systems the file descriptor is checked (except with `MAP_ANONYMOUS`) and the `MAP_EXECUTABLE` and `MAP_DENYWRITE` flags are masked out before the `do_mmap()` function itself is called. `sys_munmap()` swaps the file out and releases the memory used.

Implementation

Since in POSIX the parameter type for the system call `mmap()`is not `long *`, the C library must convert the call accordingly:

```
static inline
_syscall1(long,_mmap,unsigned long *,buffer);

caddr_t mmap(caddr_t addr, size_t len, int prot,
             int flags, int fd, off_t off)
{ unsigned long buffer[6];
   buffer[0] = (unsigned long)addr;
   buffer[1] = (unsigned long)len;
   buffer[2] = (unsigned long)prot;
   buffer[3] = (unsigned long)flags;
   buffer[4] = (unsigned long)fd;
   buffer[5] = (unsigned long)off;
   return (caddr_t) _mmap(buffer);
}
```

The system call `munmap()` simply uses the syscall macro.

Errors

EACCES – if the values specified in the flags do not match the rights of the specified file.

EBADF – if no file is opened.

EINVAL – if an invalid value has been specified for the flags, or the sum of
address and length exceeds the permitted process memory, or `MAP_FIXED`
has been specified and the address `addr` is not a page boundary.

ENOMEM – if the address (with `MAP_FIXED`) is not available.

System call	mprotect	LINUX

File: mm/mprotect.c

```
#include <sys/types.h>
#include <sys/mman.h>

int sys_mprotect(unsigned long addr, size_t len,
                 unsigned long prot);
```

This function allows the access protection for mapped areas also to be modified at a later stage. The area is defined by the address `addr`, which must lie on
a page boundary, and the size `len`. For `prot`, the values `PROT_READ` (for
reading), `PROT_WRITE` (for writing) and `PROT_EXEC` (for execution) are allowed.

As the selected area must lie within the `vma` zones belonging to the
process, the area that contains the start address is determined first. There, the
rights are re-entered, whereby the old values are overwritten. After this, all
further areas are modified via the linked list, until the whole length `len` has
been reached.

Implementation

The system call is converted via the syscall macro.

Errors

EFAULT – if there is no matching `vma` zone.

EBADF – if a parameter is invalid.

EACCES – if `prot` contains an invalid value.

EINVAL – if the sum of `addr` and `len` exceeds the permitted process memory.

System call	mremap	

File: mm/mremap.c

```
#include <sys/mman.h>

unsigned long sys_mremap(unsigned long addr,
        unsigned long old_len, unsigned long new_len,
        unsigned long flags)
```

This function allows the size of a mapped memory area to be changed. The start address `addr` must lie on a page boundary. `old_len` specifies the old size, `new_len` the new size. The old area must not exceed the limit of a virtual memory area.

When the area is reduced, the freed area is mapped out with `do_nmap()`. When a locked memory area is increased, the process resources must not be exceeded. If there is enough space free up to the beginning of the next virtual memory area, the old area is enlarged. If the `MREMAP_MAYMOVE` flag is not set, an error is returned; otherwise, a new area of the required size is created, and the old area copied and released. The return value is the (new) address of the memory area.

Implementation

The C library does not provide an interface.

Errors

EINVAL – if `addr` does not lie on a page boundary.

EFAULT – if no virtual memory area can be found for the specified address or the size is spread over more than one area.

EAGAIN – if the `RLIMIT_MEMLOCK` process resource is exceeded.

ENOMEM – if there is not enough memory available for an increase.

System call	msync	POSIX

File: mm/filemap.c

```
int sys_msync(unsigned long start, size_t len, int flags)
```

This function changes the flags of a mapped memory area. Its beginning is specified by `start`, its size by `len`. If no mapped area can be found at that location, an error is returned. As this call takes the local memory management peculiarities into account, it is *extremely* architecture-dependent. The following values can be specified as flags:

MS_SYNC – the cache buffer is written back and changes to the kernel segment are transferred to the user segment.

MS_ASYNC – the cache buffer is written back and, in addition, a `sync()` call is sent to the inode of the mapped inode.

MS_INVALIDATE – the cache buffer is written back, after which the occupied areas are released.

Implementation

The system call is converted via the syscall macro.

Errors

EINVAL – one of the passed parameters is invalid or a part of the specified area is not mapped.

EFAULT – no virtual memory area can be found for `start`.

System call	swapon	LINUX
	swapoff	

File: mm/swapfile.c

```
int sys_swapon(const char * specialfile, int swap_flags);
int sys_swapoff(const char *file);
```

`sys_swapon()` activates the swap memory which uses either the file or the block device `specialfile`. `swap_flags` can be used to assign a priority to the swap memory. `sys_swapoff()` deactivates swap memory.

The call can be executed only by the superuser and only once for each `specialfile`. Upon success, 0 is returned and a message is displayed on the console. Interestingly, during execution of this call, one may receive the message 'Unable to start swapping: out of memory :-)'. The reason for this is that before initialization the kernel allocates one more page.

Implementation

Both system calls are converted via the syscall macro.

Errors

EPERM – if a non-privileged user calls the function.

EINVAL – if `specialfile` exists, but is neither a swap file nor a block device.

EBUSY – if `specialfile` is already used as a swap file.

ENOMEM – if no memory is free. For `sys_swapon()`, two memory pages are required in the kernel for initialization.

A.5   Initialization

Initialization should theoretically do without system calls, as it is carried out only once, during booting. The fact that calls nevertheless do exist depends on how initialization works internally. A typical characteristic of these calls is that they can be called only once (or by one process only).

System call	`idle`

File: arch/i386/kernel/process.c

```
int sys_idle(void);
```

The system call *idle* is structured differently for single-processor and multi-processor systems. It is the idle process, meaning that the idle process calls the system call *once* and from then on remains only in this system call.

If SMP has been configured, the `counter` value of the current process is set to –100 (which causes the `need_resched` value to be set to 1 at the next timer interrupt) and the scheduler is called immediately. Waiting happens outside the system call (in `cpu_idle()`) in order to facilitate synchronization.

In the non-SMP case too, the `counter` value is set to –100 and the function enters an endless loop, in which the time elapsed since the last timer interrupt is stored, the assembler instruction `hlt` is executed (if this instruction is supported by the processor) and the scheduler is called. If the process is in this loop for some time after the last timer interrupt, the appropriate BIOS routines are called if *APM-BIOS* has been configured.

Errors

EPERM – if the current process does not have PID 0.

System call	`setup`	LINUX

File: fs/filesystems.c

```
#include <linux/fs.h>

void sys_setup(void);
```

When starting, the system needs an overview of the available hard disks, binary formats and file systems. `sys_setup()` initializes the device drivers for the hard disks and registers the binary formats and file systems specified during kernel configuration. Finally, the root file system is mounted by means of `mount_root()`. The system call can only be called once, which is ensured by the static variable `callable`.

Although this is not evident at first sight, this function must be a system call. On the one hand, a process is needed at this point, for in `mount_root()` a `read` function is called. This can now block, and the process has to hand over control to the scheduler. Now, however, we have a process in user mode from which it cannot access kernel internal data. Thus, a system call is the last remaining alternative (*see also* Section 6.2.1).

A.6   All that remains

Here we find the system calls that have not been implemented. However, in order to be able to work with programs and configuration scripts (such as the well-known `configure` from the world of GNU), a common interface has been implemented.

System call	acct	break	ftime
	lock	mpx	phys
	prof	profil	stty
	gtty	ulimit	ustat

File: kernel/sys.c

These system calls are not implemented. When called, they return `-ENOSYS`.

```
int sys_acct(void)
{
    return -ENOSYS
}
```

Implementation

The conversion is carried out via the syscall macro.

Kernel-related commands

Many are called,
But few are chosen.

Matthew 20:16

This chapter deals with *kernel-related* commands: in other words, with commands that exploit special properties of the LINUX kernel or operate directly with the kernel. As this is a rather elastic definition, we have made our choice and describe only those commands that have either been mentioned in the previous chapters or thematically belong to them.

Many programs, however, exist in different versions. Reasons for this are the large number of different distributions and the widespread use of the freely available LINUX system. For this appendix, we have selected programs that exploit special features of LINUX.

Some programs have versions that cooperate with the *Proc* file system. The advantage of such programs lies in increased security and independence of the kernel. Thus, for example, the `ps` command (originally `procps`) does not need to access kernel memory (`/dev/kmem`) at all.

B.1 free – synopsis of the system memory

The `free` program indicates the occupation of the available memory, differentiating between RAM and swap areas. The display shows total, used and free sizes, together with, for the RAM area, the parts used as shared memory and as buffers. Options are the switches:

-b   values are displayed in bytes.

-k   values are displayed in Kbytes.

-m values are displayed in Mbytes.

-o in addition, a line displays the size of used (free) RAM memory without (with) buffer memory.

-t a line of total sizes is displayed.

s*sec* free repeats its output every **sec**. sec can be specified as float in microseconds resolution.

-v the version is displayed.

```
$ free
               total        used    free  shared  buffers  cached
Mem:           30956       30512     444   15792     9372    9136
-/+ buffers:               12004   18952
Swap:          34236        4176   30060
```

This program works with the *Proc* file system (*see* Section 6.3). It reads the file meminfo and reformats the result.

```
$ cat /proc/meminfo
          total:      used:     free:  shared: buffers:  cached:
Mem:  31698944 31227904    471040 16183296  9584640  9351168
Swap: 35057664  4276224 30781440
```

B.2   ps – display of process statistics

The ps command gives a synopsis of the processes running in the system. This synopsis is only a 'snapshot'; for continuous monitoring, top should be used.

In LINUX, the ps command reads its data from the *Proc* file system. As a result, it runs independently from the kernel version, and does not need special privileges or s-bits set, either. The options may begin with a minus sign '–', but this is not compulsory. The following options are available:

-O The output is sorted. Several keys can be specified:

G sorting key is the TPGID.

J sorting key is the time spent in user mode (including the total time spent by the children).

K sorting key is the time spent in user mode.

M sorting key is the number of major faults of the process.

N sorting key is the number of major faults of the process and its children.

P sorting key is the PPID.

R	sorting key is the size of unswapped memory.
s	sorting key is the size of multiply used memory.
T	sorting key is the start time.
U	sorting key is the UID.
c	sorting key is the command line.
f	sorting key is the F field.
g	sorting key is the PGRP.
j	sorting key is the time spent in system mode (including the total time spent by the children)
k	sorting key is the time spent in system mode.
m	sorting key is the number of minor faults of the process.
n	sorting key is the number of minor faults of the process and its children.
o	sorting key is the SID.
p	sorting key is the PID.
r	sorting key is the RSS field.
s	sorting key is the size of the physically occupied memory.
t	sorting key is the TTY name.
u	sorting key is the user name.
v	sorting key is the sum of occupied virtual memory areas.
y	sorting key is the priority of the process (nice value).

-s	*CPU time* and *page faults* of child processes are added to the displayed values.
-X	stack and register occupation is displayed.
-a	processes of other users are also displayed.
-c	the command name currently present in the task structure is displayed.
-e	in addition, the environment of the processes is displayed.
-f	the output is formatted; child processes are indented (tree-like).
-h	no headline is displayed.
-j	in addition, PPID, PGID, TPGID and UID are displayed.
-l	a detailed display is generated.
-m	memory data are displayed.
-n	for the USER and WCHAN fields, the numeric values are displayed (UID and address).
-o	the output is not sorted.
-p	memory-oriented values are not displayed in bytes, but in pages.

-r   only running processes are displayed.

-s   in addition, set signal masks are displayed.

-u   user name and percentages of CPU and memory usage are displayed.

-v   in addition, virtual memory data are displayed.

-w   the complete command line of the process is displayed. If this option is not set, ps truncates the display to make it fit on one line. This option can be specified several times.

-x   only processes with no *controlling terminal* are displayed.

t*xx*   only processes connected to the terminal *xx* are displayed.

All running processes or (if specified) a comma-separated list of PIDs is evaluated. According to the option used, ps yields a different display format. Table B.1 shows a summary of the output of the individual options. The columns represent the indicated option, the rows the data displayed. The simple call of ps corresponds to the first (empty) column. Only one of the options j, l, s, u, v, m and X can be specified at any one time. The options a, x, S, r and n work in combination with the other options and do not modify the display format. The TTY, PID and COMMAND rows have been omitted, as they are output in any case. The individual fields have the following meaning:

ALARM	alarm timer of the process
BLOCKED	signal mask of signals blocked by the process
CATCHED	signal mask of the signals handled by the process
COMMAND	command line of the process
%CPU	ratio of system time (stime) to user time (utime)
DRS	RSS of the data segment
DSIZ	size of the data segment
DT	number of library pages accessed
EIP	EIP register
ESP	ESP register
FLAGS	flags of the process, now ranged left
IGNORED	signal mask of signals ignored by the process
LIB	memory size for shared libraries used
LIM	memory limit of the process; if no limit is set, xx is displayed
MAJFLT	number of page access faults leading to the corresponding pages being loaded from hard disk
%MEM	memory occupied by the process (RSS) in proportion to existing memory (RAM only)
MINFLT	number of page access faults where the requested page is already in memory

Table B.1 Options of the `ps` program.

	u	j	s	v	m	l	X		u	j	s	v	m	l	X
ALARM							×	PPID		×					×
BLOCKED			×					PRI							×
CATCHED			×					RSS	×				×		×
%CPU	×							SHRD					×		
DRS					×			SID				×			
DSIZ				×				SIGNAL			×				
DT				×				SIZE	×				×		×
EIP						×		STACK							×
ESP						×		START	×						
FLAGS					×			STAT	×	×	×	×	×	×	×
IGNORED			×					SWAP					×		
LIB					×			TIME	×	×	×	×	×	×	×
LIM				×				TMOUT							×
MAJFLT					×			TPGID				×			
%MEM	×				×			TRS						×	
MINFLT					×			TSIZ					×		
NI					×			UID		×	×				×
NR						×		USER	×						
PAGEIN				×				WCHAN						×	
PGID		×													

NI	the (converted) `priority` value of the process
NR	*see* `FLAGS`
PAGEIN	number of page access faults leading to the corresponding pages being loaded from hard disk (same as `MAJFLT`)
PGID	process group of the process
PID	process PID
PPID	process PPID
PRI	the (converted) `counter` value of the process
RSS	size of the program in memory (in Kbytes)
SHRD	size of shared memory
SID	process SID
SIGNAL	signal received by the process (`task->signal`)
SIZE	virtual memory size; sum of virtual memory areas occupied
STACK	start address of the stack
START	start time of the process
STAT	status of the process, with the following meaning:
	D process sleeps and cannot be woken up by a signal

R	process is active
S	process sleeps, but can be woken up by a signal
T	process is halted or runs with `ptrace`
Z	process is in zombie state

Additional information may follow:

W	process has no pages in memory (RSS=0), but is not a zombie
<	`task-<nice` is less than 0
N	`task->nice` is greater than 0
SWAP	swap memory used (in Kbytes); the `-p` option displays the size in pages
TIME	running time of the process
TMOUT	timeout set for the process
TPGID	process group of the process owning the terminal
TRS	RSS of the text segment
TSIZ	size of the text segment
TTY	terminal connected with the process
UID	process EUID
USER	name belonging to process UID
WCHAN	current kernel routine the process is executing. Normally, only the address is displayed. In order to obtain a reasonable display of the field, the `psupdate` program must be called. This generates a file `psdatabase` in the `etc` directory containing the kernel functions and their addresses in the kernel. Thus, `ps` can display the name of the function, not just its address.

For a graphic display of the process tree, there is the `pstree` program. It displays, starting with `init`, all processes in a tree structure, for example:

```
init-+-5*[agetty]
     |-amd
     |-crond
     |-gpm
     |-inetd-+-2*[in.rshd---tcsh---xterm---tcsh---vim]
     |       |-in.rshd---tcsh---xterm---tcsh
     |       |-nmbd
     |       '-smbd
     |-kflushd
     |-klogd
     |-kswapd
     |-lpd
     |-4*[nfsiod]
     |-rpc.mountd
```

```
|-rpc.nfsd
|-rpc.portmap
|-4*[rsh]
|-sendmail
|-syslogd
|-tcsh---startx---xinit-+-X
|                       '-fvwm-+-GoodStuff
|                              |-xbiff
|                              |-xload
|                              '-xterm---tcsh
|-timed
|-update
'-ypbind
```

B.3 Additional kernel configuration

The parameters for root image, swap area, RAM disk and video mode are managed by rdev.

rdev [-rsvh] [-o *offset*] [*image* [*value* [*offset*]]]
rdev [-o *offset*] [*image* [*root_device* [*offset*]]]
swapdev [-o *offset*] [*image* [*swap_device* [*offset*]]]
ramsize [-o *offset*] [*image* [*size* [*offset*]]]
vidmode [-o *offset*] [*image* [*mode* [*offset*]]]
rootflags [-o *offset*] [*image* [*flags* [*offset*]]]

When rdev is called without arguments, it displays the root file system. In the boot image of the LINUX kernel, there are areas that manage the root image, the RAM disk size, the swap area and the video mode. This information can be found in the kernel starting at offset 504 (*see* Table B.2). The values can be modified by using rdev.

Table B.2 Position of the status bytes in the kernel.

Byte	Meaning
498	Root flags
500	Reserved
502	Reserved
504	RAM disk size
506	VGA mode
508	Root device
510	Boot signature

Typical values for *image* are /vmlinuz or /dev/fd0. For *root_device* or *swap_device*, /dev/hda[1-8] and /dev/sda[1-8], respectively, might be specified. In the ramsize command, the *size* parameter specifies the size of the RAM disk in kbytes. In the rootflags command, the *flags* determine the way in which the root directory is mounted. The *mode* parameter in the vidmode command specifies the video mode.

If no value is specified, rdev reads the current value from *image*. The options have the following meaning:

-s   rdev works as swapdev.

-r   rdev works as ramsize.

-R   rdev works as rootflags.

-v   rdev works as vidmode.

-h   displays the help text.

Since recently, all the parameters described above can also be set from within LILO (*see* Section D.2.5).

B.4   top – the CPU charts

Similarly to ps, the top program provides a synopsis of the current state of the running system. However, top runs in a loop and displays a new synopsis every five seconds.

top has the following options:

dxxx top waits *xxx* seconds between two outputs. The interval may be a floating point number with microsecond resolution.

q   the waiting time is 0 seconds. With root privileges, the priority is set to –10 in order to avoid collisions with kswapd.

c   instead of the command name, the whole command line is displayed.

s   the displayed time is the total time of the process and its children. CTIME is (unfortunately) not displayed with the command line parameter.

i   processes whose status is S or Z are not displayed.

s   top runs in *secure* mode. Thus, the following interactive commands are no longer available: k (*kill*), r (*renice*) and s (*sleeping time*).

A call with the -q option lets top repeat the output without waiting. If the user is the superuser, the program runs with the highest possible priority.

While running, the program can be controlled by inputting commands. The following keys may be pressed:

[Ctrl][L]   redraws the screen.

[M]   processes are sorted by %MEM.

P	processes are sorted by %CPU.
S	displays the total time including child processes (cumulative time).
T	processes are sorted by [C]TIME.
W	current settings are saved in the file ~/.toprc.
C	toggles between display of command name and entire command line.
F	displayed fields can be modified.
H/?	give a brief summary of the commands supported.
I	toggles display of processes in *idle* status.
K	lets the user send a signal to a process. Process PID and the signal are read.
L	toggles display of *uptime* information (first line).
M	toggles display of *free* information (fourth and fifth line).
N	modifies the number of processes displayed.
Q	quits the program.
R	sets a new priority for a process.
S	lets the user modify the time span between updates.
T	toggles display of process statistics (second and third line).

The display is a mixture of uptime, free and ps. In addition, a synopsis of all processes and the CPU load is displayed. The display is sorted in decreasing order of priority.

```
10:44am  up  1:01,  5 users,  load average: 0.02, 0.06, 0.09
55 processes: 52 sleeping, 1 running, 0 zombie, 2 stopped
CPU states:  4.1% user,  3.6% system,  7.7% nice, 92.3% idle
Mem:  30956K av, 30424K used,   532K free, 24636K shrd, 4164K buff
Swap: 34236K av,     0K used, 34236K free             10840K cach

  PID USER     PRI  NI  SIZE  RSS STAT %CPU %MEM  TIME COMMAND
  352 magnus    18   0   688  688 R     5.5  2.2  0:01 top
  107 root       5   0  5952 5952 S     1.8 19.2  1:39 X
  111 root       2   0  1592 1592 S     0.4  5.1  0:04 xterm
    1 root       0   0   520  520 S     0.0  1.6  0:01 init
    2 root       0   0     0    0 SW    0.0  0.0  0:00 kflushd
    3 root     -12 -12     0    0 SW<   0.0  0.0  0:00 kswapd
```

At the beginning, some indications are given as to the current state of the system. The first line contains times and system load analogous to uptime. The second line shows the number of processes, differentiating between the individual states. CPU time used (in per cent) for processes in user mode, with a negative nice value, in system mode and idle are shown in line three.

The remaining fields correspond to the homonymous fields of the free (*see* Section B.1) and ps (*see* Section B.2) commands. They are, therefore, not explained in further detail. The current version (1.01) still has the problem that it uses a fixed page size of 4096 bytes.

B.5 `init` – primus inter pares

The *init* process with process number 1 is often called the parent of all processes. In LINUX, this is *not* the case, as this function is exercised by the *idle* process, but it is still called as such by force of habit and also in the sources.

The features described here refer to the program in version 2.6 which is compatible with System V. Its main task is a controlled initialization of the system and the management of the start processes for the individual *run levels*. It is configured by means of the file `/etc/inittab`. Several configurations can be specified in this file by indicating different *run levels*. A run level is a predetermined software configuration of the system.

When the `init` program is called, it first stores its name (without path). Then it checks its process number. If this is not equal to 1, an init process is already running, and only the run level is to be modified. This case is discussed further below.

The command line is checked for parameters, and `init boot` is entered as command name.

```
if (getpid() == 1 ) {
        maxproclen = strlen(argv[0]) + 1;
        for(f = 1; f < argc; f++) {
                if (!strcmp(argv[f], "single"))
                        dflLevel = 'S';
                else if (!strcmp(argv[f], "-a") ||
                         !strcmp(argv[f], "auto"))
                        putenv("AUTOBOOT=YES");
                else if (!strcmp(argv[f], "-b") ||
                         !strcmp(argv[f], "emergency"))
                        emerg_shell = 1;
                else if (strchr("0123456789sS", argv[f][0])
                         && strlen(argv[f]) == 1)
                        dflLevel = argv[f][0];
                maxproclen += strlen(argv[f]) + 1;
        }
        maxproclen--;

        argv0 = argv[0];
        argv[1] = ((void *)0) ;
        setproctitle("init boot");
        InitMain(dflLevel);
}
```

In the `InitMain()` function, the *root* file system can be remounted, if necessary, and a `chroot()` executed. This part of the program must be linked during compilation with the compiler option `-DROOTFS`. The `Log()` function outputs its string via syslog, console or both.

```
#ifdef ROOTFS
  close(0); close(1); close(2);

  if (mount(ROOTFS, "/root", "ext2", 0, 0) < 0) {
      Log(L_VB, "mount(%s, /root): %s", ROOTFS,
                                 sys_errlist[errno]);
      while(1) pause();
  }

  if (chroot("/root") < 0) {
      Log(L_VB, "chroot(/root): %s", sys_errlist[errno]);
      while(1) pause();
  }
#endif
```

After this, the program enables booting with Ctrl+Alt+Del and enters handling routines for the signals ALARM, HUP, STOP, TSTP, CONT, CHLD, INT, QUIT and PWR. All other signals are ignored.

The standard input and output as well as the standard error output are closed and the console is initialized with SetTerm(). The values (speed and flags) are read from the file /etc/ioctl.save, if it exists. The program enters itself as leader in a new process group and initializes a PATH variable. In addition, the *utmp* file is recreated – and the program says 'Hello'.

```
reboot(0xfee1dead, 672274793, 0);

for(f = 1; f <= _NSIG; f++) signal(f, SIG_IGN);

SETSIG(sa, SIGALRM,  signal_handler);
SETSIG(sa, SIGHUP,   signal_handler);
SETSIG(sa, SIGINT,   signal_handler);
SETSIG(sa, SIGPWR,   signal_handler);
SETSIG(sa, SIGWINCH, signal_handler);
SETSIG(sa, SIGCHLD,  chld_handler);
SETSIG(sa, SIGSTOP,  stop_handler);
SETSIG(sa, SIGTSTP,  stop_handler);
SETSIG(sa, SIGCONT,  cont_handler);

close(0); close(1); close(2);
SetTerm(0); setsid();

if (getenv("PATH") == NULL) putenv(PATH_DFL);

(void) close(open(UTMP_FILE, O_WRONLY|O_CREAT|O_TRUNC, 0644));

Log(L_CO, bootmsg);
```

For systems with special security requirements it is possible, by specifying -b, to start a shell via the sulogin program, before *anything* else is done. sulogin asks for the root password and starts a shell (which can be set via SUSHELL); by default, this is the shell entered in /etc/passwd or /bin/sh. By pressing Ctrl+D at any time, it is possible to continue the normal boot process.

```
if (emerg_shell) {
        if ((f = Spawn(&ch_emerg)) > 0) {
                while(wait(&st) != f);
        }
}
```

At this point, init reads its configuration file inittab, evaluates it and starts the necessary processes.

```
runlevel = '#';
ReadItab();
StartEmIfNeeded();
```

The file contains individual lines each of which triggers an action for a prede-termined event. A comment line begins with a #.

name:*level*:*action*:*command*

The individual elements have the following meaning:

- **name**
  This is a denominator, four characters long, which uniquely identifies the line.

  Old *init* versions (a.out and compiled with libraries <5.12.18) allow only two characters.

  Warning: for *getty* or *login* processes, the name must match the ending of the corresponding tty. The reason for this is that the name is used as utmp entry – otherwise, accounting would not work (another reason for the limited size).

- **level**
  One or more run level(s) of the system. Possible values are the numbers 0 to 9 and the letters S, A, B and C, where init does not distinguish between upper and lower case. The value S stands for single user mode. If this indication is omitted, the *action* of the process is activated at each change of the run level. With the *action* fields sysinit, oot and ootwait, the level is ignored.

- **action**
  This indication tells the process when to execute the program specified by *command*. The following actions are recognized:

boot	The program is executed once at system boot. The process does not, however, wait for it to terminate, but continues evaluating the `inittab` file.
bootwait	The program is executed once at system boot and `init` waits for it to terminate; generally, the file `/etc/rc` is usually executed in this way.
ctrlaltdel	The program is started when Ctrl+Alt+Del[1] are pressed.
initdefault	The level used at system boot. If this line is omitted, `init` asks for the level on the console at boot time. The *command* entry is ignored.
kbrequest	The command is executed when a determined key combination is pressed. For this, `KDSIGACCEPT` must be configured in the sources.
off	Nothing is executed.
once	The program is started once at the beginning of the level.
ondemand	The program is executed each time `init` changes to the corresponding run level. Usual levels for `ondemand` are `A+`, `B+` and `C+`.
powerfail	As `powerwait`; however, *init* does not wait for it to terminate.
powerfailnow	The program is started when the `SIGPWR` signal occurs and the entry `L` is found in `/etc/powerstatus` (for example, nearly empty battery packs in laptops).
powerokwait	The program is started when the mains power is restored (`SIGPWR` signal and entry `0` in `/etc/powerstatus`). Usually `shutdown -c` is called.
powerwait	The program is started when the init process receives the `SIGPWR` signal. With this signal, uninterruptible power supplies (UPS) indicate a mains failure. Normally, a `shutdown` is executed.
respawn	After it has terminated, the program, normally `getty`, is restarted.
sysinit	The program is executed at system boot. These entries are executed before `boot` and `bootwait`.
wait	The program is started once at the beginning of the level.

• *command*
  Here we find a UNIX command. Specification of parameters is allowed. If the command begins with a plus sign, it is not entered in the files `wtmp` or `utmp`.

---

[1] Also known as the 'hacker's claw' or *Three Finger Salute*.

The entries in the `inittab` file are stored in a list; if lines have the same name, only the first line is considered. In the next step, this list is worked through by starting the processes and entering them in `/etc/utmp` and `/usr/adm/wtmp`.

After all necessary processes have been spawned, `init` enters a loop in which the transitions from starting (`runlevel='#'`) via booting (`runlevel='*'`) to normal operation are realized. If no more processes are running and no signals are received, the control fifo is checked.

```
while(1) {
    BootTransitions();
    for(ch = family; ch; ch = ch->next)
        if ((ch->flags & RUNNING ) && ch->action != BOOT ) break;
    if (ch != NULL  && got_signals == 0) CheckInitFifo();
```

This file (`/dev/initctl`) allows additional control over *init*. Programs (`telnetd`) can enter requests into the file and thus trigger various actions. A request has the following structure:

```
struct init_request {
    int magic;                      /* magic number                 */
    int cmd;                        /* kind of request              */
    int runlevel;                   /* new runlevel                 */
    int sleeptime;                  /* time between TERM and KILL    */
    char gen_id[8];                 /* Beats me... telnetd uses "fe" */
    char tty_id[16];                /* TTY name without /dev/tty     */
    char host[MAXHOSTNAMELEN];      /* host name                    */
    char term_type[16];             /* terminal type                */
    int signal;                     /* signal to be sent            */
    int pid;                        /* and its receiver             */
    char exec_name[128];            /* program to be executed       */
    char reserved[128];             /* future extensions            */
};
```

Up to now, however, only four kinds of request are recognized:

INIT_CMD_RUNLVL – the new `sleeptime` is entered and a transition to the required level is carried out.

INIT_CMD_POWERFAIL – the new `sleeptime` is entered and the commands belonging to the `POWERFAIL` action are started.

INIT_CMD_POWERFAILNOW – the new `sleeptime` is entered and the commands belonging to the `POWERFAILNOW` action are started.

INIT_CMD_POWEROK – the new `sleeptime` is entered and the commands belonging to the `POWEROK` action are started.

The next function has the following background. If init notes that *respawn* processes are to be called very often during a short period of time (ten times within two minutes), an error is assumed and the inittab entry is deactivated for five minutes. This prevents unnecessary system load in case of an incorrect inittab entry. FailCheck(), which is also called after reception of the SIGHUP signal (new inittab!), reactivates the entries after five minutes. Finally, received signals are processed, the necessary processes started, and the loop is terminated.

```
        FailCheck();
        ProcessSignals();
        StartEmIfNeeded();
        sync();
    } /* while */
```

For a run level change, the old processes have to be terminated. First they are sent a SIGTERM and after five seconds (defined in sltime/sleeptime) a SIGKILL. This is carried out inside the ReadItab() function which is called at every change – a separate function would probably be more elegant.

When init receives a signal, then, depending on the kind of signal, the processes specified in inittab are activated. As handlers have been entered only for a few signals, only those few signals are reacted to.

SIGALRM   Nothing happens.

SIGCHLD   A child process has terminated. The flags RUNNING, ZOMBIE and WAITING are deleted and the utmp and wtmp files updated.

SIGHUP   init tries to read the new run level from the file /etc/initrunlvl. If it does not exist, the old level is used again. In addition, the inittab file is re-read and all 'sleepers' (FailCancel()) are woken up.

SIGINT   The program belonging to ctrlaltdel is activated.

SIGPWR   The file /etc/powerstatus is read and deleted. The DoPowerFail() function activates the appropriate commands.

SIGWINCH   The program belonging to kbrequest is activated.

Now back to the case that init or telinit are called to change the run level. This is only permitted to the superuser. After the compulsory syntax check, two strategies are employed. First, a request is assembled and written to the control fifo. This attempt is encapsulated by an alarm() to avoid blocking.

```
        signal(SIGALRM, signal_handler);
        alarm(3);
        if ((fd = open(INIT_FIFO, O_WRONLY)) >= 0 &&
                write(fd, &request, sizeof(request))
                    == sizeof(request)) {
            close(fd); alarm(0); return 0;
        }
```

If this attempt fails, the 'traditional' way is followed: `init` stores the new run level in the file /etc/initrunlvl and sends itself a SIGHUP.

The program `telinit` is a link to `init`. It is used to change the run level from the command line. The following arguments can be specified:

0–6   Change to the specified run level.

a–c   Only those processes are executed that have the specified run level in `inittab`.

Qq   The `inittab` file is re-read.

Ss   The system changes to single user mode.

-t *sec*   With the option **-t** *sec* the waiting time between the signals SIGTERM and SIGKILL can be changed. The default is 20 seconds.

B.6 `shutdown` – shutting down the system

The `shutdown` program safely shuts the system down. All users are warned and `login` is blocked.

> `shutdown [-t` *sec*`] [-i` *level*`] [-rkhncf]` *time* `[`*message*`]`

The following options can be used:

-c   A running `shutdown` is aborted. Obviously, no time can be indicated; a message is, however, possible.

-f   No `fsck` is executed after rebooting the system (*fast reboot*).

-h   After shutdown, the system halts.

-k   The shutdown is simulated; only the corresponding messages are issued.

-n   No use is made of *init*, instead, `shutdown` shuts the system down itself. This option is only possible with **-h** or **-r**.

-r   Reboot after shutdown.

-t *sec*   The program waits *sec* seconds between the sending of the signals SIGTERM and SIGKILL to all processes.

time   The time at which `shutdown` shuts the system down.

message This message is issued to all users when `shutdown` is called.

The argument *time* has two different formats. It can be indicated in the form *hh:mm* (%d:%2d), where *hh* stands for hours and *mm* for minutes. Or the format is +*m*, where *m* is the number of minutes. The specification `now` is an alias for +0.

When called, `shutdown` first of all sets its UID to its effective UID. If after this, the UID is not 0, the program aborts. It only works with root privileges. Then it checks whether the process owns a terminal. If this is not the case, `shutdown` has been called by `init` (via [Ctrl]+[Alt]+[Del]). Now `shutdown` determines which users are allowed to shut the system down. These are stored in `/etc/shutdown.allow`. If this file is not present, only the superuser has the right to shut the system down. The length of this file is limited to 32 lines. All users are identified and compared with the authorized users. Remote users are excluded. Users are recognized by their login names. Root is implicitly authorized (but not as a remote user).

Now the command line is read and evaluated. In addition, an attempt is made to determine, from the file `/etc/shutdownpid`, the process number of an already running `shutdown`. If a `shutdown` is already running and the option `-c` set, the running `shutdown` is terminated by sending it `SIGINT`. If the option is not set, the program aborts.

Now the `shutdownpid` file is created, its own **PID** stored and all signals except `SIGINT` blocked. When `shutdown` receives a `SIGINT`, it deletes all files it has created and calls `exit(0)`. The program changes to the root directory. If the option `-f` has been set, the file `/etc/fastboot` is created. As a last step, the time is evaluated. If it is `now` or `+0`, the function `shutdown()` is called immediately. Otherwise, the program waits and, in the meantime, issues warnings. The `shutdown()` function issues a last warning. If `-k` is set (simulation) all created files are deleted and the program is terminated.

With `-n` (without the deviation via *init*) all processes are terminated in the usual manner (`SIGTERM` plus `SIGKILL`), the script `/etc/rc.d/rc.halt` is executed (if present), and finally the system is halted (or rebooted). Otherwise, `shutdown()` assembles a parameter list and with it calls the `init` program. With option `-h` this leads to a transition into run level 0 and with option `-r` into run level 6. If none of the options is specified, the system changes to run level 1. This may possibly lead to a nasty surprise: some older `inittab` files contain the line 'x1:6:wait:/etc/rc.d/rc.6'. Thus, after a `shutdown -r`, one finds oneself in front of an X login, instead of having the computer boot.[2]

B.7   strace – monitoring a process

Fault detection in programs is a tiresome business. Often there is a wish to have a summary of all system calls executed, together with their parameters. This is exactly what `strace` provides.

```
strace [ -dffhiqrtttTvxx ] [ -a column ] [ -e expr ]
           [ -o filename ] [ -p pid ]
           [ -s strsize ] [ -u username ]
           command
```

---

[2] Note: Imitation not exactly recommended.

```
strace -c [ -e expr ] [ -O overhead ]
            [ -S sortby ] command
```

The `strace` program monitors the execution of the *command* command. It registers system calls and signals. Output is on standard error or, with the option -o, in a file.

Each output line contains a system call, its arguments (in parentheses) and the return value. On error (return value = –1) the error number is given as a symbolic name, together with its description (for example '`EINVAL (Invalid Argument)`'). Signals are indicated by their names.

Arguments are output, if possible, in a readable form. Pointers to structures are dereferenced and their components and contents indicated in curly brackets. Pointers to strings are also dereferenced and the string is displayed in quotation marks. Non-printable characters are indicated as escape sequences, as is usual in C. While curly brackets are used for structures, arrays are indicated by square brackets.

In order to control monitoring more precisely, there is a multitude of options. Thus it is possible, for example, to restrict monitoring to certain system calls or to follow child processes generated by `fork()`. The following options are allowed:

-c   `strace` generates time statistics for each system call and outputs them at the end.

-d   `strace` works in debugging mode and outputs information itself.

-f   If a monitored process generates children by means of `fork()`, these are monitored in their turn.

-ff   Works together with -o *filename*. Each child process writes its output into the file *filename.pid*, where *pid* is the child's PID. The -f option is switched on in addition.

-h   Help about usage is displayed.

-i   At the beginning of each line, the instruction pointer (EIP) is displayed.

-q   Information on halting and releasing processes is suppressed. This is done automatically, if the output is not redirected to a file. This option is meaningful only in conjunction with -f or -p *pid*, as only then processes are controlled by means of `ptrace(PTRACE_ATTACH,pid,data)`, *see also* page 302.

-r   For each system call, the time passed since the previous call is output in seconds and microseconds.

-t   Each line begins with the current time in the format `HH:MM:SS`.

-tt   In addition, microseconds are output.

-ttt   Each line begins with the current time in second and microseconds.

-T   The time used by the system call is displayed, measured between call and return.

-v   All complex data, such as argument vectors and structures, are displayed to their full extent. Otherwise, only the first components or characters are shown.

-V   `strace` displays its version number.

-x   Non-printable characters in strings are output in hexadecimal format.

-xx   All characters in strings are output in hexadecimal format.

-a *column*   The return value of the system call is written in the *column* column; the default is 40.

-e *expr*   Here, an expression *expr* can be specified which controls the trace procedure more precisely. The expression has the following format:

[*type*=][!] *value1* [, *value2*]...

The type can be `trace`, `abbrev`, `verbose`, `raw`, `signal`, `faults`, `read` or `write`. Depending on the type, the value can be a name or a number. The default type is `trace`. An exclamation mark negates the value. An example: -e open, which corresponds to -e trace=open, only traces open() calls, as opposed to -e trace=!open, where all calls are traced except open(). In addition, there are two special cases: `all` and `none`.

abbrev=*set*   Influences the display of individual components of large structures. The -v option sets `abbrev=none`. Default is `all`.

faults   Erroneous memory access attempts are displayed as well. This option works only with SysV.

raw=*set*   Displays the arguments of the calls specified in *set* uncoded in hexadecimal format.

read=*set*   For all read operations on the file descriptor *set*, a dump is output in both ASCII and hexadecimal formats.

signal=*set*   Only the signals specified in *set* are traced. Default is `all`.

trace=*set*   Only the calls specified in *set* are traced. Default is `all`. the following classes can be specified as *set*:

file   All system calls are traced that belong to the file system. These are:

access(), acct(), chdir(), chmod(), chown(),
chroot(), creat(), execve(), link(), lstat(),
mkdir(), mknod(), mount(), open(), readlink(),
rename(), rmdir(), stat(), statfs(), swapon(),
symlink(), truncate(), umount(), unlink(),
uselib(), utime()

ipc   All system calls are traced that belong to the IPC (SysV). These are:

msgctl(), msgget(), msgrcv(), msgsnd(),
semctl(), semget(), semop(), shmat(),
shmctl(), shmdt(), shmget()

network   All system calls are traced that belong to network communication. These are:

> accept(), bind(), connect(), getpeername(),
> getsockname(), getsockopt(), listen(), recv(),
> recvfrom(), recvmsg(), send(), sendmsg()
> sendto(), setsockopt(), shutdown(), socket(),
> socketpair()

process   All system calls are traced that belong to process administration. These are:

> _exit(), fork(), waitpid(),
> execve(), wait4(), clone()

signal   All system calls are traced that belong to signal handling. These are:

> pause(), kill(), signal(), sigaction(),
> siggetmask(), sigsetmask(), sigsuspend(),
> sigpending(), sigreturn() und sigprocmask()

verbose=*set*   Controls the display of arguments for system calls as pointers or as dereferenced structures. For *set*, the structures are displayed to their full extent, for the remainder, only the pointers as hexadecimal addresses. Default is all.

write=*set*   For all write operations on the file descriptor *set*, a dump is output in both ASCII and hexadecimal formats.

–o *filename*   The output is redirected to the file *filename*, or, with **–ff** set, to the file *filename.pid*.

–O *overhead*   Through the monitoring of system calls, an overhead is generated that distorts the statistics generated with –c. The value, heuristically determined by the program itself, can be corrected here. The precision may be checked by the user him/herself by determining the system time used by the program to be monitored with the time program and comparing it with the values determined by –c. The overhead value must be indicated in microseconds.

–p *pid*   The process *pid* is to be monitored.

–s *strsize*   By default, only the first 32 characters of strings are output. This can be changed using the –s option.

–S *sortby*   The table obtained with –c is sorted by the *sortby* column. Possible values are time, calls, name and nothing. Default is time.

A final example:

```
# strace sync
execve("/bin/sync", ["sync"], [/* 32 vars */]) = 0
sync()                              = 0
_exit(0)                           = ?
```

B.8   Configuring the network interface

The network interface is configured by `ifconfig`. Normally, it is executed at system boot and sets the parameters of the network devices.

> `ifconfig [interface [[options ...] address]]`

When `ifconfig` is called without parameters, the current configuration of the network interface is displayed. Otherwise, the interface is configured with the specified *options* parameters at IP address *address*. The following parameters are allowed:

interface   The name of the interface (for example, `lo` or `eth0`).

up   The interface is activated. If a new address is specified (*see below*), this option is set implicitly.

down   The interface is switched off.

metric *N*   The parameter sets the interface metrics to the value *N*. It should be set to zero.

mtu *N*   The parameter sets the maximum packet size.[3] For Ethernet cards, a value between 1000 and 2000 is suitable, for SLIP a value between 200 and 4096.

[-]arp   Toggles the use of the ARP protocol. If preceded by a minus sign (-), the protocol is switched off.

[-]trailer   This option is ignored by LINUX.

broadcast *aa.bb.cc.dd*   Sets the broadcast address for the interface.

dstaddr *aa.bb.cc.dd*   Sets the specified address for a point-to-point connection (PPP) as 'other end'. This option is currently not supported.

netmask *aa.bb.cc.dd*   Sets the net mask for the interface.

B.9   `traceroute` – Ariadne's thread in the Internet

The Internet is a worldwide conglomerate of extremely different networks. This makes the occurrence of connection problems unavoidable. In order to look more deeply into such problems as '`network unreachable`', `traceroute` has been developed.

> `traceroute [-dnrv] [-m max_ttl] [-p port#] [-q nqueries]`
> `[-s src_addr] [-t tos] [-w wait] host [data size]`

The `traceroute` program traces the route of UDP packets from source to destination. The destination address can be specified as computer name or as IP

---

[3] MTU – Maximal Transfer Unit

address. The program uses two techniques to trace the route of packets: a time stamp (a small *TTL value*)[4] and an invalid port address.

The first technique finds the route to the destination computer. Each gateway in the Internet that receives an IP packet decrements the TTL value and, when it has reached 0, sends back an ICMP packet of the type `ICMP_TIMXCEED`. When it starts, `traceroute` sends its packets with a TTL value of 1 and increments it with each `ICMP_TIMXCEED` message received. In addition, when `traceroute` receives the packet, it displays a status line for the gateway:

```
8  bnl-pppl.es.net (134.55.9.33)  516 ms  687 ms  771 ms
```

The line contains the TTL value, the name of the computer that originated the message, its IP address and the transmission times (`traceroute` always sends three packets).

When the UDP packet has reached the specified destination, the destination computer sends back an ICMP packet of the type `ICMP_UNREACH`. The reason for this is that `traceroute` uses packets that contain an invalid port number (33434) in order to generate this error. The program uses the following options:

-d   The `debug` flag is set in the `sock` structure. This causes more information to be displayed.

-m *ttl*   Sets the maximum time stamp to *ttl*. This allows the range to be preset. The default value is 30.

-n   The program only displays the IP address and not the domain name of the destination computer.

-p *port* Sets the port number used. The default value is 33434.

-q *nqueries* The number of packets to be sent per computer, usually three packets.

-r   `traceroute` tries, circumventing the route tables, to deliver the packet directly. This is achieved by setting the `localroute` flag in the `sock` structure. If the destination cannot be reached directly, an error message is returned.

-s *addr* Uses *addr* as IP address of the source. An Internet address must be specified, not a domain name. If a computer has more than one address, this may be used to change the sender's address. If the specified value is invalid for the machine, an error is returned.

-t *tos*   Enters *tos* into the IP packet as *type of service*. Permitted values lie between 0 and 255; additional information can be found in the IP specifications.

-v   All packets received are displayed, not only those returned with `TIME_EXCEEDED` and `UNREACHABLE`.

---

[4] TTL – Time To Life

-w *n*   Sets the waiting time for the answer to *n* seconds. The default is 5. If within the specified waiting time no ICMP packet is received, an asterisk (*) is displayed for the corresponding tests.

An example[5] for the execution of a `traceroute` call:

```
# ./traceroute ice3.ori.u-tokyo.ac.jp
traceroute to ice3.ori.u-tokyo.ac.jp (157.82.132.65),
      30 hops max, 40 byte packets
 1 delta.informatik.hu-berlin.de (141.20.20.19)  6 ms   4 ms   4 ms
 2 141.20.20.9 (141.20.20.9)  4 ms   4 ms   4 ms
 3 192.2.6.2 (192.2.6.2)  98 ms   41 ms   33 ms
 4 Berlin1.WiN-IP.DFN.DE (188.1.132.250)  653 ms   549 ms   1037 ms
 5 ipgate2.WiN-IP.DFN.DE (188.1.133.62)  856 ms   669 ms   559 ms
 6 usgate.win-ip.dfn.de (193.174.74.65)  466 ms   392 ms   506 ms
 7 pppl-frg.es.net (192.188.33.9)  2288 ms   2964 ms   1057 ms
 8 umd2-pppl2.es.net (134.55.12.162)  361 ms   1375 ms   1441 ms
 9 umd1-e-umd2.es.net (134.55.13.33)  1669 ms   2334 ms *
10 pppl-umd.es.net (134.55.6.34)  1421 ms   1346 ms   1477 ms
11 llnl-pppl.es.net (134.55.5.97)  1970 ms   1440 ms *
12 * ames-llnl.es.net (134.55.4.161)  1255 ms   2781 ms
13 ARC5.NSN.NASA.GOV (192.203.230.12)  2499 ms   2353 ms   2223 ms
14 132.160.252.2 (132.160.252.2)  2417 ms   1798 ms *
15 tko3gw.tisn.ad.jp (133.11.208.3)  1738 ms   1141 ms   1053 ms
16 uts4gw.tisn.ad.jp (133.11.210.2)  1575 ms   1505 ms   1498 ms
17 ncgw.nc.u-tokyo.ac.jp (133.11.127.127) 1740 ms 1677 ms 1170 ms
18 hongogw.nc.u-tokyo.ac.jp (130.69.254.3)  1222 ms * *
19 nakanogw.nc.u-tokyo.ac.jp (157.82.128.2) 1380 ms 594 ms 680 ms
20 origw1.nc.u-tokyo.ac.jp (157.82.128.65) 1770 ms 2006 ms 1650 ms
21 origw3.nc.u-tokyo.ac.jp (157.82.129.3) 2669 ms 854 ms 1254 ms
22 * ice3.ori.u-tokyo.ac.jp (157.82.132.65)  1262 ms *
```

Exclamation marks (!) in the output indicate problems.

!   The port is unreachable (`ICMP_UNREACH_PORT`) and the returning `ttl` value is less than 2.

!F   Fragmentation is needed (`ICMP_UNREACH_NEEDFRAG`).

!P   A protocol error occurred (`ICMP_UNREACH_PROTOCOL`).

!H   The computer is unreachable (`ICMP_UNREACH_HOST`).

!N   The network is unreachable (`ICMP_UNREACH_NET`).

!S   Use of the source address failed (`ICMP_UNREACH_SRCFAIL`).

---

[5] If you really want to know, 132.160.252.2 is a computer in Hawaii.

B.10   Configuring a serial interface

The `setserial` program sets or reads the parameters of a serial interface. With this, port number and IRQ can be modified. If an already occupied IRQ is specified, `setserial` returns the error message 'Device busy'.

> `setserial [ -abqvVW ] device [ opt [ arg ] ] ...`
> `setserial -g [ -abv ] device1 ...`

The following options can be specified:

-a   All parameters of the device are displayed.

-b   The default settings (port, IRQ and UART) are displayed.

-g   A list of devices can be specified.

-q   No display is generated with **-W** set.

-v   After setting the device, its new data are displayed.

-V   The program only displays its version number.

-W   Tries to find all unused interrupts (and displays them with **-va**).

The following options may be specified. Numbers can be specified in several formats (decimal, octal or hexadecimal). A ^ in front of an option negates it.

[^] **auto_irq**   During autoconfiguration, the IRQ used is detected.

[^] **callout_nohup**   If the device was opened as *callout*, no `hangup()` is executed when it is closed (only if `ASYNC_CALLOUT_NOHUP` was configured).

[^] **fourport**   Configures the port as AST FourPort.

[^] **pgrp_lockout**   Only one process group can access the `cua` port, others are locked out.

[^] **sak**   The *secure attention key* is used.

[^] **session_lockout**   Only one session group can access the `cua` port, others are locked out.

[^] **skip_test**   During autoconfiguration, the UART type is not tested.

[^] **split_termios**   *dialin* and *callout* devices use different `termios` entries (only if `ASYNC_SPLIT_TERMIOS` was configured).

autoconfigure   The kernel tries to configure the device automatically.

base *base*   *see* `baud_base`.

baud_base *baud_base*   This option sets the base baud rate.

close_delay *number*   Sets the waiting time of the process when it closes the device. The value is specified in hundredths of seconds.

closing_wait2 *number*   This option is no longer supported by the kernel. Originally, it meant the waiting time of the process after closing the device.

closing_wait *number*   Time during closure of the device in which the process may still accept data (only if `ASYNC_CLOSING_WAIT_NONE` was configured).

divisor *divisor*   This sets the divisor for the baud rate. The divisor is used when the option `spd_cust` is set and the port is set to 38.4 kbaud.

get_multiport   Displays the configuration of multiport devices.

hup_notify   The `getty` program is notified about `hangup` and `close` of the port.

irq *number*   The program sets the IRQ to the specified number, where *number* is a value between 0 and 15.

port *number*   The program sets the port to the specified number.

set_multiport   Allows multiport devices to be configured. The parameters must be passed via `port[n]`, `mask[n]` and `match[n]`.

spd_cust   The baud rate is calculated as *baud_base/divisor*.

spd_hi   The baud rate is set to 57.6 kbaud if the application using the decvice requires 38.4 kbaud.

spd_normal   The default baud rate of 38.4 kbaud is used.

spd_vhi   The baud rate is set to 115 kbaud if the application using the decvice requires 38.4 kbaud.

termios_restore   The terminal settings are restored after blocking is released.

uart *type*   The parameter sets the UART type used. Supported types are 8250, 16450, 16550, 16550A and `none`. If FIFOs are to be used, the type 16550A must be specified, as the other types do not support this (or only do so incorrectly). The specification `none` switches the port off.

In LINUX it is not possible for several devices to share an IRQ (special hardware, such as AST FourPort, supports this). By default, 39 ports, `ttyS0` to `ttyS38`, are initialized in the file `drivers/char/serial.c`.

If other configurations are required, they can be realized by a call to `setserial` in `/etc/rc.local`. The specification of a new IRQ is not that easy, because most IRQs are already occupied. The use of IRQ 5, which is normally responsible for LPT2, has proved convenient. Other possibilities are 3, 4 and 7, or if the card supports 16 bits, IRQs 10, 11, 12 and 15. IRQ 2 is by default mapped to IRQ 9.

To obtain the data, the device is read using an `ioctl` call.

```
void getserial(char *device, int fd)
{
    struct serial_struct serinfo;
```

```
if (ioctl(fd, TIOCGSERIAL, &serinfo) < 0) {
   perror("Cannot get serial info");
   exit(1);
}
printf("%s, Type: %s, Line: %d, Port: 0x%.4x, IRQ: %d\n",
   device, serial_type(serinfo.type),
   serinfo.line, serinfo.port, serinfo.irq);
}
```

The port number and the interrupt are set by an ioctl call. This tests, in addition, whether the specified port or interrupt is already occupied, returning an error message. When specifying the port number, special attention is recommended: specifying an incorrect number can crash the computer.

B.11   Configuring a parallel interface

Just as there exists a program to configure the serial ports, there is also one for the parallel ports: tunelp (version 1.5) It is mainly used for printer configuration. The following options are available as parameters:

> tunelp *device* [−i *irq* | −t *time* | −c *chars* | −w *wait* | −a [on | off]]
> | −o [on | off]] | −C [on | off]] | −r | −s | −q [on | off]]

−a[on|off]   This allows the user to specify whether the printer should abort the printing process when a fault occurs. If one sits at the printer oneself, this might be more convenient, as faults can be remedied immediately. If this is not the case, however, the print spooler should deal with this, terminate the job and send a mail message to the user. The choice is yours, default is off.

−C[on|off]   If this option is set, the driver defines the printer as *online* and ignores all error messages. This is useful for printers that can also accept data in *offline* status.

−c *chars*   The value *chars* specifies the number of attempts to output a character on the printer port. 120 is a good value for most printers. The default setting is LP_INIT_CHAR, as some printers take a bit more time. For very fast printers (HP-Laserjet), a value of 10 makes more sense.

−i *irq*   This sets the interrupt to be used. If the port does not use interrupts (polling), this specification aborts the printing process. A call of tunelp −i 0 restores polling and the printer should work again.

−o[on|off]   Prior to printing, the device is opened and a status check is made.

-q[on|off]   This option can be combined with all other ones. If it is set, it displays at the end of the output whether control works via IRQ (plus number) or polling.

-r   Sends a reset to the device.

-s   Displays the status of the device. This option switches **-q** to *off*.

-t *time*   This specifies how long the device driver should wait for the parallel interface after **-c***char* attempts. The parallel interface is initialized with the value `LP_INIT_TIME`. If printing needs to be carried out as fast as possible and system load plays no role, this value can be set to 0. If printing speed plays no role or the printer is slow, 50 is a good value which, in addition, puts very little load on the system. *time* is specified in hundredths of seconds.

-w *wait*   This is the waiting time for the *strobe* signal, which is a *busy waiting* signal. Most printers only require an extremely short signal, therefore this value is initialized with 0 (`LP_INIT_WAIT`). Increasing this value allows, apart from the use of corresponding printers, for a longer printer cable.

LINUX administers printers in a table. The BIOS supports up to four printers; in reality this will hardly ever happen. Therefore, only three entries are initialized.

```
struct lp_struct lp_table[] = {
    {0x3bc,0,0,LP_INIT_CHAR,LP_INIT_TIME,LP_INIT_WAIT,NULL,NULL,},
    {0x378,0,0,LP_INIT_CHAR,LP_INIT_TIME,LP_INIT_WAIT,NULL,NULL,},
    {0x278,0,0,LP_INIT_CHAR,LP_INIT_TIME,LP_INIT_WAIT,NULL,NULL,},
};
```

By means of the system call *ioctl*, the corresponding entry is filled with the data passed. The structure, together with the above initialization, can be found in <linux/lp.h>:

```
struct lp_struct {
    int base;            /* IO address                        */
    unsigned int irq;    /* interrupt                         */
    int flags;           /* flags for busy, abort and so on   */
    unsigned int chars;  /* timeout for each character        */
    unsigned int time;   /* waiting time between two characters */
    unsigned int wait;   /* waiting time for a strobe signal  */
    struct wait_queue *lp_wait_q;
    char *lp_buffer;     /* printer buffer                    */
        unsigned int lastcall; /* time of last output         */
        unsigned int runchars; /* characters in time loop     */
        unsigned int waittime; D/*
        struct lp_stats stats; /* additional statistics       */
}
```

B.12 mount

The LINUX file systems are administered using the commands mount and umount. They serve to mount and unmount file systems. The programs included in version 0.99.6 have the following parameters:

```
mount [ -hV ]
mount -a [ nfrvw ] [ -t vfstypes ]
mount [ -nfrvw ] [ -o options ] special | node
mount [ -nfrvw ] [ -t vfstype ] [ -o options ] special node

umount -a [ -t type ]
umount special | node
```

Without parameters, mount displays the list of all currently mounted file systems. Otherwise it tries, by means of the system call *mount*, to mount the file system present on the *special* device at the mount point *node*. If *special* or *node* are not specified, the missing information is read from the file /etc/fstab. The options of mount have the following meaning:

-a An attempt is made to mount all file systems specified in the /etc/fstab file. With the -t option also set, this attempt is made only for file systems of a specified type.

-f The mounting of the file system is only simulated. Together with the -v option, this makes it possible to check which actions the mount program would carry out.

-h Help about usage is displayed.

-n The file /etc/mtab is not modified. This is necessary when the etc/ directory is located on a CD-ROM.

-o *options* The -o option specifies the mount options *options*, separated by commas (,). The following options are valid for all file systems:

defaults This is the default option. It corresponds to the options:

rw,exec,suid,dev,async,auto,nouser

[no]auto The device is (is not) included in the mount -a call.

[no]dev The use of device files on this file system is (is not) allowed.

[no]exec Execution of binaries of the mounted file system is (is not) allowed.

remount A file system is remounted. Usually, this option is used to enter new flags (for example, to change from ro to rw).

ro The file system is mounted read-only.

rw The file system is mounted read and write.

[no]suid When executing binaries of the mounted file system, any set S bits are interpreted (ignored).

[a]sync All input and output operations on this file system are executed in synchronous (asynchronous) mode.

[no]users Normal users can (cannot) mount this device. This option implies noexec, nosuid and nodev, if not set otherwise.

Further mount options of individual file systems are described later.

-r The file system is mounted read-only.

-w The file system is mounted read and write.

-t *type* The file system to be mounted is of the specified type *type*. If no type is specified or -a is set, mount() tries to recognize the type by reading the superblock (supported types are *minix*, *ext*, *ext2*, *xiafs* and *iso9660*). If the specified *special* 'device' contains a colon (:), it is automatically assumed that the file system is of the NFS type. With the -a option set in addition, several file systems can be specified, separated by commas (,). In this case, the type can also be prefixed with the string 'no'. Thus, for example, the command

```
mount -a -t nomsdos,nonfs
```

mounts all file systems contained in the fstab file which are neither of type msdos nor of type nfs.

-v The program generates verbose displays to inform users about its actions.

-V Displays the version of the program.

The umount program removes mounted file systems from the file system tree. It recognizes the -a and -t options with semantics analogous to the ones described above.

The file /etc/fstab has a simple structure. Comment lines begin with a hash sign (#). The other lines contain four fields, separated by *white space* (spaces and/or tabs), of the form:

special   node   type   option

Here, all fields are compulsory, so that for an omitted device or mount point none has to be specified, and defaults for default options. In addition to file systems, the file also indicates swap devices and files. In this case, the type is swap, and the entry is ignored by mount and umount.

Both programs modify the /etc/mtab file, so that this file normally describes the current state of the file system tree. If this file is write-protected or located on a write-protected file system (CD-ROM), the option -n must be specified and the file /proc/mounts must be used.

A string of mount options specified together with the –o option or contained in the /etc/fstab file is checked by mount for the mount flags (*see* Table 6.1) and the remaining mount options are passed as parameters to the system call *mount*. An exception to this is the NFS, in which first a connection to the remote computer is established, and then the already interpreted mount options together with the socket file descriptor are passed to the system call in the structure nfs_mount_data.

Mount options of the Ext2 file system

bsddf If this option is specified, the system call *statfs* removes the number of blocks needed for the structures of the *Ext2* file system from the total number of free blocks. This is the default behaviour of the *Ext2* file system.

check=*value* This option specifies how many safety tests the *Ext2* file system should perform during normal operation: none switches all tests off, whereas the default normal checks at each mount/remount whether the number of free inodes or blocks entered in the inodes or block bitmaps corresponds to the values in the superblock. The strict option additionally checks at each allocation or release of a data block whether the corresponding block number does indeed describe a data block.

debug This option activates the debug mode of the *Ext2* file system. At each mount/remount operation, the file system issues a message containing its version number together with the parameters of the currently mounted file system, such as block size and number of block groups.

errors=*action* This option defines the behaviour of the file system in the event of an error being detected. In the default setting continue, the error is merely signalled. The remount-ro setting mounts the file system after an error in read-only mode, so that a possible error cannot spread out and e2fsck can be used. The panic setting halts the LINUX kernel when an error with a panic message occurs.

grpid, bsdgroups When this option is set, all files generated are assigned the group ID of the directory in which they are created. With the default setting nogrpid the new files are assigned the group ID of the directory only if the group S bit is set.

minixdf In contrast to the bsddf option, the system call *statfs* returns the total number of blocks on the underlying device.

nocheck Corresponds to the option check=none.

nogrpid, sysvgroups When the group S bit of the directory in which they have to be created is set, newly created files and directories are given the group ID of the directory and not that of the process. In addition, newly created directories are also assigned the group S bit. This option is the default.

resgid=*gid* The group ID of the group whose user may also occupy the reserved blocks. If none of the options is set, only the superuser may access the reserved blocks.

resuid=*uid* The user ID of the user who, apart from the superuser, may occupy the reserved blocks.

sb=*block number* The number of the block on the device that should be read as the superblock. By default, block 1 is read. The numbering is based on 1 Kbyte blocks.

quota, **usrquota**, **noquota**, **grpquota** These options are recognized, but ignored.

Mount options of the MS-DOS file system (FAT)

sys_immutable Files or inodes cannot be modified.

[no]dots Files bearing the *hidden* attribute receive (do not receive) a dot (.) in front of their names. Default is `nodots`.

dotsOK=[yes|no] see [no]dots.

blocksize=[512|1024] Sets the sector size of the MS-DOS file system. This is normally 512 bytes. As MS-DOS 3.0 could only handle partitions of a maximum of 65 536 sectors, some partition managers set the sector size to 1024 bytes, thus allowing access to partitions of up to 64 Mbytes. In order to access such partitions, the parameter `blocksize=1024` must be set.

check=*type* Activates various grades of file name checking.

> **r[elaxed]** Upper case and lower case letters are treated the same, long file names are shortened, and spaces are allowed.
>
> **n[ormal]** as `relaxed`, but file names must not contain any character contained in the `bad_chars[]` field (that is, `*?<>|"`). This is the default.
>
> **s[trict]** as `normal`, but forbidden characters also include those contained in the `bad_if_strict[]` field (that is, `+=,;` and the space).

conv=*type* Toggles conversion of MS-DOS text files.

> **auto** Conversions are carried out for 'unknown' file types. These are files whose extension cannot be found in `bin_extensions[]`. As in practice one or the other extension is always missing, programs that operate on such files with `lseek()` may react rather ungracefully. Thus, care must be taken!
>
> **binary** No conversion takes place. This is the default.

text This setting converts all files, removing all carriage return characters during reading and jumping to the end of the file when the
end-of-file character ^z (ASCII 0x1a) is encountered. When
writing the file, all newline characters are converted back into the
usual MS-DOS combination.

debug Activates the debug mode.

fat=[12|16] Specifies whether the file system to be mounted has a 12- or 16-bit
FAT. As the size of the FAT can normally be deduced from the number
of clusters on the file system, it should not be necessary to use this
parameter.

gid=*gid* The group of the owner of all files. By default, this is 0.

quiet As the MS-DOS file system does not normally support either a change
of owner of the inode or all of the UNIX access rights, these operations
return the error EPERM. Setting the quiet option suppresses this error
message; in other words, the operations appear to be executable.

showexec Only files with extensions .exe, .com or .bat are assigned an
executable flag.

uid=*uid* As MS-DOS does not recognize owners of files, with this option set
the MS-DOS file system displays the owner *uid* for all files. By default, 0
is entered.

umask=*umask* Uses the specified *umask* (in octal!) to calculate the access rights
for all files. If this option is omitted, the umask used is that of the
process that called the *mount* system call.

Mount options of the ISO file system

norock Deactivates the use of the *Rock Ridge Extensions*.

check=*type* Activates various grades of file name checking.

r[elaxed] Upper case letters are converted into lower case before access
takes place. This option is only sensible in combination with
norock and map=normal.

s[trict] No conversions are carried out.

cruft This option masks the highest 8 bits of the file length, as some CD-
ROM manufacturers use them to store additional information. As a
consequence, however, no files longer than 16 Mbytes can be read. This
option is automatically set for (presumably) defect CD-ROMs. These
include CD-ROMs with a capacity greater than 800 Mbytes and a
volume number not equal to 0 or 1.

map=[normal|off] Toggles naming conventions for CD-ROMs that do not
possess *Rock Ridge Extensions*. By default, normal is set, which converts

all filenames into lower case and semicolons into full stops. The suffix
';1' is removed. In the off position, names are not converted.

conv=[auto|binary|text|mtext] Since LINUX 1.3.54 this option is ignored.

block=[1024|2048] Sets the block size used for CD-ROM access. The ISO file
system sets it to 1024 by default.

mode=*value* Sets the file access rights for all files, in case the media does not
contain *Rock Ridge Extensions*. By default, the value is set to S_IRUGO,
that is, read access right for all users.

uid=*uid* The user identification number of the owner of all files. By default, 0
is entered.

gid=*gid* The group of the owner of all files. By default, this is 0.

unhide Also hidden files are displayed.

Mount options of the HPFS

uid=*uid* The user identification number of the owner of all files. By default, 0
is entered.

gid=*gid* The group of the owner of all files. By default, this is 0.

umask=*umask* Uses the specified *umask* to calculate the access rights for all
files. If this option is omitted, the umask used is that of the process that
called the *mount* system call.

case=[lower|asis] Toggles name conversion. In the default setting lower, file
names are converted into lower case; in the asis setting, they are left as
they are.

conv=*type* Toggles the conversion of MS-DOS text files. In the default setting
binary, no conversion takes place. In the text setting, all files are converted, converting the carriage return/line feed sequence into the usual
UNIX newline. The auto setting checks the first block of the file to be
read by means of some heuristics, to determine whether the file is a text
file or a binary file. Then the remainder of the file is converted.

nocheck Mounting is not aborted if errors occur during the consistency check.

Mount options of the NFS

acdirmax=*n* The maximum time span in seconds in which attributes of directories are buffered before updated information is fetched from the NFS
server. Default is 60.

acdirmin=*n* The minimum time span in seconds in which attributes of directories are buffered before updated information is fetched from the NFS
server. Default is 30.

acregmax=*n* The maximum time span in seconds in which attributes of regular files are buffered before updated information is fetched from the NFS server. Default is 60.

acregmin=*n* The minimum time span in seconds in which attributes of regular files are buffered before updated information is fetched from the NFS server. Default is 3.

actimeo=*n* The options `acregmin`, `acregmax`, `acdirmin` and `acdirmax` are set to the specified value.

addr=*n* This option is ignored.

mounthost=*n* Name of the computer on which the mount daemon is running.

mountport=*n* Port number of the mount daemon.

mountprog=*n* A different RPC program is to be used. Default is 100005, the normal RPC mounted number.

mountvers=*n* The mount daemon is presented this number as RPC version.

namlen=*n* Requesting of file name lengths of the remote file system is only supported since version 2 of the RPC mount protocol. This indication is used as a specification for older servers.

nfsprog=*n* A different RPC program is to be used for linking to the remote NFS daemon.

nfsvers=*n* The NFS daemon of the remote computer is presented this number as RPC version.

port=*n* The number of the UDP port for connection with the NFS server. Default is the standard NFS port 2049.

retrans=*n* The number of minor timeouts and retransmissions before a major timeout is triggered. Default is 3. After this, the operation is aborted or the message 'server not responding' is displayed.

retry=*n* The number of times of a HUHU operation. Default is 10 000.

rsize=*n* The number of bytes the NFS uses when reading files from an NFS server. Default is 1024, but a better value would be 8192.

timeo=*n* The time in tenths of a second before data are retransmitted after the first RPC timeout. Default is seven tenths of a second. Each time another RPC timeout occurs, this time is doubled, until the maximum of 60 seconds or a major timeout is reached.

[no]ac The `noac` option prohibits buffering of attributes of files and directories. This leads to a higher workload for the server, but it is very important when several NFS clients actively write to a file system on the server at the same time. Default is `ac` with the values set by `acregmin`, `acregmax`, `acdirmin` and `acdirmax`.

[no]bg If mounting leads to a timeout, the `bg` option tries to continue mounting in the background. Default is `fg` or `nobg`.

|no|cto The nocto option prohibits the requesting of attributes after creating a file. Default is cto.

|no|fg If mounting leads to a timeout, the fg option displays an error message. Default is fg or nobg.

|no|hard If an NFS operation has a major timeout, the hard option displays the message 'server not responding' on the console and tries to continue the operation. This is the default.

|no|intr If an NFS operation has a major timeout and the file system has been mounted hard, the intr option allows the operation to be interrupted by signals. In this case, the error EINTR is returned to the calling program. The default is nointr, which means that interruption of NFS operations is not allowed.

|no|posix A file system mounted with the posix option behaves according to POSIX specifications. Default is noposix.

|no|soft If an NFS operation has a major timeout, the soft option returns an error to the calling program. The default nosoft or hard continues the NFS operation indefinitely, if necessary.

|no|tcp The TCP protocol is used for communication. The default is UDP.

|no|udp UDP is used for communication. Many NFS servers support only this protocol.

wsize=*n* The number of bytes the NFS uses when writing to files on an NFS server. The default is 1024, but 8192 would be a better value.

APPENDIX C

The *Proc* file system

The computer continued, brash and cheery
as if it was selling detergent.
'I want you to know that
whatever your problem,
I am here to help you solve it.'

Douglas Adams

This appendix describes the individual components of the *Proc* file system which in LINUX is normally mounted under /proc. Some system utilities, such as ps, rely on this; the path is hardcoded in the sources. The main task of the *Proc* file system is to provide, in a simple way, information about the kernel and processes. The sometimes cryptic *ioctl*-calls are circumvented and information is made as readable as possible. The single files and directories are mostly generated when reading actually takes place (system calls *read* and *readdir*) and therefore always contain the current state of the LINUX system.

The root directory of the *Proc* file system has the inode number 1 and each existing process possesses a subdirectory in it. In order to guarantee a unequivocal matching, the name of this subdirectory is the process ID itself. In this directory, we find the files containing the process-related information. In addition, the root directory contains the following subdirectories and files. The inode numbers of the individual files are defined as enumeration constants in the file <linux/proc_fs.h> and correspond to the specified order.

C.1 The /proc/ directory

- **loadavg**
  This file provides the values of average system load for the last 1, 5 and 15 minutes. These values are updated at each timer interrupt. In addition, the number of running processes, their total, and the PID

of the last active process are displayed. The kernel function used is
get_loadavg().

    0.14 0.12 0.05 2/57 242

● **uptime**
This file indicates the time in seconds since system start and the time
used by the idle process.

    501.05 344.11

● **meminfo**
This file contains the number of total, used and free bytes of main
memory and swap area. In addition, it contains the size of memory
shared by more than one processes together with the size of cache
memory, analogously to the `free` command, but indicating the sizes in
bytes instead of Kbytes.

```
          total:    used:    free:  shared: buffers:  cached:
Mem: 31698944 26775552  4923392 27287552  1056768 11337728
Swap: 35057664         0 35057664
MemTotal:     30956 kB
MemFree:       4808 kB
MemShared:    26648 kB
Buffers:       1032 kB
Cached:       11072 kB
SwapTotal:    34236 kB
SwapFree:     34236 kB
```

● **kmsg**
This file supplies the kernel messages that have not yet been read via the
syslog system call (*see* page 333). A side effect of reading this file is that
the messages read are removed from the log circular buffer. Thus, any
kernel message can be read only once. For this reason, the `kmsg` file
should not be read while the `syslogd` daemon is running.

● **version**
This file represents the kernel variable `linux_banner` and results, for
example, in an output of the form:

    Linux version 2.0.0 (root@murdock) (gcc version 2.7.2) #16 Fri
    Aug 23 18:00:50 MET DST 1996

● **cpuinfo**
This file contains the parameters of the processor recognized during
system boot (file `arch/i386/kernel/setup.c`).

    processor   : 0
    cpu   : 586   *CPU type*
    model   : Pentium 75+   *Model*

```
vendor_id       : GenuineIntel  Manufacturer
stepping        : 5
fdiv_bug        : no            Does it calculate properly?
hlt_bug         : no            Does it halt properly?
fpu             : yes           FPU unit present?
fpu_exception   : yes           Does exception 16 work?
cpuid           : yes           Does the cpiud instruction work?
wp              : yes           WP bit in supervisor mode?
flags           : fpu vme de pse tsc msr mce cx8
                                Additional flags?
bogomips        : 39.73         Bogomips value
```

- **pci**
  Here we find information about the occupation of the PCI slots. If the kernel has not been configured for PCI (CONFIG_PCI), this file is not present.

  ```
  PCI devices found:
    Bus  0, device   9, function  0:
      VGA compatible controller: S3 Inc. Vision 968 (rev 0).
        Medium devsel.  IRQ 12.
        Non-prefetchable 32 bit memory at 0xf2000000.
    Bus  0, device   7, function  1:
      IDE interface: Intel 82371 Triton PIIX (rev 2).
        Medium devsel.  Fast back-to-back capable.
        Master Capable.  Latency=32.  I/O at 0x3000.
    Bus  0, device   7, function  0:
      ISA bridge: Intel 82371 Triton PIIX (rev 2).
        Medium devsel.  Fast back-to-back capable.
        Master Capable.  No bursts.
    Bus  0, device   0, function  0:
      Host bridge: Intel 82437 (rev 2).
        Medium devsel.  Master Capable.  Latency=32.
  ```

- **self/**
  This directory contains information about the process accessing the *Proc* file system. It is identical to the directory that bears the process's PID. For more detailed information refer to Section C.3.

- **net/**
  This directory contains some files that describe the Linux network layer. For more detailed information refer to Section C.2 and Chapter 8.

- **scsi**
  This directory contains the files (beginning with inode number 256) that contain information on the individual devices. If the kernel has not been configured for SCSI, this directory is empty.

- **malloc**

  This file allows monitoring of the kmalloc() and kfree() operations. If CONFIG_DEBUG_MALLOC has not been configured, this file does not exist.

- **kcore**

  The kcore file provides a core dump of the kernel. This allows debugging of the kernel at run-time. The dump can be obtained via

  ```
  # gdb /usr/src/linux/vmlinux /proc/kcore
  ```

  The size of this file equals the size of main memory plus the page size.

- **modules**

  This file contains information about the single modules loaded, their size and their state. This file exists only if CONFIG_MODULES has been configured.

- **stat**

  This provides general Linux kernel statistics.[1]

cpu 7191 0 1542 341934	*Jiffies in user, nice, system mode and idle process*
disk 102 6118 4 0	*Number of disk requests*
disk_rio 102 3586 4 0	*Read accesses per disk*
disk_wio 0 2532 0 0	*Write accesses per disk*
disk_rblk 108 7146 8 0	*Read sectors per disk*
disk_wblk 0 5064 0 0	*Written sectors per disk*
page 19588 5865	*Memory pages mapped and deleted*
swap 1 0	*Swap pages mapped and deleted*
intr 421905 350667 23464 0 0 41434 0 2 0 0 92 0 0 0 1 6225 20	
	Sum and number of 16 hardware interrupts received
ctxt 244058	*Number of context switches*
btime 841823772	UNIX *boot time*
processes 473	

- **devices**

  This file contains information about registered device drivers. It may be used by the MAKEDEV script in order to achieve consistency in the /dev/ directory. The first column contains the major number of the device driver, followed in the second column by its name, that is, the name specified during registration of the device.

  ```
  Character devices:
   1 mem
   2 pty
   3 ttyp
   4 ttyp
   5 cua
  ```

---

[1] With IDE devices, the indications *per disk* refer to the first four controllers; with SCSI devices they refer to the first four devices.

```
 7 vcs
14 sound

Block devices:
 2 fd
 3 ide0
22 ide1
```

- **interrupts**

  This file contains the number and names of hardware interrupts received. A plus sign in front of the name indicates a fast interrupt.

  ```
   0:    626851   timer
   1:     35551   keyboard
   2:         0   cascade
   4:     79959 + serial
   5:         0   SoundBlaster
   9:       131   NE2000
  13:         1   math error
  14:     55227 + ide0
  15:        24 + ide1
  ```

- **filesystems**

  This file contains the existing file system implementations of the LINUX kernel. The name of each file system that has been registered with the function `register_filesystem()` is output. If the file system does not need a device, the name is preceded by the string 'nodev'.

  ```
           ext2
           minix
           msdos
           vfat
  nodev    proc
  nodev    nfs
  nodev    smbfs
           iso9660
  ```

  Using this file, the `mount` program can try out all existing file system types when mounting a file system.

- **ksyms**

  This file contains all symbols exported by the kernel, which can then be used by modules. This file exists only if `CONFIG_MODULES` has been configured.

  ```
  00m1143dc register_symtab_from
  00108aa4 get_options
  001bd048 EISA_bus

      ...
  ```

- **dma**

  This file contains the DMA channels occupied. In the normal case, it contains

  ```
  1: SB16 (8bit)
  4: cascade
  5: SB16 (16bit)
  ```

- **ioports**

  This file contains the I/O ports occupied via `request_region()`.

  ```
    0000-001f : dma1
    0020-003f : pic1
    0040-005f : timer
    0060-006f : keyboard
  % 0080-009f : dma page reg
  % 00a0-00bf : pic2
  % 00c0-00df : dma2
    ...
  ```

- **smp**

  This file contains information on the individual CPUs in SMP systems. For this file, `SMP_PROF` must be configured.

- **cmdline**

  The command line passed to the kernel at startup.

  ```
  delay=700 BOOT_IMAGE=vmlinuz
  ```

- **sys/**

  This directory contains information controlling the most important algorithms of the kernel. For more details refer to Section C.4.

- **mtab**

  This file contains the list of currently mounted file systems.

  ```
  rootfs / ext2 rw 0 0
  /dev/hdb3 /usr ext2 rw 0 0
  none /proc proc rw 0 0
  /dev/hda1 /dos/c vfat rw 0 0
  /dev/hda5 /dos/d vfat rw 0 0
  /dev/hda6 /dos/e vfat rw 0 0
  /dev/hdb5 /dos/f vfat rw 0 0
  /dev/hdc /cdrom iso9660 ro 0 0
  ```

- **md**

  If *Multiple Device Driver Support* (`CONFIG_BLK_DEV_MD`) has been configured, this file contains statistics on usage.

- **rc**

  If *Enhanced Real Time Clock Support* (`CONFIG_RTC`) has been configured, this file contains the RTC values.

- **locks**
  This file contains the current file locks.

  ```
  1: BROKEN ADVISORY WRITE 72 03:42:8072 0 2147483647
  01f88d98 00000000 00000000 00000000 00000000
  1:
  ```

  Each line contains the number of the lock, its flag, its type, the PID of its owner, major and minor numbers of the device on which the file is located, together with the inode number and the start and end position of the lock. This is followed by the address of the lock itself, the previous and following list and the previous and following block. The second line contains the PIDs of the processes waiting for this lock.

C.2 The net/ directory

This directory contains some files that describe the state of the LINUX network layer. The files have inode numbers starting with 128. For more detailed information refer to Chapter 8.

The individual files are:

- **unix**
  Information about each opened UNIX domain socket, such as path, status, type, flags, protocol and reference counter.

  ```
  Num         RefCount Protocol Flags    Type St Inode Path
  00ecddfc: 00000002 00000000 00000000 0001 01  1015 /dev/log
  00ecda04: 00000002 00000000 00000000 0001 03  1014
  ```

- **arp**
  Displays the content of the ARP table in readable form.

IP address	HW type	Flags	HW address	Mask
141.20.22.210	0x1	0x2	08:00:5A:C7:10:24	*
141.20.22.203	0x1	0x2	00:00:C0:1B:E2:1B	*
141.20.22.204	0x1	0x2	00:00:C0:34:DE:24	*

- **route**
  This file contains the routing table in an unusual form. The route program obtains its information from this file.

Iface	Destination	Gateway	Flags	RefCnt	Use	Metric	Mask	MTU	Win	IRTT
eth0	C01D148D	00000000	01	0	0	0	C0FFFFFF	1500	0	0
lo	0000007F	00000000	01	0	2	0	000000FF	3584	0	0
eth0	00000000	C11D148D	03	0	0	1	00000000	1500	0	0

- **dev**

  This file contains the available network devices, together with their statistics.

  ```
  Inter-|   Receive                           |  Transmit
   face |packets errs drop fifo frame|packets errs drop fifo colls carrier
     lo: 30690    0    0    0    0     30690    0    0    0     0    0
    eth0:    73    0    0    0    0         0    0    0    0     0    0
  ```

- **raw**

  Information about opened RAW sockets.

- **tcp**

  Information about TCP sockets.

- **udp**

  Information about UDP sockets.

- **snmp**

  This file contains the MIBs (*Management Information Bases*) for the SNMP protocol.

- **sockstat**

  This file displays the statistics about the sockets.

  ```
  sockets: used 104
          SOCK_ARRAY_SIZE=256
          TCP: inuse 55 highest 55
          UDP: inuse 12 highest 13
          RAW: inuse 1 highest 1
          PAC: inuse 0 highest 0
  ```

In addition, the net/ directory can contain the following files, depending on the configuration of the kernel:

```
alias_types, aliases, at_route, atalk, atif, ax25,
ax25_bpqether, ax25_calls, ax25_route, igmp, ip_masq_app,
ipacct, ipfwfwd, ipfwin, ipfwout, ipmr_mfc, ipmr_vif,
ipmsqhst, ipx, ipx_interface, ipx_route, last, nr,
nr_neigh, nr_nodes, rarp, rtcache wavelan
```

C.3 The self/ directory

The process directories and the self/ directory have the following structure, in which the respective inodes have the value *PID* << 16 + *specified value*.

- **status [+3]**

  This file contains the characteristics of a process (in short form).

```
Name:    xman                          Command name
State:   S (sleeping)                  Process state
Pid:     120                           Its PID
PPid:    108                           Its PPID
Uid:     15216   15216   15216   15216 Its [ESF]UID
Gid:     15200   15200   15200   15200 Its [ESF]GID
VmSize:    2296 kB                     Size of VM areas
VmLck:        0 kB                     Locked VM areas
VmRSS:      308 kB                     RSS size
VmData:     500 kB                     Data segment (without Stack)
VmStk:       24 kB                     Stack segment
VmExe:       40 kB                     Loaded program
VmLib:     1620 kB                     Loaded libraries
SigPnd: 00000000                       Pending signals
SigBlk: 00000000                       Mask of blocked signals
SigIgn: 80000000                       Mask of ignored signals
SigCgt: 00000000                       Mask of signals with
                                       handling routine
```

- **mem [+4]**

While the device /dev/mem represents the physical memory before address conversion, this mem file represents the linear address space of the corresponding process.

It is generally not possible to write to this file, because owing to the lack of tests, it would be possible to write to the LINUX kernel itself. It is, however, possible to enable writing by removing the macro definition of mem_write in the file fs/proc/mem.c.

- **cwd [+5]**

This is a link to the current directory of the process.

- **root [+6]**

Through this link, the root directory of the process can be reached (*see also chroot* on page 344).

- **exe [+7]**

This is a link to the executable file.

- **fd/ [+8]**

In this directory we find an entry with the name of the file descriptor for each file opened by the process.

As both standard input (0) and standard output (1) are located here, programs which, for example, do not want to read from the standard input, can be persuaded to do so by making them read from the file /proc/self/fd/0.

This can, however, lead to problems, because no seeking is possible in the files of this directory.

- **environ [+9]**

  This file contains the current environment of the process. The individual entries are separated by a NULL byte. If the whole process is swapped out or if it is a zombie, the file is empty.

- **cmdline [+10]**

  Analogously to the environ file, this file contains the process's command line.

- **stat [+11]**

  This file provides more detailed information about the process, for example:

  ```
  120 (xman) S 108 108 89 1028 104 1048576 111 0 562 0 46 19
  0 0 0 0 -1 0 3838 2351104 77 2147483647 134217728 134257999
  3221223916 3221223432 1075085259 0 0 2147483648 0 1228420
  113 0
  ```

  The file lists in order the individual values of the process's task structure, thus providing the user with a complete state description of the process.

  As the single entries are generally evaluated in programs (*see* ps in Appendix B.2) they are listed in scanf() format. If an entry is the value of a component of the task structure, the name of the component is added in parentheses.

  The individual entries of the file are:

%d	the process ID (pid),
(%s)	the name of the executable file in parentheses (comm; also visible when the process is swapped out),
%c	the process state (state; 'R' for *running*, 'S' for *interruptible sleeping or swapping*, 'D' for *uninterruptible sleeping* or *swapping*, 'Z' for *zombie*, 'T' for *traced* or *stopped*, and 'W' for *swapped*),
%d	the PID of the parent process (p_pptr->pid),
%d	the process group (pgrp),
%d	the SID of the process (session),
%d	the terminal used by the process (kdev_t_to_nr()),
%d	the process group owned by the terminal used by the process,
%lu	the flags of the process (flags),
%lu	the number of minor faults[2] (min_flt) incurred by the process,
%lu	the number of minor faults (cmin_flt) incurred by the process and its children,

---

[2] A *minor fault* is an error in accessing memory pages which is handled without accessing external media. A *major fault*, on the other hand, must be dealt with by accessing external media.

%lu	the number of major faults[2] (`maj_flt`) incurred by the process,
%lu	the number of major faults (`cmaj_flt`) incurred by the process and its children,
%ld	the number of jiffies (`utime`) the process spent in user mode,
%ld	the number of jiffies (`stime`) spent in kernel mode,
%ld	the number of jiffies (`cutime`) the process and its children spent in user mode,
%ld	the number of jiffies (`cstime`) spent by the process and its children in kernel mode,
%ld	the maximum number of jiffies (`counter`) the process can run in a time slice,
%ld	the UNIX `nice` value (`priority`) used to calculate a new value for `counter`,
%lu	the value in jiffies before triggering a timeout (`timeout`),
%lu	the value of the interval timer (`it_real_value`),
%ld	the start time of the process (`start_time`) in jiffies since system start,
%u	the size in bytes of the memory accessible to the process,
%u	the number (`rss`) of pages of the process currently in physical memory,
%u	the maximum number (`rlim[RLIMIT_RSS].rlim_cur`) of memory pages for the process which may be simultaneously present in memory,
%lu	the start address (`start_code`) of the text segment,
%lu	the end address (`end_code`) of the text segment,
%lu	the start address (`start_stack`) of the stack,
%lu	the current stack pointer[3] of the process,
%lu	the current instruction pointer[3] of the process,
%lu	the signal vector[4] (`signal`) of the received signals,
%lu	the signal vector (`blocked`) of the blocked signals,
%lu	the signal vector of the ignored signals,
%lu	the signal vector of the signals equipped with handling routines,
%lu	the address of the kernel function the process is in,

---

[3] During determination of parameters the process is in kernel mode, so that the current values ESP and EIP are also calculated and point to the user segment. As EIP, one usually gets an address in the C library.

[4] The signal vector is a 32-bit number, in which each signal is represented by one bit.

%lu   the number of swap operations (nswap),

%lu   the number of swap operations of the children (cnswap).

- **statm [+12]**

  Here, the memory information of the process is stored. Determining these values takes some time, therefore they are not included in the stat file.

  ```
  220 143 60 4 0 139 12
  ```

  %d   the total number of memory pages used (*size*),

  %d   the number of memory pages (*resident*) currently in physical memory,

  %d   the number of memory pages (*share*) the process shares with other processes,

  %d   the number of text pages (*trs*) currently in physical memory,

  %d   the number of library pages (*lrs*) currently in physical memory,

  %d   the number of data pages (*drs*) including written library pages and the stack, currently in physical memory, and

  %d   the number of library pages (*dt*) that have been accessed.

- **maps [+15]**

  Here, we find information about the virtual address areas (*see also* vm_area structures in Section 4.2.2) of the process. For each virtual address area, the following are specified: start and end address, access rights and offset in the mapped file, identified by the major and minor number of the device together with the inode number. The access rights are indicated in the usual UNIX notation (rwxsp), where additional flags indicate whether the area is shared (s) or private (p). If a virtual memory area is mapped anonymously, the inode number is zero.

  ```
  08000000-0800a000 r-xp 00000000 03:43 28884
  0800a000-0800c000 rw-p 00009000 03:43 28884
  0800c000-08050000 rwxp 00000000 00:00 0
  40000000-40005000 r-xp 00000000 03:42 29
  40005000-40006000 rw-p 00004000 03:42 29
  40006000-40007000 rw-p 00000000 00:00 0
  40008000-4003b000 r-xp 00000000 03:43 20732
  ```

C.4   The sys/ directory

The subdirectories located in this directory allow reading of information relevant to the system. This information is held in internal tables and mapped to /proc/sys.

- **kernel/**
  This directory contains information on the kernel and its control structures. The inode numbers start with 4096.

  - **domainname**
    Domain name of the system.

  - **filemax**
    Maximum number of simultaneously open files.

  - **filenr**
    Current number of open files.

  - **hostname**
    Computer name.

  - **inodemax**
    Maximum number of simultaneously open inodes.

  - **inodenr**
    Current number of open inodes.

  - **osrelease**
    Kernel version.

  - **ostype**
    Name of operating system.

  - **panic**
    Timeout after a `panic` message.

  - **securelevel**
    Security level.

  - **version**
    Compiler information during kernel compilation.

- **net/**
  Depending on the network configuration, this directory may contain the most disparate subdirectories and files. There is one subdirectory for each network subsystem (corresponds to a device).

- **vm/**
  This directory does not contain data on the current memory occupation, but control parameters of processes responsible for memory management.

  - **bdflush**
    Control parameters of the `bd_flush()` process.

  - **freepages**
    Values of free-page levels.

  - **kswapd**
    Control parameters of the kswap daemon.

  - **swapctl**
    Control parameters of the swap process.

APPENDIX D

The boot process

To reboot the computer is faster
than first trying a brilliant stunt
after which you have to switch it off
and then back on again.

Murphy's Computer Laws

Proper starting up of the LINUX kernel has already been described in Chapters 2 and 3. There are, however, several different methods of making the kernel start. The simplest one is to write the complete kernel to a floppy disk, starting with sector 0, using the command

```
# dd if=zImage of=/dev/fd0
```

and then boot from that floppy disk. A much more elegant way of booting LINUX is via the LINUX Loader (LILO).

D.1 Carrying out the boot process

In a PC, booting is carried out by the BIOS. Once the Power-On Self Test (POST) is terminated, the BIOS tries to read the first sector of the first floppy disk: the boot sector. If this fails, the BIOS tries to read the boot sector from the first hard disk. More recent BIOS versions can invert this sequence and boot directly from the hard disk. As most BIOS systems do not have a SCSI support, SCSI adaptors must provide their own BIOS if SCSI disks are used for booting. If no valid boot sector can be found, the 'original' PC starts its built-in ROM-BASIC, or a message appears saying 'NO ROM-BASIC'.

The booting of an operating system generally then proceeds in several steps. As there is not much room for code in the boot sector, this normally

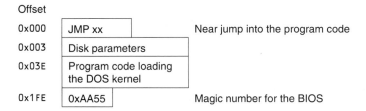

Figure D.1   The MS-DOS boot sector.

loads a second loader, and so on, until the actual operating system kernel is completely loaded.

As Figure D.1 shows, the structure of a boot sector is relatively simple; its length is always 512 bytes (so that it can be stored on either a floppy disk or a hard disk).

In this, the disk parameters are significant only for MS-DOS. It is important that the code starts at offset 0 and that the boot sector is terminated by the *magic number*.

Booting from floppy disk is now relatively simple, because each floppy disk has exactly one boot sector: the first sector. This is followed by arbitrary data. Booting from a hard disk is slightly more difficult, because it is divided into partitions. The BIOS, however, knows nothing about this; it therefore loads, as it would do with a floppy disk, the first sector, which is called the *master boot record* (MBR).

The MBR must therefore have the same structure, that is, the code starts at offset 0, the magic number 0xAA55 is found at offset 0x1FE. At the end of the MBR, the partition table is stored. This always has four entries, as shown in Figure D.2. A partition table entry consists of 16 bytes and is structured as shown in Figure D.3.

A hard disk can thus be divided into four partitions: these are called *primary partitions*. Should they not suffice, a so-called *extended partition* can be set up. This, in turn, contains at least one *logical drive*. As there evidently have been no plans to introduce any further structure at this point, the structure of the first sector of an extended partition corresponds to that of the MBR. The first partition entry of this extended partition table contains the first logical drive of the partition. The second entry is used as a pointer, if further logical drives exist. It points behind the first logical drive, where there is again a partition table with an entry for the next logical drive. The single entries of the logical drives are thus chained in a linked list: theoretically, an extended partition could contain an arbitrary number of logical drives.

The first sector of each primary or extended partition contains a boot sector with the structure described above. As booting can only be carried out from one of these partitions, the boot flag determines the *active partition*.

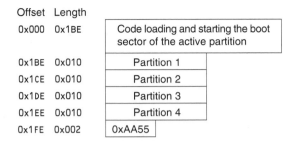

Figure D.2   The structure of the master boot record and the extended partition table.

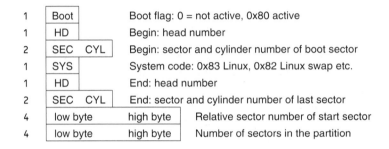

Figure D.3   Structure of a partition entry.

Originally, there were only primary partitions: therefore, fdisk under MS-DOS and most of the equivalent programs can only activate those partitions. The code in the MBR must thus only carry out the following operations:

- determine the active partition,
- load the boot sector of the active partition, using the BIOS,
- jump into the boot sector at offset 0.

The number of bytes in the MBR is more than sufficient to do this. Because, as described above, each partition in principle contains a boot sector, and furthermore, the structure of any second hard disk which may be present is similar to that of the first disk, a multitude of replacements for the standard MS-DOS MBR have come about: so-called *boot managers*. They all have in common the fact that they either substitute the MBR with their own code or occupy the boot sector of an active partition. To boot LINUX, most will use the LINUX loader LILO.

D.2   LILO – the LINUX loader

The LILO boot sector contains room for one partition table. Therefore, LILO can be installed both in a partition and in the MBR. LILO possesses the full functionality of the standard MS-DOS boot sector but, in addition, it can boot logical drives or partitions on the second hard disk. LILO can also be used in combination with another boot manager, which makes a large number of installation variants available.

D.2.1   LILO started by MS-DOS MBR

If there is at least one primary LINUX partition[1] on the first hard disk, LILO can be installed there. After this partition is activated, the boot process proceeds as follows:

- the BIOS loads the MBR,
- the MBR loads the boot sector of the active partition: the LILO boot sector,
- the loader boots LINUX or another operating system.

A deinstallation is also very simple: another partition is activated. As outside the LINUX partition no data (except the boot flag) is altered, this is the 'safest' variant.

D.2.2   LILO started by a boot manager

This approach is recommended if one does not want to renounce one's old boot manager or LILO is incapable of booting a foreign operating system. Depending on the capabilities of the boot manager, there are some more 'places' for a LILO installation:

- If the boot manager can boot extended partitions, these are an ideal place for LILO.
- If the boot manager can boot partitions on the second disk, LILO can be installed in one of these.
- Some boot managers can even boot logical drives, in which case LILO could be installed in one of those.

However, the following should be observed:

---

[1] Not a swap partition, as in this the first sector is used as well!

- The installation programs of several operating systems[2] write their own MBR to disk without checking; this might destroy the other boot manager.
- Repartitioning could destroy the boot sector of the extended partition, in which case LILO would have to be reinstalled.

A deinstallation strongly depends on the boot manager used: either the LILO boot partition used must be unregistered, or the boot manager itself offers to boot each existing partition. Then, repartitioning or formatting of partitions removes both LINUX and LILO.

D.2.3   LILO in the master boot record

If all of LINUX is on the second hard disk and there is no extended partition on the first one, then LILO must be installed in the MBR. This overwrites the existing MBR. Therefore, before beginning such an installation, one should make a backup of the old MBR (which also contains the partition table). Various DOS utilities will serve this purpose. Under LINUX, a backup is easily made by:

```
# dd if=/dev/hda of=/backup/MBR bs=512 count=1
```

Using

```
# dd if=/backup/MBR of=/dev/hda bs=446 count=1
```

the MBR is written back without the partition table. If the old partition table is also to be restored, the parameter to substitute is bs=512. But beware! In doing this, the new partition table can be easily destroyed.

D.2.4   LILO files

The LILO files are normally located in the /boot/[3] directory, the configuration file lilo.conf in /etc/. The map file contains the actual information needed to boot the kernel and is created by the map installer /sbin/lilo. For any LILO installation, the configuration file must be adapted to personal requirements.

The configuration file

In principle, the configuration file consists of variable assignments. Each line contains either a flag variable or a variable assignment. Flag variables are

---

[2] Inglorious examples for this are the installations of some versions of MS-DOS.
[3] In older LILO versions also in /etc/lilo/.

simple denominators, variable assignments consist of the name of the variable, followed by an equals-sign and the value of the variable. In addition, the configuration file is subdivided, using special variable assignments, into boot configurations, each of which boots either a kernel or another operating system. The following variables are global for all LILO configurations:

boot=*device* indicates which device (or which disk partition) shall contain the boot sector. If `boot` is not present, the boot sector is put on the current root device.

compact activates a mode in which LILO tries to carry out read requests for neighbouring sectors by means of one single request to the BIOS. This reduces loading times drastically, above all when booting from a floppy disk.

delay=*tenths* indicates the time in tenths of a second that LILO waits for a key to be pressed before the first boot configuration is booted. If `delay` is not specified, LILO boots immediately.

linear causes LILO to generate linear addresses instead of the usual sector/head/cylinder addresses. Linear addresses do not depend on the geometry of the device.

install=*boot sector* installs the indicated boot sector instead of the standard boot sector `/boot/boot.b`.

disktab=*disktab* indicates the path of the disktab file (which contains the geometry data of special disks) if it is not in `/boot/disktab`.

map=*map file* specifies the path of the map file.

message=*file* indicates the path of a file whose contents should be displayed as a startup message during booting. If `message` is not specified, the message 'LILO' appears. As this startup message is inserted into the map file, the map installer `/sbin/lilo` must be started after each modification.

verbose=*level* specifies the *debug* level for LILO. Levels 0 (no messages) to 5 (all status messages) are allowed.

backup=*backup file* indicates the name of the file in which the previous boot sector is stored. Otherwise, `/boot/boot.`*device number* is chosen.

force-backup=*backup file* as `backup`, but the file is overwritten if it already exists.

prompt forces the input of a boot configuration via the keyboard, which means that LILO no longer boots the first configuration specified.

timeout=*tenths* sets a timeout value, within which keyboard input must have taken place, otherwise the first configuration is booted. Analogously, the input of a password becomes invalid if too much time passes between two inputs. By default, this value is infinite.

serial=*port, bps parity bits* sets the parameters for the serial interface, if LILO is to accept input via this. If one of the components *bps*, *parity* or *bits* is omitted, the subsequent parameters must also be omitted. *Port* selects one of the four (standard) serial interfaces: 0 corresponds to COM1 or /dev/ttyS0. Supported baud rates range from 100 to 9600; the default setting is 2400. All parity settings (n none, e even, o odd) are supported, as well as 7 or 8 bits. The default setting is serial=0,2400n8.

ignore-table instructs LILO to ignore corrupt partition tables.

fix-table allows LILO to adapt the (sector/head/cylinder) addresses to linear addresses in each partition. Normally, a partition starts at a cylinder boundary; some other operating systems might, however, change this. As LILO can write its boot sector only on partitions in which both addresses are the same, incorrect 3D addresses can be corrected with fix-table. This does, however, not guarantee that these corrections are permanent; therefore, a repartitioning that keeps to cylinder boundaries is preferable.

password=*password* sets a password for all boot configurations.

restricted loosens the password restriction. Passwords have to be given only if one wants to pass additional boot parameters to the kernel.

optional allows one of the kernels indicated in a boot configuration to be missing. If optional is not specified, the map installer aborts with an error message.

Each boot configuration for a LINUX kernel begins with the assignments

```
image=kernel
    label=name
```

where image must contain the path of the kernel to be booted, and label the name with which the kernel can be selected at the LILO prompt. If image is specified as a device, such as /dev/fd0, the range in which the kernel can be found has to be indicated using

```
range=range
```

The range must be specified either as *start sector – end sector* or *start sector + length*, for example

```
image=/dev/fd0
    label=floppy
    range=1+512
```

Variable assignments within a boot configuration have a kind of local effect. The following assignments are possible:

append=*string*   passes the kernel the string *string* as a boot parameter. This allows, for example, hardware parameters to be passed to LINUX device drivers (*see* Section 7.4.1).

literal=*string*   as append, but the string is passed exclusively. As this might lead to the loss of vital settings, literal cannot be specified globally.

ramdisk=*size*   overwrites the kernel's default setting for the size of the RAM disk.

read-only   specifies the root file system to be mounted read only.

read-write   analogous.

root=*device*   specifies the name of the device on which the root file system is to be found.

vga=*mode*   overwrites the kernel's default screen setting. Possible modes are normal, extended and ask. In addition, the number of the screen mode can be specified.

Boot configurations of other operating systems initiate with

    other=*device*
        label=*name*

where other describes the device (or the partition) on which the boot sector of the foreign operating system is to be found. The following variables can be set for foreign operating systems:

loader=*loader*   specifies the path to be used for booting the operating system. The default is /boot/chain.b. In addition, the LILO distribution contains the following loaders:

os2_d.b can boot OS/2 from the second hard disk.

any_d.b attempts, before booting the operating system, to invert the first and second hard disk in order to boot operating systems located on the second hard disk.

table=*device*   specifies the device on which the partition table for the operating system to be booted can be found. If table is not specified, LILO does not pass information about the partition table to the boot sector of the foreign operating system.

unsafe   switches off the checking of the operating system to be booted. This switch should only be used when a configuration is to be booted from a floppy disk. Without this switch, the boot disk would have to be inserted into the disk drive every time the map installer starts running.

The disktab file

The disktab file contains information about the geometry of the device from which LILO is to boot. Normally, this information can be obtained from the device driver, so a disktab file is only needed if this does not work. In this case, LILO issues the error message

```
geo_query_dev HDIO_GETGEO (dev ...)
```

or

```
HDIO_REQ not supported for your SCSI controller.
Please use /boot/disktab
```

and the geometry data must be input manually.

```
# /boot/disktab - LILO parameter table
#
# This table contains the geometry parameters for SCSI and
# IDE disks, which cannot be recognized automatically.
# Entries in this table overwrite recognized parameters!
#
# Dev.   BIOS   Secs/   Heads/   Cylin-  Part.
# num.   code   track   cylin.   ders    offset
#                                        (optional)

#0x800  0x80   32      64       202     0       # /dev/sda
```

The fields have the following meaning:

0x800   The device number as combination of the major and minor numbers.

0x80   The BIOS code for the drive. 0x80 is the first hard disk in the system, 0x81 the second, and so on. The whole physical device, not single partitions, is considered as one unit!

32, 64, 202   The geometry data: number of sectors per track, number of heads and number of cylinders.

0   The start of the partitions in relative sectors beginning with sector 0 of the hard disk. As this information can also be read from the partition table, this specification is optional.

D.2.5   LILO boot parameters

If during booting of LILO one of the keys Ctrl, Shift or Alt is pressed, if CapsLock or ScrollLock were set or the directive `prompt` indicated, LILO switches to interactive mode. To select a boot configuration, the name, defined as *label*, must be input. Pressing the Tab key shows all available boot configurations. In addition, as with the start of a program from the shell, parameters can be passed. The combination of these parameters yields a command line which LILO passes to the kernel at start-up. Some of the parameters are used by the kernel and the device drivers. Later on, parameters containing an equals sign '=' are inserted into the environment of the init program; the others are passed on as parameters.

The following boot parameters are recognized by the kernel and/or the init program:

root=*device*

ro and **rw**   mount the root file system explicitly read-only or read/write.

debug   all kernel messages are output to the system console.

no–hlt   tells the kernel that the CPU instruction `HLT` should not be used. This is important for some processors in which this instruction is not implemented correctly.

no387   switches the FPU off and the FPU emulator on.

vga=*screen mode*   selects the kernel's default screen mode.

single   tells the init program that LINUX is to be started in single user mode.

reserve=*port address, range, ...*   prohibits hardware recognition on the I/O addresses from *port address* to *port address + range*. Normally, hardware is recognized by the drivers via the writing and reading of magic values on port addresses. This can, with hardware that by chance occupies the same ports, lead to anything from undefined behaviour to a complete system crash.[4] Thus, `reserve=0x300,8` prohibits the kernel from searching for hardware on these addresses (*see* Section 7.3.1).

ether=*IRQ, port, mem_start, mem_end, name*   sets the base address, IRQ and the mapped memory area for the network device *name*.

    ether=5, 0x280, 0xD800, 0xDFFF, eth0

sets the parameters of the first Ethernet board to IRQ 5, base port 0x280, mapped memory area from 0xD800 to 0xDFFF.

---

[4] Especially in ISA architecture, in which only 10 bits of the port address lie on the bus, this can lead to 'unwanted' overlaps. This is also the reason why S3 boards apparently occupy the port address of the fourth serial port ...

bmouse=_IRQ_   sets the IRQ channel for the Logitech MouseMan Bus Mouse.

hd=_cylinders, heads, sectors_   sets the parameters of the IDE hard disk. The parameters for the second disk must be passed via a second hd=..., for example

```
hd=721,13,51 hd=1010,12,55
```

xd=_type, IRQ, port, DMA_   sets the base port address, IRQ and DMA channel, together with the identification number, of the XT hard disk controller. Supported types can be found in the field xd_sigs[]. This field is defined in the file drivers/block/xd.c.

mcd=_port, IRQ_   sets the base port address and the IRQ channel used for the Mitsumi CD-ROM driver.

sound=_0xKPPPID, ..._   tells the sound board driver the kind and parameters of all installed sound cards. A sound card parameter is a seven digit hexadecimal number, where _K_ is the sound card identification number, as defined in <linux/soundcard.h>. _PPP_ determines the base port address of the sound card, _I_ the IRQ and _D_ the DMA channel. If more than one sound card is installed, the single entries must be separated by commas.

Thus, sound=0x222051,0x138800 defines a SoundBlaster on base address 0x220, IRQ 5, DMA 1, and an Adlib card on default address 0x388.

sbpcd=_port, interface_   sets the parameters for the SoundBlaster CD-ROM driver, where _port_ defines the base port address and _interface_ one of the interface cards supported (SoundBlaster or LaserMate).

The following boot parameters are intended for the single SCSI controllers; they set the controller type (via its name), together with its parameters (start address of mapped memory area and IRQ used).

st0x=_address, IRQ_   Seagate controller

tmc8xx=_address, IRQ_   TMC-8xx or TMC-950 controller

t128=_address, IRQ_   Trantor T128/T128F/T228

ncr5380=_address, IRQ_   generic NCR5380

aha152x=_port, IRQ, SCSI-ID, reconnect_   Adaptec AHA-1520/1522 parameters: base port address, IRQ, SCSI-ID of the AIC-6260 (0-7, default 7), together with a flag that specifies whether the reconnection mode of a SCSI disk is to be used.

Furthermore, LILO always adds the parameter BOOT_IMAGE=_label_ to the command line, together with the word auto, if the first boot configuration was booted automatically.

Passing the command line to the kernel is very straightforward. LILO writes the magic number 0xA33F to the physical address 0x9000:20 and the offset of the command line's address relative to 0x9000:0 to the address 0x9000:22.

D.2.6 LILO start-up messages

During the boot process, the loader issues the message 'LILO'. If the loading process was aborted, the characters output up to that moment can serve to diagnose the error. Some of these error messages should, however, not occur because they can only be caused by destroying LILO or by a faulty BIOS.

no message   No part of LILO has been loaded. LILO has not been installed or the partition containing LILO is not active.

Lnumber   The first step of the loader has been loaded and started up, but the second step could not be loaded. The two digit error number characterizes the problem (*see* Section D.2.7). This may be caused by a physical fault on the hard disk or an incorrect geometry (wrong parameters in disktab).

LI   The first step of the loader has been able to load the second step, whose processing then failed. This can be caused by an incorrect geometry or by repositioning the file boot.b without reinstalling the loader.

LIL   The second step of the loader has been started, but cannot read the descriptor tables from the map file. This indicates a physical defect or an incorrect geometry.

LIL?   The second step of the loader has been loaded to an incorrect address. This behaviour has the same reasons as LI.

LIL-   The descriptor table is faulty. This indicates an incorrect geometry or a repositioning of the map file without reinstalling the loader.

LILO   All parts of the loader were loaded.

D.2.7 Error messages

If the BIOS signals an error while LILO loads the kernel, the error number is displayed.

0x00 *Internal error*
    This error is generated by the read sector routine, when an internal inconsistency is detected. The probable cause of the error is an incorrect map file.

0x01 *Illegal instruction*
    This error message should not occur.

0x02 *Address label not found*
An error occurred while reading the media.

0x03 *Disk is write protected*
This error message should not occur.

0x04 *Sector not found*
This error is caused by incorrect geometry data. If the boot disk is a SCSI disk, the kernel does not recognize the geometry data or the disktab file is faulty. In rare cases, this error is also generated by the compact flag.

0x06 *Change line active*
This error is normally caused by opening and closing the disk drive door during the boot process.

0x08 *DMA overflow*
This error message should not occur.

0x09 *DMA transfer exceeds 64K limit*
This error message should not occur.

0x0C *Invalid media*
This error message is caused by defective media. It should not occur, however.

0x10 *CRC error*
The data on the media are faulty. A reinstallation of LILO might help (to rewrite the sector). If this error occurs when booting from a hard disk, its bad sector list should be updated by running fsck.

0x20 *Controller error*
This error message should not occur.

0x40 *Seek error*
This error message indicates a media problem.

0x80 *Timeout*
The disk drive is not ready. The drive door might be open.

Generally, especially when booting from a floppy disk drive, it is a good idea to repeat the boot process, if no other possible cause for the error has been explicitly indicated.

APPENDIX E

Useful kernel functions

Experience is like lead shot in your behind;
one who has never been shot
doubts that such a thing exists at all.

Hans Lippmann

There are some tasks in kernel programming that have to be carried out repeatedly. Unfortunately, in the LINUX kernel we cannot use the convenient C library that offers solutions to these tasks. There is nevertheless a plethora of functions in the LINUX kernel that facilitate developers' work.

We shall take a closer look at these functions here, in order to avoid re-implementations in future development work on the LINUX kernel. The knowledge of these functions also helps with reading and understanding the kernel sources. Many of these functions have been presented in previous chapters and are, therefore, just briefly mentioned.

Kernel function	close()	dup()	execve()
	exit()	open()	setsid()
	wait()	write()	

The kernel also provides a range of functions known as system calls. These can be used (with the known functionality) in the kernel and work via the syscall macro.

Kernel function	set_bit()	clear_bit()
	change_bit()	test_bit()
	find_first_zero_bit()	find_next_zero_bit()
	ffz()}	

These functions are programmed as inline functions in the file `<asm/bitops.h>`. Depending on the architecture, they are assembler or C functions. They provide elementary bit operations. Bit 0 is the lowest bit of `addr`, bit 32[1] the lowest bit of `addr+1`.

```
inline int set_bit(int nr, void * addr);
inline int clear_bit(int nr, void * addr);
inline int change_bit(int nr, void * addr);
inline int test_bit(int nr, void * addr);
```

The `set_bit()` function sets bit `nr` at address `addr`. The function `clear_bit()` deletes bit `nr` at address `addr` and `change_bit()` inverts it. The function `test_bit()` simply tests whether the bit is set or not. If bit `nr` previously had the value 0, the functions return 0, otherwise they return a non-zero value.

```
inline int find_first_zero_bit(void * addr, unsigned size);
inline int find_next_zero_bit (void * addr, int size, int offset);
inline unsigned long ffz(unsigned long word);
```

The `find_first_zero_bit()` function searches a range for a zero bit. The range starts with address `addr` and is `size` bits long. The function `find_next_zero_bit()`, on the other hand, searches the range starting from an offset `offset`. The function `ffz()` searches for the first free bit in the value `word` and returns its position. The behaviour of the function is undefined when the value does not contain a zero bit.[2] This must therefore be tested beforehand. All three functions return the position of the bit found.

Kernel function	iget()	iput()
	namei()	lnamei()

The four functions allow access to a certain inode structure.

```
inline struct inode * iget(struct super_block * sb, int nr);
void iput(struct inode * inode);

int namei(const char * pathname, struct inode ** res_inode);
int lnamei(const char * pathname, struct inode ** res_inode);
```

The `namei()` function splits up the path name passed as an argument and stores the address of the inode belonging to the file `pathname` in `res_inode`. The

---

[1] This obviously holds only for 32-bit architectures.
[2] The i386 version returns 0.

function ʟnameiⁿ differs from nameiⁿ insofar as ʟnameiⁿ does not solve symbolic links and therefore returns the inode of the link.

Both functions use igetⁿ and iputⁿ. The first returns the inode described by the superblock sb and the inode number nr and, at the same time, updates the hash table (by incrementing the reference counter or re-entering the inode). The inodes obtained with igetⁿ must be released with iputⁿ. This function decrements the reference counter by one and releases the inode if the counter is 0.

Kernel function	sprintf()
	vsprintf()

To store different data in a string, C uses the sprintf() function. As kernel programming has to be carried out independently from the C library, it is rather useful that the kernel sources provide such a function.

```
int sprintf(char * buf, const char *fmt, ...);
```

This function merely transforms its arguments into variable argument lists and calls vsprintf(). The return value is the number of characters written to buf. The function vsprintf() carries out the transformation itself.

```
int vsprintf(char *buf, const char *fmt, va_list args);
```

The string fmt contains two kinds of character: normal characters which are simply copied, and conversion instructions which trigger transformation and output of the following argument. Each conversion instruction begins with a percent sign and ends with a conversion sign. Between these, the following items can be placed in the specified order:

Control character   One or more characters in arbitrary order, which modify the conversion.

A space   If the first character is not a sign, a space is inserted.

–   The converted argument is output ranged left.

Numbers are output in one of several formats. If octal format is specified, the number is preceded by a 0; in hexadecimal format, it is preceded by 0x or 0X.

0   Numbers are filled up to the field width with leading zeros.

Number   Sets the minimum field width.

Dot (full stop)   Separates field width and precision.

Number   The precision. This establishes the maximum number of characters to be output from a string, or the number of digits to be output after a decimal point.

Letter   h indicates *short* arguments, l or L indicate *long* arguments.

The conversion characters are specified by the following list:

c   Type int. The character arg is output.

s   Type char *. The character string arg is output up to byte '\0' or the required precision.

p   Type void *. The address arg is output in hexadecimal format.

n   Type int. The argument arg is a pointer to an integer in which the number of characters output until now is stored.

o   Type int. The number arg is output in octal format (with no leading 0).

x   Type int. The number arg is output in hexadecimal format (in lower case letters and with no leading 0x).

X   Type int. The number arg is output in hexadecimal format (in upper case letters and with no leading 0X).

d, i   Type int. The number arg is output signed.

u   Type int. The number arg is output unsigned.

Finally, the string buf is terminated with a zero byte and the number of characters actually written to buf is returned.

Kernel function   printk()

No one who has ever written extensive pieces of software will deny the usefulness of control and debug messages. As LINUX has in the course of time also become such a piece, it obviously must not lack a function to provide these. To offer and enhance the possibilities of an ordinary printf(), the kernel provides the function printk().

```
int printk(const char *fmt, ...);
```

The printk() function is passed its parameters in the same way as printf(). In addition, the first position can be taken up by a macro that specifies the importance (called the 'level' in what follows) of the message. The following macros are available:

```
#define KERN_EMERG   "<0>" /* System no longer usable          */
#define KERN_ALERT   "<1>" /* Action to be terminated at once */
```

```
#define KERN_CRIT     "<2>" /* Critical condition          */
#define KERN_ERR      "<3>" /* Error                       */
#define KERN_WARNING "<4>" /* Warning                      */
#define KERN_NOTICE   "<5>" /* Normal, but noteworthy      */
#define KERN_INFO     "<6>" /* Information                 */
#define KERN_DEBUG    "<7>" /* Debug level                 */
```

If no level is specified, the KERN_INFO level is used by default. The level[3] can also be inserted directly into the message (as a character string).

Messages output with printk() are firstly stored in the log book, a 4-Kbyte storage area, and secondly, depending on their levels, written to the console.

```
#define LOG_BUF_LEN     4096
static char log_buf[LOG_BUF_LEN];

unsigned long log_size = 0;
static unsigned long log_start = 0;
static unsigned long logged_chars = 0;
```

The first variable describes the size of the log book; it can vary between 0 and LOG_BUF_LEN, the latter being the beginning of the current message. With an access to (log_start+log_size) & (LOG_BUF_LEN-1), we thus obtain the last position of the current entry. The total number of characters in the log book can be found in logged_chars.

In what follows, we describe how the function is processed. First of all, printk() saves the flags of the processor and blocks all interrupts. The string passed (and any parameters contained in it) are copied into a 1024-byte internal buffer. There is no overflow check, and a longish string can thus cause the kernel to crash. The first three characters are kept free for a level to be inserted later if required.

```
save_flags(flags);
cli();

va_start(args, fmt);
i = vsprintf(buf + 3, fmt, args);
                            /* hopefully i < sizeof(buf)-4 */
buf_end = buf + 3 + i;
va_end(args);
```

---

[3] Obviously, a higher level can also be entered. If 'debug' is present in the LILO boot parameters, the log level is set to 10.

Now the messages are output. If at call time no level was specified, KERN_INFO is at first inserted as the level.

```
for (p = buf + 3; p < buf_end; p++) {
    msg = p;
    if (msg_level < 0) {
        if ( p[0] != '<' || p[1] < '0' ||
            p[1] > '7' || p[2] != '>') {
                p -= 3;
                p[0] = '<';
                p[1] = DEFAULT_MESSAGE_LOGLEVEL - 1 + '0';
                p[2] = '>';
        } else
                msg += 3;
        msg_level = p[1] - '0';
    }
```

Now the message is written into the memory area allocated for this purpose in the kernel – the system's *log book*. This storage is defined as a circular buffer, writing restarts at the beginning when the size is exceeded.

```
for (; p < buf_end; p++) {
    log_buf[(log_start+log_size) & (LOG_BUF_LEN-1)] = *p;

    if (log_size < LOG_BUF_LEN)
        log_size++;
    else {
        log_start++;
        log_start &= LOG_BUF_LEN-1;
    }
    logged_chars++;
    if (*p == '\\n')
        break;
}
```

Of course, the number of characters written is also counted. If a printk() call contains several messages, separated by '\n', these are treated separately. Now the message is written to the console. Only messages that are sufficiently important (with a priority above the log level) are output. The log level can be changed with the system call *syslog* (*see* page 333). While p now points to the end of the current message, msg still points to the beginning.

```
if (msg_level < console_loglevel && console_print_proc) {
    char tmp = p[1];
```

```
            p[1] = '\\0';
            (*console_print_proc)(msg);
            p[1] = tmp;
        }
```

When the current message is finished, a new priority has to be determined.

```
            if (*p == '\\n') msg_level = -1;
        }
```

Finally, the flags are put back on the stack and all processes which are blocked by reading in an empty log book are woken up.

```
        restore_flags(flags); wake_up_interruptible(&log_wait);
        return i;
    }
```

The number of characters written into the log book is returned.

Kernel function   `panic()`

```
    NORET_TYPE void panic(const char * fmt, ...);
```

The `panic()` function is a `printk()` with the fixed priority `KERN_EMERG`. In addition, the kernel function `sys_sync()` is called, provided that the affected process is not the *swap task*. The call in the end jumps into an endless loop – and the computer can be booted again.

Kernel function   `memcpy()`   `bcopy()`   `memset()`
                   `memcmp()`   `memmove()`   `memscan()`

These functions handle storage areas. Normally these are areas consisting of character strings which are not terminated by a zero byte. None of the following functions checks for overflow conditions. Not without reason, these functions are similar to the string handling functions. Generally, the same algorithms are implemented, the difference being that an additional length indication is needed.

```
    void * memset(void * s, char c, size_t count);
```

The `memset()` function fills the area addressed by `s` of size `count` with the character `c`.

```
void * memcpy(void * dest, const void *src, size_t count);
char * bcopy(const char * src, char * dest, int count);
```

Both functions have the same effect: the area dest is filled with the first count characters of src.

```
void * memmove(void * dest, const void *src, size_t count);
```

This function copies count characters of the area src into the area dest. It is, however, somewhat more intelligent than the previous function. It checks whether the copying could overwrite the source (source address plus count is higher than target address), then starts copying at the end of the area.

```
int memcmp(const void * cs, const void * ct, size_t count);
```

The function memcmp() compares two memory areas of maximum count characters. The return value is a number greater than, equal to or less than zero, depending on whether cs is lexicographically greater than, equal to or less than ct.

```
void * memscan(void * addr, unsigned char c, size_t size);
```

The function memscan() scans size characters in the area addr for the character c. It returns the address of c's first occurrence.

Kernel function	register_chrdev() unregister_chrdev()
	register_blkdev() unregister_blkdev()

```
int register_chrdev(unsigned int major, const char * name,
                struct file_o perations *fops);
int unregister_chrdev(unsigned int major, const char * name);
int register_blkdev(unsigned int major, const char * name,
                struct file_o perations *fops);
int unregister_blkdev(unsigned int major, const char * name);
```

Both register functions register a device driver in the kernel. The first registers a character device driver, the second a block device driver. The parameters are the same in both cases:

major – the desired major number of the device,

name – the symbolic name, for example, 'tty' or 'lp',

fops – the address of the file_operations structure.

The driver is entered into the corresponding table in the kernel, with its major number as an index. If the major number is 0, the last free entry is used and its index returned. If there is no free entry in the table or the major number is already occupied, the function returns −EBUSY.

The unregister functions terminate the driver's registration by writing NULL into the table.

Kernel function	`register_binfmt()` `unregister_binfmt()`
	`register_exec_domain()` `unregister_exec_domain()`
	`register_filesystem()` `unregister_filesystem()`

These functions register and unregister formats and file systems in the kernel. As opposed to device drivers, the number of these formats is arbitrary, because they are not managed in a table, but in lists. If an attempt is made to register the same format twice in the kernel, the function returns −EBUSY.

```
int register_binfmt(struct linux_binfmt * fmt);
int unregister_binfmt(struct linux_binfmt * fmt);
```

The register_binfmt() function registers a binary format in the kernel by entering it into the list of known formats. A binary format has the following structure:

```
struct linux_binfmt {
    struct linux_binfmt * next;
    int *use_count;
    int (*load_binary)
        (struct linux_binprm *, struct  pt_regs * regs);
    int (*load_shlib)(int fd);
    int (*core_dump)(long signr, struct pt_regs * regs);
};
```

The standard format of LINUX is the a.out format. A known binary format can be removed with unregister_binfmt().

```
int register_exec_domain(struct exec_domain *it);
int unregister_exec_domain(struct exec_domain *it);
```

The register_exec_domain() function registers a new *exec domain* in the kernel. A domain may be removed using unregister_exec_domain(). An exec domain has the following structure:

```
struct exec_domain {
   char *name;
   lcall7_func handler;
   unsigned char pers_low, pers_high;
   unsigned long * signal_map;
   unsigned long * signal_invmap;
   int *use_count;
   struct exec_domain *next;
};
```

```
int register_filesystem(struct file_system_type * fs);
int unregister_filesystem(struct file_system_type * fs);
```

These functions register and unregister a file system type in the kernel. The structure passed is as follows:

```
struct file_system_type {
   struct super_block *(*read_super)
      (struct super_block *, void *, int);
   char *name;
   int requires_dev;
   struct file_system_type * next;
};
```

Kernel function	register_serial()	unregister_serial()
	register_netdev()	unregister_netdev()

These functions register devices that are different from 'normal' UNIX devices.

```
int register_serial(struct serial_struct *req);
int unregister_serial(int line);
```

Normally, the number of serial devices of a computer is fixed and does not vary during operation. This function is only of interest to owners of a PCMCIA interface (laptop owners), as it is used to add a serial port at run-time. The structure is entered into the table rs_table[] and its index is returned. If no suitable port can be found in the table, the first free unknown port is occupied. Registration is terminated with unregister_serial(). The line parameter determines the port to be unregistered. If this is still connected to a terminal, it is closed (using tty_hangup()).

```
int register_netdev(struct device *dev);
void unregister_netdev(struct device *dev);
```

These functions register and unregister abstract network devices. Working with these functions is not easy, not least because of the size of the device structure. For a more precise description, refer to Section 8.3.

Kernel function   `tty_register_driver()`
                   `tty_unregister_driver()`

```
int tty_register_driver(struct tty_driver *driver);
int tty_unregister_driver(struct tty_driver *driver);
```

These functions register a new TTY driver in the kernel. When registering a driver, an internal call is made to `register_chrdev()`. In `driver`, we find the major number and its name; the standard TTY operations are entered as file operations. If the driver does not yet possess a function to output a single character, the registering function inserts one. The driver is unregistered with `tty_unregister_driver()`. If the driver is still in use, `-EBUSY` is returned.

Kernel function   `register_symtab()`

```
int register_symtab(struct symbol_table *intab);
```

This function adds a new section to the global symbol table. Two cases have to be distinguished. The function is called internally by the kernel and as yet no module is loaded. Then, a pseudo-module is generated internally and entered into the symbol table `intab`. The pseudo-module is added to the list directly after the first module generated by the system call *init_module*.

In the other case, a loaded module wants to modify its symbol table. In contrast to the kernel, an external module can also delete its symbol table. The function checks whether an old symbol table is present and whether it is referenced by other modules. If this is not the case, the new table is inserted. Otherwise, a new table is built out of the old references and `intab` and is then inserted as a symbol table. The old table is released in both cases.

Kernel function			
	`strcpy()`	`strncpy()`	`strchr()`
	`strcat()`	`strncat()`	`strspn()`
	`strcmp()`	`strncmp()`	`strpbrk()`
	`strlen()`	`strnlen()`	`strtok()`

The functions listed here provide most of the routines known from the C library. They are defined as generic C functions in `lib/string.c`, and as optimized inline assembler functions in `<asm-i386/string.h>`.

```
char * strcpy(char * dest, const char *src);
char * strncpy(char * dest, const char *src, size_t count);
```

The strcpy() function copies the string src to dest, including the zero byte. The strings should not overlap, and the target string should have sufficient capacity. The function strncpy() works in the same way, but only copies the first count characters. If src (including the zero byte) is shorter than count, only src is copied. Both functions return a pointer to dest.

```
char * strcat(char * dest, const char * src);
char * strncat(char *dest, const char *src, size_t count);
```

The strcat() function appends a copy of the string src to the string dest. The strncat() function appends a maximum of count characters of the string src to the string dest.

```
int strcmp(const char * cs, const char * ct);
int strncmp(const char * cs, const char * ct, size_t count);
```

The strcmp() function compares the string cs character by character with the string ct over the length of cs. The return value is a number greater than, equal to or less than zero, depending on whether cs is lexicographically greater than, equal to or less than ct. The function strncmp() compares a maximum of count characters.

```
char * strchr(const char * s, char c);
```

The strchr() function returns a pointer to the first occurrence of the character c in the string s. If the character is not found, a NULL pointer is returned.

```
size_t strlen(const char * s);
size_t strnlen(const char * s, size_t count);
```

The strlen() function returns the number of characters in s, excluding the zero byte, whereas strnlen() returns the minimum of string length and count. This function is used by vsprintf() in format instructions for strings.

```
size_t strspn(const char *s, const char *accept);
char * strpbrk(const char * cs, const char * ct);
```

The strspn() function returns the size of the first part of s that does not contain characters from accept. The function strpbrk() returns a pointer to the position in cs where the first occurrence of a character from ct is found.

```
char * strtok(char * s, const char * ct);
```

The `strtok()` function returns the first character string (*token*) of the string `s` that does not contain characters from `ct`. Repeated calls of the function with a `NULL` pointer for `s` divide the string into a sequence of character strings.

Kernel function   `simple_strtoul()`

```
unsigned long simple_strtoul(const char *cp,
                             char **endp,unsigned int base);
```

The eternal problem of converting a string into a number is handled by this function. The string `cp` contains the number to be converted, `base` contains the base of the number system to be used. If it contains 0, the function tries to determine the base automatically. The standard is base 10, but if `cp` begins with '0', base 8 is used, and if it begins with '0x', base 16 is used. Then `cp` is read character by character, until a character no longer fits into the number system, and converted. The remaining string is stored in `endp`, and the calculated result is returned.

Kernel function   `verify_area()`

```
int verify_area(int type, const void * addr,
                unsigned long size);
```

This function checks whether a flag operation is allowed on a memory area identified by the address `addr` and the size `size`. Two operations are possible: `VERIFY_WRITE` as a flag checks whether write access is allowed; `VERIFY_READ` checks for read access.

Kernel function   `get_user_byte()`   `put_user_byte()`
              `get_user_word()`   `put_user_word()`
              `get_user_long()`   `put_user_long()`

The following six functions allow access to data located in the user's address space. For historical reasons, these functions also exist as `fs` functions[4] (instead of `user`); the macros for the above functions are defined in the (architecture-dependent) file `segment.h`.

---

[4] The reason behind the name `fs` lies in the addressing via the FS register in x86 processors.

get_user_byte(addr) – returns the byte found at address `addr`.

put_user_byte(x,addr) – writes the byte x to address `addr`.

get_user_word(addr) – returns the word found at address `addr`.

put_user_word(x,addr) – writes the word x to address `addr`.

get_user_long(addr) – returns the value of size `long int` found at address `addr`.

put_user_long(x,addr) – writes the value x of size `long int` to the address `addr`.

> Kernel function   `suser()`   `fsuser()`

These two functions check whether a process has superuser privileges or superuser privileges with respect to the file system. Both are simple macros in the header file `<linux/kernel.h>` of the form:

```
#define suser() (current->euid == 0)
#define fsuser() (current->fsuid == 0)
```

There is a proposal to make them into functions of their own and to protocol when which process works with superuser privileges. Therefore, these tests should always be called last.

> Kernel function   `add_wait_queue()`   `remove_wait_queue()`

The management of wait queues is not a complicated issue. But it must be ensured that no two processes or interrupts modify a wait queue at the same time. The following functions must be used for access.

```
inline void add_wait_queue(struct wait_queue ** p,
                           struct wait_queue * wait);
inline void remove_wait_queue(struct wait_queue ** p,
                             struct wait_queue * wait);
```

The first function puts the entry `wait` into the wait queue `p` (as the first entry, obviously); the second function removes it. Both functions block interrupts during the modification and afterwards restore the processor flags. If the kernel has been compiled with the `-DDEBUG` option, they also provide control messages about wait queue and entry.

Kernel function	up()	down()

```
extern inline void up(struct semaphore * sem);
extern inline void down(struct semaphore * sem);
```

These two functions allow synchronization between processes via a semaphore. The down() function checks whether a semaphore is free (greater than 0) and decrements it when successful. Otherwise, the process enters itself in a waiting queue and blocks until the semaphore is free again.

The up() function does nothing but increment the semaphore by one and execute a wake_up() on the wait queue associated to the semaphore.

Both functions have yet to be made safe against interrupts.

References

Bach M. J. (1986). *The Design of the Unix®
Operating System*. London: Prentice-Hall
International, Inc.
Describes the structure of UNIX System V
and how it operates. Together with Leffler,
McKusick, Karels and Quaterman (1989) this
is the standard work on UNIX operating
system implementation.

Burgess R. A. (1995). *Developing your own 32-
Bit Operating System*. Sams Publishing
This book describes the structure and
functioning of MMURTL, a multi-tasking
operating system for 80386 systems. The
complete source code is included, so that
everybody is welcome to experiment.

Claßen L. (1990). *Programmierhandbuch
80386/80486*. Berlin: Verlag Technik
A very compact introduction to 80386
programming. References to Claßen and
Wiesner (1990) are available in places.

Claßen L. and Oefler U. (1987). *UNIX und C –
Ein Anwenderhandbuch* 2. Auflage. Berlin:
Verlag Technik
An introduction to UNIX and the C
programming language. Referring as it does
to UNIX Version 7, it is perhaps not quite up
to date, but still readable.

Claßen L. and Wiesner U. (1990).
Wissensspeicher 80286-Programmierung.
Berlin: Verlag Technik

Comer D. E. (1991). *Internetworking with
TCP/IP*, Volume I – Principles, Protocols
and Architecture 2nd edn. London: Prentice-
Hall International, Inc.
The standard work on TCP/IP. Covers all
basic protocols including ARP, TCP, IP and
RIP.

Comer D. E. and Stevens D. L. (1991).
Internetworking with TCP/IP, Volume II –
Design, Implementation, and Internals 1st edn.
London: Prentice-Hall International, Inc.
Covers the TCP/IP implementation of the
Xinu system. The Xinu system is a free
implementation of a UNIX-compatible system.

Deering S. (1989). *RFC 1112* – Host extensions
for IP multicasting. August
This RFC deals with the extensions and
alterations which need to be made in network
implementations in order to support IP
multicast. In so doing, it only goes into the
requirements of individual computers.

Deering S. E. and Cheriton D. R. (1985). *RFC
966* – Host groups: A multicast extension to
the internet protocol. December
Describes the IGMP protocol. For IP
multicast packets to be routed efficiently, an
exchange of information between the IP
routers is required. For this purpose a new
protocol, closely modelled on ICMP, was
developed.

ELF (executable and linkable format).
A description of the Elf binary format. This
can be found on many large FTP servers,
including (in packed form) on

`ftp.informatik.hu-berlin.de` in the file
`/pub/os/linux/packages/GCC/ELF.doc.tar.gz`.

Feit S. (1993). *TCP/IP – Architecture, Protocols, and Implementation*. New York: McGraw-Hill Inc.
One of many books on TCP/IP. A more comprehensive presentation may be found in Comer (1991).

`ftp.informatik.hu-berlin.de/pub/os/linux`.
The authors' home FTP server. Along with the most important data of other LINUX FTP servers, it also contains the PC speaker drivers described in this book (in the `hu-sound/` directory) as well as some older texts by the authors on LINUX Kernel Hacking (in the `HU-Seminar/` directory).

Gircys G. R. (1990). *Understanding and Using COFF*. O'Reilly and Associates, Inc.
A comprehensive description of the COFF object format. Describes the structure and adaptation more precisely. Since the object format has arisen from the universally known `a.out` and there is no appreciable difference between the two, it is also suitable for use as literature for `a.out`.

GNU Public License. Free Software Foundation
The GNU Public License specifies the license conditions under which the LINUX kernel and most programs included with LINUX distributions may be used. The full text can be found in the root directory of the enclosed CD-ROM.

Goodheart B. and Cox J. (1994). *The Magic Garden Explained*. Prentice-Hall International, Inc.
An up-to-date description of the internals of UNIX System V Release 4.

Hetze S., Hohndel D. *et al.* (1996). *Linux Anwenderhandbuch* 6. erweiterte und aktualisierte Auflage. LunetIX Softfair
A good reference work for the budding LINUX user on installing and maintaining the LINUX system.

Intel (1997). *MultiProcessor Specification*, Version 1.4.
The Intel multi-processor specification describes the interaction of several Intel processors in a system. It can be downloaded via: `http://www.intel.com/design/pentium/datashts/242016.htm`

Johnson M. K. (1995). *Linux Kernel Hacker's Guide* draft 0.6 edition. Linux Document Project
This should really become the standard work for the LINUX kernel. The most recently published version dates from January 1995. For the future, it is rather intended to become a collection of articles. As with all other documentation on the LINUX document project, the text of this book is available on all good LINUX FTP servers, for example via `http://sunsite.unc.edu` in the directory `/LDP`.

Leffler S. J., McKusick M. K., Karels M. J. and Quaterman J. S. (1989). *The Design and Implementation of the 4.3BSD Unix Operating System*. Reading, MA: Addison-Wesley
In contrast to Bach (1986) this concerns the implementation of the BSD variants of UNIX. Also a standard work on 'How do I write my own UNIX system?' For 4.4BSD implementation, *see* McKusick *et al.* (1996).

Lewine D. (1991). *POSIX Programmers Guide*. O'Reilly and Associates, Inc.
Anyone who does not already have the POSIX standard on their desk (and who does?) should at least take a close look at this book.

LINUX Documentation Project
In many large software projects there is usually no one who writes the necessary documentation. Happily this is not the case with LINUX. There soon formed a group of developers who write important texts under the name LINUX Documentation Project. These include the detailed Manual Pages, a LINUX installation manual, the Network Administrators Guide, the LINUX Kernel Hacker's Guide and the LINUX Programmers Guide.

McKusick M. K., Bostic K., Karels M. J. and Quarterman J. S. (1996). *The Design and Implementation of the 4.4 BSD Operating System*. Reading, MA: Addison-Wesley
The successor of Leffler S.J. *et al.* (1989) describes the complete internals of the latest BSD version.

Messmer H.-P. (1997). *The Indispensable Hardware Book*, 3rd edn. Harlow, UK: Addison-Wesley
A good, understandable description of standard PC hardware. The fundamental

introduction to the thematic of DMA is highly commendable.

Pike R., Thomson K. *et al.* (1991). *Plan 9*: The early papers, July
A very interesting collection of some older works on the experimental Plan 9 operating system. If the authors' names sound familiar, that is because the same people also wrote the first UNIX systems 20 years ago. Here one can read how they now regard the UNIX concepts. These reports have also been published on the Internet and are available on many good FTP servers.

Postel J. (1981). *RFC 793* – Transmission control protocol: Protocol specification, September
This RFC is actually the basis for all implementations of the TCP protocol. If everyone keeps to it, there will be no problems with communication via TCP.

Salus P. H. (1994). *A Quarter Century of Unix*. Reading, MA: Addison-Wesley
A book not about the internals of UNIX but about the history of this fascinating operating system.

Santifaller, M. (1995). *TCP/IP and ONC/NFS: Internetworking in a Unix Environment*, 2nd ed. Harlow, UK: Addison-Wesley
Introduction to thematics whose emphasis lies in their use.

Schimmel C. (1994). *Unix Systems for Modern Architectures*. Reading, MA: Addison-Wesley
After a general introduction to the UNIX kernel, the author gives a detailed treatment of the problems and possibilities of multiprocessing and caching for UNIX systems.

Silberschatz A. and Galvin P. (1994). *Operating System Concepts*. Reading, MA: Addison-Wesley
Yet another introduction to the matter.

Stapelberg S. (1994). *Unix System V.4 für Einsteiger und Fortgeschrittene*. Bonn: Addison-Wesley

Stevens W. R. (1992a). Advanced *Programming in the Unix® Environment*. Reading, MA: Addison-Wesley
The ultimate book on programming under UNIX. Stevens describes here in over 700 pages the entire spectrum of system calls from BSD 4.3 through System V Release 4 to the POSIX standard – including the application of system calls to meaningful examples.

Stevens W. R. (1992b). *Programmieren von Unix-Netzen*. Jointly published by Carl Hanser and Prentice-Hall, Munich and London
Anyone finding the chapter on networks in Stevens (1992a) too short will find everything about programming UNIX networks here. Another very commendable book.

Stevens W. R. (1994). *TCP/IP Illustrated: The Protocols* Volume 1. Reading, MA: Addison-Wesley
Undoubtedly the book by which one should familiarize oneself with TCP/IP. Describes the subject matter in exactly the way in which the UNIX user encounters it. A set of freely usable tools helps with exploring the network.

Tanenbaum A. S. (1986). *Modern Operating Systems*. London: Prentice-Hall International, Inc.
Does not cover Minix, in contrast to Tanenbaum (1990). Describes fundamental principles of the mode of operation of classical and distributed operating systems. These are subsequently explained using, in each case, two concrete examples (MS-DOS, UNIX, Amoeba and Mach). It still remains unclear to us how the description of MS-DOS found its way into a book called 'Modern Operating Systems'.

Tanenbaum A. S. (1989). *Computer Networks*, 2nd edn. London: Prentice-Hall International, Inc.
An overview of how networks operate. Starting with the OSI reference model, the theoretical foundations of the individual layers and their realization in practice are described. A good foundation book, even though no longer quite up to date.

Tanenbaum A. S. (1990). *Betriebssysteme – Entwurf und Realisierung – Teil 1 Lehrbuch*. Jointly published by Carl Hanser and Prentice-Hall, Berlin and London
Here Tanenbaum describes the structure and functioning of his MINIX system. MINIX (Mini UNIX) was written by Tanenbaum for educational purposes. It illustrates very well the concepts of implementing UNIX systems,

but its limitations render it not entirely suitable in practice. MINIX was the first Unix system whose source texts could be obtained relatively inexpensively. For this reason it was quite popular with Information Technology students. The development of Linux began under MINIX.

Washburn K. and Evans J. T. (1993).
TCP/IP: Running a Successful Network.
Herlow, UK: Addison-Wesley
An even more comprehensive introduction to the thematics of TCP/IP. The emphasis lies clearly on the description of the protocols and their application.

Index

The index is intended as a tool for those working with the LINUX kernel. For kernel functions, variables and structures, the file in which the definition can be found is specified in parentheses '( )'. Files are specified relative to the root of the LINUX sources (*see* Chapter 2), with the exception of the header files which are located in the include path (thus mainly under /usr/include). In analogy to the include instruction of the C preprocessor, these files are enclosed in angle brackets '< >'. The word *static* following a variable or a function indicates that this variable or function is defined locally in the specified file.

If in preprocessor macros the value is a simple number, it is indicated after an equal sign '='. In addition, a file in which the macro is defined is also specified.